FILMMA
ed
ANTH(

D1430616

58. *Smile When the Raindrops Fall*, by Brian Anthony and Andy Edmonds. 1998
59. *Joseph H. Lewis: Overview, Interview, and Filmography*, by Francis M. Nevins. 1998
60. *September Song: An Intimate Biography of Walter Huston*, by John Weld. 1998
61. *Wife of the Life of the Party*, by Lita Grey Chaplin and Jeffrey Vance. 1998
62. *Down but Not Quite Out in Hollow-weird: A Documentary in Letters of Eric Knight*, by Geoff Gehman. 1998
63. *On Actors and Acting: Essays by Alexander Knox*, edited by Anthony Slide. 1998
64. *Back Lot: Growing Up with the Movies*, by Maurice Rapf. 1999
65. *Mr. Bernds Goes to Hollywood: My Early Life and Career in Sound Recording at Columbia with Frank Capra and Others*, by Edward Bernds. 1999
66. *Hugo Friedhofer: The Best Years of His Life: A Hollywood Master of Music for the Movies*, edited by Linda Danly. 1999
67. *Actors on Red Alert: Career Interviews with Five Actors and Actresses Affected by the Blacklist*, by Anthony Slide. 1999
68. *My Only Great Passion: The Life and Films of Carl Th. Dreyer*, by Jean Drum and Dale D. Drum. 1999
69. *Ready When You Are, Mr. Coppola, Mr. Spielberg, Mr. Crowe*, by Jerry Ziesmer. 1999
70. *Order in the Universe: The Films of John Carpenter*, 2nd ed., by Robert C. Cumbow. 2000
71. *Making Music with Charlie Chaplin*, by Eric James. 2000
72. *An Open Window: The Cinema of Víctor Erice*, edited by Linda C. Ehrlich. 2000
73. *Satyajit Ray: In Search of the Modern*, by Suranjan Ganguly. 2000
74. *Voices from the Set: The Film Heritage Interviews*, edited by Tony Macklin and Nick Pici. 2000
75. *Paul Landres: A Director's Stories*, by Francis M. Nevins. 2000
76. *No Film in My Camera*, by Bill Gibson. 2000
77. *Saved from Oblivion: An Autobiography*, by Bernard Vorhaus. 2000
78. *Wolf Man's Maker: Memoir of a Hollywood Writer*, by Curt Siodmak. 2001
79. *An Actor, and a Rare One: Peter Cushing as Sherlock Holmes*, by Tony Earnshaw. 2001
80. *Picture Perfect*, by Herbert L. Strock. 2000
81. *Peter Greenaway's Postmodern/Poststructuralist Cinema*, edited by Paula Willoquet-Maricondi and Mary Alemany Galway. 2001
82. *Member of the Crew*, by Winfrid Kay Thackrey. 2001
83. *Barefoot on Barbed Wire*, by Jimmy Starr. 2001
84. *Henry Hathaway: A Directors Guild of America Oral History*, edited and annotated by Rudy Behlmer. 2001
85. *The Divine Comic: The Cinema of Roberto Benigni*, by Carlo Celli. 2001

Body and Soul

The Cinematic Vision of Robert Aldrich

Tony Williams

Filmmakers Series, No. 110

The Scarecrow Press, Inc.
Lanham, Maryland • Toronto • Oxford
2004

TO JEAN ROUVEROL BUTLER

SCARECROW PRESS, INC.
Published in the United States of America
by Scarecrow Press, Inc.
A wholly owned subsidary of
The Rowman & Littlefield Publishing Group, Inc.
4501 Forbes Boulevard, Suite 200, Lanham, Maryland 20706
www.scarecrowpress.com

PO Box 317
Oxford, OX2 9RU, UK

British Library Cataloguing in Publication Information Available

Library of Congress Cataloging-in-Publication Data

Williams, Tony, 1946 Jan. 11–
  Body and soul : the cinematic vision of Robert Aldrich / Tony Williams.
    p. cm. — (Filmmakers series ; 110)
  Includes filmography.
  Includes bibliographical references and index.
  ISBN 0-8108-4993-3 (alk. paper)
  1. Aldrich, Robert, 1918–Criticism and interpretation. I. Title. II.
Series: Filmmakers series ; no. 110.

  PN1998.3.A44W55 2004
  791.4302'33'092—dc22
                                        2004000020

Contents

ACKNOWLEDGMENTS

I wish to thank the following people for their indispensable help in this project: first and foremost, Anthony Slide for encouraging me to contribute to the Scarecrow Filmmakers Series; Jean Rouverol for providing contacts and several stimulating insights of her own; Ken Hall for referring me to his translations of Cuban film critic G. Cabrera Infante, who wrote some significant essays on the early films of Robert Aldrich; the Interlibrary Loans Department of the Morris Library and Southern Illinois University; Nancy Fligor of the Undergraduate Reserve Library of Southern Illinois University; William Aldrich for granting me permission to access material at the Directors Guild of America and for stimulating comments concerning his father's work; Caroline Sisneros of the American Film Institute; Boyd Magers; Woody Wise; and last but certainly not least, Alain Silver for providing me access to several Robert Aldrich screenplays as well as loaning me his video copy of . . . *All the Marbles* (1981).

INTRODUCTION

Apart from occasional screenings of his *Kiss Me Deadly* and *The Dirty Dozen*, the name of director Robert Aldrich (1918–83) appears to have been forgotten by most critics and audiences. A director once celebrated by that doyen of critics Andrew Sarris as "an underrated genre stylist" whose direction of actors created a "subtle frenzy on the screen" accompanied by a visual style suggesting "an unstable world full of awkward angles and harsh transitions," Aldrich's status has today fallen far below that suggested by the title of Sarris's 1981 article "What Ever Happened to Bobby Aldrich?"[1] Does anybody even remember Aldrich outside of Hollywood and a few critical circles?

The title of Sarris's article is not accidental. It evokes parallels with one of the director's most successful box-office films dealing with the tragic fate of an entertainment figure whose time has passed. But Jane Hudson and Robert Aldrich were not soul mates. For at least four decades the director practiced a philosophy of staying at the gambling table and playing whatever cards were dealt to him by the Hollywood system. Unlike Baby Jane's, his work never became limited to one particular era. Aldrich was never a victim of the system. But he knew its traps and worked both inside and outside the film set to provide alternative avenues of cinematic expression. His activist work in the Directors Guild of America on behalf of those economically outside the Hollywood dream revealed him to be a hardheaded practical figure fully aware of the changing circumstances around him. His last creative achievement, *Twilight's Last Gleaming* (1977), failed at the box office, and his final films certainly do not do justice to his unique talent. Many of his films exhibit the problems accompanying Sarris's individualist definition of the "auteur theory." A director cannot function in isolation from the relevant historical, industrial, and economic issues affecting the final product. If

1

these combinations are adverse, then the film may be drastically affected, no matter how creative a director may be. Circumstances often influence the nature of any artistic product, whether literature or film. But an individual is still there who may win or lose a game depending on contextual factors.[2]

The song "I'm Writing a Letter to Daddy," from *What Ever Happened to Baby Jane?* (1962), concluded Robert Aldrich's memorial service, one that he planned himself. This appears a highly unusual choice for a director associated with macho action movies such as *The Dirty Dozen* (1967) and *The Longest Yard* (1974). But it reflects the feelings of a director toward the tragic plight of a character in a film that cannot be arbitrarily limited to "camp" definitions. Poignant tributes by figures such as Abraham Polonsky as well as heart-warming comments by studio technicians (who owed much to the director's generosity) preceded this music. Baby Jane is not entirely a monster. She is the victim of a manipulative father, passive mother, jealous sister, and the changing world of an entertainment industry that she cannot adapt to. Robert Aldrich was no victim. He often sympathized with outsiders victimized by a family unit seeking to destroy human potential whenever it could. He was fully aware of changing historical forces affecting American cinema and society, often for the worst. The cultural movements of the New Deal had an effect on his work as well as the trauma caused by the blacklist.

Despite those frequent publicity photos of "le gros Robert" deceptively reinforcing critical assaults against a culturally vulgar director promoting gratuitous images of male violence and flying across the Atlantic to see his favorite team play during breaks in filming, Aldrich's work is far more complex. The same person who directed *The Dirty Dozen* also made *Twilight's Last Gleaming*, one of the most damning indictments of American power politics ever to have reached the screen. Like *Attack!* (1956), *Twilight* condemns a corrupt military bureaucracy existing like an undiagnosed cancer within the heart of a country supposedly espousing values of democracy and freedom. It also interrogates the flawed psychic mechanisms of an American heroism that often proves impotent against an inhumane authoritarian system. This critique also occurs in *The Dirty Dozen.* It is not just a macho war film. But many audiences and critics regarded it so at the time. They still do today and use it to dismiss the director's work. Ironically, it became the director's most commercially successful film, allowing him to purchase his own studio. But Aldrich did not choose to follow up his success by making a sequel but, rather, selected some very unusual subjects that failed at the box office. *The Dirty Dozen*'s antiauthoritarian themes captured the mood of the Vietnam-generation audience. Yet the more subtle overtones contained in *Too Late the Hero* (1970) escaped this very same audience, who misread the film as an endorsement of the very values critiqued in *The Dirty Dozen*. The even more radical *Twilight's Last Gleaming* failed drastically at the box office because of an audience preferring to ignore the lessons of Vietnam and rally around the flag. Then, as now, any cinematic criticism of the American power structure fell on deaf ears.

This book intends to connect Robert Aldrich to relevant cultural and social issues affecting his life and career. By complementing other major studies by Arnold and Miller and Silver and Ursini, it aims to suggest further avenues to approach the work of a Hollywood director urgently in need of reevaluation.[3] The special June 2000 issue of the Internet journal *Screening the Past* represents one major step in this direction.

Although from a rich family, Aldrich was really an "orphan child" of the 1930s Cultural Front movement.[4] But he began directing long after the McCarthyite reaction had destroyed the social and political alternatives that briefly appeared in pre- and postwar American society. These features opposed both the dehumanizing conspicuous consumption of the 1920s (also characterized by labor injustice and racism) and the Great Depression of the 1930s. The Depression revealed that the system had failed, and many people attempted to articulate other directions. But postwar reaction would silence them. As a director, Aldrich attempted to follow the progressive ideals he had learned from such mentors as Lewis Milestone, Charles Chaplin, Jean Renoir, Abraham Polonsky, and Joseph Losey. During his brief tenure at Enterprise Studios he had worked with stars such as John Garfield. The actor's star persona in *Body and Soul* (1947) and *Force of Evil* (1949) symbolized the decline and fall of 1930s progressive ideas. It was an image that would influence the director throughout his career. How could Aldrich follow these ideals in later inhospitable decades? How could he continue interrogating the false nature of the American dream when a reactionary society had silenced other critical voices?

Body and Soul: The Cinematic Vision of Robert Aldrich attempts to answer these questions. It concentrates on those films expressing creative and cultural dilemmas affecting his individual characters, who may or may not survive the ordeals they confront. These ordeals are both personal and political. Aldrich was never an explicitly political director. He was no Eisenstein or Joris Ivens. But his films reflect the grim reality of a postwar American society that had destroyed radical 1930s hopes for a better world. Like a military strategist, Aldrich took the enemy position seriously. He never entertained any utopian illusions. His films depict a world in which hero or heroine may not succeed. Yet they also reveal that struggle is always important, no matter how overwhelming the odds. Aldrich rejected false optimism. But he never denied the possibility of things changing for the better should circumstances allow.

The issues dealt with in Aldrich's cinema often resembled those in the post–*Waiting for Lefty* (1935) plays of Clifford Odets, such as *Awake and Sing!* (1935), *Paradise Lost* (1935), *Rocket to the Moon* (1939), and *Night Music* (1940). Despite their different achievements, Odets remained a key influence on Aldrich even in his last film, . . . *All the Marbles* (1981). This relationship extended far beyond Aldrich's 1955 film version of Odets's damning indictment of Hollywood, *The Big Knife* (1949), featuring the playwright's original choice for *Golden Boy*, John Garfield. Odets's theatrical vision grimly reflects those economic and emotional dead ends affecting characters trapped within depression-era society. But it also suggests the possibility of survival, unless human potential is destroyed by material and personal contamination as in *Golden Boy* (1937) and *The Big Knife*. Like Odets, Aldrich initially believed that these suicidal avenues represented gestures of revolt. But he began to retreat from such nihilistic solutions after *The Big Knife* (1955).

Odets remained a dominant influence for Aldrich throughout his life. For anyone growing up in the 1930s it was impossible to escape that visionary apostle of the depression era. Odets's plays articulate various dilemmas affecting those who attempted to survive physically and spiritually during a grim decade that threw all previous values into question. Odets was not merely a political proletarian director as many critics believed. Political *and* personal matters influence the issues contained in *Waiting for Lefty*. The play may lead to a call to "Strike!" but it is composed of several dramatic vignettes revealing the personal and psychological dilemmas faced by many victims of the Great Depression. Although explicit historical and political issues appear absent in the later plays, personal dilemmas cannot be divorced from their relevant social context. Although *The Big Knife* and *The Flowering Peach* (1954) are postdepression plays, they parallel issues in the earlier plays because they also deal with questions of survival and integrity. The affluent, but politically limited, creative era of the 1950s also had its own set of problems. Although the biblical world of *The Flowering Peach* appears an anomaly in Odets's work, it echoes the anxieties of the atomic age. Odets's characters now attempt to survive the holocaust of the Flood as they earlier did the Great Depression. But they still have to confront the same types of personal contradictions that appear in the earlier plays. Aldrich's biblical epic *Sodom and Gomorrah* (1963) ends with a nuclear mushroom cloud destroying the wicked city. But the film also deals with significant issues of power politics, gender, and patriarchy, which characterize other Aldrich films.

Abraham Polonsky (1910–99) represents another major influence on Aldrich. They remained friends after working together in Enterprise Studios on two key productions: *Body and Soul* and *Force of Evil*. Director, screenwriter, and novelist Polonsky was a major Popular Front creative talent. The blacklist drastically affected his career until he resumed directing in 1970 with *Tell Them Willie Boy Is Here*, a revisionist western in the spirit of *Body and Soul* and *Force of Evil* that refuses easy solutions. Like Aldrich's *Vera Cruz* (1954) and the Associates and Aldrich Co. production *The Ride Back* (1957), *Willie Boy* interrogates the heroic role, showing both pursued and pursuer as victims of identical social and cultural contexts.[5] Aldrich and Polonsky examined similar issues involving the nature of an oppressive social structure, the damaging psychological aspects of hubris and self-delusion, and the necessity of struggling against overwhelming odds. Aldrich's modest first feature, *Big Leaguer* (1953), involves winners and losers. A potential winner is dropped from the training team because of a mistake made by the coach. However, he returns as a winning key player on the opposing team in the film's final game. Some losers can always return again to compete in the next season.

The ghosts of *Golden Boy* and *Body and Soul* haunt Aldrich's *The Big Knife*. It is a film combining the influences of Odets and Polonsky. *The Big Knife* may be viewed as an unconscious sequel to *Body and Soul*. What if Charley Davis and Roberts had made it up and engaged in another Faustian bargain? Whenever Aldrich found himself in a creative dilemma he would always turn to *Body and Soul* for inspiration. *The Longest Yard* and the final twelve minutes of *The Choirboys* (1977) are two such examples. But Aldrich always knew the other side of the coin. Despite *Body and Soul's* positive ending, Charley may eventually have to pay for his decision. The final climax Polonsky argued for differs from Robert Rossen's proposed ending showing Charley's dead body with his head in a garbage can. But another grim fate may await him in the near future.

Aldrich and Polonsky recognized that their struggling heroes had won only temporary victories. Yet even a brief respite is important. Although Charley Davis might have to pay his dues on the following day, the fact remains that he *had* decided not to sell out or submit to threats. He might die as an individual. But his integrity inspires others in the future, be they Jewish immigrants who look on him as their role model in *Body and Soul* or those prison inmates in *The Longest Yard* who would never again submissively accept the totalitarian rule of Warden Hazen. Aldrich's protagonists face their own personal demons as well as the oppressive nature of the social systems that created them in the first place. But they *do* have a choice, despite the fact that victory may only be temporary and the situation may change the next day. The key fact is that something *can* be reversed and the very nature of its reversal may provide seeds for more permanent change. This use of the subjunctive is deliberate. Like one of Odets's characters, Aldrich always believed in other possibilities.

But the system still remains. It is not one that will easily be overthrown. Aldrich never presented his viewers with false optimistic solutions. He also rejected the typical Hollywood "happy ending." *The Dirty Dozen* concludes with all but three of the original team dead. Despite General Denton's (Robert Webber) pompous congratulation to the survivors, the final overhead shot in the film astutely reveals what the Stars and Stripes actually involves. The three survivors are dwarfed into insignificance by this overhanging camera shot revealing three primary colors (Bowren's blue robe, white hospital sheets, and red blankets) denoting the inhumane nature of a system that has used and abused these survivors and will do so again. Aldrich usually employs this high angle shot at suggestive moments in his work to emphasize menacing overtones. It is a device he used since his contributions to the 1952 television series *China Smith* and forms a key visual metaphor within his entire work.

The days are long gone when auteur-influenced critics could blandly assume that all films directed by their chosen figures are more interesting than those produced by mere *metteur-en-scène* directors such as John Huston. Today, nobody would seriously argue that Fritz Lang's *American Guerilla in the Philippines* (1950) is more important than the achievements of Vincente Minnelli. No excuses can be made for problematic films such as *The Frisco Kid* (1979), one of the projects Aldrich had to accept to keep playing at the Hollywood card table. Not all of Aldrich's films are of equal interest, and some are—to put it frankly—terrible. No case will be made for the Sinatra western *4 for Texas* (1963). Although it has some good comic moments as well as an interesting performance by Charles Bronson clearly at odds with the material (like the later role of William Smith in *The Frisco Kid*), it is a desperate work of a director frustrated by his lack of control over the project. Problems affecting the production of *The Angry Hills* (1959) as well as Robert Mitchum's lack of interest make this film unworthy of detailed attention. By contrast, despite problems Aldrich encountered with Kirk Douglas on *The Last Sunset* (1961), the film is interesting in terms of its presentation of a dysfunctional family motif that occurs in the director's other films as well as its critique of a naive and dangerous romantic hero. *The Choirboys* is little better than a "run for cover" production enabling Aldrich to stay in the game. But even that film contains a few significant moments where the director attempts to transcend the material. Production circumstances forced Aldrich to change many elements in *World for Ransom* (1954). But this neglected film already contained the seeds of the director's critique of the American hero that he would develop in his later work. They also appear in other diverse films such as *Apache* (1954), *Kiss Me Deadly* (1955), *The Big Knife*, *Attack!*, *The Last Sunset*, *The Flight of the Phoenix* (1966), the significantly titled *Too Late the Hero*, and *Twilight's Last Gleaming*. Even *The Dirty Dozen* and *The Longest Yard* do not fully affirm the nature of male heroism but, rather, are more critical in certain ways.

Vera Cruz significantly features this critique against the background of an appropriate revolutionary context. Despite the contrasted star performances of a restrained Gary Cooper and flamboyant Burt Lancaster, these characters really represent two sides of a male ego at war with itself. Aldrich also sees masculinity as leading to not only individual crisis but also collective apocalyptic destruction. *Kiss Me Deadly* and *Twilight's Last Gleaming* reveal this. Mike Hammer's male hubris causes the end of the world. The disturbed messianic General Dell nearly begins Judgment Day, just like his more psychotic counterpart, the self-appointed violent divine savior Maggott, in *The Dirty Dozen*. Phil Gaines in *Hustle* (1975) is another example of Aldrich's psychologically "walking wounded" males who populate his films. Psychologically scarred by the discovery of his wife's adultery, Phil not only is unable to commit himself to a fulfilling relationship with Nicole but also masochistically listens to her phone-sex calls with her various clients. By the time he feels himself able to commit to her it is too late. Phil foolishly decides to act "too late the hero." As Steve Shagan's original screenplay reveals, Phil is actually a red diaper baby whose father died in the Spanish Civil War. He now lives a rootless existence in a society that has rejected those affirmative values of the 1930s.

Like Clifford Odets in *Awake and Sing! Paradise Lost*, and *Clash by Night* (1942), Aldrich was fully aware of the destructive role of the family on the human personality. Both males and females suffer from this system in many of his films. Dangerous to both himself and his men, *Attack!*'s Captain Cooney has already suffered from an abusive father who is also indirectly responsible for the dilemma the soldiers find themselves in during the early days of the Battle of the Bulge. Aldrich and screenwriter James Poe emphasized this feature in the film version of *Fragile Fox*. The military establishment, represented by Colonel Bartlett, already knows about Cooney's background. But Bartlett uses this fact to advance his own postwar military career when he intends to ascend the social ladder and enter politics. He wishes to give the judge a son he can be proud of whether dead or alive!

Autumn Leaves (1956) features two other casualties of the American family—repressed spinster Millicent Wetherby and psychologically retarded Burt Hanson. Millicent experiences loneliness arising from a false, masochistic sense of duty toward an ailing parent when she was younger. Burt suffers from a father figure who represents one of Freud's worst nightmares by enacting the "castration complex" in more senses than one. *Autumn Leaves* depicts an incestuously abusive American family scenario wherein father does *not* know best.

Jane Hudson and Charlotte Hollis in *What Ever Happened to Baby Jane?* and *Hush . . . Hush, Sweet Charlotte* (1964) also suffer in the present from the past actions of authoritarian fathers. Jane's father is directly responsible for turning a small child into an economic machine, making her into a monstrous middle-aged adult who lives in the past. Like Ray Hudson (Dave Willock), Big Sam Hollis dominates the life of his daughter. As the film's prologue reveals, he sets into motion a chain of circumstances that ruin her life. Paradoxically, he never listens to his daughter and dies before he can tell her that he was never responsible for her lover's murder. Charlotte feels guilty over a false sense of loyalty to the Law of the Father and bears her own personal cross. Jane and Charlotte are also victimized by close family relatives who prey on them like emotional cannibals.

Even *The Killing of Sister George* (1968) contains this dark aberrant family theme. The psychological problems affecting June Buckridge destroy a lesbian relationship. But it is already a macabre parody of an authoritarian mother–daughter scenario wherein an authoritarian parent abuses a vulnerable child who masochistically submits to this treatment. However, everyone is guilty in the film. There are no innocent parties. Childie is a manipulative daughter figure who encourages the attentions of the equally manipulative, competing mother figure of Mercy Croft, whose first name contradicts her actual character. June and Childie's relationship echoes the worst features of an abusive patriarchal family. The collapse of the relationship in the film comes as no real surprise. It is also associated with an entertainment industry that abuses the inherent creativity of a once-talented actress.

Aldrich viewed these various dilemmas as not solely personal. They also resulted from an inhumane system that deliberately made people antagonists instead of equal partners cooperating together against a common enemy. In *The Dirty Dozen* Major Reisman ironically recognizes the deadly nature of his assigned task. The military establishment sees the mission as a convenient way of disposing of criminal elements rather than using the apparatus of judicial execution employed in the film's prologue. It is a method they also wish to use against Reisman. But he proves that outcasts can function as team players despite the nature of their personalities and the crimes they have committed. Aldrich did not take the easy way out and imply that all twelve men are unjustly accused. They are not saintly figures. Instead, he attempts to distract any misleading audience sympathy for these characters by depicting them as manipulated players within an inhumane system that uses and abuses them. They are mere pawns in a game planned by the military establishment, which also plays with the lives of their noncriminal counterparts. During the attack on the chateau, innocent and guilty equally perish, whether they are German High Command and their ladies or French servants. The brass plan the exercise as a murderous diversionary tactic little better than the types of wartime atrocities they accuse their enemies of. The Dozen are all legally guilty of the crimes they have committed. Some, like Franko (John Cassavetes) and Maggott (Telly Savalas), deserve their sentences. But others, such as Wladislaw (Charles Bronson), Jefferson (Jim Brown), and Posey (Clint Walker), have been railroaded by an inhumane judicial system denying relevant mitigating circumstances at their trials. However, in Aldrich's satirical reinterpretation of the Savior's role as a "fisher of men," Reisman turns all these men into a fighting unit. All, except Jimenez and Maggott, perform their roles satisfactorily. But they have been placed into a "nowin" situation and ironically perform acts that are little better than atrocities for the Allied cause. All except one die in *The Dirty Dozen.* But the entire team wins in *The Longest Yard.* The Dozen operate as a team. But they individually fight to survive and escape the execution of their sentences. The prisoners in *The Longest Yard* have already received their sentences. But they function as a team to beat the system in the final game. They all attempt to struggle against the negative consequences of a competitive American system.

Aldrich understood that alternatives existed as well. But people also had to confront a deadly competitive ethos sown within the human personality by a corrupt system. *Emperor of the North* (1973) illustrates this. Set within the brutal Social Darwinist world of the Great Depression, the film depicts not only the atavistic contest between A. No. 1 (Lee Marvin) and Shack (Ernest Borgnine) but also a rivalry with the former's self-styled successor, Cigaret (Keith Carradine). Despite the opportunity of benefiting from the older man's guidance, Cigaret decides to upstage him from the very first moment. This parallels a familiar social situation wherein the younger generation arrogantly sees itself as the natural successor to a supposedly obsolescent predecessor whose experience and historical knowledge are deliberately ignored. Like George A. Romero's *There's Always Vanilla* (1972), *Emperor of the North* emerged in a decade witnessing the failure of the 1960s radicalism of the younger generation to achieve any significant change in the system. As someone personally experiencing the collapse of New Deal idealism in the postwar era, Aldrich never entertained any illusions about the younger generation as Clifford Odets does in his 1940 play *Night*

Music. In his depiction of Cigaret, Aldrich shows that the rising generation can fall into the same competitive traps of its predecessors. This judgment was well before its time and may have resulted in the film's unpopular box-office reception. After saving Cigaret from Shack, A. No. 1 throws him off the train. The emperor of the North Pole not only rejects a younger successor. He also refuses to have anything more to do with a manipulative and treacherous character who has no real moral code. Cigaret's tactics often parallel those used by Shack against the hoboes. But Shack is at least honest in his goals. Both A. No. 1 and Shack have their own type of integrity. Cigaret has nothing. The potential collective nature of the hobo brotherhood seen in one sequence in the film also remains an unfulfilled dream.

A broader social context also informs Aldrich's last film, . . . *All the Marbles.* Unfortunately, the final version dropped certain key elements from the screenplay that explained the motivations affecting the two California Dolls, echoing Aldrich's cinematic examinations of dysfunctional families. Molly (Laurene Landon) is a lesbian who has suffered parental rape in the past. Iris (Vicki Frederick) is a single mother battling with her former husband for child custody while she travels away from home to support both herself and her child. With their manager Harry (Peter Falk), they form an antagonistic, but closely knit, alternative family that struggles constantly but remains together, often facing impossible odds.

Aldrich's films contain little sympathy for conventional modes of living. Instead, they contain bleak images of a hostile twentieth-century universe that has rejected all previous systems of values. No positive value systems exist. Aldrich's cinema involves direct confrontation with the chaotic nature of human existence. Both he and certain characters never rely on old beliefs that are no longer relevant. His Vietnam-related western *Ulzana's Raid* (1972) is probably one of the best indirect depictions of the actual war. It presents a world of violent absurdity in which nothing really seems to make sense to those caught inside the conflict who attempt to understand it by redundant codes of old value systems.

Aldrich's most nihilistic film, *The Grissom Gang* (1971), also overturns established moral conventions. In this second adaptation of James Hadley Chase's *No Orchids for Miss Blandish* (1939), Aldrich deliberately presents a squalid world, giving audiences nobody to identify with. Unlike *The Dirty Dozen,* where the audience may admire

Reisman's tenacity as well as certain individuals in the group, *The Grissom Gang* provides no redeeming character—not even private eye Dave Fenner (Robert Lansing)—at least until the final seconds of the film. It is a deliberate artistic strategy. But it is also known as "box-office poison." The film's financial failure led to the collapse of Aldrich's studio, in which he attempted to re-create the brief conditions of Enterprise Studios where he worked as an assistant director in the late 1940s. *The Grissom Gang* is one of Aldrich's bleakest films. It depicts a world of nihilism, violence, and absurdity that contaminates everybody. Unlike in the 1948 British film version, Aldrich decided to place the film in the context of the Great Depression, where the callous and selfish remain rich and the poor attempt to survive by whatever means possible. The film depicts a society in which all values have collapsed and a system that cares little for its victims.

Also, various characters in *The Grissom Gang* resemble those within a bleak naturalist novel, trapped inside a ruthless deterministic world they are powerless to alter. Aldrich may have offended certain sensibilities by using the dubious theme of a woman eventually falling in love with her rapist. But the eventual fragile love between Barbara (Kim Darby) and Slim (Scott Wilson) touchingly counterpoints the dehumanizing nature of the American depression. The film also condemns a rich father who refuses to acknowledge the life-threatening circumstances that have caused his daughter to try to survive in the only way she could. Blandish coldly condemns Barbara at the climax. He thus becomes as heinous a parental figure as his outlaw counterpart, Ma Grissom. Irene Dailey's Ma represents a monstrous image of those mother figures in Odets plays, such as *Awake and Sing!* and *Paradise Lost,* whose desire to keep the family together at all costs may not be in the best interests for all concerned—especially the younger generation!

Deliberate contradictions and reversals characterize the cinematic vision of Robert Aldrich, which also parallels the bleak postwar universe depicted in David Cochran's *America Noir: Underground Writers and Filmmakers of the Postwar Era.* His book analyzes the cultural significance of talents such as Jim Thompson, Charles Willeford, Chester Himes, Patricia Highsmith, Ray Bradbury, Charles Beaumont, Samuel Fuller, Roger Corman, and Rod Serling. Cochran sees them as "ten representative figures, laboring within genres dismissed as hopelessly corrupted mass-cultural forms by elite critics, [who] managed to produce art that went to the heart of the cultural contradictions of Cold War society, that thrived on chaos, ambiguity, irony, and juxtaposition—characteristics notably absent from the period's dominant middlebrow culture."[6] Cochran recognizes that other talents were also active.

He cites Aldrich and others such as David Goodis as artists "producing work that offered a darker, more critical vision than was common in the dominant culture" rather than the more "self-consciously, avant-garde, experimental art of people such as Stan Brakhage, Jonas Mekas, William S. Burroughs, or Yoko Ono."[7] *Kiss Me Deadly*'s deliberate use of a grotesque noir expressionism anticipates Orson Welles's *Touch of Evil* (1958) as well as contemporary movements in modern art. Aldrich's later, stylistically sober films such as *Too Late the Hero* and *Twilight's Last Gleaming* also contain the chaos, ambiguity, irony, and juxtaposition that Cochran finds in this postwar movement.

Like Clifford Odets in *Awake and Sing! Clash by Night*, and *The Big Knife*, Aldrich saw Hollywood as a conveyer of false values capable of destroying human personalities. Her premature vaudeville stardom and her later humiliating position as a bad actress in the 1930s studio system both psychologically destroy Jane Hudson. Despite its many flaws, *The Legend of Lylah Clare* (1968) is an angry indictment of a corrosive Hollywood system. Director Lewis Zarkan murders his protégé not once but twice. Aldrich worked in the system as an insider. But he often rebelled against its ignominious constraints and attempted to offer alternative cinematic visions. Aldrich often inserted himself as an "author in the text," as seen in the prologue of *What Ever Happened to Baby Jane?* Bert Freed's producer wears his tie in the same manner as Aldrich did on the studio set. So does Ernest Borgnine's Barney Sheehan in *The Legend of Lylah Clare*. Perhaps Aldrich satirized his own contradictory complicity in a system he hoped to change?

The cinematic universe of Robert Aldrich involves a contradictory combination of body and soul. During the climactic moments of *Body and Soul*, Charley Davis finally makes the right decision. He decides to combine his physical prowess and emotional feelings toward defeating his opponent and the system. Charley's victory may only be temporary, but it is personally fulfilling. In *Apache*, Massai briefly discovers other values that provide a more positive avenue for his energies than dying heroically as the last real Apache warrior of his generation. Ben Trane of *Vera Cruz* finally relinquishes his material quest to restore the lost fortunes of his Southern plantation and joins a revolutionary movement. Like many characters in the plays of Clifford Odets and the films of Robert Aldrich, he learns that it is impossible to return to the past. By doing so, Trane has to kill an alter ego embodying his own worst qualities. Mike Hammer of *Kiss Me Deadly* never reaches this level of consciousness.

Minority figures often play a key role in Aldrich's films by attempting to motivate the heroes into considering other alternatives. Nalinle achieves this in *Apache* for a short time. Christina Bailey utters a condemnation of Mike Hammer that falls on deaf ears. Heroes are often flawed figures in the university of Aldrich. Despite his potential as a savior figure, Lt. Costa in *Attack!* allows negative emotions to get the better of him. His actions parallel General Dell's in *Twilight's Last Gleaming*. Dell's cause is noble, but psychological contamination by false heroic values makes his messianic crusade pathologically insane. He becomes a perversely destructive savior figure who will unleash a nuclear Judgment Day similar to that in the final scenes of *Sodom and Gomorrah*. Willis Powell briefly succeeds in changing Dell's mind, but it is too late for this hero. When President Stevens arrives, Dell again relapses into the naive illusion that he can individually change the system. It is an illusion Aldrich always critiques in his various films. Individuals can never do this on their own.

The director offers no false solutions or easy alternatives. The game may be lost, as in *Twilight's Last Gleaming*, or victory, temporary. But if a brief respite exists, it does represent an achievement. It also delivers a lesson to any audience member watching the film critically. As in *Waiting for Lefty*, viewers have a final option of collectively calling "Strike!" and actively opposing an oppressive system. Odets's play ends with the death of the savior-hero. But the playwright's message is a collective one that his ideal audience understands after witnessing the various personal vignettes structuring the play. Saviors are not necessary for change to occur. In fact, they may be harmful and redundant.

Despite current academic dismissal of the work of Andrew Sarris, his brief comments on Aldrich in *The American Cinema* are informative. Sarris sees Aldrich's deliberately baroque, stylistic noir exercises in *Kiss Me Deadly, The Big Knife*, and *Attack!* (as well as his neo-noir *Hustle*) as exhibiting a "distinctively personal signature."[8] But it is also one having social significance. Sarris describes Aldrich as "a moralist in a man's world."[9] But he also recognizes his role as an intuitive chronicler of his era: "His films are invariably troubled by intimations of decadence and disorder. The titles of even his lesser films—*World for Ransom, Autumn Leaves, Ten Seconds to Hell, The Last Sunset, Sodom and Gomorrah*—suggest a mood befitting the Decline of the West."[10] It is a decline that can lead to apocalyptic destruction, as *Ten Seconds to Hell* (1959), *The Last Sunset, Sodom and Gomorrah,* and *Twilight's Last Gleaming* demonstrate.

Like Stanley Kubrick, Aldrich recognized that decline and destruction result from contradictory tensions involving personal dilemmas related to the surrounding social environment.[11] Aldrich and Kubrick never provide easy answers. However, influenced by the alternative cultural movements of the New Deal and the progressive work of talents in the pre-blacklist era, Aldrich showed sympathy toward alternative possibilities. His films always envisage that tentative goal of "the Big Tomorrow" that has haunted American society since the progressive movement of the 1930s.[12] But, like Stanley Kubrick, Aldrich also believed in the necessity of destroying false illusions before any real progress could be made. Ed Lowry notices that Aldrich has much in common with Kubrick. His films often exhibit a critical sense of irony also revealing "a cynicism so bitter that it could only arise from a liberal sensibility utterly disillusioned by an age in which morality has become a cruel joke."[13] Lowry also recognizes that the critical establishment often hides behind a convenient repugnance to the surface values of Aldrich's films so as to deliberately ignore "their savage, multi-layered critiques of Hollywood's genres and American ideology."[14] But Aldrich's critical vision derived from a broader cultural movement in twentieth-century American society. It is one significantly represented by the work of Clifford Odets, who influenced Aldrich throughout his entire career.

NOTES

1. Andrew Sarris, "What Ever Happened to Bobby Aldrich?" *Village Voice* 29 (28 October 1981): 49.

2. See the final section of John Caughie, *Theories of Authorship* (London: British Film Institute, 1981), 199–207, a work that complicates poststructuralist axioms concerning the "death of the Author."

3. Edwin T. Arnold and Eugene I. Miller, *The Films and Career of Robert Aldrich* (Knoxville: University of Tennessee Press, 1986); Alain Silver and

James Ursini, *What Ever Happened to Robert Aldrich? His Life and His Films* (New York: Limelight Editions, 1995).

4. For a key analysis of the creative context of the 1930s, see Michael Denning, *The Cultural Front: The Laboring of American Culture in the Twentieth-Century* (London: Verso, 1997). Several movements emerging from this era later influenced key achievements of 1940s Hollywood cinema, as several critics have noted. Among these were Orson Welles and the Mercury Theatre, the early work of Joseph Losey, and the cinema of Nicholas Ray. The blacklist effectively ended any possibility for this creative energy to really develop and become the dominant force in Hollywood a decade later. However, many blacklisted writers did work underground during this period. As Jean Rouverol notes in her stimulating book, "One could only wonder what the Motion Picture Academy would have done for Oscar-winning screenplays all those years if the blacklistees had really been driven from the industry!" (*Refugees from Hollywood: A Journal of the Blacklist Years* [Albuquerque: University of New Mexico Press, 2000], 208).

5. See Paul Buhle and Dave Wagner, *A Very Dangerous Citizen: Abraham Lincoln Polonsky and the Hollywood Left* (Berkeley: University of California Press, 2001), 204–9. The authors note that "close-ups of Robert Blake were strikingly reminiscent of the young John Garfield" (*A Very Dangerous Citizen*, 204). Furthermore, despite differences between the characters of Garfield in *Force of Evil* and Redford in *Willie Boy*, both operate as agents of an inhumane system.

6. David Cochran, *America Noir: Underground Writers and Filmmakers of the Postwar Era* (Washington, D.C.: Smithsonian Institution Press, 2000), xiii.

7. Cochran, *American Noir*, 223.

8. Andrew Sarris, *The American Cinema: Directors and Directions 1929–1968* (New York: Dutton, 1968), 84.

9. Sarris, *The American Cinema*, 85.

10. Sarris, *The American Cinema*, 85.

11. For the relationship between Aldrich and Kubrick in terms of black comedy, see Ed Lowry, "Robert Aldrich," in *International Directory of Films and Filmmakers*, vol. 2: *Directors*, ed. Tom Prendergast and Sara Prendergast, 4th ed. (New York: St. James Press, 2000), 7–8.

12. For the significance of this evocative image within American culture, see Lary May, *The Big Tomorrow: Hollywood and the Politics of the American Way* (Chicago: University of Chicago Press, 2000).

13. Lowry, "Robert Aldrich," 8.

14. Lowry, "Robert Aldrich," 8.

ONE

ODETS AND ALDRICH

Apart from the 1955 film adaptation of *The Big Knife*, featuring Odets's original choice for the title role of *Golden Boy*, John Garfield, the work of playwright Clifford Odets and the cinema of Robert Aldrich appear to be distinct entities. *The Big Knife*'s theatrical condemnation of Hollywood did not reach the screen until six years after the play was written. The film version was the only time both talents became linked. But both playwright and director share a common cultural context, which they developed in different ways. Odets was the theatrical spokesman for the grim era of the Great Depression. After that era, his later plays never attracted the kind of attention his 1930s productions did. His interests changed both personally and professionally. For any creative individual growing up in the 1930s, it would have been impossible not to have been influenced by the plays of Clifford Odets, for they formed an indispensable part of that creative movement defined as the Cultural Front by Michael Denning and others. Odets made a great impression on the director, who frequently cites him in his films. For example, during one scene in *The Angry Hills* (1959), Mike Morrison (Robert Mitchum) finds it difficult to pronounce the name of Greek resistance worker Eleftheria (Gia Scala). He decides instead to nickname her "Lefty," stating that "where I come from it's a name for very special people." Aldrich not only inserts an in-joke into a film made during the blacklist but also adds a touch of irony. Like Odets's characters in *Waiting for Lefty*, Morrison will wait in vain for a character who dies offscreen.

Robert Aldrich began his career as a film director in the year following Odets's infamous testimony to the House Un-American Activities Committee (HUAC) in spring 1952. Although the playwright only mentioned the names of individuals who had already been named and supplied no further information, the spectacle of one of the major influences of the 1930s groveling before this appalling institution must have affected all those who were inspired by his plays. Odets later mentioned that the act gave him a "sense of incalculable revulsion."[1] However, the damage was already done. A few months later, Golden Boy John Garfield died of a heart attack brought on by the blacklisting that threatened his career. Among the many factors leading to his death was despondency after hearing Odets's testimony. Although the playwright faced questions concerning Garfield's presumed communist associations, he pleaded ignorance on that score. Despite the fact that Odets did not name Garfield, the nature of his testimony damned the actor by silence rather than giving him the affirmative support he so desperately needed.

An entire era had ended. Riddled by guilt for many years, Odets wrote relatively little. Apart from his screenplay contributions to *Sweet Smell of Success* (1957) and *Wild in the Country* (1961), his major creative period was now over. He died of cancer on 14 August 1963 still believing that he could regain his lost talents. Now overshadowed by the theater of Arthur Miller and Tennessee Williams, Odets appeared to be an anachronism. He was stereotyped as belonging to another era whose significance was now irrelevant to a new America typified by novels such as Sloan Wilson's *The Man in the Gray Flannel Suit* and sociological studies such as William H. Whyte's *The Organization Man* and David Reisman's *The Lonely Crowd*. The optimism generating the various Cultural Front movements had now disappeared because of the blacklist. Norman Mailer's picture of General Cummings's vision of postwar fascism in *The Naked and the Dead* (1948) appeared a grim reality. After World War II, the national mood had begun to change, manipulated by right-wing spin doctors in the Republican Party who wished to destroy any further extensions of the New Deal. They attempted to turn America into a milder version of the totalitarianism they had defeated in the "Good War."

Many submitted to the new order either by changing their allegiance from the Democratic Party to the Republican Party or by informing on their colleagues to the FBI, as did future president Ronald Reagan. Some such as John Berry and Joseph Losey fled abroad to escape the effects of blacklisting on their careers or moved across the border to Mexico.[2] Others such as Abraham Polonsky and Dalton Trumbo went underground and continued writing under pseudonyms. For those who remained in America, the choices involved either total conformity or subversively expressing the cultural contradictions of the new era within the safety of either low-budget cinema or popular genres such as the western or melodrama. Samuel Fuller, Douglas Sirk, Anthony Mann, and Vincente Minnelli are among the group who chose this route, as is Robert Aldrich. For Aldrich, the situation was different. As he mentioned in several interviews, he had worked in Enterprise Studios alongside many talents who would soon face the blacklist. He had also assisted Charlie Chaplin at a time when the "Little Tramp" had been radicalized by the progressive movements of the 1930s and 1940s and cast a critical eye on the contradictions within the society he lived in, in many ways. *Monsieur Verdoux* (1947) suffered limited distribution because of boycotting by the American Legion and blacklisting for daring to suggest that its title character's activities were less dangerous than capitalist militarism. As Aldrich stated, had he fallen under the influence of future blacklistees earlier, he would have suffered the same fate. But the victims were already on the run, and his Rhode Island family connections probably saved him. When liberal actor Robert Ryan was once asked why J. Edgar Hoover never placed him under surveillance, he replied that he had the right combination of associations in being both an ex-Marine and a Catholic. Although the actor's activism was well known, his military and religious background saved him from investigation. For Aldrich, who remained in Hollywood, the problem was how to keep faith with this formative 1930s cultural tradition. He must also have recognized that the dark era of the 1950s contradicted any sense of naive optimism. He had to find other avenues for his cinematic visions.

One of the avenues lay in his intuitive understanding of the diverse implications existing in the plays of Clifford Odets, which made them much more than the supposedly outdated political tracts associated with the Great Depression. Associations between Aldrich and Odets deserve further exploration. They suggest that the director developed and expanded themes within the playwright's work within his own generic explorations in cinema. According to William Aldrich, Odets was a formative influence on his father, who had driven him around Hollywood when he returned to the colony in the 1940s.[3] But the era in which Aldrich worked was completely different from the one that had witnessed Odets's theatrical successes. His films take a much less optimistic and more cynical view of the human experience than Odets's plays because of the changed historical circumstances.

Although recent critical studies are moving beyond unfairly stereotyping Odets as a "proletarian playwright" and are taking a broader understanding of his work, the influence of the Great Depression is still important. That era resulted in economic and psychological dislocation when it became clear that the old values were no longer relevant and something different had replaced them.[4] Odets's work does lend itself to artistic and psychobiographical interpretations.[5] But his achievements cannot be divorced from their historical context. Although his first three plays directly reflect the influence of the Great Depression, their yearnings for a socialist solution are often qualified by the fact that personal contradictions may defeat any utopian aspirations. Many contemporary critics condemned Odets for moving away from ideological considerations in later plays such as *Golden Boy* (1937). But Beth Fleischman critiques this accusation: "Actually, this charge has little validity; an examination of Odets's plays reveals that his basic theme, the struggle of the individual to maintain his integrity, remains constant, and that it is Odets's tone which undergoes change—from militancy to moderation."[6]

Born into a Philadelphian middle-class Jewish family, Odets suffered from an antagonistic relationship with his domineering father. Wishing to become an actor, he worked at several jobs in the theatrical world until he joined the Group Theatre in 1930. This body was one of the most creative influences on the American stage in the 1930s. Founded by Harold Clurman, Lee Strasberg, and Cheryl Crawford, the company operated as a collective. It attempted to produce plays reflecting progressive values in an attempt to change the surrounding society. Modeled on the theories of Konstantin Stanislavsky, the Group Theatre attempted to unite its actors into a single organism to reflect the values of the production rather than provide vehicles for individual star performances. Although contradictions existed between utopian ideals and personal dissensions echoing the dilemma of Nathaniel Hawthorne's *The Blithedale Romance,* the Group Theatre had a major impact in its era. It also provided a catalyst for the dramatic talents of the young Clifford Odets.[7]

Despite its eventual collapse, the Group Theatre was, as Irwin Shaw later commented to Clurman concerning the 1945 first edition of *The Fervent Years,* "a glorious crusade, not a funeral."[8] It appeared during a period that naturally led to artistic, personal, and political radicalization, in which many people, such as Odets, joined the Communist Party, seeing in it the only movement actively campaigning against the evils of the Great Depression. Furthermore, the 1930s reflected a similar spirit to that of the Weimar Republic before the emergence of Hitler. As Odets testified to the HUAC in 1952,

Literature was passed around, and in a time of great social unrest many people found themselves reaching out for new ideas, new ways of solving depressions or making a better living, fighting for one's rights. . . . The right to be steadily employed, for instance, I believe at that time there were perhaps fifteen or sixteen million unemployed people in the United States, and I myself was living on ten cents a day. . . . They were horrendous days that none of us would like to go through again. . . . [I] finally joined the Communist Party, in the belief in the honest and real belief, that this was some way out of the dilemma in which we found ourselves.[9]

Odets's membership lasted for the brief period of eight months. But it was less an act of dogmatic political commitment and more of a personal response to contemporary conditions. His first performed play, *Waiting for Lefty* (1935), was instantly hailed as a proletarian classic articulating the need for constructive social action. Ostensibly about a taxi driver strike, its hero never appears, and his murder occurs at the end of the play. *Waiting for Lefty* contains a series of brief vignettes emphasizing personal predicaments conditioned by the surrounding political context.

Set in a Union Assembly Hall, *Waiting for Lefty* uses the theatrical stage politically, with thespian union officials facing the audience. Actors playing union members are also strategically placed among the spectators. The play begins with union organizer Harry Fatt attempting to stop a taxi driver union strike. Everyone waits for the arrival of leader Lefty Costello. As one man argues for a strike, the stage lighting changes to introduce the second scene, where a husband and wife argue over economic deprivation. The husband listens to his wife's grievances and moves into action. He becomes the man who argues for the strike in the concluding scene of the play. The next scene features Miller, a former laboratory assistant in a poison gas company, now driving a taxi. He has been fired from his previous job for refusing to spy on his coworker and for hitting his boss.

Scene 3 features a young couple forced to separate because the girl's brother refuses to allow her to marry a poor taxi driver. This incident is a draft for a later scene in *Awake and Sing!* (1935) in which Ralph loses his girlfriend because of similar economic circumstances. "The Interne" scene features a victim of anti-Semitism in the medical profession who decides to remain in America as a taxi driver rather than move to Russia, whereas the final scene features a union member urging the others to strike immediately rather than wait for Lefty. We finally learn that Lefty has been murdered. The play ends with the men rising to their feet calling, "Strike!"

Although Odets's first play is political agitprop, it also deals with relevant personal issues caused by an oppressive social and historical background: "*Waiting for Lefty* asserts the right of every individual to have his share of human dignity. The villain in the play is not just capitalism, but any system or set of values which strips a man of his self-worth and destroys personal relationships."[10] It is a philosophy very close to the cinema of Robert Aldrich. Significantly, enough, the play ends with the lack of a hero and a call toward collective action on the part of both actors and audience members, who have observed several episodes depicting the devastation of human relationships in an inhumane situation. No hero is really needed. Perhaps this is why Aldrich often undermined the heroic image so entrenched within Hollywood cinema? The play concludes with an ideal: a call to collective action, needing no hero, which the audience may choose to follow. It is "too late the hero" but not too late for an audience to act collectively and attempt to change the system.

Awake and Sing! concentrates on the personal dynamics of a Jewish family trapped by the Great Depression both economically and psychologically. Taking its title from Isaiah 26.19, *Awake and Sing!* expresses the same type of optimism articulated in the concluding call to strike in *Waiting for Lefty*. But this time optimism is more qualified because of several conflicting and contradictory factors. The play also contains many themes occurring in Aldrich's cinema.

Awake and Sing! focuses on the Berger family. The father, Myron, has known nothing but failure in his personal and business life. But he never admits defeat and chooses to live in the past. His wife, Bessie, aims at preserving family unity despite the fact that instability rules. Like Ma Grissom of *The Grissom Gang* and Jane Hudson of *What Ever Happened to Baby Jane?* she resorts to force to keep her power over her family, as seen when she smashes Grandfather Jacob's collection of Caruso's music. Her act anticipates Mike Hammer's similarly callous action in *Kiss Me Deadly*. Bessie also forces her pregnant daughter Hennie into a loveless marriage with a man she deludes into thinking the baby is his. Her motivations involve family respectability, now irrelevant in the changing world of the 1930s. Bessie's actions cause nothing but misery for the entire family. Her son Ralph is a naive and romantic dreamer, constantly hoping for his chance "to get to first base." This line also foreshadows Aldrich's later cinematic use of sporting metaphors. But Ralph loses his girlfriend, Blanche, because of economic circumstances as well as his inability to act decisively. Uncle Morty is a businessman who has sold out to the system. Grandfather Jacob is a Marxist idealist who also lives in the past like his son Myron. Despite the activist nature of his political beliefs, he nostalgically lives in a dream world and constantly plays classical music like Carmen Trivago in *Kiss Me Deadly*. His only affirmative action in the play is ironic. Jacob commits suicide after urging Ralph toward some form of action, a path he has never been able to follow himself: "This . . . I tell you—Do! Do what is in your heart and carry in yourself a revolution. But you should act. Not like me. A man who had golden opportunities but drank instead a glass of tea."[11] Replace the "glass of tea" with a Hollywood contract and the world of Charlie Castle in *The Big Knife* is not too far away.

Jacob names Ralph as the beneficiary to his insurance policy and gives him the opportunity to break away from a dysfunctional family situation caused by the Great Depression. *Awake and Sing!* ends on a supposedly optimistic note with Ralph's speech: "I'm twenty-two and kickin'! I'll get along. Did Jake die for us to fight about nickels? NO! 'Awake and sing,' he said. Right here he stood and said it. The night he died, I saw it like a thunderbolt! I saw he was dead and I was born! I swear to God, I'm one week old! I want the whole city to hear it—fresh blood, arms. We got 'em. We're glad we're living."[12] This appears like a clarion call for personal and political action against both an oppressive family and the depression. However, despite the speech's affirmative nature involving the yearnings of a younger generation to escape from the past, several problems exist, calling into question these idealistic premises. First, Ralph is as romantic as his grandfather and may fall into the same trap of inactivity. His call to action may be merely a verbal act of self-gratification as futile as Jacob's library of Marxist texts, which never motivated the old man into any form of political activism. Furthermore, Jacob's suicide may really resemble the same type of nihilistic actions Aldrich later criticized when reflecting on the conclusion of *The Big Knife*. The other younger member of the Berger family, Hennie, also seeks some form of escape and runs away with a lodger and petty gangster, Moe Axelrod, who has lost a leg in the Great War. But Moe and Hennie run away to Cuba, which was then ruled by a ruthless political dictatorship.[13] Unlike Dr. Benjamin in *Waiting for Lefty*, Hennie takes the easy way out and does not remain in America to struggle for her rights as an individual. She also runs away with the most morally compromised character in the play.

As Fleischman points out, the conclusion of *Awake and Sing!* is really ambiguous. We have no real evidence that Ralph will have the courage to follow his convictions. He anticipates the ambivalent figure of Lt. Woodruff in *Attack!* Despite the Hays Code–imposed ending of him doing the right thing, we have no firm evidence to support this contention. The case of Ralph Berger is similar in many ways: "Additionally, Ralph's alleged transformation does not truly indicate that his life will be any different in the future. The audience is merely *told* Ralph has changed. His final speech is impassioned and seems full of conviction, but there is no proof that Ralph is now capable of action, nor is there any concrete suggestion of what he will do to improve his situation."[14]

Furthermore, both the older and younger members of the Berger family fall victim to the same types of self-deception dominating their elders. C. W. E. Bigsby suggests this when commenting on Hennie's abandonment of her family:

> The flouting of convention is offered as itself adequate evidence of rebellion, but it is difficult to sustain this interpretation given Hennie's weakness and her casual abandonment of her child, and given Moe's strategy of neutralizing the crude immorality of society with his own homeopathic corruption. Marx did not propose adultery as a solution for capitalism, nor the exchange of one failed capitalist paradise for another. But the confusion does not only operate in Odets's mind; it is endemic in the play.[15]

This confusion may be deliberate. Odets probably recognized that there are no easy answers or set formulas to any dilemma—a factor that Aldrich seized on and developed in his films. Also, as Harold Cantor notes, many delusive traps exist in the society Odets depicts, not the least of which is the illusionary escapism of a Hollywood system that dominates the dreams of several characters. *Awake and Sing!* develops the critique of Hollywood movies begun in *Waiting for Lefty* that continued throughout Odets's work. Both the older and younger members of the Berger family constantly refer to the dream machine, whether represented by the past world of silent cinema or 1930s Hollywood. Cantor points out that because the Hollywood dream remains out of reach, "the myths underscore the lack of progress for the young. For the old, however, they are comforting—proof that America is the land of opportunity and that the poverty in the streets is a temporary aberration."[16] The dark implications of these delusionary mechanisms culminate in *Clash by Night* and *The Big Knife*, as Cantor notes:

> Long before *The Hidden Persuaders*, Marshall McLuhan, and the Yippie media freaks, Odets was aware of the potent forces that could lure the common man into creating a fantasy life more real than real, and of the none-too-subtle manipulations by means of which the poor could be made to accept their status quo in the capitalist system. In *Clash by Night*, Joe Doyle denounces the use of media as an opiate: ". . . Earl, Jerry, Mae, millions like them, clinging to a goofy dream—expecting life to be a picnic. Who taught them that? Radio, songs, the movies—you're the greatest people going. Paradise is just around the corner. Shake that hip, swing that foot—we're on the Millionaire Express! Don't cultivate your plot of ground—tomorrow you might win a thousand acre farm! What farm? The dream farm!" (II.2).[17]

Awake and Sing! contains several motifs, such as the harmful nature of a dysfunctional family unit that wrecks human personality, that would later appear in Aldrich films, as in *Attack! Autumn Leaves, What Ever Happened to Baby Jane? Hush . . . Hush, Sweet Charlotte,* and *The Grissom Gang*. The redundancy of old ideals in a constantly changing, hostile environment exists in other films, such as *Apache, Kiss Me Deadly, The Big Knife, The Legend of Lylah Clare, Ulzana's Raid,* and *Twilight's Last Gleaming*. Using the legacy of Clifford Odets, Aldrich developed a cinema that would clash by night and day with the delusionary mechanisms of a system he was a part of and attempted to change. Both *Baby Jane* and *The Legend of Lylah Clare* contain damning indictments of the Hollywood machine, continuing the critiques begun by Odets.

Till the Day I Die (1935) is the last of Odets's explicitly political plays. It is also one of his weakest achievements in terms of durability. Dealing with the dilemma of a communist worker arrested by the

Nazis and then released to capture other members of the resistance, it is a schematic and stereotypical production. The play ends with the suicide of the leading character after he has pleaded in vain with his brother to kill him. *Till the Day I Die*'s conclusion also reveals Odets's fascination with a solution Aldrich later regarded as futile in terms of any serious struggle for personal and political survival.

Odets's fourth play, *Paradise Lost* (1935), features another family economically and psychologically damaged by the Great Depression. As in *Awake and Sing!* the unit is middle class rather than working class. Odets once commented that the hero of the play is "the entire middle class of liberal tendency."[18] It is this class that suffered most from the Great Depression because the values it put its trust in were catastrophically destroyed. Head of family Leo Gordon is a small businessman who designs handbags. His wife, Clara, finds fulfillment in her children, all of whom embody middle-class status symbols. Ben is a former Olympic hero, Julie is a bank clerk hoping for financial success, and Pearl is a classical pianist. Other characters outside the family are Leo's friend Gus, a failed businessman; his daughter Libby, who will marry Ben; Leo's unscrupulous business partner, Sam Katz; Ben's friend Kewpie, a small-time crook; and Mr. Pike, a casual worker representing the type of early-twentieth-century downwardly mobile American pioneer stock, familiar from novels such as Jack London's *The Valley of the Moon* (1913), who espouses Marxist ideals. All these characters symbolically embody the uneasy coexistence of American middle-class ideals with dark alternatives emerging from the Great Depression.

During the play the Gordons experience one crisis after another until they finally face eviction following the collapse of Leo's business. The family tragedy is personal and political. Leo discovers that Sam is little better than an embezzler. But despite the fact that it will lead to bankruptcy, Leo agrees to union demands for a living wage. Former Olympic hero Ben has a weak heart and is now unemployed. Succumbing to Kewpie's temptations to participate in a robbery, he is killed by the police. Although Julie has made a fortune on paper, she suffers from an incurable disease, whereas Pearl (like Ralph in *Awake and Sing!*) loses her lover for economic reasons because he has to go to another city and find a job. Although the play contains more pessimistic overtones than *Awake and Sing!* it also concludes with an optimistic speech. Despite his personal and professional collapse, Leo dreams about the future:

That was the past, but there is a future. Now we know. We dare to understand. Truly, truly, the past was a dream. But this is real! To know from this that something must be done. That is real. We searched; we were confused! But we searched, and now the search is ended. For the truth has found us. . . . Oh yes, I tell you the whole world is for men to possess. Heartbreak and terror are not the heritage of mankind! The world is beautiful. No fruit tree wears a lock and a key. Men will sing at their work, men will love. Ohhh, darling, the world is in its mourning . . . and *no man fights alone!*[19]

Leo's speech expresses a romantic optimism evoking those earlier visions of William Blake and William Morris, two creative talents who confronted the early ravages of industrialism, which would have more devastating effects in the twentieth century. But it also anticipates the false ideological optimism of Willie Loman in Arthur Miller's *Death of a Salesman*, who dies as a tragic victim of his false beliefs. The speech is double sided. It expresses hope for the future, but it is a hope as far from realization today as it was in the time of Blake and Morris.

If we read this speech as representing another false illusion by a character refusing to confront hard facts by disavowing the necessity for relevant action, then it would further link Aldrich's cinema to an influential predecessor. If so, Odets and Aldrich share a common perception of the false nature of a misleading ideology influencing the American psyche. Odets witnessed a depression that never resulted in a revolutionary change. Working in Hollywood a generation later, Aldrich was more cynical than Odets. But he also sounded a wake-up call to his audience by the very bleak and cynical nature of his apocalyptic, crisis cinema, influenced by the bleak nature of historical circumstances. Aldrich would never end his films with the optimistic finale characterizing several Odets plays. He realized how this formula would soon become incorporated into the Hollywood "happy ending" mechanism. However, Leo's lines— "Truly, truly, the past was a dream. But this is real!"—may also define Robert Aldrich's cinematic vision. It applies to both the consolations offered by religion and those New Deal visions destroyed by American right-wing reaction in the postwar era.

R. Baird Shulman sees parallels between *Paradise Lost* and the plays of Sean O'Casey, such as *Juno and the Paycock*. He also understands the connection between the personal apocalypse affecting the Gordon family and the historical context: "Odets is not for a moment

trying to imply that only *a* family is destroyed; indeed, a huge segment of society is being swallowed up—morally, economically, spiritually—in one of the most pervasive upheavals to occur in the
United States during its history. The author is concerned in *Paradise
Lost* with this all-encompassing social situation which he portrays
microcosmically through one very limited group of characters."[20]

After his first disappointing venture into Hollywood leading to a
screenplay for the inconsequential Lewis Milestone melodrama *The
General Died at Dawn* (1936), Odets both wrote and subsidized *Golden
Boy* for the Group Theatre in 1937. Developing several minor themes
in *Awake and Sing!* and *Paradise Lost* concerning the conflict between
artistic creativity and economic restrictions, Odets moved further
into the realm of personal tragedy. But relevant social factors indirectly influencing individual dilemmas are still present. *Golden Boy*
deals with Joe Bonaparte, the artistically talented son of an Italian
fruit vendor, who forsakes his potential career as a successful concert violinist to become a boxer. Treated as a commodity by his manager, Tom Moody, and gangster Eddie Fuselli, who buys a "piece of
him," Joe accidentally kills a black opponent, Chocolate Drop, in the
ring. He also injures his hand so that he can never play the violin
again. Realizing the nature of his tragic fall, Joe dies in a car crash
with Lorna, Tom Moody's girlfriend, whom he thinks he has fallen
in love with. *Golden Boy* never settles the question of Joe's death. It
may be suicidal or accidental. But Joe dies in a Deusenberg automo-
bile, a contemporary symbol of materialism and speed.

Odets wrote *Golden Boy* specifically for John Garfield. But Harold
Clurman overruled his choice by casting the more professionally experienced (if an unusual choice for a young boxer) Luther Adler in
the title role. Angered at this incident, Garfield then accepted a Hollywood contract, but he finally managed to play the title role ten
years later during a Broadway revival. He also lost out to William
Holden in the 1939 Columbia film version directed by Rouben
Mamoulian when Warner Bros. refused to loan him out for the role.

Like *The Big Knife*, *Golden Boy* reflects tensions between the loss of
personal integrity and material success, something close to the
hearts of both Odets and Garfield. Although less explicitly political
than his other plays, *Golden Boy* reflects the same concerns involving
sympathy for human beings caught by forces that pervert their personalities and trap them in deadly circumstances. *Golden Boy* would
become the basis for the Robert Rossen/Abraham Polonsky Enterprise Studio production *Body and Soul* (1947).

Rocket to the Moon (1938) suffered adverse criticism upon its initial production by critics condemning Odets for leaving his political roots to become a playwright totally concerned with subjective issues. However, Odets rejected charges that his play lacked substance by arguing that "the roots of love and the meaning of it in the present world need surely to be comprehended as much as the effect of a strike on its activists."[21] Despite its highly personal nature, *Rocket to the Moon* is a play owing as much to the surrounding context of the depression as Odets's earlier work. Social and political issues remain in the background, allowing the play to concentrate on personal dilemmas; but the depression still functions as an invisible Lacanian "structured absence" within the context of the play.

Timid dentist Ben Stark is dissatisfied with his personal and professional life. Married to a woman, Belle, little better than a domineering shrew, he experiences daily frustration because of his wife's refusal to allow him to risk his secure business by moving to a new location. Although no potential artist like Ralph, Pearl, and Joe Bonaparte, Ben experiences creative frustration resulting from an unsatisfactory marriage and the gargantuan nature of a Great Depression that has already destroyed many businesses. Cleo, a young naive girl seeking love and excitement, enters his life when she begins work as his secretary. The two begin an affair. But Ben has other rivals for Cleo, such as Mr. Prince, his father-in-law, who has suffered from an unhappy marriage, and Willy Wax, a philandering Broadway director. The three men represent different personal choices for Cleo. At the climax she rejects them all and decides to follow her individual path toward personal happiness. Ben loses Cleo because he cannot break away from his environment. But although he remains trapped within the same mundane set of circumstances depicted in the beginning of the play, he finally reaches some form of self-awareness: "For years I sat here, taking things for granted, my wife, everything. Then just for an hour my life was in a spotlight. . . . I saw everything, realized who and what I was. Isn't that a beginning? Isn't it?"[22]

This final note of revelation is ambiguous. With Cleo gone, it is doubtful whether Ben will ever again think of changing his personal and professional life. As for Charlie Castle in *The Big Knife* and General Lawrence Dell in *Twilight's Last Gleaming*, self-awareness has arrived too late. *Rocket to the Moon* is a tragedy of the depression. It depicts an inertia, passivity, and lack of personal growth suffocating any type of personal and social alternatives. The possibilities represented by the New Deal were only temporary. Right-wing reaction began to mobilize before Pearl Harbor occurred, and McCarthyism was only a decade away. As Gerald Weales notes, the very title of the play refers to taking chances, a movement depicted in the lines Mr. Prince says to Stark: "Why don't you suddenly ride away, an airplane, a boat! Take a rocket to the moon! Explode!"[23] But, as in _Awake and Sing!_ and _Paradise Lost,_ the decision is problematic and often determined by personal characteristics. Inertia cripples Ben's personality. Odets also depicts his heroine Cleo as hopelessly naive. Although she rejects three unsatisfactory suitors who represent different personal and social alternatives, there is no guarantee that she will ever achieve her dreams. The ideological grip of the depression may affect everyone. As Fleischman notes, "The failure of the Starks's marriage seems to be due as much to the Depression, thus undermining the ideological foundations of the play."[24] However, _Rocket to the Moon_ concentrates more on personal insecurities. Apathy and passivity characterized most Americans in this era, hindering any possibility of personal and social revolution succeeding. Ben, Belle, and Mr. Prince are also victims of dysfunctional family situations similar to characters in _Awake and Sing!_ and _Paradise Lost._ Ben's self-realization is questionable—he may also be seen as an older and sadly wiser version of Ralph Berger in _Awake and Sing!_

The Great Depression's malign influence on personal growth is also present in the play, as witnessed by two secondary characters, Phil and Frenchy. Phil's personal happiness and career have suffered as a result. He complains to Ben, "Who's got time to think about women! I'm trying to make a living!"[25] Chiropodist Frenchy muses about the conflict between personal happiness and the work ethic. He speaks lines relevant not just to Ben but also to most of Aldrich's future characters:

> FRENCHY: Love is no solution of life! Au contraire, as the Frenchman says—the opposite. _You have to bring a whole balanced normal life to love if you want it to go!_
> STARK: Yes, I see your point.
> FRENCHY: _In this day of stress I don't see much normal life._[26]

Night Music (1940) attempts to express personal optimism. Odets experimented with a different type of theatrical structure aiming at a tonal experience whereby text, performance, music, and sets collaborated in depicting a prevailing mood.[27] Using a "boy meets girl"

formula he previously avoided, Odets depicts the growing relationship between wisecracking movie employee Steve Takis and struggling young actress Fay Tucker. They meet on a Saturday and fall in
love by Monday at the play's conclusion. The action resembles similar events in Odets's later screenplay for Harold Clurman's *Deadline
at Dawn* (1946), even featuring a philosophical older man who acts
as mentor to the young couple.[28] The play was a commercial failure
and has never been successful in any revivals. This may be partly because of the superficial nature of the two leading characters as well
as an ambiguity surrounding the forces that influence their characters. Odets hints that Steve suffers from his search for a missing
mother whereas Fay experiences psychological malaise resulting
from the suffocating nature of her family. This time the depression
does not appear as an explicit element in the text. But for Clurman
the roots of the problems facing Steve and Fay were obvious. Odets
may have assumed that his audience would understand the
legacy of insecurity that the depression left on the American psyche: "The play stems from the basic sentiment that people nowadays are affected by a sense of insecurity; they are haunted by the
fear of impermanence in all their relationships; they are fundamentally *homeless,* and whether or not they know it, they are in search of
a home, of something real, secure, dependable in a slippery, noisy
and nervous world."[29]

Insecurity in a hostile universe also features in many Aldrich
films. Both Steve and Fay have associations with an entertainment
industry providing an illusionary escapist "haven from a heartless
world" during the depression. Steve and Fay's professional choices
conflict with the affirmative lines spoken to them by their dying
guardian angel, Lincoln Rosenberger: "I am in love with the possibilities, the human possibilities." *Night Music* suggests that the
worlds of mindless entertainment provided by most forms of cinema and theater will frustrate the type of possibility envisaged in
Rosenberger's utopian vision.

Taking its title from Matthew Arnold's poem "Dover Beach"
(1867), *Clash by Night* (1941) examines again the domestic family entrapment treated in *Awake and Sing!* and *Paradise Lost*. But this time
the ending is entirely bleak. *Clash by Night* depicts the stale marriage
of Jerry and Mae Wilenski and suggests that the future union of
young Joe and Peggy may be little better. The play presents 1941 as
a modern version of Arnold's "darkling plain" where no real hope

exists. Most critics see few connections between the sociological and psychological issues in this play. But they do exist. As in *Night Music,* the former operates as an offstage element determining the lives of individual characters. The world of the play is one where the cultural and social hopes of the New Deal are now in retreat. It is an environment in which "possibilities" are absent, giving ironic resonance to Arnold's line, "Where ignorant armies clash by night."

Despite contemporary criticisms, the play uses the device of an eternal triangle theme to good effect. *Clash by Night* is melodramatic, but it belongs to a melodramatic tradition in which the nature of the social environment indirectly affects personal dilemmas.[30] The various characters are trapped in a personal situation with little hope for the future. Bored by her marriage to the childlike Jerry, Mae begins an affair with his friend Earl that eventually leads to his murder. Earl is a projectionist whom Jerry ultimately murders in a projection booth during the showing of an escapist movie. *Clash by Night* continues Odets's critique of the negative effects of banal popular culture on the American people. Although this anticipates the 1950s attacks of highbrow critics against "masscult," David Cochran notes that similar critiques were made by many working within the underground culture of that time.[31] Cochran not only demolishes the deceptive premises of postmodernist critics who argue that *all* attacks against popular culture emerge from elitist representatives in society. He also documents the fact that talents working within the popular arena can also be criticizing the worst examples of that particular culture. It is also an approach common to both Aldrich and Odets.

Adrift from alternative political and cultural movements, the various characters of *Clash by Night* inhabit their own types of "darkling plain" and clash because of ignorance. Odets suggests that an American working-class society lulled into a sense of false security by the banality of certain types of popular culture may harbor forms of repressed violence resulting in fascism. Mae hums escapist songs such as "The Sheik of Araby" and "Avalon," whereas Earl's occupation promotes cinematic illusions. The failure of past traditions also occurs in the play. Jerry's Polish immigrant father, Joe, has never learned to speak English. He is constantly afraid that he will be deported back to Poland (a serious fear in 1941). Jerry's uncle Vince represents fascist elements within the American psyche. He is the one who pushes Jerry into killing Earl. Although Joe finally utters the same type of optimistic speech in the tradition of Ralph Berger of *Awake and Sing!* he also sees fascism lurking around the corner to take advantage of American disillusionment: "I see what happens when we wait for Paradise. Tricky Otto comes along, with a forelock and mustache. Then he tells them why they're blue. 'You've been wronged,' he says. 'They done you dirt. Now come along with me. Take orders, pack your brains, don't think, don't worry; poppa tucks you in at night!' And where does that end? in violence, destruction, cripples by the carload."[32]

Traumatic family relationships also affect Mae and Jerry. Mae constantly compares Jerry with her former lover, a big politician who gave her "confidence." This theme evokes the malignant dominance of the father over adult children such as Aldrich's future characters—Captain Cooney, Burt Hanson, Jane Hudson, and Charlotte Hollis. Jerry exhibits infantile behavior and has a definite mother fixation. When he learns of Mae's betrayal, he acts in a manner anticipating Captain Cooney's regressive behavior in *Attack!* "I can go sleep in poppa's room, if you don't wanna talk to me, momma, I mean Mae." The scene concludes with him embracing a teddy bear like a fetish object in the same way that Cooney clutches his slipper in *Attack! Clash by Night* also anticipates several important features in future Aldrich films.

The Big Knife (1949) contains autobiographical elements involving the Hollywood experiences of both Odets and John Garfield. The play contrasts the depression-era optimism of its leading figure, Charlie Castle, with his present position as a victim of the Hollywood machine. The play may be looked on as an unconscious sequel to *Golden Boy*. It deals with the final evolution of a character who has sold out his integrity at the altar of material success. But like *Clash by Night, The Big Knife* also recognizes that character flaws, as well as the influences of a corrupt society, can lead to destruction. Although *The Big Knife* was criticized as a self-serving Hollywood diatribe by two artists biting the hand that fed them, it is another example of Odets's exploration of psychological factors leading to personal and social entrapment. Despite Odets's personal and political vacillations, his work intuitively moves away from taking easy options, such as blaming everything on the surrounding social structure, toward considering a complex number of relevant factors. Society is influential, but other mechanisms are also present, such as internal psychological aspects making individuals their own jailers.

Such factors play a dominant role in *The Country Girl* (1950). Although the political aspect is entirely absent in this dramatic representation of theater life, Odets uses this new environment to develop his insights into the personal dilemmas he examines in his other plays. Like cinema, theater is an entertainment medium that can create deliberate illusions or "willful blindness."[33] Like *Clash by Night*, *The Country Girl* employs the romantic triangle theme but develops it in terms of the limited perspectives dominating the three protagonists, who are more privileged than the working-class characters of the earlier play. Theatrical producer Bernie Dodd wishes to stage a new play with former star Frank Elgin, now a hopeless alcoholic. He believes that Frank's wife, Georgie, is responsible for Frank's condition and attempts to restore his confidence so that he can return to the stage. However, as Weales points out, Bernie not only attempts to "fit Frank and Georgie into preconceived roles" but also engages in a "salvage operation" that has more to do with his own family situation than the reality he confronts: "Frank is Bernie's father all over again, the alcoholic he did not save from the subway wheels."[34]

The three major characters live lives of deliberate falsity, a fact emphasized by the play's theatrical setting. Frank performs the role of a happy man and refuses to admit that lack of confidence has made him an alcoholic. Although dependent on Georgie, he pretends that she is neurotic and blames her for his condition. But Georgie also lives a self-created lie. She believes that Frank is dependent on her and that she must protect him like a mother figure. Georgie often refers to herself as an "old lady," dresses up to resemble one, and behaves more like a mother than a wife. Bernie falls in love with Georgie, but because his dysfunctional family background influences his character, he may unconsciously re-create the role of the son in an old thespian melodrama hoping to displace the father and appropriate the mother.

By the end of the play all of the characters have reached some form of self-realization that may enable them to break away from their former damaging behavioral patterns. Frank recognizes the truth about himself and achieves his theatrical comeback. Georgie decides to remain with Frank and advises Bernie to "stay unregenerate. Life knocks the sauciness out of us soon enough."[35] However, the play qualifies its optimistic conclusion by recognizing that problems will still remain in the future. As Georgie tells Frank, "Neither of us has really changed. And yet I'm sure that both our lives are at some sort of turning point. There's some real new element of hope here—I don't know what. But I'm uncertain ... and you, Frank, have to be strong enough to bear that uncertainty."[36] Her speech echoes the Enterprise screenplays of Abraham Polonsky as well as Aldrich's later films, especially his Hollywood trilogy *The Big Knife, What Ever Happened to Baby Jane?* and *The Legend of Lylah Clare*, all of which deal with the dangerous nature of manufactured illusions and individual self-deceptions.

Following his humiliating appearance before HUAC, *The Flowering Peach* (1954) became Odets's last play. Although well received, it lost the Pulitzer Prize nomination to Tennessee Williams's *Cat on a Hot Tin Roof*. It is the playwright's adaptation of the Noah story and has both contemporary and classical relevance. Several contemporary critics regarded the ark as a symbol of the bomb shelter. Although this may not have been deliberate, we must remember that the atomic bomb cast an ominous shadow upon the American cultural landscape during the 1950s. Like the influence of the 1930s plays of Clifford Odets on the depression generation, the Bomb was inescapable in both politics and mass culture.[37] Aldrich's *Kiss Me Deadly* (1955) is one such example, as is the conclusion of *Sodom and Gomorrah*.

The Flowering Peach follows the well-known outlines of the biblical story but adapts its premises to contemporary times by using the theme of mass destruction as well as exploring the competing psychological mechanisms of various characters caught in the drama. Noah is an alcoholic patriarch accepting the will of God. His son Japheth challenges the dominance of a God of destruction and refuses to enter the ark until physical force is used. Father and son argue throughout the voyage. One of their differences involves using a rudder to steer the ark. The deterministic Noah refuses, believing strongly in God's will until he finally admits that God may accept human assistance in certain circumstances. His other sons, Shem and Ham, reflect the negative sides of both the biblical and the American dream. Like Uncle Morty and Moe of *Awake and Sing!* and Sam Katz and Kewpie of *Paradise Lost*, Shem is an opportunistic character who nearly sinks the ark by hoarding dried manure, which he intends to manufacture as briquettes in a postapocalyptic world. The Freudian implications are unmistakable, as well as Shem's cynical "business as usual" attitude. Ham is a playboy who lusts after Japheth's intended bride, Goldie. Noah's wife, Esther, tries to keep the peace among warring members of her family and dies of old age as a result. Odets thus extends the dysfunctional family themes he has explored in his earlier depression plays. *The Flowering Peach*'s dysfunctional family dynamics foreshadow the conflicts within Lot's family in *Sodom and Gomorrah*. But this time the Flood (or the Bomb) threatens human survival.

Noah changes during the course of the play from a rigid patriarch to a person accepting the different patterns of human behavior. When the ark lands on a mountaintop in April, the month of rebirth, Noah and Japheth have also changed and accept each other. Noah finds that love, rather than expecting blind obedience, is the best way to run his family; thus, Japheth becomes less rebellious. Noah's final speech also affirms the qualified optimism characteristic of most of Odets's plays: "Thank you, Lord, above, thank you. . . . But what I learned on this trip, dear God, you can't take away from me. To walk in humility, I learned. And listen, even to *myself* . . . and to speak softly, with the voices of consolation. Yes, I hear you, God— Now it's in man's hands to make or destroy the world."[38]

Odets died in 1963 after seeing his achievements overshadowed by the plays of Arthur Miller and Tennessee Williams.[39] By then he appeared to be a tarnished figure whose work was no longer relevant to the concerns of a new era. Yet, as Fleischman notes, although his dramatic techniques changed considerably throughout his career, his message always involved the dilemma of "the individual trying to maintain his sense of identity in the midst of an often hostile world" as well as exhibiting "a profound belief in the dignity of the human race."[40] These beliefs also influenced Abraham Polonsky and Robert Aldrich. Like Odets, they owed much to the cultural legacy of the 1930s articulated by Odets and others. For Aldrich working within the Hollywood studio system's "Big Knife," the legacy of Clifford Odets served as both inspiration and warning. It inspired his better efforts as a director but also warned him that the path was fraught with danger. Aldrich rejected the problematic optimism expressed in Odets's works because he knew that no easy solutions existed. He would not fall into the trap of the Great American idealistic Awakening that Bigsby sees as marring Odets's works:

The realist texture of Odets's work itself implies rejection—a rejection of fantasy and dream. His characters have to be weaned from their self-conceits, from the myths to which they pledge their lives, because, ostensibly at any rate, it is that tactile world which has to be reforged, shaped so as to contain the freedom they would claim. And yet there is a problem here for Odets insofar as he is himself a visionary. He rejects the myths with which society has sought to validate greed and self-concern, but wishes to endorse the potential sentimentality of love and to parade his own visionary ideals.[41]

Aldrich would emphasize rejection but avoid idealism. His pragmatic involvement in the battleground of the Hollywood film industry would shape his films much more strongly than Odets's temporary flirtation with the system. However, the playwright remained one of the most influential legacies on his work. Summing up the achievements of Clifford Odets, Harold Cantor makes some relevant comments that also intuitively apply to the work of Robert Aldrich:

> Odets's plays . . . are peopled by men and women filled with passion and loneliness, desperately reaching out for community. And if we read them correctly, we can see that far from being merely plays of social realism, they are poetic visions, purgatorial plays in which man struggles to achieve fulfillment against the sinister forces in American life. Nor should we read them for solutions to our social problems, remembering Hank's remark to Charlie Castle, 'I can't invent last-act curtains for a world that doesn't have one' (*The Big Knife*, III.1). Odets's plays, even those that end safely, are dramas of hopeful beginnings, in which men are brought to the threshold of wisdom by understanding themselves and their world.[42]

In Aldrich's cinema, sometimes they do. At other times, they do not. But the audience does have the opportunity of learning from the complex nature of the dilemmas faced by Aldrich's various characters and drawing relevant conclusions.

NOTES

1. See Beth Fleischman, "Clifford Odets," in *Twentieth Century Dramatists: Dictionary of Literary Biography*, vol. 7, ed. John McNicholas (Detroit: Gale Research Press, 1981), 137.

2. For one stimulating account of this period, see Jean Rouverol, *Refugees from Hollywood: A Journal of the Blacklist Years* (Albuquerque: University of New Mexico Press, 2000). In her opening chapter, the author makes these

pertinent comments: "The year was 1951. Our troubles had begun a few months before in January. No, that's not quite true. The seeds of our troubles had really begun in the midforties when the country's wartime alliance with the Soviet union had fallen apart and the Cold War had taken its place." She then mentions other factors, especially HUAC's goal "in discrediting the infant labor movement in the film industry" (*Refugees from Hollywood*, 1). Writing in the Cold War era, Group Theatre producer Harold Clurman believed that there was "considerable truth" in the idea that a "sharp reaction" set in with the death of Roosevelt. See Clurman, *The Fervent Years: The Story of the Group Theatre and the Thirties* (New York: Hill and Wang, 1957), 285.

3. William Aldrich, phone conversation, 20 February 2002.

4. The first part of one major historical study paints a grim picture of the beginning of the American depression and the inability of the Republican Party headed by President Herbert Hoover to understand this disastrous change in American history. See Arthur Schlesinger Jr., *The Age of Roosevelt: The Crisis of the Old Order* (Boston: Houghton Mifflin, 1957). In his autobiography Arthur Miller makes some relevant remarks concerning a masochistic disposition within the American psyche that prevented any revolution in society: "It has often been said that what kept the United States from revolution in the depths of the Great Depression was the readiness of Americans to blame themselves rather than the system for their downfall. A fine dusting of guilt fell upon the shoulders of the failed fathers, and for some unknown number of them there would never be a recovery of dignity and self-assurance, only an endless death-in-life down to the end" (*Timebends* [New York: Grove Press, 1987], 113). He then mentions the huge number of suicides in New York during the early 1930s. Miller also makes some other pertinent comments as he looks back in retrospect concerning the dark era of the late 1940s: "Ten, twenty, thirty years later it became clear that a good part of what drove this domestic campaign was a conscious decision first by a sector of the Republican Party, out of power for nearly two decades, to equate the basic New Deal ideas with disloyalty, and then by acquiescent Democrats to see the light. But at the time, to most people, it all had the feel of a natural phenomenon, an unstoppable earthquake rolling through the political landscape. Despite the Democrats' only spotty resistance to him, McCarthy would soon be calling the whole Roosevelt–Truman era 'twenty years of treason.' And indeed, by the eighties under Reagan, the structural supports of the New Deal had largely been repudiated even if they could not be totally dismantled without the country collapsing" (*Timebends*, 311). Similar comments could be made about the British experience under Thatcher and Blair.

5. See the excellent study by Margaret Brenman-Gibson, *Clifford Odets, American Playwright: The Years from 1906–1940* (New York: Athenaeum,

1981). Although influenced by the psychoanalytic work of Erik H. Erikson and fully aware of the playwright's character flaws as well as his dysfunctional family background, the author superbly relates Odets's work to its important historical context. See, for example, where Brenman-Gibson recognizes this factor in addition to the various personal factors influencing Odets (*Clifford Odets, American Playwright*, 248–49). She makes an interesting observation concerning Odets's final draft of *Awake and Sing!* in which its young protagonist, Ralph, struggles with both the personal problems of family life and the necessity for political action: "Equally apparent, however, in successive drafts—and in all of his subsequent work—is the deeper struggle born in his own family *but inseparable from the larger sweep of developing history*" (*Clifford Odets, American Playwright*, 249, emphasis added).

6. Fleischman, "Clifford Odets," 127.

7. For the key account of this movement, see Clurman, *The Fervent Years*. Gerald Weales comments on another influence that also has relevance to the teamwork effort on a Robert Aldrich film: "Perhaps more important than the ideational influence and one that he could have got only from the Group was the structural effect that organization had on his plays. Odets is one of the few American playwrights who did not fall automatically into the pattern which saw to it that a star part or parts dominated a scene with minor figures" (*Clifford Odets: Playwright* [New York: Pegasus, 1971], 32).

8. Clurman, *The Fervent Years*, ix.

9. Fleischman, "Clifford Odets," 127–28. Brenman-Gibson has a different interpretation of Odets's reasons for artistic and political involvement at this time. Influenced by Erik Erikson's psychoanalytical school, she makes the following comments: "At this point of his *personal* history, Odets' need for solutions to his economic and spiritual crises was being met by the Group Theatre. It is thus an irony that this playwright—to be celebrated as the 'dramatist of social protest of the thirties'—had less necessity to discover a political formula for changing the world than to discover a creative concept of theater that would elicit his profoundest talents" (*Clifford Odets, American Playwright*, 249). However, despite her comments concerning the "tacked-on quality of his self-conscious Marxist metaphor" in the various drafts leading to *Awake and Sing!* Brenman-Gibson cannot really avoid the existence of relevant historical influences, as her work actually reveals.

10. Fleischman, "Clifford Odets," 129. The conflict between Harry Fatt and Lefty may be read as a father–son contest rooted in the playwright's problematic relationship to his father. Commenting on Odets's identification of Fatt with capitalism, Brenman-Gibson notes that "while Odets's recently embraced Marxist ideology dictated this symbol, he is at the same time dramatizing once again the outer struggle between himself and his father and the inner one between the warring identity-elements" (*Clifford Odets, American Playwright*, 304). Such a conflict may result from a complex

number of personal and political factors, which are intertwined inextricably in the play and need not necessitate the dominant individualist Eriksonian interpretation that Brenman-Gibson employs. On the interplay between personal lives and collective action, see Michael J. Mendelsohn, *Clifford Odets: Humane Dramatist* (Deland, Fla.: Everett/Edwards, Inc., 1969), 22.

11. Clifford Odets, *Awake and Sing!* in *Waiting for Lefty and Other Plays* (New York: Grove Press, 1979), 78. C. W. E. Bigsby makes some relevant parallels between Odets's critique of inactivity in *Awake and Sing!* and Roosevelt's second inaugural speech, which stressed wiping out "the line that divides the practical from the ideal" (*"Awake and Sing!* and *Paradise Lost,"* in *Critical Studies on Clifford Odets,* ed. Gabriel Miller [Boston: G. K. Hall, 1991], 154). Jacob's suicide represents an "exemplary warning of the futility of a commitment and vision not rooted in practical action" (Bigsby, *"Awake and Sing!* and *Paradise Lost,"* 155). Comparing Jacob's self-deception with that of Willie Loman in *Death of a Salesman,* Bigsby also remarks that in both cases "the weakness lies as much in the individual, willfully self-blinding, vacillating, visionary without cogent perception, as it does in society" (*"Awake and Sing!* and *Paradise Lost,"* 156).

12. Odets, *Awake and Sing!* 100–1.

13. Citing Odets critic Gerald Weales, Fleischman ("Clifford Odets," 130) points out that the Cuban Tourist Commission promoted advertisements in American newspapers to assure American tourists that they would be safe in Cuba. Further, "the point of Hennie's action is that of emphasizing the moral chaos which Odets saw about him as a result of the depression and, by extension, of the capitalist system" (R. Baird Shuman, *Clifford Odets* [New York: Twayne, 1962], 61).

14. Fleischman, "Clifford Odets," 130. Shuman writes, "One cannot be sure that Ralph will be any more successful in attaining his ends than Jacob was, because Odets does not give one evidence that Ralph is a man of action, but rather suggests the contrary; he has shown some signs of being willing to rebel, but he demonstrates an inability to rebel in a situation so commonplace as that involving his relationship with Blanche, the young woman with whom he has fallen in love" (*Clifford Odets,* 60). Edward Murray notes that although Ralph will remain at home, he does show a potential for change because "his situation will not be the same as it had been with the family" (*Clifford Odets: The Thirties and After* [New York: Frederick Ungar, 1968], 40).

15. Bigsby *"Awake and Sing!* and *Paradise Lost,"* 158.

16. Harold Cantor, "The Family as Theme in Odets's Plays," in *Critical Essays on Clifford Odets,* ed. Gabriel Miller (Boston: G. K. Hall, 1991), 135. Cantor notes that Odets shows a strong concern with breaking out of the family trap. He also notices the dangerous nostalgia for a past world no longer tenable within American society as well as the deceptive lures of the mass me-

dia. His comments have several connections with many themes in Aldrich's films, such as *What Ever Happened to Baby Jane? Hush . . . Hush, Sweet Charlotte, The Flight of the Phoenix* (1965), and many others. Cantor writes: "Since the forces of the mass media and the pull of the past conjoin to seal the family trap, we may wonder what happens to those who remain and attempt no break-out . . . either they become hapless victims of social forces they cannot control or a kind of walking dead like Myron and Julie. But the analysis would be incomplete without noting still another Odetsian motif—that of mendacity and hypocrisy—which affects those who remain in the trap and motivates those who would flee. The Moloch-god of materialism corrodes the family's moral values, and each play usually contains a pivotal scene of deceit which shows the trap closing on an unanticipated victim" ("The Family as Theme in Odets's Plays," 137).

Shuman also notes the theme of "general fraud" existing in this play, whether it be characters living in the past, such as Jacob and Myron who still hero-worship Theodore Roosevelt, or following contemporary examples. He quotes Odets's comments from a contemporary *Time Magazine* interview where the playwright condemned "the Cinderella approach to life, the American success story." Shuman observes that the playwright's concern with these issues results in his emphasizing Hennie's interest in the movies, representing "her one easily obtainable means of escape" (*Clifford Odets*, 170). It is "the great American lie" (Shuman, *Clifford Odets*, 171). The dysfunctionally psychological nature of the family trap occurs throughout most of Odets's plays. See, e.g., Mendelsohn, *Clifford Odets*, 115–16; Murray, *Clifford Odets*, 45, 67, 84–85, 131–32.

17. Cantor, "The Family as Theme in Odets's Plays," 136. As Gabriel Miller notes, economics has now replaced the old gods of classical tragedy. But Odets's vision is never deterministic because he "concentrates not on the broad economic disaster of his time but on human reactions to the conditions they live under. If Odets's characters fail, he makes it clear that they have no one but themselves to blame for their plight. A character's own weakness or inability to act may prevent him from escaping or rising above his circumstances, but he is not allowed to claim external opposition for his excuse" (Miller, *Clifford Odets* [New York: Continuum, 1989], 36–37).

18. Quoted in Fleischman, "Clifford Odets," 131.

19. Clifford Odets, *Paradise Lost*, in *Waiting for Lefty and Other Plays* (New York: Grove Press, 1979), 229–30.

20. Shuman, *Clifford Odets*, 73. For comparisons between Odets's ear for New York language and Sean O'Casey's "ear for Irish rhythms," see Mendelsohn, *Clifford Odets*, 103.

21. Quoted in Fleischman, "Clifford Odets," 133.

22. Clifford Odets, *Rocket to the Moon*, in *Waiting for Lefty and Other Plays* (New York: Grove Press, 1979), 418.

23. Weales, *Clifford Odets*, 132. Brenman-Gibson points out that during a period when war seemed inevitable Odets was moving away from the simple solutions expressed in his earlier plays. However, despite changes in his perspective, the social angle still remained, as his notes for an abandoned play reveal: "I am not interested in portraying human nature—that is easy—but in portraying human nature as modified and conditioned by society and social conditions. It is the only way I set out to work. A character is a social type when I set out. On this foundation an individual appears" (in Brenman-Gibson, *Clifford Odets, American Playwright*, 495). Cantor also notes that "the strength of his [Odets's] plays lies in his portrait of the submerged and paralyzed American will" ("The Family as Theme in Odets's Plays," 134).

24. Fleischman, "Clifford Odets," 134. Another critic notes the deterministic nature of the society on relationships: "The marriage of Ben and Belle is presented as a product of the society they live in. Ben sees them as 'two machines counting up the petty cash,' and Prince says, 'She runs his life like a credit manager.' The implication is that for the Starks, as for the Bergers, the family is an economic unit and that social fact has made a tyrant of Belle, a younger, more frightened and more waspish Bessie" (Weales, *Clifford Odets*, 133).

25. Odets, *Rocket to the Moon*, 352.

26. Odets, *Rocket to the Moon*, 404, emphasis added.

27. Weales points out that "the Group had always worked for an effective ensemble, a total impression, and Mordecai Gorelik had been insisting that sets must contribute to a play's dramatic and ideational bridges between scenes, but in *Night Music*, design and music reached out as bridges between scenes" (*Clifford Odets*, 143). This practice resembles the type of overtonal cinematic experiment associated with Sergei Eisenstein and followed by others such as Michael Powell and Emeric Pressburger in *The Red Shoes* (1948) and *Tales of Hoffmann* (1951). These types of practices were also indebted to Soviet theatrical movements of the 1920s, which both Odets and Clurman were familiar with.

28. *Deadline at Dawn* resembles the problematic amalgamation of diverse talents, similar to Francois Truffaut's adaptation of Cornell Woolrich's *The Bride Wore Black* (1968) and *Mississippi Mermaid* (1969). Neither Odets nor Truffaut could appropriately render the dark paranoid world of Woolrich because of the very different nature of the creative personalities. On the nature of these adaptations, see the excellent biography by Francis M. Nevins, *Cornell Woolrich: First You Dream, Then You Die* (New York: Mysterious Press, 1982), 460–62, 482–85.

29. Harold Clurman, "Introduction," in *Night Music*, by Clifford Odets (New York: Random House, 1940), viii. For the gradual erasure of the various movements of the New Deal by reactionary politicians in the late 1930s, see also Michael Denning, *The Cultural Front: The Laboring of American Cul-*

ture in the Twentieth-Century (London: Verso, 1997), 45, 80, 104, 364–66. We must also remember that the HUAC began mobilizing at this time. Its activities were temporarily postponed by World War II. In his final chapter, "Farewell to the Thirties and Now—," Harold Clurman makes the following eloquent observations: "When Roosevelt's remedies had allayed the people's worst fears, reaction set in. Many who still sat in the saddle of power began to notice that the artists and intellectuals were clamoring that they wanted 'more' before they would sing songs of satisfaction. A new worry crept into the strong men's hearts. Too many writers, actors, teachers, professional people of all kinds, had taken to habits that might spell mischief. . . . Thus there arose malevolent allusions to 'Left' writers, 'foreign' ideas, 'un-American' ideals and other spurious epithets that serve to confound everyone so that the world may more easily be set back on the old anarchic path that people of power find normal and pleasant" (*The Fervent Years*, 271).

30. See Peter Brooks, *The Melodramatic Imagination: Balzac, Henry James, Melodrama and the Mode of Excess* (New Haven: Yale University Press, 1976), and other relevant studies. For a cinematic context, see, e.g., Jack Bratton, Jim Cook, and Christine Gledhill, eds., *Melodrama: Stage, Picture, Screen* (London: British Film Institute, 1994).

31. See David Cochran, *America Noir: Underground Writers and Filmmakers of the Postwar Era* (Washington, D.C.: Smithsonian Institution Press, 2000), 1–15. Cochran also espouses the critical aspect of modernism, a feature ignored by so-called postmodernist critics who believe that modernism is dead. For an early critique of this attitude by one of the most stimulating defenders of the modernist heritage, see Marshall Berman, *All that Is Solid Melts into Air: The Experience of Modernity* (New York: Simon & Schuster, 1982), 33–34, 351n24. Frank R. Cunningham has also explored the modernist elements in Odets's plays and notes connections between the earlier and later works that contemporary critics neglected. Recognizing the modernist heritage of historical discontinuity, Cunningham comments that "the dramas from *Waiting for Lefty* (1935) through *Rocket to the Moon* (1938) manifest technical attributes of the modernist style, emphasizing the dynamic, the fragmentary, and the subjective, with which the two conceptual faces of modernism are also evident in *Night Music* and *Clash by Night*" ("*Night Music* and *Clash by Night*: Clifford Odets and Two Faces of Modernism," in *Critical Essays on Clifford Odets*, ed. Gabriel Miller [Boston: G. K. Hall, 1991], 228). Seeing these two later plays as exhibiting modernist concepts of both permanence and confusion, Cunningham also notes key features of the psychoanalytic aspects of conflict and suffering affecting the major characters in these plays: "In his wistful romance *Night Music* and in the following dark psychological tragedy *Clash by Night* (1942), the dramatist reveals in theme and form a continuing awareness of

the twentieth century as a fragmented, inconclusive time in which people endeavor to resist the period's institutionalization and dehumanization, searching for meaning and coherence in an attempt to replace the vanished stabilities and consistencies of the past" ("*Night Music* and *Clash by Night,*"229).

As Michael Denning points out, the 1930s witnessed an explosion of modernism within many diverse forms of representation, not the least of which was a proletarian avant-garde (see *The Cultural Front,* 27–29, 64–67, 118–23, 242–43, 287–88). One of the many devices employed by talents in this era was melodrama, a genre employed both in *Clash by Night* and by Aldrich in *Autumn Leaves, What Ever Happened to Baby Jane? Hush . . . Hush, Sweet Charlotte,* and *The Killing of Sister George* (1968). Denning points out that 1930s ghetto pastoral writers often adopted "the crime stories of the popular thriller, to lay a melodramatic plot over the sketches of everyday life" (*The Cultural Front,* 243).

Gabriel Miller intuitively recognizes the dynamic nature of Odets's modernism in his early plays, which "vividly re-create the parameters of the social world his characters inhabit, articulating in dialogue—unsurpassed in the naturalism of its tone, texture, and rhythm—the tensions produced in the individual who harbors within himself the impulses and energies of that world's competitive materialism and social injustice" (*Clifford Odets,* 14). This social message is crucial to understanding the type of modernism employed by Odets, Polonsky, and Aldrich in their various works. Miller also quotes from Harold Clurman's obituary essay on Odets: "His central theme was the difficulty of attaining maturity in a world where money as a token of success and status plays so dominant a role" (*Clifford Odets,* 14).

32. Quoted in Fleischman, "Clifford Odets," 135.

33. Weales, *Clifford Odets,* 171.

34. Weales, *Clifford Odets,* 171. Murray sees Frank Elgin as Odets's projection of "an accurate portrait of an orally regressed neurotic" (*Clifford Odets,* 197). Like Captain Cooney of *Attack!* and the title character of *What Ever Happened to Baby Jane?* he substitutes the bottle for the breast. Murray also notices "a strong element of latent homosexuality in Bernie's attitude toward Frank," which also echoes features contained in *Golden Boy* and *Clash by Night* concerning Joe Bonaparte and Eddie Fuselli, and Jerry and Earle (*Clifford Odets,* 67–68, 150, 194).

35. Clifford Odets, *The Country Girl* (New York: Viking Press, 1951), 124.

36. Odets, *The Country Girl,* 122.

37. See, e.g., Mark Osteen, "The Big Secret: Film Noir and Nuclear Fear," *Journal of Popular Film and Television* 22, no. 2 (1994): 79–90. Noting his emphasis on humility and avoiding self-deception and easy answers by listening to oneself, Weales points out the playwright's legacy to a future generation far removed from the political commitments of the depression era:

"Obviously, Noah's Flood is a workable image for potential atomic destruction. Such a reading of the play is sanctioned by Rachel's 'There is idealism now in just survival,' a line that finds its dramatic context in the fact that Japheth and Noah, idealists both, work for survival, finally at the cost of principle" (*Clifford Odets,* 178).

Gabriel Miller also makes several salient observations about the play: "The earth is suffering from a heat wave; the drought motif recalls at once *Rocket to the Moon* and *Clash by Night,* but the world of this play is on the verge of actual destruction, and the rain that is to come will eradicate rather than revive it. Clearly this theme of destruction was intended as an allusion to the dropping of the atomic bomb, the Flood being an entirely appropriate image for what had happened in Odets's world a few years earlier" (*"The Flowering Peach,"* in *Critical Studies on Clifford Odets,* ed. Gabriel Miller [Boston: G. K. Hall, 1991], 252).

38. Quoted in Fleischman, "Clifford Odets," 138.

39. However, in many ways Odets paved the way for his successors, as Harold Clurman has noted: "The outstanding new playwrights of the thirties were Lillian Hellman and Clifford Odets. . . . In the late forties Arthur Miller and Tennessee Williams emerged; men who kept alive—this is particularly true of Miller—some of the impassioned social conscience of the thirties" (*The Fervent Years,* 281). For Arthur Miller's reactions to the work and persona of Clifford Odets, whom he regarded as an "American romantic," see Miller, *Timebends,* 227–43. Speaking of 1930s playwrights, he states that "there were no Americans who seemed to be working a vein related to what I had come to sense was mine, except for Odets," whom he compares with Eugene O'Neill in being "playwrights of political consequence, not merely theatrical talents" (*Timebends,* 227–28, 232). For Odets's influence on Miller, William Gibson, Lorraine Hansberry, and others, see Mendelsohn, *Clifford Odets,* 107.

40. Fleischman, "Clifford Odets," 138. The screenplays of Clifford Odets deserve further study, especially *None but the Lonely Heart* (1944) and *Sweet Smell of Success* (1957). Even his screenplay for one of the better Elvis Presley films, *Wild in the Country* (1961), contains suggestions that the love between the younger man and older woman (Hope Lange) may contain dark aspects of the familial relationships found in his plays. In *The Story on Page One* (1960), which Odets both wrote and directed, one character played by Gig Young is a lonely widower still dominated by his mother at the age of thirty-five! Does this character represent the origins of Victor Buono's Edwin Flagg in *What Ever Happened to Baby Jane?* a role originally intended for Peter Lawford? There may be further gems awaiting discovery in future analyses of Odets's screenplays such as *Wild in the Country.* As James Goodwin notes: "That Odets was credited as screenwriter astounded film reviewers. But the storyline and dialogue exhibit, in an extreme form, characteristics to be found even in the best of Odets's work. The premise that a

backwoods juvenile delinquent is destined to become a world-famous novelist is not, finally, any more exaggerated than the connections between the fight arena and the concert stage in *Golden Boy*" ("Clifford Odets," in *Dictionary of Literary Biography,* vol. 26: *American Screenwriters,* ed. Robert E. Monsberger, Stephen O. Lesser, and Randall Clark [Detroit: Gale Research Co., 1984], 239). Weales also notes that Jean Renoir and Richard Boone tempted Odets into writing for television at the end of his life for a production that resembled a "distant mass-media echo of the Group Theater" (*Clifford Odets,* 184). Toward the end of his life Odets's remarks in a *Time* interview unconsciously anticipated the future work of director George A. Romero: "We don't know who the enemy is with a capital E. This is a frightening thing. Who gives a goddam about moon shots when you see zombies walking around with lost souls?" (quoted in Murray, *Clifford Odets,* 101).

41. Bigsby, "*Awake and Sing!* and *Paradise Lost,*" 163. Murray argues that "in his best work Odets manages to project both the horror and faith that characterized the 'vision' of the thirties" (*Clifford Odets,* 22).

42. Harold Cantor, *Clifford Odets: Playwright, Poet,* 2d ed. (Metuchen, N.J.: Scarecrow Press, 2000), 177. For Weales, Odets always believed in the power of human possibility, hoping that some of his characters would "reach the moment of change, of recognition that will allow the play to look into a better future" (*Clifford Odets,* 188). For Aldrich this optimism was always qualified by whatever circumstances challenged his protagonists.

TWO

ENTERPRISE AND AFTER

Before directing his first film in 1953, Robert Aldrich underwent a long period of apprenticeship in the American studio system, which benefited him enormously. Upon leaving college in 1941, he was hired at RKO as a production clerk, a position little better than a gofer. From that point on, Aldrich worked his way up the ladder, refusing any easy advantages that his family connections could have given him, until, as Arnold and Miller state, "he obtained such a thorough knowledge of both the art and mechanics of film, and that accounted, in part for his appreciation and consideration for the crew on his set."[1] The testimonials made at his memorial service, especially from the latter group of people, are eloquent enough in terms of the latter factor. From 1943 to 1945, Aldrich worked on a number of assignments, such as two-reel comedies and the "Music Master" Series, as well as several different films made by various studios such as United Artists, Columbia, and Paramount, giving him the opportunity to see directors as varied as Jean Renoir and William Wellman in action.[2] He learned the importance of the atmospheric effects of location shooting when working as assistant director on Renoir's *The Southerner* (1945); the rehearsal of action scenes from William Wellman and Lewis Milestone on *The Story of G.I. Joe* (1946), *The Strange Lover of Martha Ivers* (1946), and *Arch of Triumph* (1948); the visual empathy that must exist between camera and audience from Charlie Chaplin on *Limelight* (1952); and the importance of communicating with actors from his work with Joseph Losey on *M* and *The Prowler* (both 1951).[3] Aldrich's most formative experience arose from his apprenticeship with Enterprise Studios during 1946–48. He not only acquired experience in the roles of assistant director, unit production head, and studio manager but also assisted on key productions such as *Body and Soul* and *Force of Evil* in collaboration with talents such as John Garfield and Abraham

Polonsky. His association with Joseph Losey also represented another formative social context that would appear in Aldrich's own
work as director.

Several critics have already emphasized the important influence
of Enterprise on Robert Aldrich, citing the work of Allan Eyles in
this area.[4] But the studio had many points of contact, not only in
terms of its attempt to maintain the goals of the Cultural Front
movement in a period of developing historical reaction but also in
its associations with the philosophy and practices of the artistic
ideals of the Group Theatre and other bodies. In its short-lived existence Enterprise did attempt to make films criticizing the state of
American society and hoping for radical change in much the same
manner as the Group Theatre and the developing wave of new playwrights such as Arthur Miller and Tennessee Williams. It is important to see this studio against the background of these historical and
cultural associations.

Talents such as John Garfield, Art Smith, and Abraham Polonsky
were all products of the proletarian avant-garde modernism that
characterized the Cultural Front. Like Clifford Odets, Garfield had
gone to Hollywood but became dissatisfied with the limited opportunities for extending his talent that Warner Bros. offered him. However, both Odets and Garfield were attracted by the possibilities that
film offered in establishing a wider audience for the type of socially
conscious work that they had performed on the stage. But they
knew full well the nature of the oppressive system that confronted
them, a beast defined metaphorically by Odets's 1949 play *The Big
Knife,* which featured John Garfield. Although plays such as *Awake
and Sing!* and *Clash by Night* show that Odets was fully aware of the
dangerous nature of Hollywood ideology, he also recognized that
cinema contained important possibilities for promoting social messages. As Gerald Weales notes:

> Yet the technical quality, the size of the audience, the possibility of say-
> ing something significant, socially or artistically—these always at-
> tracted [Odets]. Beginning with his first trip to Hollywood, he offered
> interviews praising and blaming the industry, the relative weight of
> praise or blame depending on whether he was arriving or leaving, be-
> ginning a new film that interested him or running home to the stage.
> There is a large helping of rationalization in all those interviews, but
> there is truth too.[5]

Irwin Shaw's definition of the Group Theatre as a "glorious crusade" reflects the company's ideas. As Harold Clurman has stated, the company idea was not exclusively a "Left theatre movement but rather a 'theatre of the united front'—that is a theatre with a wide appeal to all the best elements in our society, regardless of political sympathies."[6] Eschewing the star system and repertory revivals, the Group Theatre operated as a collective that attempted to reflect the spiritual ideals motivating many living in the grim decade of the depression. This spirit was less political and more utopian, as Clurman would define it in his final chapter, "Farewell to the Thirties and Now—":

> The objective of all our creative forces must be—what it always was— to make man's hands work in conformity with the movement of his free spirit, to make his active life the reflection of his noble dreams, to make the deeds of all his days rise from the springs of his love. The tragedy of modern life is the forced separation and contradiction between the "way of the world" and the "way of man" between the power motif of our external machinations and the love motif of our subjective desire.[7]

This was an "Awake and Sing" ideal fully aware of the corrosive effects of a dehumanizing system on individual personality as well as the crucial fact that isolated individualism is both damaging and impossible. Clurman defines a utopian ideal that must also have motivated those attempting to change Hollywood as well as Broadway: "The theatre, to be fully understood and appreciated, must be seen as a manifestation of the process of interchange between society and the individual. It must be judged as a continuous development of groups of individuals within society, a development which becomes richer, acquires greater force and value as it grows within the society in which it originates. Only in this way can the theatre nourish us."[8]

This mood, which undoubtedly reflected many of the feelings of those who worked in Enterprise Studios, is also summed up by Arthur Miller. Looking back at previous decades, Miller comments that "the playwright's challenge was to please not a small sensitized supporting clique but an audience representing, more or less all of America."[9] He also affirms the work of Tennessee Williams, whom he does not regard as an isolated aesthete but, rather, as someone expressing "a radical politics of the soul."[10] Significantly enough, Clurman regarded both Miller and Williams as responsible for keeping alive "some of the impassioned social conscience of the thirties."[11] This evaluation of Williams by both Clurman and Miller may possibly explain Aldrich's sympathies toward minorities, especially lesbians, in his films. *The Killing of Sister George* (1968) may not be as exploitative and sensationalist as several critics believe.[12]

Speaking about the necessity of a play to reach beyond the converted, Miller makes the following comment:

> For a play to do that it had to reach precisely those who accepted everything as it was; great drama is great questions or it is nothing but technique. I could not imagine a theatre worth my time that did not want to change the world, any more than a creative scientist could wish to prove the validity of everything that is already known. I knew only one other writer with the same approach, even if he surrounded his work with a far different aura. This was Tennessee Williams.[13]

These statements are not intended to assert a direct connection between the world of the theater and Enterprise Studios (and, by implication, Robert Aldrich). They are merely designed to show that all these personalities were influenced by contemporary ideals that were part of the cultural currency of their era. Although not overtly political, Williams's plays cannot be read in isolation from the developing Cold War homophobia that would grip American society in the late 1940s and 1950s.

Significantly enough, Miller had worked uncredited on the original screenplay of *The Story of G.I. Joe.* Much of his work in a film dealing with the sacrifices on the battlefront must have led him to his critique of "the selfishness, cheating and economic rapacity on the homefront" in *All My Sons.*[14] The destruction of the human spirit by the system in *Death of A Salesman* also appears in *The Big Knife* as well as Odets's 1930s plays. Miller's theatrical utopian ideals expressed in *Timebends* also apply to those who attempt to use cinema for positive ends. He comments that the "real theatre—as opposed to the sequestered academic one—is always straining at the inbuilt inertia of a society that always wants to deny change and the pain it necessarily involves. But it is in this effort that the musculature of important work is developed."[15] Arguing against the idea that a renaissance occurred in the American theater of the 1940s, Miller comments that "there was a certain balance within the audience—a balance, one might call it, between the alienated and the conformists—that gave sufficient support to the naked cry of the heart and, simultaneously, enough resistance to force it into a rhetoric that at one stroke could be broadly understandable and yet faithful to the pain that had pressed the author to speak."[16]

Such issues of balance would occupy Robert Aldrich throughout his career, as his comments concerning the ways in which audiences read certain films such as *Attack!* and *The Dirty Dozen* in his Directors Guild of America lecture show.[17] For Aldrich, these films were not merely entertainment because they contain elements attacking the status quo. He always hoped that the conformist elements within his audiences would see the light, become appropriately alienated, and "awake and sing" in their own ways. These issues also involved key personnel at Enterprise Studios and, in particular, Abraham Lincoln Polonsky, who would soon be named the "most dangerous man in America."[18]

As several critics have noticed, *Body and Soul* belongs to a group of films that Paul Buhle and Dave Wagner define as "the culmination of the Depression generation's struggle to emancipate American dramatic art from the film corporations' control. From the perspective of the generation that surveyed the wreckage of the McCarthy era well into the 1960s, they would be among the last examples of the classic American film making that could compare, on its own terms and within its own traditions, to the best of the new international cinema."[19] If Buhle and Wagner see Enterprise Studios as the real beginning of Abraham Polonsky's "cinematic story," the same is also true for Robert Aldrich, who worked as assistant director on *Body and Soul.*

Body and Soul was originally intended to be a biopic about middleweight professional boxer and Jewish war veteran Barney Ross, who had been arrested on a charge of drug possession shortly before production began. Wary of the profitability of boxing movies, Enterprise executive Charles Einfeld gleefully saw this as an excuse to end a project he had doubts about.[20] But John Garfield, Bob Roberts, and Robert Rossen wanted to continue. According to Polonsky, he had to come up with an idea on very short notice when he had decided to return to New York. According to him, he conceived the fundamental premises of *Body and Soul* while walking the two blocks that separated the offices of Paramount and Enterprise Studios. As he put it, "I know all about that Clifford Odets stuff."[21] The idea was to rework *Golden Boy* into a film that would tell a romantic story as well as make a social comment. Polonsky also commended himself on Garfield's later return to the New York stage to appear in the title role of a play originally written for him by Odets: "He was very good, as he would be, having already played it in my picture!"[22] Despite Polonsky's later opinion of the film as "a fable of the empire city" and its associations with Warner Brothers 1930s social conscience movies, *Body and Soul* has many positive features.[23] It was the only Enterprise Studios film to make a profit featuring elements common to the progressive visions shared by both Polonsky and Aldrich in his later work as a director. The question of the ending is a good example of such elements.

Originally director Robert Rossen wanted the film to end with the death of its hero, who ends up gunned down in an alley with his head in a trash can after defying the mob's order to throw his fight. Polonsky claimed that this was not in his original screenplay and took his case to producer Roberts and star Garfield. Both endings were shot and previewed, with Polonsky winning his case.[24] Despite Robert Aldrich's later reservations concerning Polonsky's interference on the set (obviously reflecting his perspective on the importance of the director's role) and objections by critics such as Robert Sklar, the current ending of *Body and Soul* is appropriate for the film as it stands today.[25] Rossen's perspective is far more cynical and pessimistic than the vision shared by both Aldrich and Polonsky. Both men were realists who looked at disturbing facts directly and never engaged in naive escapism. But they also shared a common vision of progressive possibility that might exist even in the most grim circumstances. Even if Charley Davis dies the next day, he has gained a temporary victory and achieved a sense of moral redemption far more important than the fact of his continuing survival. Cutting Charley down at the exact moment of his triumph would be too nihilistic. The entire construction of *Body and Soul* denies any validity for Rossen's cynical conclusion. Furthermore, although Polonsky borrowed from *Golden Boy*, he creatively reworked its premises both stylistically and thematically. During a 1969 interview he remarked that his films never employed the naturalist style associated with Odets. Rather, they were "very classical" in nature.[26] He elsewhere commented that *Tell Them Willie Boy Is Here* has more in common with *Body and Soul* than with *Force of Evil*, which he regarded as a modern realistic film. For Polonsky,

Body and Soul was "a fairy tale, a myth of the streets of New York, just as *Willie Boy* is a myth, a parable."[27]

Some comments are necessary at this point concerning Polonsky's understanding of myth. The concept is usually associated with illusion and false consciousness, elements that have been particularly prominent in American culture (and elsewhere!) from its very beginnings, as the work of Richard Slotkin demonstrates.[28] In the final chapter of *Gunfighter Nation* Slotkin interrogates the crisis of public myth in American society. He argues that rather than discarding myth itself, a democratic community should be aware of the shifting parameters of the concept and move toward a more inclusive definition that is not dominated by "the imperatives of the commercial corporation or the preferences of a managerial or proprietary elite."[29] Slotkin argues for a more oppositional use of myths, especially those based on the narratives of resistant communities as well as those present in certain sections of the mass-culture industries. Fully aware of the existence of a broader mythic definition of an American nation, representing the best example of an imaginative community encompassing inclusiveness and progressive movements, Slotkin concludes his work with a rallying call for cultural activity:

> Myth is not only something *given* but something *made*, a product of human labor, one of the tools with which human beings do the work of making culture and society. The discourses of myth are, and have been, medium as well as message: instruments of linguistic and ideological creativity as well as a constraining grammar of codified memories and beliefs. We can use that instrument to reify our nostalgia for a falsely idealized past—to imagine the nation as a monstrously overgrown Disneyworld or Sturbridge Village—or we can make mythic discourse one of the many ways we have of imagining and speaking truth. By our way of remembering, retelling, and reimagining "America," we too engage myths with history and thus initiate the process by which our culture is steadily revised and transformed.[30]

It is this type of activity that Polonsky and others attempted in the late 1940s, an activity that reactionary forces, which had curtailed the cultural work of the New Deal a decade before, were fully aware of. Without the distraction of a world war, they used the developing Cold War paranoia to continue their work to crush any dissident political and cultural force. *Body and Soul* must be viewed as a legacy of the ideals of the depression era in its attempt to formulate a new inclusive national myth within Hollywood conventions. It uses the conventions of the Warner Bros. social consciousness movies and the boxing movie genre to formulate a different type of cultural front. Red-baiting commentators such as Ed Sullivan were fully aware of what they were dealing with at this time.[31]

Body and Soul opens with a long shot of a deserted training camp at night. A punching bag swings in the wind, creating a shadow on the canvas.[32] This object is employed in the beginning of the film and is returned to at the end of Charley's flashback; its full significance will finally become understood by an audience that will receive relevant background knowledge later in the film. Polonsky uses the familiar flashback film noir convention in a significantly intellectual manner. This device represents a particular artistic type of cinematic experimentation within the Hollywood system that would soon be brutally curtailed. James Wong Howe's camera then cranes up a tree, moves to a verandah, and views Charley (John Garfield) from an overhead exterior shot lying on a bed and framed by window bars. The camera cuts to a close-up as he wakes up from a nightmare calling, "Ben. Ben." This abrupt close-up represents a shock effect in more than one way. As Buhle and Wagner note, the "scarred and swollen face" we see is "John Garfield's, shriven of its 1930s optimism and possessed now of a postwar familiarity with death."[33]

The tormented fighter gets into his car and drives to New York. Attempting to appeal to an alienated mother (Ann Revere) and girlfriend Peg (Lilli Palmer), he ends up at a nightclub at 3:00 a.m. for bodily comfort from Alice (Hazel Brooks), who represents a vulgar femme fatale noir version of Lauren Bacall.[34] The following morning during the weigh-in, Charley's competitor, Texan Jackie Marlowe, taunts him—"Nightclub fat. Whisky fat. Thirty-five year fat"—before another remark provokes Charley into hitting him. Although Marlowe's manager cynically apologizes—"I'm in charge of the muscles, not the brain"—his remarks also apply to Charley, who has divorced body and soul for the sake of material gain. Later that night, shady businessman promoter Roberts (Lloyd Goff) articulates the moral universe within the nightmare world that has trapped Charley: "The books are all balanced. The bets are all in." He then attempts to banish the last vestiges of conscience Charley has: "You still thinking about Ben, Charley? Everybody dies. Ben, Shorty, even you." Roberts's henchman Quinn (William Conrad) then steps in as chorus: "You've got to be businesslike, Charley, and businessmen have to keep their agreements." Roberts concludes with the statement, "Everything is addition and subtraction. The rest is conversation."

Charley orders Quinn outside and lies down before the fight. The camera angle changes to an overhead shot as Charley's repeated voice-over dominates the soundtrack—"Everything down the drain"—before the image blurs into flashback. These opening scenes are significant not just in articulating the parallels between the business and criminal world emphasized throughout the film but also in stressing the commodified object that Charley's body has become. We also hear an echo of the yet-unseen Ben in Roberts's speech, which counterpoints the cry awakening Charley from his nightmare. For Roberts, death represents the final elimination. Nothing has any significance beyond addition and subtraction. The rest is just empty "conversation." *Body and Soul* will move toward rebutting this nihilistic philosophy on its own realistic and nonidealistic terms.

Despite Charley's individual anguish, the film will reveal that he is not alone in his dilemma. Although he is the nominal hero, his plight is not unique but, in fact, echoes the problems of others existing in his own society.[35] The opening scene of the flashback reveals Peg exhibiting herself as a bodily commodity for $25.00 a night at a Democratic fundraising party for the media-conscious Jack Shelton (Ed Begley), campaigning for city alderman during the late 1920s. Peg is fully aware of her performative role, as she later comments: "I get $25 and the crowd get to whistle." She first meets Charley there accompanied by his friend Shorty (Joseph Pevney). Now downwardly mobile, European-educated Peg is working her way through art school hoping to become a major artist.[36] She later becomes a fashion designer in a world where artistry pays no dividends, as Joe Bonaparte recognizes in *Golden Boy*. However, like Mrs. Davis, Peg represents the values of honesty and integrity in a deceitful world. When Charley announces, "I want to be a success," she replies, "You mean you want other people to think you're a success." The naive Charley replies, "Sure. Every man for himself." Charley will never understand Peg's values until it is nearly too late, especially her quotations from William Blake's "The Tyger" ("Tyger! Tyger! burning bright . . . ") a poem by one of the earliest protestors against the dehumanizing nature of industrial society.

As played by Group Theatre veteran Art Smith and future black-listee Ann Revere, Charley's parents are Jewish immigrants who hold fast to the moral values of the old society in a different urban environment. When Mr. Davis accidentally dies during a speakeasy bombing, Mrs. Davis attempts to take out a loan to send her son to college during the beginning of the Great Depression. But Charley's anger at the social worker who arrives one night to begin a means test of Mrs. Davis results in a "tiger, burning bright" with anger, moving into an urban jungle populated by predatory capitalists such as Roberts. Despite Mrs. Davis's pleas to her son to "fight for something, not for money," he soon becomes little better than a "money machine," regardless of Shorty's warnings. Postponing his marriage to Peg, Charley gets a crack at the title, oblivious to the fact that his opponent, Ben Chaplin (Canada Lee), suffers from a blood clot and the fight has been fixed. Like Joe Bonaparte's, Charley's as-cent comes at a bloody cost. Even if Ben does not die in the ring like Chocolate Drop in *Golden Boy*, he is left with a serious injury that not only ends his career but results in a future life of poverty and inse-curity from which Charley rescues him after the death of Shorty. The noble Ben will not accept charity but willingly agrees to act as Charley's trainer.

Despite Shorty's warnings and Peg's refusal to be a part of the corruption, Charley becomes seduced by the material values repre-sented by Roberts, who frequently doles out money to place him into debt and economic slavery. Roberts regards the fight game as a "business" in which "debts have to be paid, otherwise it won't be business."[37] Before Shorty dies, he emphasizes the economic corrup-tion contaminating Charley: "He's money and people want money so bad, they make it stink. They make *you* stink." Shorty, Mrs. Davis, and Peg represent alternative values to those affecting Charley, as Polonsky's dialogue makes clear. Immediately recognizing Alice's greedy nature, Mrs. Davis replies to her with the critical remark that she does not need money because "I'm beautiful." When Alice de-scribes herself as "nobody," Peg responds with lines revealing her compassionate nature: "You know who nobody is? Anybody who belongs to somebody. If you're nobody, you belong to somebody." These comments also compare selfish individualism to communal values.

Eventually, Charley becomes entrapped in the same type of deadly game that ruined Ben. Despite the character's subordinate role in *Body and Soul,* the casting of Canada Lee was by no means accidental.[38] Played by an actor prominent in the New Deal Theatre of the 1930s who later suffered a tragic death caused by blacklisting, Ben acts as Charley's moral conscience throughout the film. During brief, sparse cutaways, he reads Charley's motivations in the same way that Nalinle does with Massai in Aldrich's *Apache* (1954). Despite Charley's denial, Ben immediately discerns that his friend has decided to throw the fight. The night before the fight, Ben also knows the real situation and tries to persuade Charley to do the honorable thing. Although Roberts then orders him to "start running," Ben literally decides to go down fighting. Telling Roberts, "I don't scare anymore," he fights to the last in the training camp ring before dying of his blood clot.

Ben's death represents the final catalyst that will eventually spur Charley into action on the fateful night. It also parallels the effect the death of Chocolate Drop has on Joe Bonaparte in *Golden Boy* but in a more positive manner. Charley goes through the motions by fighting badly against Marlowe. But when it becomes clear that he faces the same type of setup as Ben, the close-up on his eyes reveals that Ben's comments, "I don't scare anymore," have the desired effect. Furthermore, his eyes also resemble those of William Blake's tiger, burning bright in the urban jungle.[39] He goes on to win the fight and then finally encounter Roberts's threat outside the ring.

Having regained his self-respect and Peg's love, Charley faces Roberts for the last time. He throws Roberts's threat back in his face: "What are you going to do to me? Everybody dies." He walks away a poor but free man in the ending Polonsky fought for, embodying and articulating hope and inspiration for not just one man but an entire community.[40] As Arnold and Miller point out, *Body and Soul* influenced future director Robert Aldrich in many ways, not the least of which involved the possibility of some form of hope existing in extreme circumstances, especially that containing some form of moral regeneration, no matter how temporary this might be.[41]

As the director of his own screenplay, Polonsky had more control over the shooting of *Force of Evil.* Unlike *Body and Soul,* which contains its share of characters such as Peg, Mrs. Davis, and Shorty who would never sell out, *Force of Evil* shows that everybody is contaminated by the system responsible for the downfall of Charley Davis. Developing *Body and Soul's* parallels between the business and gangster worlds, it grimly depicts a system that is unredeemable.

For Robert Aldrich, the environment of *Force of Evil* would implicitly lead to the apocalyptic resonances of *Kiss Me Deadly*, *Sodom and Gomorrah*, and *Twilight's Last Gleaming*.

Featuring "the graceful and tormented face of John Garfield," whose visage "becomes a landscape of moral conflicts" in the role of crooked corporation lawyer Joe Morse, *Force of Evil* represents one of the most uncompromising attacks on the dehumanizing nature of capitalism ever filmed.[42] Visually influenced by film noir and Edward Hopper's Third Avenue paintings, the film also develops the rhetorical dialogue techniques Polonsky began in *Body and Soul*.[43] Based on Ira Wolfert's naturalist novel *Tucker's People* (1943), *Force of Evil* focuses on two brothers caught in different webs of a corrupt capitalist system. Joe Morse has sold out and become a corporation lawyer for a former bootlegger now moving into the New York numbers racket. This is no aberrant activity but, indeed, a fundamental part of the American dream, which has now become contaminated. *Force of Evil* opens with an overhead shot of Wall Street depicting its inhabitants as scurrying ants. Joe's voice-over comments, "This is Wall Street, and today was important, because tomorrow, July 4, I intended to make my first million dollars. An important day in any man's life." Tucker and Joe intend to use the number associated with Independence Day to break up a number of small illegal businesses and force them into a planned merger. As Joe's voice-over comments later when he visits his brother's business, "These collection offices were called banks and they were *like* banks because money was deposited there. They were *unlike* banks because the chances of getting money out were a thousand to one. These were the odds against winning."

Force of Evil reveals that human beings are not just manipulated by the system. They are also flawed by personal defects, which facilitates their daily oppression and final betrayal. Like Charley Davis, Joe has betrayed his Jewish working-class roots for material gain.[44] But unlike the case in *Body and Soul*, there are no real viable alternatives for him to consider because the omnipresent nature of the system renders them all unviable. Were this a Warner Bros. social consciousness gangster movie, Joe would see the light and join his brother in a crusade against the racket. Fortunately, Polonsky recognized the illusionary aspects of a generic formula.[45] But at the same time he uses it for the purposes of radical reconstruction in the sense of using the familiar to draw attention to the unfamiliar in popular entertainment.[46] As Brinckmann comments concerning the blurring of the boundaries between law and crime in *Force of Evil*, "The equation of crime with business in general, of the criminal world with society, or of gangsterism with Americanism becomes the equation of crime with the established countermeasure directed against it, the law itself."[47]

This emerges in a particularly subtle manner in one scene involving the unseen figure of District Attorney Hall during the film. Unlike with the type of heroic attorney played by Humphrey Bogart in *Marked Woman* (1937) and Walter Abel in *Racket Busters* (1938), we never see Hall throughout the entire film. This omission is deliberate because he is part of the hostile urban forces threatening Joe Morse and others. We have no real assurance that a deal will not be made in the future between two opposing forces similar to that made between Tucker (Roy Roberts) and his former bootlegging partner, Ficco (Paul Fix). The one personal fact we learn about Hall is questionable. Joe discovers that his Harvard-educated partner, Whelock (Paul McVey), once knew the Hall family until his financial losses in the Wall Street crash exiled him from their polite upper-class society. Later, Whelock returns to the class that exiled him in 1929 by betraying Joe. As Joe ironically comments to Edna Tucker (Marie Windsor) later in the film, "Hall is in the business and Ben Tucker is his stock in trade." But stock can change hands, and former enemies such as Tucker and Ficco can become partners again.

Although Leo (Thomas Gomez) wears the mask of a respectable businessman and delights in making his prodigal brother feel guilty, the relationship between them is no one-dimensional Cain and Abel pattern, no matter how much Leo wishes to see himself as the injured party. Both brothers have been shaped by their environment, and, as Brinckmann and others have recognized, Leo's very character contains a self-destructive masochistic element leading him to seek a form of martyrdom that is indispensable in terms of his relationship to society.[48] He also refuses to understand Doris Lowry's (Beatrice Pearson) reasons for quitting her employment and instills guilt feelings over her decision.

Angered by his brother's refusal to join Tucker, Joe phones the police, who then raid Leo's business. Although Leo refuses his brother's offer of help after his appearance at the magistrate's court, he requests that he find Doris a job. Despite Doris Lowry's character expressing more resilience than the original in Wolfert's novel, she also is trapped by a system that offers her no form of employment other than working in an illegal business.[49] As she tells Joe: "I went to a business college for ten weeks because my mother wanted to give me advantages." On the other hand, the victimized and eventual Judas figure of Bauer (Howland Chamberlin) represents the insecurity that failure in the capitalist dream breeds in its victims.[50] He will eventually betray his mentor, Leo, twice. The cop Egan betrays Bauer after he has informed on Leo, whereas gangster Wally ("What do you mean gangsters. It's business.") will finally betray Bauer. There is really no difference between supposedly oppositional forces in the capitalist jungle.

Joe eventually plunges his brother further into the depths of corruption, a level that is little better than the legitimate concerns Leo once worked in. Arguing against his wife's naive understanding of business, Leo responds: "A lot you know. Real estate business! Living from mortgage to mortgage, stealing credit like a thief. And the garage! That was a business! Three cents overcharge on every gallon of gas . . . two cents for the chauffeur and a penny for me. A penny for one thief, two cents for the other. Well Joe is here now. I won't have to steal pennies anymore. I'll have big crooks steal dollars for me."

Joe eventually reaches the point of change and moral redemption after he learns of his brother's kidnapping. Prior to that event, he had sat in a nightclub with Doris masochistically drowning his sorrows following his betrayal by Whelock. After settling scores with Tucker and Ficco, he goes in search of his brother's body where it has been callously dumped. Although Joe descends level by level, David Raksin's score acts as a moral counterpoint depicting both his realization of his responsibility for his actions and his understanding of his real relationship to the world, which he had previously denied. The final lines in Garfield's monologue represent eloquent testimony: "I found my brother's body at the bottom there, where they had thrown it away on the rocks by the river, like an old dirty rag nobody wants. He was dead . . . and I felt I had killed him. I turned back to give myself up to Hall. Because if a man's life can be lived so long and come out this way, like rubbish, then something was horrible and had to be ended one way or another and I decided to help."

Many critics have commented on the supposed incongruity in these final lines. What can Joe expect from a system where even Hall is suspect? Does it not represent the old Hollywood Hays Code of going over to the system in the familiar Warner Bros. social consciousness manner? Not entirely. As John Schultheiss eloquently argues, Joe's decision represents less moral redemption and more a form of existential revenge.[51] By going to the system, he is using it to get back at the crooked establishment that has caused the death of his brother. At the same time, the idea of moral redemption is not entirely ruled out. Polonsky himself recognized that "as in any tragedy, there are complex motivations that cannot be completely explained."[52] Joe's redemption is neither Capraesque nor one involving any acceptance of the status quo. As Polonsky put it, "He's choosing revenge. Just like Charley in *Body and Soul*."[53]

But both aspects may be complementary, involving a different type of moral redemption to that usually found in classical literature and Hollywood cinema necessitating ultimate acceptance of the status quo. The entire film has shown how impossible that is. Instead, *Force of Evil* concludes in a highly unusual manner involving ambiguity and complexity more than anything else. Life has no happy endings, a fact common to both the work of Abraham Polonsky and the cinema of Robert Aldrich.

Force of Evil is a masterly cinematic experiment, the like of which would never be seen (or heard) again in American cinema. It represents a fusion of sound and image that influenced the later films of Robert Aldrich. Although the future director could not experiment in the same way as Polonsky, he would make films noted for excessive visual style and, sometimes, distinctive use of sound. Aldrich learned much from both Odets and Polonsky but could not directly employ their techniques in the films he directed from the 1950s onward. Several reasons explain this, such as the association of Odets and Polonsky with the blacklist and the conservative nature of the studio industry concerning the employment of radical artistic styles. *Force of Evil* was an isolated experiment, artistically as well as politically. The blacklist intervened to prevent Polonsky from developing his ideas further. But, as William Pechter has noted, *Force of Evil* gives the impression of really hearing on the screen "the sound of city speech, with its special repetitions and elisions, cadence and inflection, inarticulateness and crypto-poetry."[54]

As Buhle and Wagner point out, Polonsky succeeded on the screen where Clifford Odets failed, by combining a stylistic form of dialogue with the visual image.[55] Aldrich would never achieve the type of artistic experimentation exhibited in *Force of Evil*. But he would break the boundaries in his own particular stylistic and thematic manner, as *World for Ransom* and *Kiss Me Deadly* show. However, *Force of Evil* does contain several features that Aldrich would employ in his later work as director. Polonsky's first shot ends ironically with the "God's-eye view" of classical Hollywood cinema revealing the redundant nature of religion in a new world order where money rules. Later in the film, Joe walks with Doris through the Trinity Church cemetery. However, Polonsky undercuts the romantic nature of their relationship not just by the location but also by a succeeding shot of the dominating Wall Street skyscraper skyline. When the "prodigal brother" leaves his office for the last time, Polonsky shoots him from a high angle so that he appears little different from the antlike human figures of the opening shot. The sequence ends with Joe approaching the narrowly confined vicinity of Trinity Church. Although Polonsky's screenplay notes that "Come ye yourselves apart and rest awhile" represents the comforting words of the church, it is obvious that Joe will receive neither rest nor comfort in the deadly environment he inhabits. As in Aldrich's later films, religion is little better than useless in a changed world.

Earlier in the film, a shot of hands reaching above a safe introduces the audience to Tucker. However, Tucker's apartment contains a selection of classical Western artifacts similar to those seen in the Allied Headquarters and the German chateau in *The Dirty Dozen*. A classical bust lies awkwardly on the top of Tucker's safe. Also, when Tucker begins escorting Joe down the stairs, whose bars cast shadows on the wall depicting the latter as a fly caught in a trap, he passes a classical Greek statuette as he begins his lines with "You know, I didn't have to invest all this money, Joe" before remembering his earlier violent bootlegging days with his former partner Ficco. Finally, during the scene in Tucker's office when the human calculating machine performs his routine and ends by mentioning, "I was born that way. It's my gift," Polonsky shows that Tucker uses small classical Greek busts as bookends in his library. Like religion, the world of classical values occupies the same status it will later have in *Kiss Me Deadly*.

However, before Aldrich began to direct he was involved in three films with Joseph Losey, two in the capacity as assistant director and another in his only appearance as an actor. *The Prowler, M,* and *The Big Night* (1951) also belong to the same postwar cultural movement destroyed by the blacklist. These films involved the collaboration of talents who would soon suffer from the McCarthyite reaction. In addition to Losey, they included screenwriters Hugo Butler, Dalton Trumbo, and Ring Lardner Jr. as well as actors such as Howard da Silva, Karen Morley, and Dorothy Comingore. *The Prowler, M,* and *The Big Night* are films that attempt to explore the dark underside of American society. But, like *Body and Soul* and *Force of Evil,* they represented a threat to a monolithic status quo that became intolerant of any dissenting views. These films must also have been a formative influence on a young assistant director who escaped the blacklist. Perhaps his Rhode Island connections may have saved him in the same manner as Robert Ryan's Catholic and Marine Corps background hindered the attentions of J. Edgar Hoover?[56] However, Aldrich's involvement as assistant director on *The Prowler* and *The Big Night* represented much more to Joseph Losey than a personal gift from Sam Spiegel. During the late 1970s Losey spoke highly of Aldrich to Michel Ciment: "I respect his professionalism, his honesty, his vigour. I've seldom had a closer relationship with anybody professionally."[57] Like his Enterprise apprenticeship, Aldrich's involvement with Losey not only would continue his formative experiences with the progressive wing of Hollywood cinema but also began his association with Hugo Butler, with whom he would also work on *World for Ransom* (1954), *Sodom and Gomorrah* (1963), and *The Legend of Lylah Clare* (1968).[58]

Scripted by Hugo Butler and Dalton Trumbo (who remained uncredited), *The Prowler* bears a strong resemblance to Billy Wilder's *Double Indemnity* (1944). But unlike in that earlier film, the emphasis is more social than psychological. Set in the spiritually barren environment of Los Angeles during its first half, *The Prowler* is as much an indirect cultural testimony to the effects of the blacklist as Peter Lorre's *Der Verlorene* (1950) is to post–World War II Germany. Both Webb Garwood (Van Heflin) and Susan Gilvray (Evelyn Keyes) are psychological victims of a culture that elevates material success above all other values. But even achieving the consumerist goals of 1950s America results in dissatisfaction, self-deception, and spiritual unfulfillment. The opening pre-credits scene shows the camera (and, by implication, the audience) voyeuristically watching Susan before she becomes aware of its presence and screams. Patrolmen Webb Garwood and Bud Crocker arrive on the scene to investigate the incident. Both Losey and set designer John Hubley wished Susan's house "to reflect the tawdriness of those expensive Hollywood imitations of Spanish houses which were neither comfortable nor beautiful but status symbols."[59] When Webb sees it, he comments, "Quite a hacienda," admiring a status symbol well beyond his reach. After investigating the incident, he replies resentfully to Susan's "I'm all right now" with, "*I'm sure you are!*" For Webb, material success is everything. Resentful of his downwardly mobile status as an ordinary cop and bored with Bud's fascination with Californian history while refusing to learn the lesson of the boom-and-bust ghost town, Calico, that his partner is fascinated with, Webb decides to use Susan for his own avaricious purposes.

Discovering that he and Susan share the same Indiana background, he tells her of coming "from the wrong side of the tracks." He lost his athletic scholarship because of arrogant behavior, which he describes as "individual playing" rather than being part of a team. As a result he lost his ticket to the American dream of 1950s affluence, involving the "soft job with the big house" and "lunch at the University Club." He sneers at the memory of his father, who was content to earn $1.20 an hour at Union rates on the oilfield rather than risk self-employment as an independent "roughneck." For Webb, his father was "too yellow to lose his buck twenty an hour and never made it." However, Webb never considers whether his father considered job security and raising a family more important in the long run. Webb is a resentful, manipulative character who sees Susan as the means to his dream of upper-middle-class status by acquiring a dream motel in the gambler's paradise of Las Vegas.

Susan has attempted to build an acting career in Hollywood. But recognizing that she was "a little short of talent" and tired of fighting the casting couch, she succumbed to cozy domesticity by marrying an older affluent man who she hoped would give her a family. However, her own attempt at economic prostitution has failed because her husband is impotent and prefers to work for the fun of it, even though he has "earned enough to retire." The Gilvray marriage is sterile, and Susan faces her own form of imprisonment. Webb is trapped in the occupation of patrolman, and Susan has to listen to her husband's late-night show every evening. Obviously, the frustrating state of their marital relationship has led Gilvray to seek solace in work and demand that she listen to his nightly performance. Though left alone, she is controlled by his voice, ending his nightly broadcasts with the same monotonous signature: "Good-night folks. The cost of living is going down. I'll be seeing you, Susan." Uttered by the unseen Dalton Trumbo, John Gilvray's closing lines are ironic. Although his reference to the "cost of living" has manifest economic undertones in terms of the American dream of material success, it has another nuance. "Living" in an emotionally fulfilling sense has certainly gone down in this materially stagnant society. Furthermore, Gilvray will later find that his own life means absolutely nothing when, outside his own home, he finally confronts Webb, who has decided to set him up as a prowler and kill him. Before he dies, we see a frightened, older man (Sherry Hall) confronting a lower-class avaricious predator.

Although suspicious of Webb's action, Susan cannot testify to the coroner's court concerning their adulterous affair. Eventually, she becomes swayed by Webb's manipulative actions and marries him. As Losey points out, the scene of their wedding occurs in one take in a 180-degree crane shot revealing a funeral occurring in a church across the street.[60]

The couple moves from one sterile environment to another in a film where mise-en-scène plays a prominent role. Arriving at Webb's Las Vegas dream motel, they enter an environment that is as emotionally barren as Susan's former domicile. As Foster Hirsch notes, "A flashing sign of 'vacancy' in front of the motel is an appropriate indicator of the characters' own vacancy."[61] It is a place where Webb casts a wandering eye on another attractive female soon after his marriage. However, Susan's revelation of her pregnancy leads Webb to remove them from the eyes of the probing media, which will immediately discern that they knew each other well before Susan's testimony in court. Ironically, they relocate to Calico, Bud's favorite ghost town, emblematic of the past historical dream of material success that still rules individual consciousness a century later. Hubley's set design reflects a naturalistic context as the two characters gradually descend into downward mobility, leading to the revelation of their real inner selves. Webb lives in a furnished room whose seediness not only embodies his economic insecurities but also indirectly influences his murderous schemes. Although suspicious of Webb, Susan allows her desire for a family to dominate her personality. As Paul Mayersberg later noted, "In *The Prowler* the human development is reflected in the decor. . . . In his analysis of human behaviour and in the scale of his themes, Losey is already the von Stroheim of the post-war cinema."[62] This comment also shows the connections between literary naturalism and film noir noted by many scholars, as well as the influence of Zola's *Thérèse Raquin* on films such as *Double Indemnity*.[63] However, in Losey's film Susan is really an unconscious accomplice, rather than a conscious one like Thérèse, for she allows her maternal instincts to overrule her rational suspicions concerning her husband's murder.

After helping a doctor to escape with her newborn child, Susan confronts Webb for the last time, fully aware of the doubts she has suppressed in her own mind. He finally confesses, relating his sickness also to society in a manner reminiscent of Leo in *Force of Evil*: "So what? So, I'm no good. But I'm no different from anybody else. You work in a store—you knock down on the cash register. You're a big boss—the income tax. Wardheeler—you sell votes. A lawyer—bribes. But whatever I've done I've done for you. . . . How am I different from those other guys? Some do it for a million, some for ten. . . . I did it for sixty-two thousand. Do you take me for a sucker?" Following this revelation, Webb attempts to escape but is shot down by a cop as he vainly attempts to climb up a high, slippery mine tip. He falls down, now a dead waste product of a society whose values he had murderously subscribed to.

The next film Aldrich worked on with Losey was a new version of Fritz Lang's *M* (1931). Set predominantly in urban locations representing a naturalistic counterpoint to the affluent American dream presented in most contemporary films, *M* makes good use of the dilapidated downtown Bunker Hill Los Angeles area, the Bradbury Building (later used in *Blade Runner*), and a credit shot of an unusual, noirish night shot of the Angels' Flight funicular railway. In *Kiss Me Deadly* Carmen Trivago lives in a similar area.[64] *M* also features several players who would soon suffer from the blacklist, such as Howard da Silva and Karen Morley as well as the famed Group Theatre actor Luther Adler, whose role of *M*'s defending lawyer is far more significantly realized than the original in Lang's version.

As Edward Dimendberg has shown, Losey's *M* is not only a product of late modernity; it is also a film fully aware of the social contradictions existing in its era. It is another key cultural text that influenced Aldrich. Following *M*'s opening murder, a police chief appears on television, warning the public to be on the alert for suspicious characters. As Dimendberg notes, the chief's discourse addressed to a passive audience replaces the reading of newspapers in Lang's original film, thus binding "isolated individuals into a community," which soon enacts the vigilante aspects of the blacklist by accusing innocent people.[65] Unlike Lang's original, Losey's film contains no character such as Otto Wernich's Inspector Lohman with whom the audience may identify. Instead, representatives of law and order are often indistinguishable from the underworld. Both Lt. Carney (Howard da Silva) and his subordinate Becker (Steve Brodie) are assigned the task of tracking the child killer. The momentum really builds up not after the murder of working-class child Elsie Coster but following that of a councilman's daughter. The vote-conscious mayor (Jim Backus) orders both cops to the hunt. At one point in the film the otherwise sleazy Carney expresses doubts about the electric chair as a solution to the problem, "Yeah. And that'll fix everything!" to Becker's gleeful, "He'll burn." But unlike Lang's Inspector Lohman, Carney is just another cog in a remorseless contemporary social machine out to victimize "un-American" outsiders. Relishing the torture of suspects, Becker also expresses his desire for "one genuine stool pigeon," an obvious blacklist reference similar to another line of dialogue: "A red dress! What are you, a communist?"

Headed by Marshall (Martin Gabel), the Los Angeles criminal fraternity sees the murders as hindering business. As he tells his colleagues, "We're in a business with a take of millions from your race wires and book making, from your gambling houses, from your baseball and football pools, from your slot machines." Business now comprises legal and illegal enterprises, with Harrow representing a threat to the profit margin. Marshall does not mobilize Lang's army of beggars but, rather, uses street kids and a satellite taxi service ironically titled "Ajax." Did this inspire Aldrich's critique of old values in his later films? The final pursuit and capture of Harrow occur in the old Bradbury Building. As Dimendberg points out, "Once associated by writers and critics such as Emile Zola and Walter Benjamin with the phantasmagoria of capitalist visuality, the iron and glass architecture that appears in *M* in the form of the Bradbury building is a degraded remnant of this earlier thinking, the 'new' of the modern that has long since become antiquated."[66]

Like Peter Lorre's original M, David Wayne's Martin Harrow is also a pathetic figure. But, as Losey points out, he is also a victim of the dark side of the wholesome American family ideology promoted particularly in the 1950s.[67] When we first see him he lies on his bed fastening a child's shoelace to a bedside lamp, his face in shadow.

He then moves a plasticine model of a child to a dressing table near a picture of his stern-looking mother. After gazing at himself in a mirror, he winds a string around the doll's neck until the head becomes severed. This action typifies M as a precursor of Hitchcock's Norman Bates in *Psycho* as well as revealing an action designed to be a surrogate castration directed against a figure who symbolically performed the same action toward him in the past. Losey's M is a character whose deviant sexuality has definite social causes.[68] While testifying in his own defense at the criminal court in an underground garage above which is a central exit ramp reading "KEEP TO THE RIGHT," Waldo Salt clarifies Harrow's position as a victim of a dysfunctional family situation: "Mother told me that men were the source of all evil. . . . My father would have been hanged for the things he did. She said so!" Despite the nature of his crimes Harrow is a figure needing medical and psychological help. Although Aldrich mostly presented the father figure as the victimizer in later films such as *Attack! Autumn Leaves, What Ever Happened to Baby Jane?* and *Hush . . . Hush, Sweet Charlotte,* the figure of David Wayne's Martin Harrow obviously influenced later images of his psychologically tortured adult children.

The role of Luther Adler's drunken lawyer Langley, who turns against Marshall and dies defending the rule of law in his last moments, not only represents a symbolic protest against the illegal aspects of the blacklist but also foreshadows motifs in Aldrich's later films.[69] Constantly humiliated by Marshall because of his alcohol addiction, Langley regains his self-respect by defending Harrow. He also turns on Marshall by blaming him for causing his fall. Langley's change of character represents his finest moment in the film before Marshall shoots him. The film ends with the arrival of the police, who arrest Harrow and Marshall, leaving Langley's body in the right foreground of the frame. Some L.A. cops stand in the background like Gestapo agents. It is a bleak ending suggesting little resolution. But with Langley's protest, it contains a brief moment intimating that things could be different.

Losey's final American film, *The Big Night,* has not fared well with most critics. David Caute dismisses it as "inferior in almost every respect to his previous Hollywood films," whereas Foster Hirsch notes the visual significance in Losey's "ability to recycle pulp."[70] However, Alain Silver notes important rite-of-passage psychological elements existing in the film.[71] Despite Aldrich's unavailability to be assistant director, he did perform a brief uncredited role as a Madison Garden ringside fan. Although credited to Losey and author Stanley Elfin from his novel *Dreadful Summit*, the screenplay mainly belongs to Hugo Butler and Ring Lardner Jr., who worked on it after Butler became blacklisted.[72] *The Big Night*, however, does contain many features that would reappear in Aldrich's work as director, such as the son's difficult relationship to the father and the tortured attempt to find some stability in a discordant universe, which may not be successful.

Reedited during Losey's absence, *The Big Night* opens with a shot of a gas tank framed between two narrow buildings as George La Main (John Barrymore Jr.) enters the shot and suddenly departs. The viewer catches a glimpse of his anguished face before he disappears as the credits roll. Repeated later in the film, this shot is the only remnant of the flashback structure Losey intended before the producer insisted on a chronological framework. After the credits, we see the naive and inexperienced George physically and sexually bullied by his classmates. His father Andy (Preston Foster) looks on but decides not to intervene. Before his father can celebrate George's birthday with the customers in his diner, the intervention of Al Judge (Howard St. John) and two thugs disrupts the celebration. Watching his respected father passively submit to a humiliating beating evokes in George a psychological crisis. Neither Andy nor his partner Flanagan (Howland Chamberlin) informs George of the reasons why this has happened. Wearing his oversized father's jacket and hat, he begins an urban odyssey to avenge himself on Judge. During his search he encounters various father figures, such as the vicious hoodlum Peckinpaugh (Emile Meyer) and slumming journalist/professor Lloyd Cooper (Philip Bourneuf), before he finally faces Judge and discovers why his father was beaten. Judge informs him that his sister committed suicide when Andy refused to marry her. After Judge attempts to exact further revenge by handing George over to the police, the ensuing fight supposedly results in Judge's accidental death. Rejected by Cooper and expelled from the brief emotional sanctuary he has enjoyed with Marion Rostina (Joan Lorring), the sister of Cooper's girlfriend, George returns home. His father intends to take the blame until the police inform them that Judge was only wounded. Andy then tells George that he could not marry Judge's sister because his own wife was still alive and not dead as he had told him. The film ends with Flanagan removing the birthday cake as the reconciled father and son go away with the police. George has moved from late childhood into a more adult understanding of the world around him. His father realizes that he should have treated his son more as an adult than a child.

Unlike the case in Aldrich's later films, reconciliation occurs between parent and child. But *The Big Night* does anticipate the psychological confusions lying at the heart of the family relationships dealt with more pessimistically by Aldrich. As played by John Barrymore Jr., George is as much a victim of gender crisis as Captain Cooney, Burt Hanson, Jane Hudson, Charlotte Hollis, Trucker Cobb, June Buckridge, Childie, and Slim Grissom. As Losey has pointed out, the fictional character matched the person who played him, for John Barrymore Jr. was obsessed with a father he had seen only two or three times in his life and "had a very ambiguous and strange relationship with his mother Dolores Costello."[73] The director was certainly aware of the actor's vulnerability and relationship to his father, which certainly influenced the casting. It must have been common knowledge to Aldrich and others working on the film.

The future director had now served an apprenticeship within the classical Hollywood film industry. Because of the blacklist, his association with Losey ended. The two men had bought two scripts. One dealt with the life of Aimee Semple McPherson, and the other, *Apache*, would later be filmed by Aldrich.[74] One wonders how Aldrich's attitude toward religion would have affected the Aimee Semple McPherson project, which would have starred Evelyn Keyes. However, Aldrich benefited both professionally and artistically from his involvement with Enterprise and Losey, and was now ready to begin his own long-awaited directorial career.

NOTES

1. Edwin T. Arnold and Eugene I. Miller, *The Films and Career of Robert Aldrich* (Knoxville: University of Tennessee Press, 1986), 3.

2. For a list of Aldrich's credits at this time, see Alain Silver and James Ursini, *What Ever Happened to Robert Aldrich? His Life and His Films* (New York: Limelight Editions, 1995), 320–23.

3. Arnold and Miller, *The Films and Career of Robert Aldrich,* 7.

4. See Allan Eyles, "Films of Enterprise," *Focus on Film* 35 (1980): 13–27.

5. Gerald Weales, *Clifford Odets: Playwright* (New York: Pegasus, 1971), 110.

6. Harold Clurman, *The Fervent Years: The Story of the Group Theatre and the Thirties* (New York: Hill and Wang, 1957), 151.

7. Clurman, *The Fervent Years,* 276.

8. Clurman, *The Fervent Years,* 289.

9. Arthur Miller, *Timebends* (New York: Grove Press, 1987), 179.

10. Miller, *Timebends,* 181.

11. Clurman, *The Fervent Years,* 281.

12. See, most recently, Kelly Hankin, "Lesbian Locations: The Production of Lesbian Bar Space in *The Killing of Sister George,*" *Cinema Journal* 41, no. 4 (2001): 3–27.

13. Miller, *Timebends,* 180.

14. Miller, *Timebends,* 223.

15. Miller, *Timebends,* 181.

16. Miller, *Timebends,* 181.

17. Robert Aldrich, "The American Film Institute Seminar with Robert Aldrich," transcript, Center for Advanced Film Studies, 2 November 1971 (Beverly Hills: American Film Institute, 1978), 40–42.

18. For the context of this remark, see Mark Burman, "Abraham Polonsky: The Most Dangerous Man in America," in *Projections,* vol. 8, ed. John Boorman and Dennis Donahue (London: Faber and Faber, 1998), 258.

19. Paul Buhle and Dave Wagner, *A Very Dangerous Citizen: Abraham Lincoln Polonsky and the Hollywood Left* (Berkeley: University of California Press, 2001), 108. Thom Anderson's magisterial study places both *Body and Soul* and *Force of Evil* among this key group of films, which includes examples such as *They Live by Night, Knock on Any Door, Thieves Highway,* and *We Were Strangers* (all 1949); *Night and the City, The Asphalt Jungle, The Breaking Point,* and *The Lawless* (all 1950); and *The Prowler, Try and Get Me,* and *He Ran All the Way* (all 1951). See Thom Anderson, "Red Hollywood," in *Literature and the Visual Arts in Contemporary Society,* ed. Suzanne Ferguson and Barbara Goseclose (Columbus: Ohio State University Press, 1985), 183–84. The list could also be extended by including other films such as Lewis Milestone's *The Strange Love of Martha Ivers* (1946) and Joseph Losey's *M* and *The Big Night* (both 1951), which also represent apprentice work for Robert Aldrich. The year 1947 was key in more ways than one: "If anyone wishes to chart the death throes of the major motion-picture studios, the cancer began in 1947, when they succumbed to the virus of reaction. Witch-hunting and suppression of free thought were personified by the House Un-American Activities Committee and the dawn of the Age of McCarthyism. In many ways the studios began their own downfall: they were scrapping themselves" (Jerome Lawrence, *Actor: The Life and Times of Paul Muni* [New York: G. P. Putnam's Sons, 1964], 295).

20. Eyles, "Films of Enterprise," 16.

21. Burman, "Abraham Polonsky," 245.

22. Burman, "Abraham Polonsky," 259. Buhle and Wagner comment that *Body and Soul* represents one of the best examples of postwar cinematic treatments of the American depression, "a revision of the Group Theatre's *Golden Boy,* with none of that film's sentimentality or social ambivalence" (*A Very Dangerous Citizen,* 113). Rouben Mamoulian's 1939 film version had diluted the play and utilizes the clichéd Hollywood happy ending.

23. Buhle and Wagner, *A Very Dangerous Citizen,* 117; Mark Rappaport, "Abraham Polonsky's *I Can Get It for You Wholesale* (1951) Reconsidered," *Senses of Cinema* (available at www.sensesofcinema.com/contents/02/20/ polonsky.html, 2002): 3. For an outstanding analysis of *Body and Soul,* see John Schultheiss, ed., *Body and Soul: The Critical Edition* (Northridge: Center for Telecommunication Studies, California State University, 2002).

24. See Polonsky's graphic account of this incident in "Abraham Polonsky," in *Tender Comrades: A Backstory of the Hollywood Blacklist,* ed. Patrick McGilligan and Paul Buhle (New York: St. Martin's Press, 1999), 485–86. See also Burman, "Abraham Polonsky," 247.

25. Eyles, "Films of Enterprise," 16. Speaking of Polonsky's hopes that the film would be understood as "an allegory of the actual and spiritual corruption of human values in the American capitalist system," Sklar believes that Polonsky made a serious error in winning his battle over the ending because it diluted this social analysis by making it into a drama of individual redemption. See Robert Sklar, *City Boys* (Princeton: Princeton University Press, 1990), 186–97. But the two aspects are not contradictory. Polonsky often operated from a more humanistic vision than contemporary interpretations of Marxism allowed. He was also very clear about the differences between *Body and Soul* and *Force of Evil.* As he stated, *Body and Soul* is a "romance of the streets" allowing for the possibility that some form of victory may prevail over overwhelming circumstances. It offers hope to the audience in a postwar era still hoping for the continuation of progressive dreams that would soon vanish overnight. See Burman, "Abraham Polonsky," 247–48. The climax is not entirely related to box-office concerns as Sklar suggests.

26. See Jim Cook and Kingsley Canham, "Interview with Abraham Polonsky," *Screen* 11, no. 3 (1970): 68. Earlier, Polonsky commented on John Howard Lawson initiating a school of playwriting "of which Clifford Odets is the flower" (Cook and Canham, "Interview with Abraham Polonsky," 65).

27. Quoted in Buhle and Wagner, *A Very Dangerous Citizen,* 117, from Michel Delahaye, "Entretien avec Abraham Polonsky," *Cahiers du Cinema,* September 1969: 69.

28. See Richard Slotkin's *Regeneration through Violence: The Mythology of the American Frontier, 1600–1860* (Middletown, Conn.: Wesleyan University Press, 1973); *The Fatal Environment: The Myth of the Frontier in the Age of Industrialization, 1800–1890* (New York: Atheneum, 1985); and *Gunfighter Na-*

tion: The Myth of the Frontier in Twentieth-Century America (New York: Atheneum, 1992).

29. Slotkin, *Gunfighter Nation*, 658.

30. Slotkin, *Gunfighter Nation*, 659–60.

31. In 1952, newspaper columnist Ed Sullivan saw *Body and Soul* as setting "the pattern that the commies and their sympathizers in TV networks, agencies, and theatrical unions would like to fasten on the newest medium" (Buhle and Wagner, *A Very Dangerous Citizen*, 117). See also Schultheiss, *Body and Soul*, 376–81.

32. Buhle and Wagner see this object as having a metaphorical significance expressing lynching. Associated with Ben (Canada Lee), whom we will not meet until later in the film, it also parallels Eisenstein's theories concerning the role of mise-en-scène in evoking intellectual consciousness.

33. Buhle and Wagner, *A Very Dangerous Citizen*, 113.

34. She also sings one of the songs associated with Lauren Bacall in her first screen appearance in *To Have and Have Not* (1944)—"Am I Blue?" Anthony Slide has noted that the song was also associated with Ethel Waters.

35. Buhle and Wagner note that the central narrative of *Body and Soul* represents a common thread running through most of Polonsky's novels and films in being, namely, "the story of an immigrant's son, an individual who has turned his back on his working-class background for personal gain. Later, he discovers a moral and (in the broadest sense) political need to rejoin the working-class, regardless of the personal price" (*A Very Dangerous Citizen*, 112).

36. Allan Eyles is mistaken in describing Peg as a "sensitive young violinist" ("Films of Enterprise," 16). This is true in the literal sense, but Eyles unconsciously evokes the symbolic influence of *Golden Boy* by making this error. According to Jerome Lawrence, the character of Joe Bonaparte was actually based on Paul Muni, who told Clifford Odets about this unlikely combination of boxer and violinist: "Muni quit boxing at the gym for fear he might break his fingers and wouldn't even be able to grub a living with a violin" (*Actor*, 72).

37. As well as having obvious political connotations, Roberts's frequent repetition of the word *business* anticipates the more sophisticated rhetorical screenwriting techniques Polonsky would employ in *Force of Evil*.

38. For Canada Lee's significance, see Glenda E. Gill, "Canada Lee: Black Actor in Non-traditional Roles," *Journal of Popular Culture* 25, no. 3 (1991): 78–89. Although Ben lacks the dubious masculinity associated with Joe Bonaparte's trainer, Tokio, in *Golden Boy*, he does share several traits with him. According to Edward Murray, "Tokio has been seduced, corrupted and emasculated through compromise with the values of a commercial society" (*Clifford Odets: The Thirties and After* [New York: Frederick Ungar, 1968], 63). But unlike Tokio, Ben is fully aware of his predicament. He agrees to fight

Charley to save his manager from Roberts and acts as a decisive moral conscience throughout the entire film. Polonsky merged *Golden Boy*'s Chocolate Drop and Tokio into a fascinating new creation.

39. Other insights may flash across his mind as well as the audience's, the most notable being that he is not an isolated individual but, rather, a symbolic representative of his own community. As stated by a deliveryman, Simon, over his $5.00 bet, "It isn't the money. Over in Europe, the Nazis are killing people like us just because of our religion. But, over here, Charley Davis is champeen, and of that, we can be proud." When Peg slaps Charley after she learns of his proposed betrayal of his people, she mentions the "lonely nights" she has had to endure because of his personal betrayal of her with Alice.

40. Buhle and Wagner understand the exact reverberations of this ending. Had Charley died as Rossen intended, this would have been merely a cynical grimace to a world-weary audience: "What matters most is the clarity of understanding that Charley attains at that moment. For Polonsky this was nothing less than the hope that all of the world's Charleys one day would make the same declamation. Hence Polonsky's frequently expressed frustration with Rossen's ending: this is not a fable about Charley Davis, it is a fable of the working class" (*A Very Dangerous Citizen*, 115).

41. Arnold and Miller, *The Films and Career of Robert Aldrich*, 10.

42. The comments are from Martin Scorsese's introduction to the 1995 Republic Studios video rerelease of the film. See John Schultheiss and Mark Shaubert, eds., *Force of Evil: The Critical Edition* (Northridge: California State University, 1996), 8. For Polonsky, the moral of *Force of Evil* was that "under a system based on profit there's the destruction of morality and judgement and therefore people should all be romantic socialists, I guess, but I don't say that in the picture" (Burman, "Abraham Polonsky," 252).

43. For Hopper's influence, see Christine Noll Brinckmann, "The Politics of *Force of Evil*: An Analysis of Abraham Polonsky's Preblacklist Film," in *Prospects: The Annual of American Cultural Studies*, vol. 6, ed. Jack Salzman (New York: Burr Franklin, 1981), 360; and Burman, "Abraham Polonsky," 251. In an earlier interview, Polonsky described his motivations for using Hopper as follows: "Third Avenue, cafeterias, all that backlight, and those empty streets. Even when people are there, you don't see them, somehow the environments dominate the people" (Eric Sherman and Martin Rubin, *The Director's Event: Interviews with Five American Filmmakers* [New York: Atheneum, 1970], 20).

Polonsky also criticized the tendency of others to describe his dialogue as blank verse: "They thought I wrote poetry; in fact, I used the rhetorical devices of poetry, but it was street talk all the way through" (Burman, "Abraham Polonsky," 250). As Buhle and Wagner note, Polonsky succeeded in screenwriting where Clifford Odets failed. Although the playwright had succeeded in giving "English language audiences the feeling for immigrant and second-generation vernacular in a community where capitalism's ravages were most likely to be interpreted in political terms" (Buhle and Wagner, *A Very Dangerous Citizen,* 128), Odets's theatricality and Jewish sentimentalism limited his work. On the other hand, by "utilizing some of the same stock of experiences, Polonsky's task was to render the quasi-Yiddish of Odets's English more universal, to place characters in filmable circumstances, and to add one more crucial distinctive element" (Buhle and Wagner, *A Very Dangerous Citizen,* 128). It involved avoidance of gender stereotypes and the recognition of a New York Jewish appropriation of popular culture most notably embodied in the star persona of John Garfield. For Polonsky, he was a star who represented a social phenomenon embodying the radical dreams of the 1930s. See Abraham Polonsky, "Introduction," in *The Films of John Garfield,* by Howard Gellman (Secaucus: Citadel Press, 1975), 8–9.

44. Although no explicit clues are given as in *Body and Soul,* this feature has been recognized by Brinckmann ("The Politics of *Force of Evil,*" 364). It was a deliberate change of name from "Minch" in *Tucker's People.* See Schultheiss and Shaubert, *Force of Evil,* 193n39.

45. For an analysis of the conservative aspects of genre, see Judith Hess, "Genre Films and the Status Quo," *Jump Cut* 1 (1974): 1, 16, 18.

46. See Brinckmann, "The Politics of *Force of Evil,*" 372.

47. Brinckmann, "The Politics of *Force of Evil,*" 373.

48. Brinckmann writes, "It is as much Leo's rigidity and eagerness to victimize himself as it is Joe's involvement in the racket that finally results in Leo's death" ("The Politics of *Force of Evil,*" 373). See also Theodor Reik, *Masochism in Sex and Society,* trans. Margaret H. Beigel and Gertrud M. Kurth (New York: Grove Press, 1962). Brinckmann also notes, "Even Leo's physical appearance expresses his painful intractability—he is fat, unhealthy, elderly and seedy. But most of all it is his *traditionally Jewish rhetoric of futility, guilt and victimization* that characterizes the scenes between the brothers and makes it clear to us from the beginning that Joe will be unable to save Leo" ("The Politics of *Force of Evil,*" 364, emphasis added).

49. See Schultheiss and Shaubert, *Force of Evil,* 131–32. Polonsky changes the novel's character, who embodies the worst aspects of naturalist determinism, into an appealing figure embodying innocence and experience as well as illustrating self-sufficiency and personal responsibility.

50. For the original deterministic image of Bauer, who embodies the death instinct bred in an insecure people following World War I, see Schultheiss and Shaubert, *Force of Evil,* 167–68. In the novel Wolfert "designed a baroque parallel between the rise of Nazism (fascism) and business—both destroy the possibility of the self and hold the promise of wholesale death" (Schultheiss and Shaubert, *Force of Evil,* 167). Polonsky manages to suggest these characteristics

in his version of Bauer without resorting to this historical framework. As he later commented, Bauer is afraid of life and thus untrustworthy, a figure who is "going to cause the death of almost all the people who died in this picture because of his character" (Schultheiss and Shaubert, *Force of Evil*, 137).

51. See the excellent discussion in Schultheiss and Shaubert, *Force of Evil*, 174–81.

52. Schultheiss and Shaubert, *Force of Evil*, 180. Schultheiss discussed these issues with Polonsky in 1990 and 1995.

53. Schultheiss and Shaubert, *Force of Evil*, 181.

54. William Pechter, "Abraham Polonsky and *Force of Evil*," *Film Quarterly* 15, no. 3 (1962): 48.

55. Buhle and Wagner, *A Very Dangerous Citizen*, 122–23.

56. For Aldrich's comments on this period, see Arnold and Miller, *The Films and Career of Robert Aldrich*, 13–14.

57. Michel Ciment, *Conversations with Losey* (London: Methuen, 1985), 125.

58. As Jean Rouverol has mentioned in correspondence, Aldrich provided solid support during the dark days of blacklisting and afterward. See also David Caute, *Joseph Losey: A Revenge on Life* (New York: Oxford University Press, 1994), 383–84; and Jean Rouverol, *Refugees from Hollywood: A Journal of the Blacklist Years* (Albuquerque: University of New Mexico Press, 2000), 51, 205, 210, 246, 249.

59. Ciment, *Conversations with Losey*, 104–5.

60. Ciment, *Conversations with Losey*, 105.

61. Foster Hirsch, *Joseph Losey* (Boston: Twayne, 1980), 50. The three major locations of Spanish-style house, utilitarian plain-wall motel, and crumbling ghost town cabin are all important here. Caute writes, "The Spanish house was built as a composite set, with arched doorways, to convey emotional emptiness within material comfort. Paintings, tapestries, and expensive furniture don't make the house lived in: it lacks and awaits a child. The same emotional vacuum extends to the motel with its plain white walls. . . . The desolation of the desert shack is reinforced by piles of packing crates, a lonely phonograph, a traveling first aid box" (*Joseph Losey*, 92).

62. Quoted in Caute, *Joseph Losey*, 92, from a 1988 National Film Theatre program note.

63. See Alain Silver and Elizabeth Ward, eds., *Film Noir: An Encyclopedic Reference to the American Style*, 3d ed. (New York: Overlook Press, 1992), 379, 384, 388.

64. Even if Trivago does not live in the Bunker Hill area, which underwent fundamental transformation in the 1950s, he lives in a similar area. For an excellent analysis of the geographical differences affecting the two versions of *M*, see Edward Dimendberg, "From Berlin to Bunker Hill: Urban Space, Late Modernity, and Film Noir in Fritz Lang's and Joseph Losey's *M*," *Wide Angle* 19, no. 4 (1997): 62–93. Dimendberg writes, "The film's opening sequence on

the Angels' Flight funicular railways conveys the spatial separation of its setting, the Bunker Hill neighborhood whose destruction by the agents of urban renewal coincides with Losey's filming. Bunker Hill was one of the oldest neighborhoods in the city, dating back to the nineteenth century and full of irregularly shaped streets and Victorian-era mansions converted into long shabby rooming houses memorialized by writers such as Raymond Chandler and John Fane" ("From Berlin to Bunker Hill," 78).

65. Dimendberg, "From Berlin to Bunker Hill," 93n55. Dimendberg also notes that the very shot of the film shows a stack of immobile newspapers on the street as the Angels' Flight railways ascend, as if suggesting the increasing distance between the cultures of newspaper and television. He writes, "Notably, in Losey's film the murderer Harrow never writes to the newspaper, an insinuation that in the social world constituted by television in fifties America communication was increasingly visual and unidirectional" ("From Berlin to Bunker Hill," 72).

66. Dimendberg, "From Berlin to Bunker Hill," 83. A smaller version once existed in the now-demolished Swansea Arcade in South Wales. Another still exists in Cardiff. Dimendberg also notes that the building's manifestation in a 1951 Los Angeles film also calls the present into question because it represents "an earlier mode of urban public space in danger of becoming forgotten" at a time of massive urban development expelling residential districts from the city's central business district ("From Berlin to Bunker Hill," 83).

67. Ciment, *Conversations with Losey,* 109–10, 114.

68. Originally, the print contained a scene of M masturbating with a shoestring and destroying a clay image of his mother with a poster on the wall reading, "Did You Write to Your Mother?" See Ciment, *Conversations with Losey,* 113. Bellamy in *Hustle* is another victim of a physically abusive parent.

69. Dimendberg, "From Berlin to Bunker Hill," 85–87, 93n55.

70. Caute, *Joseph Losey,* 95; Hirsch, *Joseph Losey,* 52–53.

71. Alain Silver, "*The Big Night,*" in *Film Noir: An Encyclopedic Reference to the American Style,* 3d ed., ed. Alain Silver and Elizabeth Ward (New York: Overlook Press, 1992), 32–33.

72. Ciment, *Conversations with Losey,* 116; Caute, *Joseph Losey,* 95; Rouverol, *Refugees from Hollywood,* 5.

73. Ciment, *Conversations with Losey,* 115.

74. Ciment, *Conversations with Losey,* 124.

THREE

TELEVISION WORK

Although Robert Aldrich gained considerable experience from working with directors such as Chaplin, Losey, Milestone, Polonsky, and Renoir, he was still an assistant director by the beginning of the 1950s. Frustrated at the lack of opportunity to direct in the Hollywood film industry, he relocated to New York to work in television. According to Aldrich, the growing medium was in a primitive state of development and producers "really didn't know how to make filmed television there."[1] Thanks to Walter Butler (who became an associate producer on Aldrich's later films), moving to New York allowed Aldrich to work on television productions in the role of director. Aldrich also directed other television shows in Hollywood during the early 1950s such as *China Smith, The Schlitz Playhouse of the Stars,* and *Four Star Playhouse,* before he finally made his first film in 1953. Apart from directing Charles Boyer in "The Bad Streak" for *Four Star Playhouse* in 1954, Aldrich never worked in television again until 1959, when he directed the pilots for *The Sundance Kid* and *Adventures in Paradise,* as well as one additional episode from the latter series.

It is tempting to assume that Aldrich's early television work was merely a pragmatic move to break into film directing. But Aldrich's television experiences represented another type of important apprenticeship, allowing him to use cinematic techniques within the limited production schedules peculiar to the new medium. Aldrich also utilized many techniques he learned while working as an assistant director, such as rehearsing actors. He also made the necessary quick decisions needed for television based on his cumulative experience.[2] Aldrich faced the challenge fully conscious that the final product would only run some twenty-two minutes with commercial breaks. But his early 1950s television work transcended the world of a New York television industry that paid directors scale because candidates "had never directed or couldn't get a shot."[3] Aldrich worked with not only seasoned film actors such as Beulah Bondi, Dick Powell, Dan Duryea, and Charles Boyer but also new talents such as Charles Buchinski (Bronson), Jack Elam, and Richard Jaeckel, who would form part of his future cinematic repertory company. Aldrich had watched Lewis Milestone direct Charles Boyer in *Arch of Triumph* (1948) when he was assistant director. He now had the opportunity of firsthand contact in two episodes of *Four Star Playhouse*. As assistant director on Jean Renoir's *The Southerner* (1945), he observed the acting talents of Beulah Bondi and would work with her again in 1952 on "The Guest" episode of *The Doctor* television series. Aldrich would also direct Dan Duryea in *World for Ransom* and feature him among the ensemble of *The Flight of the Phoenix* a decade later. Aldrich's television work is cinematic in several ways and deserves more detailed consideration by critics than it has so far received.

Despite the disdain exhibited by certain veteran Hollywood stars and directors for the new medium, the 1950s was the "Golden Age of Television" in more ways than one. As well as the challenge of live television drama, many Hollywood stars were eager to explore the new opportunities offered by television. Not all of these people turned to television because of failing Hollywood careers, as did Errol Flynn and Loretta Young. Others such as David Niven and Dick Powell were still at the height of their fame and sought diversity in other areas. Loretta Young added a final footnote to her distinguished Hollywood career with her dramatic anthology *The Loretta Young Show*, which ran on NBC from 1953 to 1961. Dick Powell became a noted television actor and producer before his death in 1962. He often gave emerging talents such as Peter Falk and Sam Peckinpah opportunities, as in his dramatic anthology *The Dick Powell Show*, which ran on NBC during 1962–63. Also shown on BBC, *The Dick Powell Show* represented the best of contemporary American television. During the 1950s, Dick Powell, Ida Lupino, Charles Boyer, and David Niven all acted in individual episodes of *Four Star Playhouse*, which they also produced. Unlike in Hollywood, here they could exercise some degree of control over the roles they played.

Like most of early Hollywood silent and sound cinema, many of these television productions are now either lost or in the hands of private collectors and archives that have not cataloged their material. Some series were reissued and often altered for resyndication. *Four Star Playhouse* reappeared as *NBC's Best in Mystery and Suspense,* and surviving episodes of *The Dick Powell Show* (renamed *The Dick Powell Theatre*) often lack the stimulating introductions Powell filmed to introduce every episode, including those he appeared in.[4] Aldrich's early television work belongs to this creative period in the history of the new medium.

During 1952–53, Aldrich directed seventeen episodes of *The Doctor* in New York for NBC. He also wrote three teleplays. *The Doctor* was an anthology series starring Warner Anderson and emphasizing emotional rather than medical problems. It was later retitled *The Visitor* for syndication and eliminated Anderson, reducing his presence to a voice-over narrator with his back to the camera, introducing and concluding each episode.[5] Because of the lack of relevant documentation, it is impossible to say when "The Guest" was filmed or its chronological relationship to the entire series. Television episodes were often filmed out of synchronization to their actual broadcast. "The Guest" may be one of the earliest examples of Aldrich's television work. Like the future director's contributions to *China Smith* and *Four Star Playhouse,* it reveals a unique cinematic talent creatively operating within a three-day television shooting schedule.

The opening shot begins with a taxi stopping in an affluent residential area. Framed in long shot, Joe Langan (Charles Bronson) exits from the vehicle and pauses to pay his fare. The camera pans right as Langan walks across the frame. It then tracks back as he moves up the path toward the camera. The movement ceases the moment Langan moves into close-up. A milkman passes him from behind. The camera tracks left to follow him as he delivers the milk before tracking right to follow his progress in the reverse direction and then finally pausing to reframe Langan again in close-up. After the milkman leaves the frame, the camera follows Langan, who repeats the milkman's movement to the front door. The scene changes to an interior shot of the kitchen, showing Joe looking through the glass frame of the door masquerading as a milkman announcing the delivery. The next shot returns to the exterior. It reveals Joe moving to the left of the frame. Shot four shows Gwen West (Joan Camden) entering from the right of the kitchen. Shot five is in low angle, revealing Gwen kneeling to pick up the two milk bottles on the ground before her. The instant she picks up the two bottles Joe's gun suddenly moves into the frame. Then the next shot reveals Joe pushing Gwen inside the kitchen. The camera swiftly pans right and tracks in to frame them both in tight, low-angle medium close-up.

These quickly edited shots reveal a creative use of cinematic technique adding vitality to the familiar theme of "hood breaking into suburban home." They anticipate a sophisticated use of cinematic grammar, which *Cahiers du Cinema* critics later recognized in Aldrich's early films when contrasting auteurs to the *metteur-en-scène* directors represented by John Huston. Bronson's very appearance (wearing a gaudy tie) marks him as incongruous with his surroundings. Television actress Joan Camden represents the archetypal 1950s middle-class daughter threatened by an outside working-class figure. The narrative of "The Guest" involves a fugitive criminal seeking refuge in a suburban house after a jewelry robbery. However, he finds himself in a situation that will soon change his whole personality. Joe later makes a decision similar to those made by characters in *Body and Soul* and *The Longest Yard*. Gwen informs Joe that her brother has died in the Korean War and her mother suffers from heart problems. When Mrs. West (Beulah Bondi) enters the scene, Gwen introduces Joe as a friend of her brother. During the scene when Joe and Mrs. West sit down at a table, a coffeepot separates them. However, they are both equally balanced in the frame, suggesting a potential union between them that will eventually overcome the barrier represented by the symbolic position of the coffeepot. Gwen appears in the background of the frame. Aldrich places his actors in a triangular position, visually articulating their different motivations. Gwen worries about her mother. Joe wishes to hide from the police.

Mrs. West becomes attracted to a surrogate son. She tells Joe, "It's what's in a man that sets him apart. I taught my children to believe," and later criticizes Gwen for "intolerance" toward Joe: "If Ken liked him he saw some good in him." Aldrich repeats this triangular composition in another scene when Joe and Mrs. West play gin rummy. When Joe wins the game, Mrs. West makes the remark, "You play like a thief." The camera abruptly cuts to a close-up shot of her at this point before changing to a reverse close-up of a sinister looking Joe as he replies, "That's what they keep saying." This is one of the first examples of Aldrich's use of alternating close-ups between characters to punctuate visually significant lines of dialogue after introducing them in long shot. He usually closes sequences by reframing his characters in long shot, making them self-contained in a polished Hollywood manner. Joe has made himself

at home as a "guest" and intends to remain there for some unspec-
ified period of time.

In an earlier scene Joe gives Gwen some money to buy steaks. The
following shot shows her at the butcher's. Aldrich uses an overhead
shot framing Gwen at the right and a cop at the left. The composition emphasizes her emotional conflict over the situation as her
mother's voice-over fills the soundtrack. Should she tell the cop? Or
will concern for her mother's health overrule her feelings to act as a
law-abiding citizen? Aldrich often uses an overhead camera shot in
his television and film work to illustrate the complex dimensions of
a particular situation. It is one of his key visual signifiers. He even
uses it to vary the shot composition in his most unsatisfactory films,
such as *4 for Texas* (1963). For example, during one scene when Harvey Burdon (Victor Buono) returns to his office, an overhead camera
position also featuring a chandelier diminishes his bulky figure in
the frame as he enters to encounter Joe Jarrett (Dean Martin) and Angel (Nick Dennis), who verbally threaten him with knowledge of his
involvement in maritime sabotage.

When Gwen's boyfriend, Bob (James Brown), arrives at the house
to ask Gwen to drive him to the airport, his encounter with Joe ends
with the camera tracking in to a close-up of the two lovers. It subtly
parallels the earlier shot when the camera tracked in to place Joe and
Gwen tightly within the frame. Threat represents a common de-
nominator linking both scenes. Gwen wishes to conceal Joe's real
identity from Bob. She does not tell him anything over concern for
her mother's health. But Aldrich suggests that Bob has already recognized Joe by focusing on his facial expression. This suspicion becomes confirmed when Bob arrives at the house the following day
accompanied by two cops.

The next day's opening sequence begins with a close-up of a
newspaper headline revealing the robbery Joe has committed. The
camera tracks out to show Joe asleep on the sofa and Mrs. West
seated beside him. She gives him a watch she once gave to her deceased son because she sees him as both a surrogate and a person capable of redemption. Although Aldrich never answers the question
as to whether Mrs. West really knows who Joe actually is, the possibility exists that she has seen the newspaper headline while Joe
slept. But the important element in this drama involves Mrs. West's
kindness, conscious or not, toward a criminal who has never had a
break in his entire life.

When Bob arrives with the police, Joe decides to perform his final masquerade. He tells Mrs. West that he did not intend to inform her of his imminent departure and says good-bye to her in the gentlest possible manner. Mrs. West looks on him in a loving way as if saying good-bye to her own son. When Gwen thanks Joe for his gracious behavior, as he is about to leave with the cops, he replies: "I didn't want her to know what kind of a guy I am." Joe recognizes Mrs. West's fragile condition. But he has also been affected by a positive encounter with someone who recognizes his better self. He leaves with the gift of the watch presented to him by a mother who temporarily adopted him as a surrogate son and played a key role in his redemption.

Written by Don Ettinger and photographed by veteran Hollywood cameraman Joseph Biroc, "The Guest" is a significant creative achievement despite limitations of budget and time. It is also the first occasion that Aldrich worked with Charles Bronson as well as with a cinematographer he would again collaborate with in *The Ride Back, Hush . . . Hush, Sweet Charlotte, The Flight of the Phoenix, The Killing of Sister George, The Legend of Lylah Clare, What Ever Happened to Baby Jane? Too Late the Hero, Ulzana's Raid, The Grissom Gang, Emperor of the North, The Longest Yard, Hustle, The Choirboys,* and *. . . All the Marbles.*

"Shanghai Clipper" is the first of four episodes Aldrich directed in 1952 for the *China Smith* series starring Dan Duryea.[6] As with "Straight Settlement," it is another example of Aldrich gaining valuable experience for his future role as film director. Aldrich shot the episode in Hollywood, as he did the remainder of his early television work. After an opening shot of a plane, the following dissolve reveals a nervous Hexter (John Deering) squirming in his seat. The shot changes to show hostess Miss Soong (Marya Marco) attending to a mother and baby. A close-up then reveals Hexter getting up from his seat, the framing changing to medium shot as the camera tracks left to follow him to a restroom. He passes Anya Karenski (Marian Carr) and Pilok (Marc Krah). The next shot shows Anya looking suspicious before the image changes to return to the restroom door seen in the previous scene. Then the camera reverses its previous movement, tracking right, away from the door, as wind engulfs the passengers. As a distressed Miss Soong rushes to the door aware that a passenger has fallen from the plane, the shot ends with a track in on a close-up of Anya's ambiguous expression.

These introductory shots complement the nature of a narrative stressing mystery and suspense. Who is responsible for Hexter's death? Marian Carr's Anya suggests that her character represents the deadly femme fatale of film noir. She is an actress Aldrich will again use in "The Witness" episode of *Four Star Playhouse, World for Ransom,* and *Kiss Me Deadly.* Aldrich's familiarity with film noir conventions appears in China Smith's introduction to the viewer. The camera tracks left along a hotel lobby to show Smith relaxing on a sofa. Conscious of Hexter's death, Duryea's voice-over fills the soundtrack: "In the Orient, the cheapest commodity is human life." The next shot represents his point of view, showing the view tilting up from Anya's legs to show her face. Then the framing returns to the previous shot. But it now shows Smith immediately removing his hat and adjusting his tie, ready to begin his role in the drama. During the next scenes camera movements complement Smith's deliberate cat-and-mouse game with Anya and Pilaki. He masquerades as an acquaintance of Hexter to Pilok and uses him to get an introduction to Anya. Following Smith's success, the scene dissolves to a shot of a jukebox. The camera tracks out and dollies right to a low-angle medium shot framing Smith and Anya at a bar. As they interrogate each other, Aldrich uses a succession of close-ups to emphasize significant phrases such as "police," "White Russian," and "profession: hostess" in their cat-and-mouse game. He concludes the sequence by returning to the opening medium shot showing them both at the bar.

The main characters in "Shanghai Clipper" seek a map that Hexter concealed before he died. As the narrative continues, Aldrich employs several devices he will later use in *World for Ransom.* When Smith investigates Anya's room, the sequence begins with an overhead shot revealing the dominant position of a ceiling fan, which appears later in *World for Ransom.* It suddenly stops revolving, alerting Smith to Anya's presence. As she switches the fan back on, the camera tracks right, following her movement toward Smith, who begins bargaining for the map. The camera then descends to ground level, framing them both occupying equal portions of the frame as their verbal duel commences. When Smith makes Anya an offer of $1,000, the image changes to a medium close-up of Smith before cutting to a medium shot framing them both. The camera then tracks in to frame them in close proximity as they engage in further economic negotiations.

An overhead camera shot also occurs in another scene involving Smith in Anya's apartment. But this time Pilok suddenly enters the frame from below the camera. He identifies himself and explains his motivations as the representative of an exploited people seeking the location of oil concessions discovered by Hexter, which will make them independent of the British colonial government. When Anya enters her room, an overhead camera angle dominates her. The camera then pans right before descending to ground level as she moves toward Smith and Pilok, and they all begin another round of negotiations involving the missing map concealed by Hexter before his murder.

Another significant example of Aldrich's cinematic techniques occurs in an earlier sequence set in the office of Lord Ratcliff (Lewis Russell). As Hexter's employer, he is anxious to gain access to the map containing information involving the oil deposits. After showing his company logo, the image dissolves to a shot of Ratcliff at his desk. The camera suddenly makes a swift zip pan to the left as Smith enters the office before panning right to place him left of frame. This results in a triangular composition with Miss Soong's back to camera at the apex as they discuss the location of the missing map. The framing suggests that Miss Soong may hold the key to the problem.

The final sequence occurs at Killong Airport. After dissolving to Miss Soong announcing a plane departure, the camera tracks out as Smith arrives. Following a shot of the plane, the next scene shows the waiting area outside the terminal. The camera moves from long to medium shot as Smith encounters Anya. After Smith suspects where the map is hidden, the next scene shows Smith and Miss Soong inside the plane, framing both in medium shot. Smith finds the map in the lining of Miss Soong's overnight bag where Hexter hid it before he died. Smith and Miss Soong occupy the left and middle parts of the frame during this point of the narrative. But Pilok then makes another surprise entry from behind the camera as he did in the earlier scene in Anya's apartment. This time he moves into the frame from the right, his shoulder visually announcing his presence. Pilok moves forward to retrieve the map from Smith before returning to his original position, with his shoulder right of frame.

Smith and Pilok suddenly fight for the map before Pilok falls to his death from the plane as it moves across the runway. Retrieving the map from Pilok's body, Smith returns to Anya in the waiting area. As Anya kisses him good-bye, the camera cuts to a close-up of her picking his pocket to obtain the map. This scene follows a tracking shot framing them both in medium shot. Aldrich subversively turns the typical cinematic conventions of a romantic farewell into another example of Anya's strategic game playing. Inspector Hobson (Douglas Dumbrille) arrives. Following a shot of Anya framed in the circular window of the plane as she waves good-bye to Smith, the final scene places Smith and Hobson in medium shot. Smith retrieves the real map from his hat and hands it over to Hobson.

The basic narrative of "Shanghai Clipper" is familiar. But as with "The Guest," Aldrich revitalizes it by his sophisticated use of camera techniques and framing, which owes more to Hollywood practices than to contemporary television modes of directing. He would employ such devices constantly in his 1950s television episodes, keeping himself in training like a quarterback for his future role as a film director as well as cinematic coach.

Like "Shanghai Clipper," Aldrich's next contribution to *China Smith* originates from a story by Robert C. Dennis. But this time the teleplay of "Straight Settlement" was written by Lindsay Hardy. It opens with an overhead shot showing a streetlamp, which dominates the image in a similar manner to the overhead fans of "Shanghai Clipper" and *World for Ransom*. A car is parked beneath the lamp. Krantz (Lucien Prival) exits, moving left to leave the frame. Two men then emerge from the right of the frame and enter the car. Krantz returns, entering the screen from the left frame. After he goes inside the car, Aldrich cuts to an interior shot. He places the camera in a low-angle position from the perspective of the dashboard as the two men mug Krantz from behind.

The next sequence introduces Smith, the camera tracking right to left as he walks down a Singapore street. It pauses as Smith sits down and talks to a cat. The camera tracks in to a medium close-up during this dialogue and then tilts up as he moves toward the right frame. The image dissolves to show the police station. Inspector Hobson talks to Maria Torres (Susan Alexander), her back to camera. Sergeant Withers (Gil Herman) is at the right of frame. Opening with a medium shot of Hobson, the camera tracks out to frame them all in a triangular composition similar to the group composition used in "Shanghai Clipper." Following a succession of alternating medium close-ups involving Hobson and Maria, the camera returns to its original position and then tracks back to Hobson as Maria leaves. The image changes to a medium shot of Hobson before the camera pans left as Krantz enters the room. It follows him as he sits down in the chair formerly occupied by Maria. Unlike Maria, Krantz identifies Smith as one of the assailants.

Hobson visits Smith's apartment and threatens to convict him for the crime. The next sequence begins in Shira's (Myrna Dell) apartment. When she appears, the camera tracks back from its introductory medium position to pan left, showing a lamp beside her. When Smith arrives, a succession of alternating medium close-ups similar to those between Smith and Anya in "Shanghai Clipper" punctuates their conversation. Smith needs her help to escape conviction. The sequence ends with the mysterious Johnny Fong (Clarence Lung) suddenly entering the frame like Pilok in "Shanghai Clipper." He presents Smith with information leading him to Chinese businessman Sing Ho (Paul Guilfoyle).

The scene in Sing Ho's office begins with a medium shot of Sing Ho before the camera tracks out to show Smith at the left of the frame. During this sequence, Smith walks back and forth, occupying foreground and background space as he interrogates the businessman about his role in the crime. Smith's movements represent a more sophisticated version of Pilok's in the penultimate scenes of "Shanghai Clipper." When Smith's questions become too assertive, Sing Ho calls in his bodyguards. The camera pans left to show one entering the door and then pans right as another arrives. The sequence ends by returning to the original framing shot of Sing Ho. He is clearly in command of the situation and, presumably, the guilty party in Smith's frame-up.

The final denouement occurs in Shira's apartment. Johnny confronts Smith and Shira, who now know too much about his involvement in the actual theft. Before Johnny can shoot Smith, a knock on the door distracts him, allowing Smith to get the gun from his opponent. The camera pans right as Hobson enters before tilting up to an overhead shot framing all inside the room. It then tilts down to a medium close-up of Hobson. A lap dissolve follows, showing Hobson in medium close-up in his office. The camera tracks out to an overhead shot as the viewer learns of the plot between Sing Ho and Johnny to rob Maria. Aldrich varies the composition by swiftly cutting between shots of Hobson in left foreground and Smith in right background to avoid a theatrical "talking heads" effect that would slow down the scene. The sequence ends with an overhead shot as Maria embraces Smith.

The visual composition of "Straight Settlement" again shows that Aldrich was already a film director in all but name. His work with Dick Powell on three *Four Star Playhouse* episodes would confirm this.[7] "The Witness" is the first teleplay he directed with Powell in the leading role. It also reunited him with Charles Bronson and Marian Carr as well as introducing Nick ("Va Va Voom! Pretty Pow") Dennis to audiences in an amusing cameo. Aldrich also directed future Sam Peckinpah alumnus Strother Martin in a courtroom scene. He would use the actor again in *Kiss Me Deadly* and *Attack!*

"The Witness" opens with a medium close-up of a reporter phoning in his story inside a telephone booth. He comments to his editor that defense attorney Mike Donegan (Dick Powell) has once more astonished the court by failing to appear. After he finishes his call, the camera tracks swiftly right to show him entering the courtroom and pausing before the barrier separating spectators from judge, jury, and lawyers. Following the question, "Why isn't he here?" the image changes to a long shot of the entire courtroom viewed from behind the judge's back as he complains about Donegan's behavior. Donegan's partner, Philip Baedecker (Robert Sherman), again persuades the reluctant judge to grant a recess.

The next sequence begins with a dissolve to Donegan seated at a restaurant table as Nick (Nick Dennis) awaits his order. Donegan orders a sweet for his harassed partner. A succession of shot/reverse shot medium close-ups occurs from different angles as Baedecker informs Donegan about the court's impatience with the delays. Baedecker leaves. Private eye Peterson (Walter Sande) arrives. Another succession of reverse shots occurs as he tells Donegan about his failure to track the woman who could supply the necessary alibi for Frank Dana (Charles Bronson), who faces capital punishment for the death of a guard in a robbery. The framing returns to medium shot as Nick arrives with an apple pie intended for Baedecker. Nick remarks, "My you've changed!" Aldrich uses humor to lighten the serious problem of the missing witness in this sequence. When Donegan finally traces her, they meet at the same restaurant. As she sits down at Donegan's table, Nick comments, "The one last night was pretty," before Donegan dismisses him.

Nick's second comment also lightens the oppressive weight of the previous scene when Donegan visited his client in prison. After dissolving to a medium shot of the prison walls, the scene shows Donegan and Dana from a high overhead perspective, the bars ominously casting shadows over the two men as they discuss the hope-less task of finding the missing woman who can supply the neces-sary alibi. Following the change to a medium low-angle shot fram-ing the two men, the camera tilts down as Dana sits next to Donegan. It then tilts up as Dana walks toward the bars of his cell. At the moment he stops, Dana's face is framed in the foreground of the left frame between two bars. Donegan sits in the right frame of the background, his face also framed between two bars. Both men are metaphorically imprisoned by their inability to find Alice Blair (Marian Carr) at this point of the film. She is either a fantasy figure from Dana's imagination or a treacherous woman who has disap-peared when he needs her most. Dana tells Donegan that Alice left the money in his safekeeping before she vanished. Considering that Marian Carr performs several femme fatale variations for Aldrich in "Shanghai Clipper," *World for Ransom,* and *Kiss Me Deadly,* the odds do not look good at this point.

Donegan eventually traces Alice and tries to persuade her to tes-tify. He finds that Dana's idealized image of her is correct but is un-able to discover the reasons for her reluctance to testify. The next scenes occur in the courtroom as various witnesses, including Dana, take the stand. Aldrich often uses the old-fashioned wipe technique moving left across the frame as witnesses begin their testimony. When all appears lost, Alice finally enters the courtroom to testify. She faces brutal interrogation by the district attorney, and her testi-mony does not help Dana. However, sensing that she is covering up for someone in the courtroom, Donegan insists that individual male members of the audience walk past the bench. He finally focuses on Alice's brother Ted (Strother Martin), who was injured in the rob-bery and confesses his guilt. During these scenes Aldrich uses a suc-cession of varying camera angles such as low-angle shots of Done-gan, medium shots, and overhead medium shots of the trusting Dana, both to bring suspense to the narrative and to avoid the static type of visual composition characteristic of future courtroom televi-sion dramas such as *Perry Mason* (1957–74). The final shot occurs in Donegan's office with the reunited Frank Dana and Alice Blair tact-fully refusing the offer of a celebration at Nick's.

Because of the short running time, it is never made explicit why Alice refuses to admit her brother's guilt when her lover faces the death penalty. This represents the major problem of the narrative. But reading the episode in the light of Aldrich's later perverse family melodramas, several explanations are possible, ones that mainstream Cold War television can never supply. Is Alice the victim of some dark dysfunctional family relationship in being too close to her brother? Who knows?

"The Witness" was broadcast on 22 October 1953. The next two Aldrich–Powell collaborations, "The Squeeze" and "The Hard Way," were broadcast on 1 October and 19 November 1953, which may not represent the actual order in which they were shot. Both were written by Blake Edwards and feature Powell in the role of nightclub owner Will Dante, which he performed in several other episodes of *Four Star Playhouse.* Like future *Dick Powell Show* episodes "Who Killed Julie Greer?" and "Savage Sunday" (which became the basis for the future 1962–63 NBC series *Saints and Sinners* starring Nick Adams and John Larkin), the "Dante's Inferno" segments of *Four Star Playhouse* led to the 1960–61 NBC series *Dante,* starring Howard Duff in the title role.[8] As with "The Guest" and "The Witness," "The Squeeze" saw the first appearance of another key member of Aldrich's future repertory company, Richard Jaeckel. He would also appear in the director's first film, *Big Leaguer.* Unlike Charles Bronson, who began his film career in 1951, this former 20th Century–Fox delivery boy had appeared in *Guadalcanal Diary* (1943) and was already a well-known presence in supporting youthful roles in films such as *Sands of Iwo Jima* (1949), *The Gunfighter* (1950), and *Come Back Little Sheba* (1952). Despite his age, he was already a veteran actor, as he shows in his performance here.

"The Squeeze" also represents an unusual lighthearted entry in the work of Robert Aldrich thanks to the collaboration of Blake Edwards and Dick Powell. The actor performs another version of the nonchalant, urbane Philip Marlowe persona he displays in *Murder My Sweet* (1944), when he was trying to find another star image other than the juvenile singer lead he was identified with from Warner Bros. 1930s musicals. Following an establishing shot of Dante's Inferno nightclub, the next image shows the arrival of Stanley Warren (Richard Jaeckel). He walks into camera and pauses before it in a close-up position similar to Charles Bronson's in "The Guest." The camera tracks out and moves left as Stanley goes to the bar. It then pauses in medium shot as he asks Monty (Herb Vigran) about Dante's whereabouts. Another succession of establishing shots follows, showing Dante's arrival. He descends the staircase and exchanges a few words with a cigarette girl. The camera returns to the previous medium shot of Stanley and Monty at the bar. It tracks right as Stanley approaches Dante and then moves in the reverse direction as both men go to the bar. The brash politician's son wishes access to Dante's illegal casino. As they debate the issue, Aldrich uses a series of reverse-shot medium close-ups between both men until Stanley gets his way by threatening that his father will close down the casino. The camera then tracks left as both men move toward the crowded back-room casino and then stops at the cashier's cage. A shot next frames Dante and Stanley behind the bars of the cage. Dante reluctantly tells his employee to furnish Stanley with chips.

A few shots later the camera moves left as petty criminal Dutch passes Stanley. Dutch will play a key role in this narrative. A shot of him watching Stanley in the background of a medium shot stresses his recognition of the young man. After Stanley's sister Susan (Joan Camden) arrives in the nightclub and informs Dante about her brother's lack of financial resources, Dante reenters the casino and orders Stanley out. He now knows that his IOUs are worthless. By this time Dutch is at the cashier's desk. But he does not cash his chips. A low-angle shot showing him from inside the cashier's cage framed by bars suggests another ominous power play in the narrative. It parallels the previous scene showing Dante and Stanley together in the same position following Stanley's successful blackmail tactics allowing him to gamble.

A close-up shot shows Dutch at the phone. He phones racketeer Deras (Mario Siletti). The following shot is a close-up of a newspaper headline mentioning the indictment of Deras by Stanley's father. The paper drops down, showing Deras in close-up. The camera then tracks out to frame Deras in medium close-up before returning to the previous close-up of Dutch on the phone. The sequence ends in long shot with Deras framed in an arch on the right as his henchman Ernie (Karl Lukas) arrives from the left of the frame. It resembles the close-up of the newspaper headline in "The Guest" where the camera tracked out to frame two characters in medium shot.

Deras decides to obtain Stanley's IOUs from Dante. When he and Ernie arrive in Dante's Inferno they sit down at the right of Dante's table. As in his earlier television episodes, Aldrich employs different camera angles in his sequences to vary the visual composition. A close-up shows Deras and Ernie together in a tightly constructed frame. When Ernie takes exception to Dante's attitude, he moves across the frame. His head now fills the center of the frame, blocking Deras from sight. This concluding angle reveals Ernie as a major threat to Dante who will physically enact the orders of a boss hidden behind his presence. Deras obtains the IOUs from Dante. The sequence ends with a low-angle medium shot of Deras as he states, "You're too independent, Dante."

Dante and Monte later burgle Deras's apartment to reacquire the IOUs. Suspecting that a painting conceals the safe—"Where else?"—former safebreaker Monte breaks the combination. As both men reach for the documents, a circular close-up from the interior of the safe reveals Dante and Monte within the frame of the shot. However, Aldrich uses a deep focus shot, the rationale of which becomes clear as Deras appears in the background with a gun in his hand. The shot then changes to Aldrich's characteristic overhead angle emphasizing a threat before cutting to a medium shot framing all three men together. Dante tricks Deras before Ernie arrives, allowing him and Monte to escape. Dante and Monte then await Deras in the nightclub. As Deras arrives, Aldrich uses a low-angle shot of Dante's table. Deras then threatens Dante over returning the IOUs. However, Lt. Waldo (Regis Toomey) arrives on the scene and arrests Deras. The sequence ends with Susan's arrival. It ends with a medium close-up of her kissing Dante. Both depart, leaving Herb to clear up.

"The Squeeze" is another competently filmed television episode showing Aldrich's abilities as a director. He not only varies shots and camera movements consistently throughout the episode but also uses actors in the best possible manner, obviously owing to the rehearsal time he managed to obtain.

Broadcast on 19 November 1953, "The Hard Way" introduced Aldrich to another character actor he would later use in *Vera Cruz, Kiss Me Deadly,* and *4 for Texas*—Jack Elam. Like Richard Jaeckel, Elam already had several film credits. But Aldrich elicited a distinguished acting performance from him in this twenty-two-minute television drama. Although the narrative again involves timeworn themes of theft and the underworld, Elam's role as gangster Vick is never stereotypical. It contains nuances ranging from menace to humor, which again reveal Aldrich's beneficial rehearsal techniques.

Like "The Squeeze," "The Hard Way" opens with establishing shots of the city at night, the exterior of Dante's nightclub, and its owner leaving his car. As before, the first interior shot shows Dante descending the staircase. He pauses to talk to a hatcheck girl and then moves to a table to check a book as the camera tracks out before him. The camera tracks left as Dante goes to the bar to talk to Monte, who tells him that Vick is in the back room winning $80,000 at dice. The scene changes to a medium close-up of Vick inside before returning to the previous shot as the camera tracks left to follow Dante into the gambling room. One of Aldrich's spatially distinctive close framing shots occurs, showing a low-angle medium close-up of Vick at the left foreground of the frame with the croupier in the right background of the shot. The croupier announces Vick's $90,000 win. A medium shot follows as the camera tracks left to follow Dante walking to the cashier's cage. When Dante learns that he has only $115,000 in the bank, a reverse shot from the interior of the cage visually complements the serious nature of this information. The bars frame Dante outside. Another significant shot follows. It depicts the gambling table in an ominous overhead camera position. Dante faces the threatening position of trying to cut his losses without offending the feelings of a dangerous gangster.

A consecutive series of reverse close-ups involving Dante and Vick follows. The gangster insists on the game continuing. Tension develops when a reverse medium close-up shot of Vick in the left foreground with his bodyguard Tino (Lennie Breman) follows a solitary low-angle medium close-up of Dante. These shots not only show that Dante is on his own but also reveal Tino's resemblance to Ernie in "The Squeeze." He is the guy who will break bones (or worse) on the orders of his boss. However, Dante finishes Vick's winning streak by picking up the dice before they fall, closing his bank for the night. The disgruntled Vick leaves. But Dante worsens his mood by commenting on his excessive aftershave lotion, a gift from his mother.

The following sequence involves Dante romancing Southern belle Janice Howl (played by comedienne Elizabeth Fraser). However, Vick and Tino interrupt this idyllic scene by announcing that Dante has given them counterfeit money. After Janice leaves abruptly, Dante has to talk his way out of a dangerous situation. Believing that his cashier has passed dud money, Dante persuades Vick and Tino to visit the man's apartment. But they find him murdered and the police already there. The scene dissolves to the exterior of the police station viewed from a barred window. Another dissolve follows, showing Lt. Waldo at his desk in medium close-up. As he moves from his desk to a cabinet, the camera tracks back showing the three suspects. The camera then stops to frame them all in a slight over-head angle. When the suspected men leave Waldo's office, the camera frames them in medium shot in the corridor. The camera tracks left as they walk toward a bench, stopping as Dante explores the situation. When Tino sits down and drops the dice Vick used at the gaming table, Dante picks them up and discovers that they are loaded. Aldrich then uses another unusual shot similar to the one from the interior of Deras's safe in "The Squeeze." As Dante rolls the dice twice to check them, both Dante and Vick are seen in low-angle medium close-up from *the perspective of the bench*. When they leave the police station the sequence opens with the original overhead shot. But this time no window bars appear framing the scene, suggesting that Dante has already solved the problem. He has not only deliberately cued Lt. Waldo with misleading evidence but discerns that another of his employees may have been involved. The camera tracks left following their departure from the station, stopping again as Dante explains the solution. The sequence ends with a cut to a medium low-angle shot of Lt. Waldo outside the police station watching the three men.

Dante, Vick, and Tino decide to visit the apartment of Stan the Stickman (Robert Osterloh). The penultimate sequence of "The Hard Way" illustrates remarkable cinematic grammar. It opens with a dissolve to a medium close-up of Stan. The camera tracks back into long shot as he hears a knock on his door. It cuts to a low-angle medium shot of Dante, Vick, and Tino outside. When they enter Stan's room, he pulls a gun on them and threatens to kill them. Aldrich emphasizes the serious nature of this threat by employing an overheard camera angle. However, the next shot shows Lt. Waldo outside Stan's door framed in the same angle as the trio before they entered. When Waldo's knock on the door distracts Stan, Dante immediately seizes the moment to disarm him, much like China Smith's action against his opponent in "Straight Settlement."

The final sequence occurs in Dante's nightclub. Awaiting Janice's arrival to continue his romantic tryst, Dante discovers that she has decided to go on a date with Vick. He informs his rival that she approves of his aftershave lotion. Dante then decides to drown his sorrows at the bar, but the arrival of a blonde passing him in medium shot moving left to right across the frame sends Dante in the same direction. "The Hard Way" again reveals accomplished directing techniques that Aldrich would further develop later.

Like "The Guest," "The Gift" had a personal resonance for the future director. It reunited him with an actor he had worked with before. Aldrich now had the opportunity of directing Charles Boyer, whom he had previously worked with as assistant director on Lewis Milestone's Enterprise Studio production *Arch of Triumph* (1948). The plot of "The Gift" involves a cold executive who has disowned his son after he has not followed him into the family business. Although Aldrich's breach with his father may not have been as severe as the situation in "The Gift," Charles Boyer's unemotional Carl Baxter from Amory Hare's story and John and Gwen Bagni's teleplay may have had certain nuances for a young director never close to his own father.[9] Broadcast on network television on Christmas Eve 1953, "The Gift" has a happy ending. But its dominant mood is pessimistic. Dealing with a cold authoritarian businessman who fails as husband, father, and human being, the episode contains the first example of Aldrich's negative father figures who appear in his future work.

"The Gift" opens with a close-up of Carl Baxter sipping coffee. Offscreen, the voice of his wife Minna (Maureen O'Sullivan) asks if he wants more coffee. The camera then tracks out to frame them in long shot, positioning them as isolated figures in a room. Neat and spartan furnishings suggest Minna's loneliness as well as the sterile nature of their relationship. By initially focusing on Carl's solipsistic involvement with his coffee, the opening shot deceptively suggests that he is the only person present. When Minna's voice occurs offscreen, it marks her irrelevance to his isolated existence. Carl has erected an emotional barrier between them because his wife supported his son's decision to be a geologist rather than a businessman. Carl refuses to acknowledge his son's existence. Before leaving for the office, he unconvincingly attempts to express his feelings for Minna: "I have you." Minna responds, "Do I have *you*?" Alternating low-angle medium shots of Carl and Minna significantly emphasize this exchange. When Carl states, "We live in the present," the camera angle changes to an isolating overhead shot of the hallway before tracking into a medium shot of the couple as Carl again destroys Minna's hopes for reconciliation between father and son: "Martin is gone, *gone!*" Minna sadly replies, "You talk of him as if he were dead." Her remarks also apply to their marriage, as future events reveal.

The scene changes to Carl's office as the camera tracks left along a group of workers looking forward to Christmas before Carl enters.

The camera then moves right as Carl goes to his office. One worker comments to his female colleague about their boss: "Don't ever wish him a Happy Christmas. He used to be a human being." This judgment receives further confirmation in the following sequence. It begins with the camera tracking left as Carl's partner, George Lennox (Dan Tobin), moves to the desk of Mrs. Mitchell (Joan Camden). As he goes to his partner's office, the camera moves in a rightward direction. These movements are not redundant because the leftward direction expresses a vitality lacking in Carl's own life, whereas the opposite movement operates contrapuntally, complementing Carl's dehumanized character. The following medium shot shows Carl at his desk. He expresses disbelief at the number of $600 bonus payments for Christmas, which he terms "blackmail." Lennox then reminds Carl that they started the practice "in 1934 when we weren't drawing salaries ourselves" and reminds him of his more humane attitudes when his son was a small boy: "Why don't you stop torturing yourself, Carl. So your plans didn't work out the way you planned it. He's still *your* son." Despite George's pride in Carl's son now being a first-class geologist, these remarks anger his partner even more. Carl callously orders a Salvation Army woman (Amy Doran) collecting for charity out of his office. He refuses to allow Mrs. Mitchell to leave early on Christmas Eve, resulting in her resignation: "I don't understand what kind of man you are." Attributing her motives to a desire to finish Christmas shopping, Carl learns from his partner that she wished to purchase a plane ticket to see her husband returning from the Pacific after an absence of two years (perhaps from the Korean War?).

Aldrich frames the evening meal between Carl and Minna in a long shot. He again emphasizes their empty relationship in an alienating environment. They sit at opposite ends of a long table. The camera tracks in as the couple again converse. Minna attempts to plea for a son who "never had your sense of business" and "tried to follow in your footsteps." Carl refuses to open a present his son has sent him from Arabia. When he expresses disappointment in his son, Minna argues, "You can't invest in children. They're not stocks and bonds." But possessiveness rules Carl's feelings, as he reveals in his angry comments about children leaving home: "Then he grows up and he's gone. You have nothing, *nothing.*" These lines foreshadow future Aldrich films dealing with the dark aspects of possessive parental control.

Unwilling to confront these issues, Carl decides to go to his club. But before he leaves, the image of Minna holding out his hat briefly dissolves into that of the Salvation Army woman who appeared earlier in his office. Carl finds no refuge in his gentleman's club. As he sits in a chair sipping his brandy in the left frame of the image, an excited young father (Eddie Firestone) attempts to interest him in a Christmas present he has purchased for his young son. While Carl remains static in this shot, the live emotions he once felt over his past relationship with his son symbolically appear in the young father's movements. He repeatedly walks from foreground to background in the right of the frame as he tells Carl about his excitement over Christmas. The young father briefly circles around the seated older man before returning to his alternating movements across the right part of the frame. After he leaves, Carl hears the voice of the Salvation Army woman. He turns to see an apparition. But this time the woman has Minna's face as she pleads, "Please Sir." Carl's retreat to his club bar also supplies no refuge. He listens to a traveling salesman from Virginia (Gene Hardy) who misses being away from his parents during Christmas.

Touched by these incidents, Carl decides to visit a store to purchase a gift for Minna. The sequence begins with a dissolve to a Toyland sign as the camera tracks down to show Carl entering frame left. As he requests a mink stole from an assistant (Virginia Christine), he sees Minna escorting some young children to see Santa Claus. The assistant explains that she is well known for her presence every Christmas Eve bringing children from an orphanage to visit Santa Claus and buying them presents. Carl then receives the final blow to his self-esteem when the assistant tells him that they all believe Minna to be a widow: "There is something about a widow you can't mistake." Struck by this revelation, Carl returns home loaded with presents, greeting Minna warmly. The scene begins with the same isolating overhead shot that framed his departure. But it moves into a medium shot of *both* Carl and Minna, now occupying equal portions of the frame. Aldrich's episode of *Four Star Playhouse* concludes with a medium close-up of Carl kissing Minna and wishing her, "Merry Christmas."

Unlike other fathers in Aldrich's films, Carl changes before it is too late. He has the opportunity to reconcile with his son as he has done with his wife. Although the narrative moves toward a network "happy ending" for the Christmas Eve audience, its conclusion is more than formulaic. Personal feelings appear in this episode. Every viewing of this episode reinforces the fact that Aldrich invested his very emotions into this production. It speaks to the heart. Maureen O'Sullivan's performance also shows Aldrich's skill in directing women, which Ida Lupino later praised on *The Big Knife*. As an early work of a director who lost his own mother when he was young and who had a distant relationship with his own father, "The Gift" operates as a positive alternative to the bleak conclusion of *What Ever Happened to Baby Jane?* when Jane speaks those poignant lines, "All that time—we could have been friends?"

Also scripted by John and Gwen Bagni, "The Bad Streak" was broadcast on 14 January 1954. It again features Charles Boyer but this time in the very different role of debt-ridden Reno casino owner Barry Renneck. Facing the "bad streak" of the title and reluctant to become a front man for a corporate organization represented by Bentridge (John Hoyt), Renneck discovers that his estranged son also contributes to his financial problems. Angry at his father for "deserting him," David Renneck (Robert B. Arthur) seeks to ruin him economically by breaking the casino bank. After David insults his father as a "tin horn," Renneck wins all his son's inheritance money in a blackjack game between them. The winnings will enable him to continue owning his casino. But he also wishes to teach his high-society son a lesson in responsibility: "If you've got to gamble, you've got to learn how to lose." David's affluent lifestyle has not offered him any chance of learning mature and responsible behavior. Although David's grandmother, Mrs. Weston (Esther Dale), has isolated her grandson from a father whom she regards as a "bad influence," his high-society lifestyle does not seem to have given him any moral foundations. David's arrogant behavior also parallels the conduct of Richard Jaeckel's Stanley in "The Squeeze."

However, unlike most television productions, "The Bad Streak" avoids an unconvincing forced conclusion of reconciliation between father and son. David leaves condemning his father: "You taught me one thing. I hate gamblers." But Renneck decides to return the money to his son without his knowledge. He requests his lawyer to draw up a watertight trust fund. He then leaves his casino and devoted mistress, Angela (Virginia Grey), who he suspects is only interested in his money: "It's all over, all over." Although lacking the unemotional overtones of Carl Baxter, Boyer's Renneck is also an isolated individual. He distrusts Angela, perhaps seeing in her another embodiment of the economic disease that not only destroyed his own marriage but alienated him from David. However, after deciding to gamble again by inserting a coin in a diner slot machine, he finds that his bad streak has suddenly changed. Angela then arrives, deciding to commit herself to somebody she previously expressed frustration with for being a "loser" in terms of their personal relationship. Renneck decides to trust Angela. They leave the diner together to face an uncertain future.

"The Bad Streak" contains few innovative cinematic techniques because Aldrich concentrates more on his actors, as he did with "The Gift." He is by now self-assured in his new role as director. However, significant framings and camera angles occur in this episode. Renneck and Angela often appear in alternating close shots, expressing tension between them, similar to scenes in "The Gift" involving Charles Boyer and Maureen O'Sullivan. Renneck and Bentridge also appear in tight close-ups when they discuss the financial problems that may lead to a shadowy organization taking over the casino. Aldrich also uses a choker close-up shot to frame Renneck when he learns of his son's presence at the casino. When father and son go to his office to play blackjack, the camera moves from Renneck's desk to crane up into an overhead shot, bringing the gambling table into prominence. Other high-angle shots show Renneck winning and David losing. Renneck's employee Chick (Horace McMahon) suggests the deadly nature of the Oedipal game expressed in the overhead shot when he informs Angela about Renneck's cold and calculating attitude toward his son.

"Hotel de Paree" (*The Sundance Kid* pilot) and Aldrich's two contributions to *Adventures in Paradise* occurred midway through his career at a time when prospects looked grim following his Hollywood exile and problems affecting his European films. I have been unable to find a copy of "Hotel de Paree," a CBS pilot episode for a series with Earl Holliman as the Sundance Kid, which also reunited Aldrich with Jack Elam and Strother Martin. However, Aldrich's surviving contributions to ABC TV's *Adventures in Paradise* contain several significant features.

Shot on a ten-day schedule in May 1959, the pilot episode of *Adventures in Paradise* aired as the second episode of the series on 12 October 1959. Cowritten by James A. Michener (whose short stories formed the inspiration for the series) and Thelma Schnee, "The Black Pearl" involves a disparate group of passengers traveling on

Adam Troy's boat *The Tiki*. Their personalities are all affected by economic greed following the discovery of a rare black pearl. As well as featuring series regulars Troy (Gardner McKay) and his Polynesian partner, Oliver Kee (Weaver Levy), other characters in this episode include female adventuress Celeste Soulange (Patricia Medina), who may or may not have murdered her husband; her alcoholic lover and alibi Charles Remley (Anthony Steel); and racist European businessman Wagner (Kurt Kaznar). The suspected passengers have different motivations for murdering the pearl's rightful owner, One Arm (Lon Chaney Jr.). He was traveling to Australia to sell the item at a much higher price than he would gain in the island community. But their motivations are all linked to one common factor, as One Arm recognizes when he observes the passengers lustfully gazing at his pearl on the evening before his death: "Disgusting! That's what you are! Displaying your greed! Drooling over your greed. You'd do anything to get this pearl, rob or kill!" After One Arm leaves with his pearl, Wagner disdainfully remarks, "He won't last two days in Australia if he's lucky."

As Aldrich was now a seasoned professional film director, he did not need to prove cinematic expertise as much as he did in his earlier television work. However, certain scenes in "The Black Pearl" use framing effectively. When individual close-ups show the pearl's effect on the passengers, Aldrich inserts a contrasting medium close-up showing Adam and Oliver on opposite ends of the frame, objectively viewing barely concealed economic lust on the faces of their passengers. The human cargo turn against each other after One Arm's murder. Sharks devour One Arm after an unseen assailant throws him overboard. The nature of his death aptly symbolizes those cannibalistic consumerist desires infecting his fellow passengers. After the murder of One Arm's partner, Timaui (Abraham Sofaer), Adam discovers the real murderer. He is first mate Thompson (Hal Baylor), forced to leave America because of a financially crippling divorce. Whereas Adam wishes to earn enough money legitimately to eventually return home and own his own ranch, Thompson wishes to pursue his own version of the American dream by illegitimate means.

A struggle occurs. The pearl accidentally falls on the deck. Quickly edited shots show the pearl rolling across the deck as the hands of the greedy passengers attempt to grab it in vain.[10] The sequence ends with the pearl rolling over into the sea. Adam comments, "It's gone back to the depths where it belongs. Maybe the saltwater will wash it clean."

Like "The Black Pearl," "Safari at Sea" was cowritten by James A. Michener in collaboration with Bill Barrett. As Michener's style differs from that of Aldrich, "The Black Pearl" could not explicitly employ those noir features common to *World for Ransom, Kiss Me Deadly, The Big Knife, Attack!* and *The Garment Jungle.* But "Safari at Sea" contains many noirish overtones. It is also one of Aldrich's most personal contributions to a television series.[11] "Safari at Sea" deals with a dysfunctional marital relationship in which a deceased father's influence acts as a negative emotional constraining factor on his daughter's adult life. The episode parallels themes treated in *Attack!* and *The Garment Jungle* as well as foreshadowing Aldrich's future dark Gothic family narratives *What Ever Happened to Baby Jane?* and *Hush . . . Hush, Sweet Charlotte.*

The episode opens with Adam expecting the arrival of Jeff (John Ericson) and Nicole Hazen (Diana Lynn). They approach *The Tiki* in a motorboat that Nicole pilots. As Jeff greets his former college friend, the Hazens initially appear to be an archetypal happy 1950s American couple on vacation. But the mood changes abruptly. Nicole suddenly accelerates and circles dangerously around *The Tiki.* Jeff's smile turns to anxiety. Nicole clearly enjoys humiliating her husband before his old friend. Not all is well with this couple. Viewers soon learn why.

The following sequence begins at the Hazen apartment with a medium shot of Jeff ominously placed before a cocktail table consuming a drink. After an exterior shot of Adam ringing the doorbell, the camera returns to its previous position inside the apartment. It then tracks left as Jeff goes to the door to greet his old college friend from the class of 1954. During their conversation, the audience learns that Jeff proved himself to be incredibly successful, beyond the expectations of his former classmates. He became a flourishing Hollywood actor. Adam congratulates him: "I saw one of your films in Hong Kong long ago. You were good, very good."

However, the mood changes when Nicole enters. The camera dollies right as she moves toward the two men. Nicole not only now dominates the frame. She also changes the scene's amicable mood. The Hazens have returned from an African safari and wish to continue hunting in the South Seas by spearing a dangerous eel. Despite Adam's warning Nicole about her inexperience in deep-sea diving

and the nature of the quarry she wishes to pursue, she acts aggressively toward Adam and seeks every opportunity to humiliate Jeff,
who calls her by the male nickname "Nick."[12] Nick shows Adam her
watch. A close-up reveals it to be a man's watch. It belonged to her
late father. Adam attempts again to warn Nick about the dangerous
nature of deep-sea fishing. But she persists in an attitude resembling
male arrogance more than female stubbornness. Upset by her behavior, Jeff mixes another drink. Failing to defuse the situation after
offering to take them out to dinner, Adam leaves the Hazen apartment, requesting their presence on *The Tiki* at 4:00 a.m. for a 10:30
a.m. departure.

   During the following jetty sequence, Nicole boards *The Tiki* and attempts to seduce Adam: "I'm doing my best to get that early start."
However, Adam refuses her advances, not just out of loyalty to his
old friend but also recognizing that she enjoys emasculating and
possessing chosen victims: "Why do you say things when you mean
people?" She has obviously hunted Jeff like an animal on safari and
now possesses this handsome Hollywood star like a trophy. Nicole
enjoys seeing her husband masochistically submit to her verbally
sadistic behavior. She leaves Adam to confront his old friend, who
has become a hopeless alcoholic.

   The next day they begin their own version of a safari to spear the
dangerous eel. Nicole gives her watch to Jeff for safekeeping. She exhibits surprise when she learns that her supposedly weak husband
intends to join them. Nicole passes her watch to Adam: "My father's
initials are on the back. His name was Nick too." However, during
the underwater hunt, Jeff freezes when a dangerous eel later threatens Nicole. She accuses him of cowardice and wishing her dead. The
confused Jeff turns to Adam: "Did I want her dead?" They all visit a
nightclub later that evening. The sequence begins with Aldrich's
ominous overhead framing shot showing a fan revolving above as
they sit at the table in a triangular composition. Nicole is at the apex
with Adam at the left and Jeff at the right. The camera tracks down
to frame them all in medium shot. Nicole refuses Jeff's invitation to
dance. She instead diverts his attention to an attractive woman
(Genevieve Aumont). The woman looks at the table from the bar.
But the camera cuts to a close-up of Nicole, not Jeff. She looks back
at the woman *before* the camera cuts to a close-up of Jeff.

   This shot sequence is interesting on several levels. It breaks the
normal gender sequence of the Hollywood shot–reverse shot pat-

tern whereby the attractive woman looks at a man. A woman looks at a woman here followed by a shot of her husband. Usually, a woman looks at a man. Then a shot of a jealous girlfriend irritated at the attraction follows. The two initial shots implicitly suggest a lesbian attraction between two women. Nicole returns the gaze of the attractive woman as if recognizing the sublimated attraction of a woman toward a strong female rather than a weak male. Nicole then pushes her husband toward the other woman: "Don't let me stop you." It is almost as if she uses her husband as a surrogate object to accomplish a desire she cannot actually fulfill—at least for television audiences at this time! Jeff moves over to the woman. A deep-focus long shot of the nightclub occurs, showing Adam in the left foreground and Jeff in the right background, with Nicole clearly in control at the center. She has also usurped the typical male role in film by acting as a pimp in a similar manner to Astaroth (Stanley Baker) in *Sodom and Gomorrah,* who offers his mistress (Rosanna Podesta) to the captain of the guard (Antonio De Teffe) in a deliberately perverse family sequence during the later part of the film. Adam and Nicole then depart.

On one level this interesting sequence suggests a gender contest of wills. Nicole clearly wishes to humiliate her husband, as Adam recognizes: "What have you done to Jeff? He was a different person when I knew him." However, the exchange of looks between Nicole and the woman also suggests another interpretation. Nicole resembles here an early version of the powerful lesbian Queen Bera (Anouk Aimée) of *Sodom and Gomorrah,* who uses Ildith (Pier Angeli) to sexually enslave Lot (Stewart Granger). Bera not only rules her land with an iron fist but also dominates her weak, effeminate brother Astaroth, who also resembles Jeff. Bera and Astaroth have engaged in an incestuous marital relationship. Jeff and Nicole's relationship also perversely resembles a family struggle between warring brother and sister. Jeff expresses indecision over whether he did intend to kill Nicole. But Astaroth has no hesitation about murdering his sister, despite their intimacies.

"Safari at Sea" can only hint at such possibilities. The narrative returns to the more familiar ideological concerns of the decade. It suggests that the real problem arises over Nicole performing the role of the castrating mother figure condemned by Philip Wylie in *A Generation of Vipers* (1943). This text influenced Cold War fears about powerful women and impotent sons who could turn homosexual. Jeff decides not to seduce the woman at the bar. He is still in love with Nicole. So he decides to return to a masochistic relationship with a wife who also resembles a castrating mother figure.

"Safari at Sea" also supplies another motivation for Nicole's behavior. But we do not have to accept it as the only one. Adam discovers that Nicole has given Jeff impossible demands to live up to. She speaks of her husband as a "white knight" when she married him. Despite Adam's reply, "White knights look pretty silly these days," Nicole confesses that her deceased father influences not only her own personality but also her expectations concerning the other sex: "He was quite a guy, Adam. He was kind and gentle. But he knew how to be ruthless and fearless." Her attitude toward Jeff changed immediately after her father died. Nicole is as much a victim of the patriarchal family as Jane Hudson and Charlotte Hollis.[13] Aldrich has also criticized the knightly Galahad ideal in *World for Ransom* and *Kiss Me Deadly.*

However, Jeff decides to reject his masochistic self-pity and dives on his own to spear the deadly eel. He refuses to allow Nicole and Adam to accompany him. Jeff succeeds but injures his foot by trapping it in a coral reef. Adam dives down to rescue him after telling Nicole that Jeff is now acting in a more affirmative, rather than suicidal, manner. He not only wishes to live up to her idealized image of masculinity but also wishes to regain his self-respect. However, after rescuing Jeff, Adam advises him to rest and suggests that Nicole attend to her husband.

The cabin sequence begins with husband and wife displaying the type of acrimonious behavior characteristic of their marital relationship. Nicole reluctantly goes to her husband's side. But she now finds a changed person who no longer will subordinate his personal feelings to her will. Jeff tells her, "I love you but not on your terms. I can't be somebody I'm not. I can't be your type. All I want to be is myself." Nicole married a successful Hollywood actor whom she obviously wishes to mold into a living image of her dead father. Her behavior foreshadows Lewis Zarkan's activities in *The Legend of Lylah Clare* (1968). But Jeff now refuses to perform the role Nicole intends for him. Rather than accepting Jeff, Nicole returns to humiliating her husband like a bullying film director. Aldrich then employs a formal strategy similar to that used in *The Garment Jungle,* in which a restaurant booth divides Alan Mitchell and Theresa Renata on opposite sides of the frame. The camera tracks right as

Nicole moves to a partition behind her husband's bed, placing them on opposite parts of the frame. Nicole looks at her reflection through a mirror in the next shot. Her insecure expression contrasts with her harsh words to Jeff. Alternating close-up shots of the couple follow as Jeff announces his decision to divorce. When he tells her that she can keep all their property, Nicole realizes that she is dealing with a person rather than a thing. She responds, "What about me?" Her deceased father's mask now drops. A lonely vulnerable woman asks this question.

When they reach shore, a hospital doctor (Anthony Eustral) informs Adam and Nicole that Jeff's condition is serious. A life-saving operation may result in amputation of the infected leg. Adam influences a reluctant Nicole to give permission. She initially realizes that if Jeff loses his leg he will no longer be able to play the strong heroic role she wants for him. Jeff will be neither Hollywood star nor substitute for her dead father. Adam then tries to mend the broken relationship between Jeff and Nicole: "Don't try to make him something he's not. Your father's dead. Stop trying to make him live in somebody who's alive. Give up! Stop tormenting yourself!" Nicole responds in her usual aggressive, masculine manner: "You're just like Jeff, just like every other man I've known. My father was the only man who ever really loved me." Her lines evoke Jane Hudson and Charlotte Hollis here. Adam argues that Jeff really loves her and that she must give up the past: "Nicole. You're trying hard to make the dead live again. . . . Jeff loves you and I think you love him."

The scene changes to a noir-like depiction of the hospital corridor leading to the operating room. Now convinced by Adam, Nicole goes to Jeff as he is on his way to the operation. The camera tracks left, following the trolley's progress. Both Jeff and Nicole appear framed in medium shot as she encourages him. "Safari at Sea" concludes with news of a successful operation. The doctor mentions that Jeff "keeps calling for Nick." Believing the reference to involve a man, he asks Adam whether another person is missing from the waiting room. After Nicole goes to her husband, the doctor notices her father's watch on a table. Aldrich cuts to a close-up of this highly symbolic object as Adam remarks, "I don't think she'll be needing it again."

Written for network television, "Safari at Sea" appears to end positively. But visual overtones within the concluding scenes speak otherwise. The deep-focus shot of the hospital corridor with noir lighting symbolically articulates a more pessimistic interpretation. It suggests that Nick's ghost will still continue to haunt Jeff and Nicole. Jeff could die on the operating table. Or his amputated leg may exaggerate his already castrated position in this perverse marital relationship. Had Aldrich directed "Safari at Sea" as a film, these alternatives could have emerged.

A discussion of the television work of Robert Aldrich may seem unusual for a book dealing with a film director. However, like his apprenticeship involvement with Enterprise Studios, these television episodes represent important phases of his development. Aldrich's contributions to *China Smith* are not entirely "pedestrian" or memorable merely for the occasional opportunity of experimenting "with an unusual camera angle or movement prefiguring the later features that made him famous."[14] As Silver and Ursini comment, like Aldrich's *Four Star Playhouse* contributions, these television episodes offered him the opportunity to develop "the nascent methods of narrative and organization which would mark his later films."[15]

The Angry Hills (1959) represents one such example. Although a failure because of an undeveloped screenplay, Robert Mitchum's lack of interest, and producer cuts, the film does illustrate the presence of several techniques Aldrich developed from his television work. A sequence in an Athens hotel foyer begins with the camera tracking to frame the grip of Mike Morrison (Robert Mitchum) carried by an unseen bellboy in medium close-up. The shot then pauses briefly as another unseen bellboy picks up the grip and walks away with it right of frame. This movement changes the framing into a long shot as we see Morrison in the background at the hotel desk. This change of framing within the sequence without resorting to cutting recalls Aldrich's earlier experiments in "The Guest" and "The Squeeze." Second, movement within the frame often symbolizes the type of changing relationships between characters seen in Aldrich's television work. One sequence in *The Angry Hills* demonstrates this superbly. Camera movement complements verbal seduction gamesmanship techniques employed by the infirm Commander Oberg (Marius Goring) when he temporarily appropriates the mistress of Gestapo chief Conrad Heisler (Stanley Baker) and moves with her across the screen. He demonstrates to the more virile Heisler who holds the real power. Another scene shows Heisler's mistress, Maria (Jackie Lane), and her fifth columnist brother Tassos (Theodore Bikel) gravitating toward Oberg, leaving Heisler isolated in the frame as the stakes for survival become higher. Also, when Heisler attends the interrogation of Leonides (Peter Illing) by Tassos, he moves constantly from the right foreground to the background of the shot. His movement expresses distaste. But it also develops Aldrich's use of similar movements within the frame illustrated by Pilok in "Shanghai Clipper" and the young father in "The Gift." Finally, when Greek resistance agent Cheyney (Sebastian Cabot) meets Tassos in a nightclub to do a deal, the shot begins with an overhead camera angle showing a fan ominously revolving above them before the camera cranes down to ground level. It is a familiar technique Aldrich employed in his earlier 1950s work such as his *China Smith* contributions, *World for Ransom,* and *Four Star Playhouse.* Other features reminiscent of early Aldrich also appear in *The Angry Hills,* such as a check floor used as a predominant mise-en-scène element in both the hotel foyer and the archaeological institute Morrison visits at night a few scenes later. It resembles the check floor of Mike Hammer's apartment in *Kiss Me Deadly,* revealing Morrison to be little better than a pawn in a deadly game over which he has no control. Such scenes illustrate how important Aldrich's television work was in developing his future cinematic techniques. His visually grotesque contributions to film noir reveal this clearly.[16]

However, Aldrich did not entirely abandon television. During 1965 he intended to produce a television series titled *Nightmare* based on a concept by future director Larry Cohen. This was to be a one-hour suspense series about a man undergoing ESP experiences while sleeping. Despite the fact that Lukas Heller wrote a pilot script for a series to be jointly produced by the Associates and Aldrich Co. and 20th Century–Fox for ABC, the network dropped the idea.[17] But two years later Aldrich attempted to launch a television series modeled on the *Four Star Playhouse* concept. According to the Associates and Aldrich Co. 20 January 1967 treatment, Aldrich reminded his readers that the original Four Star Company "was a tremendously successful anthology series in which the four stars were owners of the production company, as well as artistic participants."[18] Ironically, the series faltered because of its success, rather than failure, when it boosted the careers of its participants.

Aldrich then pitched the idea of a ninety-minute weekly series based on a hotel that would have the advantage of continuing characters featured in every story as well as accommodating guest stars, resembling the later TV series *Hotel.* These continuing characters would be a public relations expert (chosen from a group of five possible stars: Joan Crawford, Bette Davis, Olivia de Havilland, Vivien Leigh, Merle Oberon), house doctor (Ernest Borgnine), hotel manager (Robert Ryan), permanent guest (Telly Savalas), public stenographer (Shirley Eaton), bell captain (Nick Dennis), night desk man (Gabriele Tinti), and housekeeper (Ruby Dee). Aldrich's "Big Five" artists could be secured for five appearances each in any one television season, allowing them regular appearances and flexible schedules for their other commitments. The deal would allow stars the necessary exposure for their careers as well as avoid problems associated with the Screen Directors Playhouse, in which directors submitted stories to stars, therefore guaranteeing their appearance. Aldrich noted that more often than not "name" directors pulled out treasured, but tattered, yarns, and the results were disastrous. He suggested better scripts and organization. However, the idea collapsed after the failure of *The Grissom Gang*. This idea reveals that Aldrich did not entirely discount television but only its rushed schedules and the lack of preparation time. His greatest achievements lay in the area of cinema, particularly where he could operate in as subversive a manner possible. Aldrich's contributions to film noir represent one such example.

NOTES

1. Alain Silver and James Ursini, *What Ever Happened to Robert Aldrich? His Life and His Films* (New York: Limelight Editions, 1995), 345.

2. Edwin T. Arnold and Eugene I. Miller, *The Films and Career of Robert Aldrich* (Knoxville: University of Tennessee Press, 1986), 14–15.

3. Silver and Ursini, *What Ever Happened to Robert Aldrich?* 345.

4. Powell died of cancer on 2 January 1963. According to Tim Brooks and Earle Marsh, "In deference to his family the filmed introductions that he had already prepared for future telecasts were deleted and a succession of guest stars appeared as hosts for the remainder of the season" (*The Complete Directory to Prime Time Network TV Shows 1946–Present*, 5th ed. [New York: Ballantine Books, 1992], 227). I can remember John Wayne introducing one of the shows in 1963 on BBC. But the excision of Powell's introductions may also have affected earlier shows. My copies of "Who Killed Julie Greer?" in which Powell played millionaire detective Amos Burke, and "The Losers," directed by Sam Peckinpah, lack these characteristic introductions. Like several episodes of *The Dick Powell Show*, "Who Killed Julie

Greer?" inspired a later series, *Burke's Law,* starring Gene Barry, which ran on ABC between 1963 and 1966. On the other hand, "The Losers" is a forgettable twentieth-century version of themes Peckinpah had treated much better in his 1960 NBC series *The Westerner.*

5. See Silver and Ursini, *What Ever Happened to Robert Aldrich?* 323. My copy of "The Guest" belongs to *The Visitor* resyndication and never shows Anderson facing the camera.

6. According to Silver and Ursini (*What Ever Happened to Robert Aldrich?* 323), Aldrich directed four episodes. I have only been able to trace two.

7. Silver and Ursini, *What Ever Happened to Robert Aldrich?* 324–25.

8. See Brooks and Marsh, *The Complete Directory to Prime Time Network TV Shows 1946–Present,* 207–8.

9. Arnold and Miller, *The Films and Career of Robert Aldrich,* 4.

10. I first saw this episode in 1960. Although the intervening forty-three years had wiped most of the episode from memory, the image of the hands attempting to grasp the pearl remained in my mind. Like John Ford, Aldrich achieved the director's dream of stamping a few good minutes into the spectator's memory. As this was a television production, he deserves special acclaim for doing so here.

11. For information about the shooting schedules of Aldrich's contribution to this series, see Silver and Ursini, *What Ever Happened to Robert Aldrich?* 327.

12. Although we are meant to understand the nature of the abbreviation, the female "Nic" is clearly subordinated to "Nick" throughout most of this episode. I use the more appropriate latter nuance here.

13. *What Ever Happened to Baby Jane?* and *Hush . . . Hush, Sweet Charlotte* are also key candidates for inclusion in the family horror genre along with *Psycho* (1960) and other well-known examples. See Tony Williams, *Hearths of Darkness: The Family in the American Horror Film* (Cranbury, N.J.: Fairleigh Dickinson University Press, 1996).

14. Francis M. Nevins, "From the Dawn of Television: *China Smith,*" unpublished MS, 3. I am grateful to Professor Nevins for access to this article.

15. Silver and Ursini, *What Ever Happened to Robert Aldrich?* 185, see also 63–64. The authors aptly define these episodes as "TV Noir." Bill Krohn also recognizes the importance of Aldrich's *Four Star Playhouse* contributions. See Krohn, "Adorno on Aldrich," available at www.latrobe.edu.au/screeningthepast/firstrelease/fr0600/bk2fr10b.htm, 30 June 2000.

16. For an interesting examination of certain stylistic devices in *The Angry Hills* and Aldrich's other films, see Adrian Martin, "The Body Has No Head: Corporeal Figuration in Aldrich," available at www.latrobe.edu.au/screeningthepast/firstrelease/fr0600/rmfr10e.htm, 30 June 2000.

17. See Silver and Ursini, *What Ever Happened to Robert Aldrich?* 335–36.

18. Associates and Aldrich Co., *The Plaza* (Los Angeles: Associates and Aldrich Co., Inc., 20 January 1967), 1.

FOUR

APOCALYPTIC NOIR

World for Ransom, Kiss Me Deadly, The Garment Jungle, The Grissom Gang, and *Hustle* belong to the earlier and later phases of Robert Aldrich's career. But they all represent different examples of the director's idea of apocalyptic noir, both personal and social. By questioning the very foundations of individual existence and showing their social construction, these films are Aldrich's own type of crisis cinema. It is one that may conclude in personal devastation or even nuclear annihilation as in *Kiss Me Deadly.* The first three films belong to the classical phase of American film noir, which lasted from 1940 to 1958. Shot in black and white on low budgets, these films are also part of what David Cochran has termed an "underground culture" challenging a Cold War consensus designed to instill conformity and fear into the American public.[1] This consensus effectively ended those brief cinematic challenges to the status quo that emerged during 1947 in the areas of film noir such as *Crossfire* and *Body and Soul.* *The Grissom Gang* represents Aldrich's idiosyncratic stylistic and thematic reworking of classical film noir conventions. Although not "neo-noir," both its content and its characters firmly align it with the postwar grotesque modernism analyzed by Cochran of which film noir was a key representative.

Hustle belongs to a different evolutionary stage of film noir. It is an early example of what later became termed "neo-noir." Aided by the development of high-speed lighting film stock and other technological equipment that would reproduce the stylistic features of the classical phase, the neo-noir movement began in the 1970s as an intuitive response to the post-Vietnam/Watergate malaise in American society, which witnessed the return of a repressed right wing in the election of Ronald Reagan as president.[2] *Hustle* not only evokes the mood of this era but also continues Aldrich's explorations into the vulnerable male psyche he began in *World for Ran-*

som and would continue in *The Big Knife, Attack!* and *Twilight's Last Gleaming.* Lt. Phil Gaines in *Hustle* represents a 1970s embodiment of those alienated figures in the depression plays of Clifford Odets struggling to find some meaning in a changing world and often retreating into a dangerous nostalgia for a past world no longer relevant either to him or to society. Hiding his vulnerability beneath a cynical persona, Gaines does the right thing and wins a minor battle. But he loses the war by allowing himself to be influenced by redundant patterns of heroism that no longer mean anything in his own particular world.

Similar ideas appear in other Aldrich films. But *World for Ransom, Kiss Me Deadly, The Garment Jungle,* and *Hustle* are united by employing a certain noirish mood originating in the historical context of the 1950s. They also employ a significant modernist sensibility embodying a mixture of criticism, satire, and despair. As Cochran demonstrates, a critical type of modernism was very much alive in the 1950s, involving all aspects of art such as literature, painting, cinema, and music. Robert Aldrich expressed dissatisfaction with David Raksin's score for *Apache,* stating that he preferred the contrapuntal aspect of modern music, a technique also characterizing John Lewis's score for *Odds against Tomorrow* (1959), directed by Robert Wise but scripted pseudonymously by Abraham Polonsky.[3] This technique often emphasizes the alienation and paranoia dominating the land of democracy and freedom during the 1950s. Although the progressive aspects of the New Deal and postwar optimism became crushed during the Cold War, dissonant voices still existed. Recognizing the failure of the utopian dreams of earlier decades, many talents engaged in interrogating artistically the foundations of their so-called democratic society based on suppressing minority movements and any radical political alternatives. Robert Aldrich also belonged to this contemporary movement. Unlike Odets, he no longer believed that it was now time to "awake and sing!" Instead, he would concentrate on the first goal by attempting to wake up his audience in an iconoclastic manner.

Liberal critics of the 1950s such as Arthur Schlesinger Jr. and Lionel Trilling believed in consensus and unity. But they often faced "a concept of cultural pluralism that viewed society as being in a constant state of struggle."[4] Despite an official culture of censorship and suppression, alternative forces of dissent invoking violence, chaos, moral ambiguity, and alienation opposing the bland optimism of the Eisenhower era simply went underground:

> This return of the repressed encompassed a wide-ranging cultural cri-
> tique of American society of the most fundamental type. It took the very
> basis of the Cold War consensus—that American society fundamentally
> worked—and challenged it at every level of economics, technology, for-
> eign policy, quality of life, modal personality, and race relations. What
> Geoffrey O'Brien has written of the hard-boiled paperback of the post-
> war period is more generally true of the underground culture: "The pa-
> perbacks . . . tell of a dark world below the placid surface, a world
> whose inhabitants tend to be grasping, dissatisfied, emotionally twisted
> creatures. Here, all is not well; from the looks of it, all could not be much
> more worse. . . . Worse yet, at the heart of it all, there is an implied lack
> of meaning. Unlike the settling of the West or the second World War, the
> events transcribed by hardboiled fiction serve no particular purpose;
> they just happen. A nation gets the epic it deserves, and not necessarily
> the one it wants."[5]

This quotation also applies to the films of Aldrich, which Cochran sees as part of this movement.[6] Cochran notes that the underground culture kept alive the critical spirit of modernism at a time when it had been co-opted into the dominant culture. One such critical aspect involved a modernist grotesque that had largely disappeared in the postwar period.[7] This concept may represent a survival of the hybrid and revolutionary New Deal cultural movement known as the prole-tarian grotesque.[8] Michael Denning believes that this movement rep-resents one of the few important avant-gardes in U.S. culture. It at-tracted many artists initially influenced by European modernism who then blended it within narrative formations in a counter-cultural fashion. Denning cites *Citizen Kane, Modern Times, The Cradle Will Rock,* and *Black, Brown, and Beige* as examples of a revolutionary so-cial modernist movement that opposed the apolitical world of high art. It was a political modernism typified by works such as Edmund Wilson's *Axel's Castle.*[9] Citing Kenneth Burke's 1935 "Revolutionary Symbolism in America" address to the American Writer's Congress, Denning sees the "proletarian grotesque" as central to understanding the artistic movements of the 1930s. Baroque and grotesque images appearing in such Welles films as *Citizen Kane* and the distended vowels of Billie Holiday's "Strange Fruit" attempted to plunge audi-ences into different forms of perception. Rather than allowing audiences to bask in the aesthetic appreciation or indulge in "harmless entertainment," the grotesque movement represented an "unstable, transitional modernism" designed to stimulate perceptions.[10] Denning describes this movement as follows:

> The oxymoron—the apparent contradiction—is, Kenneth Burke argued, the characteristic trope of the grotesque, and the grotesque is the poetic form most appropriate to moments of crisis and transition, a form in which "the perception of discordances is perceived without smile or laughter." "Humor tends to be conservative," Burke suggests, "the grotesque tends to be revolutionary." The grotesque creates gargoyles that violate accepted classifications, human heads on the bodies of birds. For Burke, the grotesque way of seeing characterizes both communism and surrealism, both Marx's account of class consciousness, which grotesquely realigns our categories of allegiance, and the "modern linguistic gargoyles" of Joyce. Indeed, Burke categorizes two of the young proletarian writers of the time, Robert Cantwell and Erskine Caldwell, as instances of the grotesque imagination. One could take Burke's suggestions further: in retrospect, the arts of the cultural front are better characterized as a "proletarian grotesque" than as any kind of social realism.[11]

Denning also sees Orson Welles and the Chaplin of *Modern Times* as part of this movement. Both men influenced Aldrich during the early part of his career. Although unable to depict the revolutionary aspects of this tradition, some Aldrich films do contain significant parallels. He often employs techniques designed to stimulate viewers into realizing the true causes of the hysteria and violence embodied in his films. The two Depression films, *The Grissom Gang* and *Emperor of the North,* offer relevant examples of this critical grotesque. Ernest Borgnine's Shack in *Emperor of the North* is a brutal company employee. But Aldrich often films him in such a way that he resembles an Eisenstein "type" and social gargoyle. *The Grissom Gang* emphasizes the sweaty faces of its protagonists, making them grotesque icons embodying the social ugliness of the American depression.

By the 1950s the cultural climate of America had drastically changed. But Cochran shows that the grotesque still remained within certain fields of popular culture, which also anticipated many aspects of 1960s counter-cultural movements. Talents such as Jim Thompson, Charles Willeford, Chester Himes, Patricia Highsmith, Samuel Fuller, and Richard Condon employed ideas also occurring in the films of Robert Aldrich. These involved worlds of "grotesque characters, products of a social order that twisted and perverted people physically and psychologically," taking issue with audiences "untrained in irony" to promote an underground culture that "thrived on irony, ambivalence, paradox, and complexity."[12]

Kiss Me Deadly illustrates this as well as *World for Ransom*'s ironic gender critique of the "Galahad" heroic ideal. Aldrich's cinematic vision sees old values as no longer relevant to a dehumanized atomic age. But Aldrich also employed a similar critical strategy as Willeford, Highsmith, and Fuller. As Cochran notes, they "made frequent reference to traditional high-cultural texts but, not in midcult fashion, to give their works a patina of respectability while cutting away any critical aspects of high culture. Rather they used high culture in various ways as a means of criticizing the dominant cultural sensibilities."[13] These talents also adopted a tone of moral neutrality to avoid the didactic moralizing and pontification of questions of "good taste" characterizing the prevailing culture. However, critical elements featured in their vision too. Aldrich also employed these critical aspects of twentieth-century modernism in his work in addition to the other influences of Odets, Polonsky, and others.

The Aldrich–Bezzerides adaptation of Micky Spillane's *Kiss Me Deadly* has several associations with Jim Thompson's oppositional pulp fiction rather than the work of the original author. Cochran believes that Thompson deliberately creates "an absurd universe based on a fundamental core of insanity" by refuting the dominant ideology and "showing the psychic ravages inflicted on the victims of the American economic and political system."[14] Thompson later contributed to the bleak satirical visions contained in Stanley Kubrick's *The Killing* (1956) and *Paths of Glory* (1957). Many figures in the film industry knew his work and must have dreamed of cinematically recreating his bleak vision. Thompson also ironically treated Christian symbolism in a manner similar to Aldrich's. Opposed to the values of the American political and economic system, Thompson placed his characters in material versions of hell on earth. His vision reflects the "existential despair that was a dominant theme of postwar modernism."[15] *Kiss Me Deadly* has several points of contact with Thompson's fictional world "filled with godlike figures who act as ultimate powers, playing with people's lives for arbitrary reasons, a world in which guilt and innocence are utterly meaningless."[16] *The Dirty*

Dozen (1967), *Too Late the Hero* (1969), *The Longest Yard* (1974), and *Twilight's Last Gleaming* (1977) all belong to this dark cultural canvas.

In an era firmly committed to family values, Thompson's fiction also "portrayed the American family as beset by a generational, Freudian crisis, more often than not the source of the ravaged psyches of its protagonists."[17] It is a vision appearing frequently, often in those Aldrich films that depict the family as an emotional wasteland, such as *Autumn Leaves*, *Attack! What Ever Happened to Baby Jane? Hush . . . Hush, Sweet Charlotte*, and *The Killing of Sister George*.

Cochran also notes that paradox and the breaking down of artificial divisions form key components of Thompson's universe. Very few of his characters emerge as sympathetic. His only heroes are those not only having a general vision of what is good but also employing a ruthless and amoral approach to achieving it: "All these characters realize they are fighting a losing battle against an absurd system in which even the concept of success is problematic; and yet, like Sisyphus, they keep rolling the stone back up the hill."[18] It is an apt description of characters such as Major Reisman of *The Dirty Dozen* and Paul Crewe of *The Longest Yard*.

Aldrich's noir films embody several features relevant to this critical twentieth-century modernist movement. Cochran sees this movement as an attempt to deconstruct rigid dualistic nineteenth-century oppositions between morality and immorality, civilization and primitivism, conscious and unconscious, rationality and irrationality. The basic idea involved revealing the dark side of a world that official thought denied the very existence of. Ironically, only certain avenues of popular culture offered the opportunity to depict subversively those deadly ambiguities governing human existence that the Eisenhower era hoped to suppress. Like Jim Thompson, Aldrich delighted in ambiguity and paradox and aimed to show that "such seeming oppositions as sanity and insanity, order and chaos, success and failure, god and devil, were merely differences of shading."[19] Both Aldrich and Thompson existed in the contradictory Cold War–era climate, understood its values, and reacted against them. They represented different aspects of a postwar underground modernist movement aiming to challenge official certainties. This movement offered Aldrich the opportunity of developing the critiques contained in the works of Clifford Odets to an even bleaker level by revealing the true nature of official society as violent, chaotic, and absurd.

This modernism contained an apocalyptic overtone, as Marshall Berman recognizes. It involved understanding that the destructive nature of contemporary bourgeois society would logically culminate in Marx's vision contained in *The Communist Manifesto* of "all that is solid melt[ing] into air." This often happens in the films of Robert Aldrich. Mike Callahan's solid masculine securities psychologically melt into air in the climax of *World for Ransom*. The world moves toward its logical apocalyptic destruction in the final scenes of *Kiss Me Deadly*. Cochran's quotation of Berman in relation to Chester Himes also evokes Aldrich's *Kiss Me Deadly* and *Twilight's Last Gleaming*. Himes's sensibility captures Berman's definition of "the glory and modern energy and dynamism, the ravages of modern disintegration and nihilism, the strange intimacy between them; the sense of being caught in a vortex where all facts and values are whirled, exploded, decomposed, recombined; a basic uncertainty about what is basic, what is valuable, even what is real; a flaring up of the most radical hopes in the midst of their radical negations."[20] It represents imagery common to most of Aldrich's work but especially his noir explorations.

Despite production difficulties and censorship problems, Aldrich always retained a fondness for his second film, *World for Ransom* (1954). Aldrich described it as the first film "towards which I have a personal feeling."[21] Aldrich's statement appears unusual because *World for Ransom* resembles an apprentice work. Shot on a low budget during a ten-day shooting schedule with a screenplay by uncredited blacklisted writer Hugo Butler, the film represents a feature-length version of the *China Smith* television series Aldrich worked on in 1952.[22] Dan Duryea reprises his *China Smith* role as Mike Callahan, appearing with series regulars such as Douglas Dumbrille and Keye Luke. Aldrich employed and developed the same types of cinematic techniques he used in directing his early 1950s television work. Both Michael Grost and Silver and Ursini notice several remarkable cinematic techniques in the film.[23]

Despite a rushed shooting schedule, *World for Ransom* operates as a film noir interrogation of gender issues anticipating themes common to *Attack! Autumn Leaves, What Ever Happened to Baby Jane? Hush . . . Hush, Sweet Charlotte, The Legend of Lylah Clare,* and *Hustle.* As with Aldrich's entire work, it is difficult to place it within any rigid generic categories because his films often complement each other. Also, as Robin Wood has significantly noted, all Hollywood genres have common social foundations because "they represent different strategies for dealing with the same ideological tensions."[24] Such tensions also involve definitions of masculinity and femininity in Western society. *World for Ransom* foreshadows gender crisis themes in "Safari at Sea," *The Legend of Lylah Clare*, and *The Killing of Sister George*. But it also contains Aldrich's deconstruction of the heroic ego ideal contained within *Kiss Me Deadly, Hustle, Too Late the Hero*, and *Twilight's Last Gleaming*.

World for Ransom begins and ends in the circular manner characterizing most Aldrich films. No happy ending exists, only a feeling of entrapment within a circuitous personal maze where the main characters often find themselves back where they started and frequently ready to begin another futile odyssey. The opening scene deceptively evokes those Hollywood Orientalist landscapes where a white male adventurer encounters the deceptive lures of the East. An ominous establishing overhead long shot of a noir-lit Singapore street appears. The image then changes to a medium shot as fortune-teller Mai Ling asks Mike Callahan (Dan Duryea) to "take a chance." Mike declines the offer: "Thanks Mai Ling. Not now. Maybe tomorrow." *World for Ransom* concludes in a similar manner. Callahan again declines any further involvement in a game of chance. He has already discovered that the certainties he took for granted no longer exist. Although once again wearing the white suit of his first appearance, he ends the film as a disillusioned adventurer fully comprehending the ironic implications of Mai Ling's final words: "Take a chance, Mr. Callahan. Love is a white bird, yet you cannot buy her."

World for Ransom follows the narrative format of the *China Smith* television series but extends the limiting duration of the usual twenty-two-minute running time into feature-film length. Hired by his former wartime girlfriend, Frennessey (Marian Carr), to investigate the activities of her husband Julian March (Patric Knowles), Mike Callahan finds himself not only trying to help a friend but also believing that he has a fighting chance to win back his ex-girlfriend's affections. He discovers that international gangster Alexis Pederas (Gene Lockhart) has employed March in a scheme to kidnap nuclear scientist Sean O'Connor (Arthur Shields) and ransom him to the highest bidder. Ironically, March impersonates a British officer and returns briefly to his former authoritarian role in colonial Singapore after living outside the margins of society. After discovering O'Connor's whereabouts, Callahan infiltrates the jungle hideout with Major Bone (Reginald Denny), the officer whom March impersonated when he kidnapped the scientist. Callahan has also escaped being framed for the kidnapping by Pederas. He survives to confront the kidnappers and kills them all, including March, who he hoped would take up his offer of escape. Callahan is left alive to tell the tale. But despite his hopes of winning Frennessey, she blames him for her husband's death. She informs him of the life of prostitution she lived in Shanghai when Callahan left her during World War II. Frennessey condemns him for misunderstanding her real character, affirming her devotion to a man who loved her for what she actually was. The film ends as it began with Callahan again representing the "luck of your father and mother," refusing Mai Ling's offer of taking a chance. From this brief synopsis, it becomes evident that *World for Ransom* leads toward this revelation rather than emphasizing the typical action heroics of contemporary film and television.

World for Ransom employs the action formula of 1950s television adventure series such as *Dangerous Assignment* (1952), starring Brian Donlevy; *Soldiers of Fortune* (1955), featuring John Russell; *Sailor of Fortune* (1957), starring Lorne Greene; and *Man with a Camera* (1958), with Charles Bronson. These series all featured an American adventurer pursuing danger in different parts of the world during the post–World War II period. But other factors differentiate Aldrich's second film from its television contemporaries. These involve a noir sensibility and a progressive undermining of the heroic character. Several Aldrich themes of duality and the deceptive nature of appearances characterize this early work, which he regarded as the "first film towards which I have a personal feeling" as well as "a parody on the usual exotic espionage adventure films."[25]

Several scenes in *World for Ransom* reveal the presence of noir devices Aldrich already employed in his *China Smith* episodes. After an introductory scene showing Callahan, the next shot shows him beginning to climb a long, narrow staircase. Shot in deep focus, the image evokes an abstract modernist aura. The camera follows Callahan ascending the stairs until a figure appears at the top. A reverse-angle overhead shot dominates Callahan as he sees another figure blocking the entrance to the alley below. As Grost and Silver and Ursini note, the imagery exhibits the connotations of a trap affecting Callahan both physically and psychologically, foreshadowing the limitations affecting human agency contained throughout *World for Ransom*.[26]

The two men lead Callahan to the office of Singapore racketeer Chan (Clarence Lung). The scene begins with a lap dissolve as the camera moves left to right and ascends into an overhead position. This not only minimizes Callahan within the frame but also distracts the viewer's attention from him. The angle also reveals an overhead fan in motion above Chan's desk, casting multiple noirish shadows on the walls. Although Callahan initially plays the tough guy by refusing to investigate his friend Julian March for Chan, the mention of Frennessey's name changes his mind.

When Mike confronts March in his office, he finds his friend studying a map and exhibiting a slight degree of apprehension at his sudden arrival. Julian (Patric Knowles) responds to Mike's concern, "I'd hate to see you in trouble again," with, "What are you talking about? Me or Frennessey?" The decadent Julian informs Mike of his intention of cheating on Frennessey that evening. He also challenges Mike's authority: "You shouldn't play Galahad. You're way out of character." Julian also affirms that his relationship with Mike's former girlfriend does not follow normal social conventions: "Has the thought ever occurred to you that I may not want to hurt her, that I might not want to hurt her, that I can't help what I am? By most people's standards, I'm not a good husband. But in a strange sort of way, I am." The enigmatic nature of his comments becomes clear at the end of the film. But Aldrich and Hugo Butler have already begun to critique the knightly male heroic role as well as cast doubt on the reliability of Mike's perceptions.[27]

Like Humphrey Bogart's Rick in *Casablanca* (1943), Mike carries a torch for his former lover, but he also perversely continues to watch over both her and her husband. The next scene shows Julian with criminal mastermind Pederas. Seated before a chessboard as he goes over the kidnapping plans, Pederas dominates Julian in the same way the latter dominated Mike in the earlier sequence. Despite their different natures, Mike and Julian are similar in certain ways. Both wish to be heroes. But Julian not only chooses a criminal path but also verbally betrays Mike before Pederas, foreshadowing his final action in the film. Mike describes Julian as a "friend," rather than "partner," to Chan. But Julian disavows any obligation to a friend who once saved his life in Shanghai. When Pederas comments, "Your undertaking is much more important to us than Callahan. I believe he saved your life in Shanghai," March replies, "I didn't ask him for it." When Pederas remarks, "He's still your friend," March replies, "I didn't ask him for that either." The comments evoke the futility of Raymond Chandler's knightly heroism in Robert Altman's version of

The Long Goodbye (1973), when Marlowe finds that his friend Terry Lennox has betrayed him. Pederas, however, admires Julian's cynical "refreshingly detached attitude toward your friend."

The next scene shows Mike entering the Golden Poppy nightclub where Frennessey works. He buys some plum blossoms from a little girl but leaves them at the bar during Frennessey's performance. She appears dressed in a tuxedo smoking a cigarette before she begins a performance deliberately evoking Marlene Dietrich's nightclub scene in *Morocco* (1930). Censorship resulted in Aldrich eliminating a scene showing Frennessey kissing a female at the table along with other evidence of her lesbianism. But Frennessey's very appearance and Julian's earlier enigmatic comments concerning their relationship alert any active viewer toward discerning the naive nature of Mike's romantic desires. The following scenes involving Mike and Frennessey involve visual elements questioning the very nature of their relationship.

Aldrich shot the first scene between Mike and Frennessey in her dressing room in one take. She has picked up the plum blossoms Mike left at the bar and thanks him for them. Frennessey expresses concern over Julian to Mike, mentioning that her husband's male insecurities have led him toward criminal activity: "He keeps talking about how he can't keep living on my money. He should be the one who supports me." Mike interprets Frennessey's remarks in the way that *he* wants to hear them. When he remarks, "You couldn't run out on anybody you'd loved," Frennessey changes the verb to "liked." Mike believes that she still has feelings for him but misinterprets the very nature of what they actually involve. Frennessey's change toward him not only gives him false hope but also makes him forget Julian's earlier comment: "Frennessey was never for you." As Mike approaches a woman keenly aware of his romantic dependence on her, a shadow falls over him. It subversively accompanies his following line, "Are you saying I've got a chance"; and she answers, "More than a chance." Despite the suggestive romantic overtones of the dialogue, both lighting and framing operate in a more critical manner. When Mike replies, "But how do I know?" the image reveals Mike and Frennessey contained within the spiral frames of her bed. Like Mike Hammer in *Kiss Me Deadly*, Mike Callahan has already become trapped. But Aldrich suggests that he has constructed his own spider's web.

In *World for Ransom*, the trap involves male romanticism rather than Mike Hammer's grubby materialism. However, like Hammer,

Callahan also thinks: "What's in it for me?" But he desires the resumption of a relationship that never really existed in the first place. He is a victim of his own heterosexual romantic illusions. Mike is also living in the past and entertains naive illusions about the validity of past values. He resembles those characters in Odets's plays who cannot distinguish between illusion and reality. Silver and Ursini also notice an "underlying tension" within the composition of this scene, suggesting that something is not entirely right.[28] Other scenes between Mike and Frennessey in her apartment also involve destabilizing levels of mise-en-scène and camera movement. Mike Callahan is a trapped individual. His heroic knightly mission to rescue Julian fails. So do his hopeless romantic yearnings for the lady fair.

World for Ransom also evokes Josef von Sternberg's *The Shanghai Gesture* (1941) as well as *Morocco*. Like Madam Gin Sling, Frennessey seeks to trap a Caucasian male in her spider's web. Frennessey has also suffered a "fate worse than death." But she survives to take revenge on the man who abandoned her. Although Callahan is not as callous as Sir Guy Charteris in *The Shanghai Gesture*, he did leave a vulnerable eighteen-year-old female alone with "no parents, no profession or training" to fend for herself. As Frennessey states, she solved her "problems in the only way I could." Her manipulation of Mike contains feelings of revenge for his earlier abandonment as well as dissatisfaction with someone who can only see her in a certain way.

The next scenes between Mike and Frennessey occur in her apartment. Aldrich introduces two succeeding sequences by revealing the spiral wire head of her bed frame dominating not only the room but also Mike when he first enters. It anticipates a setup Aldrich will use again in *Kiss Me Deadly* when Mike Hammer first meets Lily Carver. But Frennessey is no mere spider woman like Lily Carver. She does use Callahan in a manner similar to Lily's manipulation of the egotistic Hammer. But she is a more complex character than the woman who will open the Pandora's box in the later film. Frennessey has had to survive on her own in a male-dominated world. She marries a man who makes no demands on her but who also feels insecure over his dependence on her. She wishes Mike to save him from harm. But she also manipulates a man who abandoned her years before, one who refused to acknowledge the very nature of her character, by using the misleading romantic yearnings ingrained in his character for her own ends. Although Frennessey deserves blame for her actions, she merely wishes the safe return of a husband who understands her and will not make her become something that she is not. Like Aldrich's other films, *World for Ransom* contains morally ambivalent characters reflecting a world where no secure values exist.

Costume plays a key role in two scenes involving Mike and Frennessey. She wears male pajamas during the first bedroom scene and an attractive negligee in the second. She wears the first for convenience. But her second, more feminine attire represents a deliberate attempt to ensnare Mike by using his romantic illusions against him. Mike may believe that the girl he left behind is still waiting for him. But Frennessey has other motives for her actions.[29] *World for Ransom* is a film carefully structured on multilevel duality.

Duality dominates the entire film. When Julian impersonates Major Bone, he decides to use his own decorations rather than the fake ones provided by Pederas. He obviously relishes the opportunity of returning (if only briefly) to his former sense of masculine assurance and heroic military glory. Callahan later forms a brief friendship with the real Major Bone (Reginald Denny) when they attack the Village of Death containing the captured nuclear scientist, O'Sullivan. Callahan obviously relishes the opportunity to relive the male adventure bonding he once had with March. However, the audience knows something that Callahan does not. Julian March has already told Pederas that he never regarded Mike as a friend, though he has clearly encouraged him in this belief in the past. His actions also parallel Frennessey's in making Mike believe that she is still "his girl." When Bone earlier defended Callahan against a murder accusation, he mentioned that the charges in Shanghai involved "false pretenses" rather than murder. This ironically evokes the actions of Frennessey and Julian, who engage in different forms of "false pretenses" to manipulate Mike. Bone represents a positive version of Julian March in terms of the fraternal bond that he and Callahan later form. When Callahan remarks that his father "was a general in the IRA," Bone responds, "My father was a colonel in the Black and Tans." Callahan concludes, "As they say, rank is everything in life." Grost recognizes that "Bone has the integrity and character that March lacks, and which Callahan is desperate to find in other people."[30] Callahan is a man more at home in the world of male adventure. But it is a doomed world. March betrays him, and Bone, the only British colonial official to believe in Callahan's innocence, dies in the attack on the village.

Like *Kiss Me Deadly*, *World of Ransom* presents a world where civilized distinctions between good and evil do not exist. Sinister overhead shots of fans appear in the offices of Chan and the governor (Nigel Bruce), who supposedly represent opposing forces. The governor has no scruples over Callahan being accused of a murder he did not commit. When Pederas enters the governor's office, fan blades cast shadows on the ceiling. It evokes the earlier scene when Chan threatened Callahan. A chessboard pattern appears on the governor's floor. Pederas plays a game of chess as he plans O'Connor's kidnapping. O'Connor, Callahan, and March are all pawns in a deadly game played by competing sides that resemble each other in the ruthless methods they employ. When Pederas leaves the governor's office he gives his address as the Colonial Room of the Raffles Hotel, remarking, "Ironic, isn't it gentlemen?" Raffles was the gentleman thief of pre–World War I fiction. But neither British colonial authorities nor Pederas acts in gentlemanly ways. That world has now gone. Pederas arranges the death of the tailor who made March's uniform. He also doubts whether March could survive British colonial interrogation: "With the future of a man like O'Connor at stake, even the British would forget their cricket for a while." After Inspector McCollum (Douglas Dumbrille) successfully frames Callahan for murder, he remarks to a subordinate that once his chosen victim leads him to O'Connor, then "we can hang him." Chan earlier threatened Callahan that his men would "interrogate" Frennessey if Callahan did not investigate March's activities.

A small fan also appears in Frennessey's apartment when she and Callahan meet for the last time before he goes on his rescue mission. She paces back and forth in the frame before she pauses and stands above him in a dominant position. After discussing Julian's possible involvement in the murder of Mike's friend Wing (Keye Luke), a shadow appears over her face. She obviously plans the next move in her sexually duplicitous chess game. When Mike rises to kiss her on the mouth, she reacts against his romantic gesture by retreating from him. Her abrupt manner is revealed to the audience, but Callahan does not read the writing on the wall. When he is about to leave, Callahan informs her about his previous sexual involvements. But he idealistically puts her on a pedestal: "You were the only one that was way out there on the hill, the only one that was straight from beginning to end." It is almost as if he sees her as an untarnished "city on the hill." By viewing her in this way, he employs a highly charged ideological metaphor that has caused nothing but disaster from the very beginning of American cultural and political history.[31] The same is true of rigidly enforced traditional codes of sexual behavior that bear no relationship to the actual diversity of human character. Mike is not only a hopeless romantic; he also reveals to Frennessey his own contradictory pattern of behavior. As a male, he may indulge in many affairs but not his lady fair, who has married his "best friend" and who is expected to transfer her fidelity from one male to another. Before Mike leaves, Frennessey rushes to him and finally fulfills his romantic yearnings by kissing him on the mouth. It appears spontaneous. But we viewed an entirely different reaction earlier in the scene. Callahan leaves to rescue March. Silver and Ursini note, the "ultimate irony or tragedy in *World for Ransom,* then derives from the narrative revelation that Frennessey has indeed been lying, that a blind side in Callahan has prevented him from seeing her as the real peril to his survival."[32] However, the film clearly demonstrates that the real blindness results from a man who sees and hears nothing that does not fit into his rigid code of male behavior.

When Callahan finally confronts March and three other members of Pederas's group, the shadows falling on the wall in this long shot are only two, rather than five, thus symbolizing those two rivals for Frennessey. Despite Callahan's offer of help, March refuses. He intends to kill his old friend. March is dominated by his own form of male illusion, hoping to return to his former heroic status. Mike manipulates March into killing his three associates, but March intends to betray him, dreaming of returning to Singapore as a "national hero" by rescuing O'Sullivan. Callahan saves himself by throwing two grenades at his betrayer. Finding O'Connor alive, he leaves him with the words, "I wouldn't be a good hero, either," bidding Julian good-bye.

Mike's most emotionally devastating betrayal occurs in the penultimate scene of *World for Ransom.* Although Mike genuinely attempted to save Julian, Frennessey condemns him for murder. She also reveals her real nature to a romantic knight who wears not shining armor but, rather, the film noir hero's trench coat. Mike no longer resembles Bogart's romantic Rick of *Casablanca* but Robert Mitchum's betrayed masochistic Jeff Bailey of *Out of the Past* (1947).

During his last meeting with Frennessey, Callahan does not wear the neat, tailored white suit of his earlier scenes. He looks much older, resembling the prematurely aged, similarly betrayed heroic figure portrayed by Dennis O'Keefe in the final scene of *Angela* (1955). Frennessey greets Mike in her dressing room. She decides to reveal her past life to him, expecting Julian to appear at any moment. Her confession echoes Mike's own in their last scene together. But it undermines his privileged male perspective. Frennessey implies that she lived a life of prostitution in Shanghai. But her confession is articulated in such an ambiguous manner to imply a lesbian subtext that the censor refused to explicitly allow it on the screen. She tells Mike that she survived his abandonment of her "in the only way I could," as well as marrying the decadent Julian. Frennessey sarcastically comments that "plum blossoms are nice." But she now reveals that she lied to Mike and really loves Julian. When she hears of Julian's death, her shadow falls on Mike, this time more prominently than in their earlier scene together. She now discloses her true nature, condemning Mike for "looking at me as if I were a saint" and his lack of perception: "Couldn't you see? The way I look! The way I sang." After criticizing Mike for being "in love with a goofy 18-year-old, a lily white doll in your own mind," she proclaims her undying love for Julian, who loved her *"for what I really am."* She physically and verbally abuses Mike before collapsing on a sofa covered with several dolls. A revealing picture of a female pinup appears on the wall above the sofa. These objects visually affirm Frennessey's real nature.[33] Mike's world has ended in an apocalyptic personal explosion as devastating as any nuclear device O'Sullivan could invent. He can never again return to his formerly secure world as an archetypal heterosexual American adventurer.

World for Ransom ends with Mike again refusing to take a chance. He finds that luck does not necessarily involve a patriarchal illusion of romantic love. Despite Mai Ling's tempting words, Mike now finds that he does not "wear the luck of your father and mother." As he disappears into the Singapore crowd, Mai Ling proclaims that "love is a white bird, yet you cannot buy her." But the film ends on an ambiguous note. A few seconds before the final credits, Mike enters the Golden Poppy, the last place on earth we would ever now expect him to enter. Frennessey still works there. His final exit in *World for Ransom* suggests masochistic overtones as well as casting doubt on whether he has really learned anything. Mike's final

"Shanghai gesture" thus suggests a self-destructive streak that is also a part of his national character. Mike Callahan is a man belonging to a nation that learns nothing from personal experience or history and always makes the same mistakes. But these mistakes may have devastating apocalyptic consequences, as *Kiss Me Deadly* and *Twilight's Last Gleaming* reveal.

Kiss Me Deadly represents a further development of the complex issues raised in *World for Ransom*. Personal dilemmas and global destruction symbiotically interact. Set in the Hollywood metropolis of Los Angeles rather than the original novel's New York environment, the film intuitively not only depicts key elements in the cinema of Robert Aldrich but also reveals a postwar modernist dilemma informing his work. As Marshall Berman comments, the very nature of being modern "is to live a life of paradox and contradiction. It is to be overpowered by the immense bureaucratic organizations that have the power to control and often to destroy all communities, values, lives; and yet to be undeterred in our determination to face these forces, to fight to change the world and make it our own."[34] Like his predecessor, Mike Callahan, Ralph Meeker's Mike Hammer lives in a world for ransom where his movements are much more circumscribed. Although he loses his fight by his inability to resolve the deadly contradictions affecting his existence, this is not necessarily true for the audience. Aldrich and scenarist A. I. Bezzerides change Mickey Spillane's Cold War avenger Mike Hammer into an intellectual pygmy who violently confronts a modern world that will destroy him and others. As Berman further remarks, "To be modern is to be part of a universe in which, as Marx said, 'all that is solid melts into air,'" and Hammer parallels figures within the midst of this maelstrom who "are apt to feel that they are the first ones, and maybe the only ones, to be going through it."[35] *Kiss Me Deadly* concludes ironically with everything solid melting into air as the final credits appear.

The film also belongs to a critical modernism characterizing the work of Robert Aldrich. As Berman comments, "To be modern . . . is to experience personal and social life as a maelstrom, to find one's world and oneself in perpetual disintegration and renewal, trouble and anguish, ambiguity and contradiction: to be a part of a universe in which all that is solid melts into air."[36] It is a vision linking *Kiss Me Deadly* to Aldrich's last great achievement, *Twilight's Last Gleaming*. However, the tragedy in both films lies in the fact that the main characters cannot resolve their contradictions in the appropriate critical manner. A world for ransom will move toward its twilight's last gleaming.

Kiss Me Deadly depicts not only a world in which old values have become debased but also one containing faint echoes of the 1930s Cultural Front. This latter appears in Frank Devol's theme song, "I'd Rather Have the Blues than What I've Got," sung by Nat King Cole over the credits and mimed by Madi Comfort in the Club Regallo sequence. Its occurrence is much more than a convenient opportunity to feature a song by a popular artist whom Aldrich would again use (unseen) in *Autumn Leaves*. Performed by Comfort in the manner of a cabaret torch singer, the lines "The web has got me caught" and "I'd rather have the blues than what I've got" evocatively complement the film's narrative, as well as representing a link to the ironic Popular Front political cabaret illustrated in Billie Holiday's "Strange Fruit."[37] In the context of their eventual fate, Aldrich's ironical version of Nicholas Ray's "last romantic couple" may well wish that they had the blues rather than the radiation they eventually get. Furthermore, as Denning notes, Billie Holiday's love songs were not "dance tunes for jukeboxes but torch songs for the intimacy of the cabaret."[38] Madi Comfort employs a performance style also characterizing Holiday's successors at Café Society such as Hazel Scott and Lena Horne.[39] Furthermore, unlike the cabaret scene in *Force of Evil* where black musicians perform before a mostly white audience, Aldrich uses a real-life black nightclub as the setting for this scene.

Kiss Me Deadly opens with a breathless Christina Bailey (Cloris Leachman) running in a diagonal pattern across the frame. Her feet often intersect the traffic markings in a fragmentary manner. After attempting to stop several cars, she succeeds in halting Hammer's sports car by standing in front of it, her arms in a crucified position. This posture is not accidental, for it reoccurs throughout the film. When Mike is later interrogated by Dr. Soberin (Albert Dekker), he is tied to a bed in a similar position. Although Nicky (Nick Dennis) compares Mike with "Lazarus risen from the grave," Mike has also been unconscious for three days. He "rises again" in hospital before Pat Chambers (Wesley Addy) and Velda Whitman (Maxine Cooper). But Mike is no savior figure who will redeem the world but, rather, an unknowing and accidental participant in its destruction. Significantly, in an era equating female sexuality with the atomic bomb, it will be no male Angel Gabriel sounding the trumpet for the Day of Judgment.[40] Instead, it is a female agent of destruction, Gabrielle/Lily Carver (Gaby Rodgers), who gives the savior figure his "Judas kiss" before shooting him. She then opens the mysterious howling box and initiates the apocalyptic era of Revelations. It is the final culmination in a film using classical film noir techniques of mirror imagery and reversals, the latter appropriately beginning with the inversion of the classical Hollywood credit technique.[41]

Kiss Me Deadly juxtaposes many features in deliberate contradiction, whether detective thriller or film noir, in a ruthless vision of a 1950s era moving toward a logical conclusion of complete annihilation. Materialism and greed constitute *Kiss Me Deadly*'s world for ransom. Nick's brother Sammy tries to warn his doomed sibling about Mike's quest: "You should ask what it's worth to him, what *he's* going to get out of it." Mike Hammer's revealing comment to Pat after his interrogation by the FBI, "What's in it for me?" as well as Lily Carver's persistent question to Dr. Soberin, "What's in the box?" echo features within the bleak world of pulp fiction writer Charles Willeford, "in which the predatory cannibalism of American capitalism provides the model for all human relations, in which the American success ethic mercilessly casts aside all who are unable or unwilling to compete, and in which the innate human appreciation of artistic beauty is cruelly distorted by the exigencies of mass culture."[42]

The grim fate of poetry-loving Christina Bailey immediately springs to mind as well as the redundancy of Western civilization. *Kiss Me Deadly* reveals a world in which they have all become disposable, tarnished, or appropriated in demeaning ways. For example, once-powerful classical cultural worlds represented by Britain, Greece, and Rome are now futile in defining any alternative cultural values in the world of Mike Hammer. Christina's poetry does not save her; nor does its important message redeem Hammer or the brutal L.A. environment he inhabits.[43] The seedy middle-aged clerk (Leonard Mudie) at the L.A. Athletic Club represents the worst aspects of British snobbery and almost deserves his assault at Hammer's hands. Classical Greek culture has now descended into the persona of Nick, and its poetic patterns are reduced and reassembled in a verbal modernist collage of the technological era. Nick's perennial line, "Va Va Va. Boom! Pretty Pow," ironically foreshadows the climax of *Kiss Me Deadly* and satirically reworks the chorus technique from classical Greek tragedy. The old mover (Silvio Minciotti) thanks Mike for helping him lift a heavy trunk and speaks of inhabiting the "house of my body," a dwelling he moves into at birth and leaves at death. When Mike finds Carmen Trivago, he discovers an embodiment of Italian grand opera now living in a seedy downtown apartment.

The old mover's earlier line, "Every time I pick up a trunk, I take a deep breath," evokes *Kiss Me Deadly*'s most prominent aural referent on the soundtrack. In a film that Silver and Ursini regard as containing depths that have never fully been explored, Aldrich's creative use of sound deserves further investigation.[44] Although *Kiss Me Deadly* is usually regarded as a baroque example of film noir, having many associations with the style employed by Orson Welles in *Touch of Evil*, it also employs the disjunctive tradition of modernism by using certain particular sound devices. For example, although Christina's torture scene begins with her legs writhing in agony, it ends with her body still but the sounds of her screaming still occurring on the soundtrack. When Mike violently responds to the morgue doctor's greedy demands, the sounds of the latter squealing in pain do not synchronize with his lips. Occurring in a film indebted to contemporary underground modernism, such techniques are not unusual. But they are often ignored by viewers appalled by the contexts of the particular scenes. However, the jarring nature of such scenes makes the old values of classical Hollywood editing patterns obsolete. Flinn notices that Christina's labored breathing in her pre-credits introduction creates a "break in cinematic verisimilitude."[45] But in addition to other prominent sound effects such as the sound of the box, Billy Mist's snoring, Evello's release of breath at his death, the prominent traffic sounds outside Lily's apartment, and the hissing voice of Percy Helton as the morgue doctor, another context is relevant. It represents an ironic reversal of the very act of creation that began the world according to the book of Genesis. The actual meaning of the "spirit of God" hovering over the deep in the opening sentence of the Bible really means "breath of God" in the original Hebrew. Thus, it is an act of irony that breathing begins the film and concludes it, with the heavy breath of the box substituting for the trumpet heralding both the Day of Judgment and the end of the world. Another reference to breath also occurs in the conversation between Mike and boxing manager Eddie Yeager (Juano Hernandez), a character who looks as if he has emerged from the world of *Body and Soul*. When Mike asks what (monetary) offer Evello's thugs made to him, Eddie simply replies, "They said, they'd let me breathe." Ironically, the breath that created the world will now inaugurate its destruction, in the postwar atomic era inhabiting a modernity that will literally destroy everything in its path.

The acting styles of hero and villain in *Kiss Me Deadly* are also important. Both Albert Dekker and Ralph Meeker began their careers on stage. Dekker began acting in the 1930s. As Dr. Soberin he deliberately employs classical theatrical acting techniques in his poetic delivery of lines. He often uses religious terminology, as in his reference to "rais[ing] the dead" following Christina's death, and makes references to Pandora, Lot's Wife, and "Cerberus barking with all his heads at the gates of hell" to an uncomprehending Lily Carver, who speaks like a Brooklyn broad. Naturally, his comparison of the contents of the box to the "head of the Medusa," which will change anyone who looks at it into "brimstone and ashes," falls on deaf ears. Like those characters described in the Bible who are "seeing but do not see and hearing but do not hear," Lily is not interested. It is doubtful whether she would change her course of behavior even if she were intuitively aware of Soberin's references. She represents a 1950s era in which "book learning" was under suspicion. And Ralph Meeker took over the role of Stanley Kowalski in *A Streetcar Named Desire* from Marlon Brando. His acting style differs from Albert Dekker's. The anti-intellectual Hammer is the most appropriate companion for Lily, rather than the cultured Dr. Soberin.

Modernist contradiction, rather than classical narrative coherence, is the ruling factor in the world of *Kiss Me Deadly*. It results in several unusual juxtapositions. When a hoodlum follows Mike during a night scene, the clock on the wall rapidly changes from 2:10, to 2:15, to 2:20 in the course of a few seconds, suggesting a violent modernist world rapidly moving forward to its own destruction. Although Aldrich admitted that this was a shooting error, it does fit into the context of the film, and one wonders why he did not change it if it was a mistake that is so noticeable.[46] Soberin wears a neat tailored suit with incongruous blue suede shoes, making part of him easily identifiable before we actually see his face toward the end of the film. Before Mike briefly escapes from Sugar (Jack Lambert) and Charlie (Jack Elam) outside Dr. Soberin's beach house, he inquires why they are so solicitous about his welfare. One of them replies in a manner strangely out of character, stating that we are "on this world for such a short time." In an earlier scene at Evello's mansion, Sugar ordered a "broad" (Leigh Snowden) away from his card game, comparing women with flies. This line anticipates Soberin's later reference to Pandora's box, for in the original myth flies represented the ills that this classical Greek heroine unleashed onto an unsuspecting world. At this point of the film, the "broad" merely distracts Sugar's attention from the card game. When Mike invades Billy Mist's art gallery, a strangely incongruous musical theme by Frank DeVol, more relevant to a traditional gangster movie, contrasts with the modernist paintings on the wall. *Kiss Me Deadly* is a film containing many literal and aural contradictions in its postwar apocalyptic modernist world.

The modernist artifacts in Mike's apartment and his attentiveness to the classical music played on Christina's favorite radio station suggest a sensibility at odds with his brutal character. Such a split personality also appears in Willeford's fiction, which often reveals the artistic sensibility and potential creativity existing in characters contrasting with their everyday ruthless social personalities. Although Mike Hammer differs from Willeford's characters, they have certain similarities. Cochran comments that Willeford "sympathetically portrayed the artistic urge to create as a logical outgrowth of the tedium and banality of the work culture of modern America."[47] Although Velda performs ballet exercises to classical music, this may represent not just a "workout" accompanied by background Muzak but also an expression of her own split character. This particular scene involves not only mirror-image film noir duality. It also plays on audience perception, making the viewers as schizophrenic and unaware as the main characters concerning the implications of their involvement in the "great whatzit." The shot begins with what appears to be an actual shot of Velda performing her ballet exercise, with Mike watching her reflected in a mirror, until the camera moves to show the false nature of this initial perception. Both characters are reflected in the mirror in the beginning of the shot. This location functions as Mike's office and Velda's apartment. It has a checkered floor similar to the governor's office in *World for Ransom*, implying that both Mike and Velda are merely pawns in a deadly game far beyond their comprehension. Soberin and Lily play with Mike like a disposable pawn. Mike uses Velda as Soberin uses Lily, for both "creature comfort" and bait. Soberin also recognizes Lily's "feline" power of intuition, a concept foreshadowed by the presence of a white cat near the female telephone-answering service employee whom Mike earlier gains information from.

Several critics have noticed the influence of Orson Welles on Robert Aldrich. Grost comments that many scenes in *Kiss Me Deadly* exhibit deep-focus three-dimensional techniques. Although *Citizen Kane* has been canonized as a classical Hollywood narrative, Jonathan Rosenbaum has pointed out that it has little to do with the classical Hollywood tradition and should be viewed more as an experimental film demonstrating alternative perspectives that the industry could also employ.[48] *Kane* is also regarded as a work of cinematic modernism belonging to a tradition influencing both Welles and Aldrich. Welles's theatrical work in the New Deal era is well known. In his analysis of *Kiss Me Deadly,* Grost notes several significant modernist features such as the gas station resembling "an elaborate piece of sculpture, like one of Louise Nevelson's friezes," and the "irregular" depiction of the Angels' Flight of Los Angeles (was this location deliberate?) neighborhood, exhibiting many rectilinear and angular "protuberances."[49] L-shaped patterns occur in the gas station and Mike's apartment in a manner evoking Welles's *The Lady from Shanghai* (1948), whose title may have influenced Frennessey's character in *World for Ransom. Kiss Me Deadly* is also a visual homage to the type of cinema represented by *Citizen Kane* that many hoped would change the traditional patterns of classical Hollywood narrative cinema. It may not be accidental that two actors from *Citizen Kane* appear in *Kiss Me Deadly.* Both Paul Stewart and Fortunio Bonanova resemble "fallen angel" variations of their earlier roles in *Citizen Kane.* Raymond could have moved into the world of crime as a result of knowing where "the bodies are buried" following the death of his employer, whereas maestro Signor Matisti would be cast into the outer darkness after the failure of Susan Alexander Kane's operatic career.

Before her abduction Velda informs Mike about there being "new art in the world and the doctor's starting a collection." The doctor is Soberin. His collection involves not only art but the Bomb, that symbol of apocalyptic modernity that will literally melt all that is solid into air. This happens at the climax. Mike rescues Velda, but she also helps a wounded Mike stagger out of a beach house now being consumed by a nuclear holocaust whose extensions are unfathomable. Having discovered his involvement in a game far beyond his capacities and realizing that he would not have acted any differently any-way, Mike Hammer witnesses not only the end of his world but the likely annihilation of a universe that has been heading toward de-struction all along. His destructive masculinity has contributed to the end of the world. Like Velda, Mike has suffered radiation expo-sure. Survival for both is doubtful.

The conclusion of *Kiss Me Deadly* thus complements the entire style of the film, which G. Cabrera Infante applauded upon its ini-tial release. By using the camera as an "aesthetic cyclotron," Aldrich "bombarded the absurd truculences of Spillane with inner action protons, megatons of baroque photography and electrons of move-ment and mobile actors: he has achieved—as the French magazine *Cahiers du Cinema* so well said—the first film of the Atom."[50] The critic also saw the film as "the first great example of the modern movie Gothic since Orson Welles left Hollywood."[51] Unlike Mickey Spillane, Aldrich views the American heroic ideal as both self-destructive and destructive toward others in a postwar world ren-dering old ideals and securities redundant and desperately needing other alternative directions.

Although Aldrich rejected *The Garment Jungle* following his re-moval from the set, the final version credited to Vincent Sherman contains several of his predominant themes.[52] As well as involving familiar Aldrich figures such as director of photography Joseph Biroc and actor Wesley Addy, the film also features two actors asso-ciated with Clifford Odets at the beginning and end of the play-wright's career. Lee J. Cobb had appeared in both the stage and film versions of *Golden Boy*, whereas Richard Boone later began a short-lived collaboration with Odets in television production. The casting of these two actors suggests certain resonances in *The Garment Jun-gle*, especially in terms of the father–son conflict common to both Aldrich and Odets. Furthermore, Cobb played the role of Willy Lohman in the original stage production of *Death of a Salesman*, and elements of this do appear in the final version. It may also have been Aldrich's idea in the first place.

Before his removal from the set, Aldrich spoke optimistically about making one of the first pro-labor films in Hollywood empha-sizing the tragedy of the small businessman trapped between large corporations and the pressures of organized labor.[53] Both Columbia head Harry Cohn and Lee J. Cobb criticized the original script and wanted to tone it down. When Aldrich refused, he was fired. Studio fears concerning the profitability of union pictures at the box office, Cobb's memories of his humiliating testimony before the House Un-American Activities Committee, and Aldrich's own independent attitudes may have all contributed to this event. Aldrich also commented that he became less interested in the union/hoodlum angle of the original conception and more interested in the dilemma faced by the Lee J. Cobb character. His remarks evoke the world of Clifford Odets and Abraham Polonsky. Aldrich envisaged Cobb's character as a Jewish immigrant caught among big business, unionism, and gangsterism: "He was robust, dynamic and active, and also fettered by being Jewish, of which he was proud but, perhaps, also sub-consciously angry, since it interfered with his complete freedom due to the survival of some brands of anti-Semitism."[54] It is a marvelous conception that does not survive in the film, except for some faint traces. The big business angle is absent as well as the Jewish background of the Cobb character. Instead, the father–son conflict and the romantic involvement between the son and the widow of a union leader become major elements of the final film. These features are not surprising for a film made in the Cold War with the blacklist still in operation. It is also possible that Aldrich may have intended to direct a picture along the lines of Abraham Polonsky's *I Can Get It for You Wholesale* (1951), directed by Michael Gordon, which deals with issues of capitalist dehumanization common to *Body and Soul* and *Force of Evil*.[55] However, despite alterations to the original screenplay, *The Garment Jungle* contains several recognizable Aldrich features such as certain deliberately dislocating visual stylistic features, a father–son conflict over issues of integrity, and ironic dualistic narrative elements.[56] Although Arnold and Miller are correct in saying that "it is impossible today to determine just how different the picture would have been if Aldrich had been allowed to finish it," the final version does echo some familiar Aldrich themes.[57]

The Garment Jungle begins with a pre-credits voice-over in a manner similar to *I Can Get It for You Wholesale*. After a familiar tourist view of Manhattan, the commentary accompanies location shots of the Garment District, where thousands of garment workers are employed in the real world behind the depicted streets, a "teaming jungle of conflict, brutal competition, and terror." It is a commentary worthy of Polonsky's Enterprise Studio work. After the credits, the film begins with a close-up of Walter Mitchell (Lee J. Cobb) arguing with his designer partner, Fred Kenner (Robert Ellenstein), over unionization in the business he has founded. As Mitchell angrily speaks of firing workers to maintain profit margins, he tears the dress of a model in a manner similar to Susan Hayward's in one striking scene in *I Can Get It for You Wholesale*. With the exception of the streetwise model who accepts her objectification in the dehumanized world of the garment industry and casts her eyes from one partner to the other to see who will win the debate, this opening shot copies Polonsky's earlier scene revealing verbal aggression in the brutal world of the garment jungle. The camera moves from a close-up to frame both men on opposite sides of the cynical model. Kenner responds that his partner could make a profit as well as giving his workers a living wage, "rather than paying gangsters a percentage of every dress to keep the union out." Kenner storms out, adamant about signing a union contract before his murder in a rigged elevator shaft.

The following sequence shows the arrival of Alan Mitchell (Kerwin Matthews), a Korean War veteran who has returned to America after a three-year absence in Europe. He announces his intention of joining his father's business. However, this father–son reunion appears brittle, evoking those dysfunctional family scenarios common to Odets's plays and Aldrich's cinema. We learn that Alan's deceased mother never wanted him to go into the business. The arrival of Walter's mistress, Lee Hackett (Valerie French), immediately causes tensions to rise, especially when Alan notices a key to his father's apartment, which Lee clumsily attempts to conceal. He also resents his father's habit of concealing things from him. Alan's three-year absence from America may suggest a reluctance to deal with family matters as well as his alienation from a changed post–Korean War American society. Walter's apartment has some modern art paintings and African sculptures on the wall, which seem at odds with his character. But they subtly denote that critical modernist presence in Aldrich's film noirs, suggesting the presence of disturbing contradictions existing beneath the surface of 1950s affluence.

The relationship between Walter and Alan also echoes that between father and son in Arthur Miller's *All My Sons*. In both works, a son discovers not only that his father has clay feet but that he has also been involved in murder. Although the film presents Walter as having no real understanding of what his involvement with racketeer Artie Ravidge (Richard Boone) actually involves, he is as conveniently blind to this profitable working relationship as the father in Miller's play. Alan condemns his father for concealing things from him: "Still the same. When did you ever bother to talk anything over with me?" But the suggestion exists that he really wants to continue a destructive Oedipal conflict rather than investigate gangster involvement in his father's business. Unresolvable issues such as the death of his mother and the workaholic tendencies of his father have prevented any close relationship from developing between them. Alan's discovery of the dark side of the garment jungle may give him the excuse he really wants to punish his father because of unresolved psychological factors deeply buried within his own personality.

Alan's interaction with Tullio Renata (Robert Loggia) and his wife Theresa (Gia Scala) appears to provide him with the convenient excuse he needs to begin a mission against his father. Alan begins to learn about the facts of life in the garment industry, especially differences between union and nonunion labor. When Ravidge's men beat up Tullio at a secret union meeting, a location filmed with the prominent shadow shots of fan blades on the wall (evoking similar scenes in *World for Ransom*), Alan brings him to Walter's office the next morning to illustrate the violent implications of his nonunion strategy. Alan acts very much like similar self-righteous savior-hero figures in other Aldrich films such as Lt. Costa in *Attack!* and Lawrence Dell in *Twilight's Last Gleaming*. But Alan is unaware of the consequences of his action, which now makes Tullio a marked man. Also, when Alan condemns his father, "Never once did I hear anything about right and wrong," Walter responds, "There's no such thing in the garment business." His comment echoes Walter's manager, Tony (Harold J. Stone), who said to Alan during his first day at work: "Every minute is like a war. You got to fight to stay alive." Alan does not really understand the complex forces dominating the ways his father's business operates. Nor is he yet in a knowledgeable position to begin forming some pragmatic solution to the dilemma. As Mike Hammer does with Nick, Alan makes Tullio a sacrificial victim for his own ends.

Similar dysfunctional family dynamics affect Tullio. Although he may appear the noble union activist and martyr for the sins of others betrayed by his own members, his actual motivations are suspect. During their first meeting, Theresa told Alan that Tullio "is not in it for himself but to help others." However, his frequent absences from home for union activities parallel Walter Mitchell's earlier failure as a husband and father. After pleading with Tullio to leave a picket site, Theresa leaves him, caustically remarking: "E finita. From now on you sleep with the union." The following shot is a revealing track in to Tullio's face shadowed in darkness, as if he realizes the darker implications motivating his altruistic sacrificial acts for the union. This family aspect is not entirely accidental. Certain shots imply a dualistic relationship between Alan and Tullio. After Theresa arrives by taxi at the site, Aldrich shot a scene of her pleading with Tullio to return home in a significant way. He employs a low-angle shot from inside the taxi with the arched handle of the baby carriage dominating the left-hand side of the frame. The curved open door of the taxi is at the right side of the frame, with Tullio and Theresa dwarfed in the middle. Aldrich returns to this composition after it becomes clear that Tullio will not listen to his wife's pleas. He tells her, "I'm doing what I've got to do. You take care of the baby. That's what you've got to do." It is almost as if the obsessive Tullio welcomes his approaching martyrdom. He places his wife in the protection of a disciple. This time, Alan's head clearly appears within the frame. Both Alan and Tullio equally court violence and death. Tullio appears to seek martyrdom as an escape from his family responsibilities. Alan and Tullio are Korean War veterans. During Tullio's memorial service, a photo of him in military uniform prominently appears on the wall. Although two decades would elapse before Aldrich could ever depict the traumatic consequences of the "forgotten war" affecting Marty Hollinger in *Hustle, The Garment Jungle* subtly implies that the aftermath of the Korean War may have something to do with the obsessive crusades of both Alan and Tullio.

When Alan and Theresa go to a nearby restaurant, she moves to an adjoining booth to feed her baby. Aldrich and Biroc frame both their heads in a mid-shot. Alan and Theresa look in opposite directions with the booth dividing them. However, their complementary positions within the frame suggest both similarity and difference. Alan cannot understand what separates Tullio from his family. Theresa replies that Tullio's father is the reason: "His father was a soft man, a dreamer who only wanted to make life better for others. A poor tailor." Aldrich then cuts to a close-up of Alan, who appears aware of a family resemblance, his own father being hard rather than soft: "There never was any choice for Tullio, was there?" Theresa replies, "They were like one person, the same dreams, the same hopes." Alan responds, "But if he had to choose, would Tullio have turned against his own flesh and blood? What kind of son would do that?" She replies, "Blood is blood. But there is always a right and a wrong." The dialogue finishes with Alan's revealing remark: "Yes. And the choice has to be made." The next sequence is Tullio's betrayal and murder.

Shot, composed, and acted in a revealing manner, this sequence can only have emerged from Robert Aldrich rather than Vincent Sherman. It reveals a contradiction and complexity making *The Garment Jungle* much more than a compromised production. The "good guys" are psychologically flawed. Walter dies at the hands of Ravidge's thugs. But Alan's revenge is questionable. Ravidge's dark father figure beats him mercilessly at the climax without any real opposition. It is almost as if Alan masochistically wishes to be punished in a perverse performance of Freud's "A [Son] Is Being Beaten."[58] He has no idea whether Theresa has managed to bring incriminating evidence to the police. Alan is also a younger man with combat experience. But he allows a middle-aged nonveteran to beat him mercilessly. Before the police arrive, the final beating ironically occurs in the fashion display room, which usually witnesses more glamorous performances. This time audiences witness not only the dark side of the fashion business but also a macabre reenactment of the tortured relationship Alan had with his own father.

Such glimpses suggest what the film could have been had Aldrich continued on the set. But the final version of *The Garment Jungle* does end ironically. Alan now runs his father's business, which is now unionized. He experiences similar limitations on his leisure time. He enjoys the company of two women who are both widowed mother figures: Lee and Theresa. Lee earlier attempted to intervene like a mother during the first tense meeting between father and son. As an Italian mother, Theresa embodies a Madonna figure whom Alan may have yearned for after the death of his mother temporarily postponed the unresolved Oedipal conflict he had with his father. Perhaps the son will become the father? Silver and Ursini suggest this by referring to the film's sardonic ending of a Roxton Fashions operator informing a caller, "Mr. Mitchell is busy."[59] Although Aldrich disowned *The Garment Jungle*, it does contain significant features that could have resulted in another dark, satirical American world for ransom.

The Grissom Gang originated from a novel even more grotesque than Mickey Spillane's *Kiss Me Deadly*. Based on James Hadley Chase's *No*

Orchids for Miss Blandish, a brutal thriller written by a British writer under a pseudonym, Aldrich's version aims to be as provocative as his earlier version of Mickey Spillane.[60] As before, Aldrich took an iconoclastically subversive approach. He not only undermined the gratuitous violence within the original source material but also critiqued Hollywood's superficial fascination with the 1930s. Following the success of *Bonnie and Clyde* (1967), the depression era again became fashionable, and several films appeared exploiting glamorous costumes and violence. Unlike in *Kiss Me Deadly,* Aldrich chose to follow the plot of *No Orchids for Miss Blandish.* But this time he engaged in a more radical approach by subverting the material from within rather than rewriting it. *The Grissom Gang* contrasts with *Bonnie and Clyde's* "beautiful people" and Roger Corman's vulgar Freudian *Bloody Mama* (1970) to engage in a more socially relevant attack on an era that wreaked havoc on the human personality, resulting in violence and psychological destruction. Unlike in *Bonnie and Clyde,* characters are never glamorized. Instead, they are archetypal types from a nightmare postwar gallery of grotesque modernism whom audiences are discouraged from identifying with. Accurately exuding sweat in the pre-air-conditioned world of the 1930s, Aldrich's characters represent the dark underside of a world depicted glamorously in most Hollywood productions.

Barbara Blandish (Kim Darby) is a selfish manipulator. Her character will not change until the final hours before her rescue. Scott Wilson's Slim Grissom is a dangerous psychopath. But he is also a character who expresses a genuine love for his rich fairy princess, unlike his predecessor in both versions of the novel.[61] Abducted after leaving the Golden Slipper roadhouse, heiress Barbara Blandish will not be awakened by a kiss from a handsome prince. Instead, she will be touched by an aberrant figure from the dark side of an American depression she would not ordinarily encounter. Robert Lansing's Dave Fenner is one of many people doing a job and attempting to survive the rigors of the depression. He first appears as a manipulative individual out to make a fast buck. But like Barbara and Slim, his character radically changes toward the end of the film. He becomes the only person to understand the tragic nature of Barbara's plight and unsuccessfully tries to evoke sympathy from her uncaring father, who would rather see her dead than alive. However, Aldrich avoids the mistake of manipulating audience feelings toward misleading empathy. Instead, he depicts a cruelly grotesque social universe that exercises callous and unforgiving attitudes. Although *The Grissom Gang* contains few parallels to the plays of Clifford Odets, they both belong to a similar historical context that undermined previous conceptions of a secure American universe.

The film opens with an overhead shot of a diner situated on a dusty Kansas road in 1931. As Rudy Vallee's voice on the soundtrack croons "I Can't Give You Anything but Love, Baby," the credits roll before a car arrives. Three small-time crooks plan the theft of Barbara's $60,000 diamond necklace. However, a simple theft turns into capital offenses when the hoods murder Barbara's escort and kidnap her. When members of the Grissom Gang learn of this, they appropriate the heiress and kill her abductors. They plan a $1,000,000 ransom and the eventual murder of their victim. However, the emotionally disturbed Slim falls in love with Barbara and disobeys his mother for the first time, wishing to keep her alive. In a perverse variant of *Beauty and the Beast*, Slim attempts to change his character to win an upper-class lady disgusted by his very presence. Seeing the influence she has over her captor, Barbara constantly humiliates him until she learns that he is the only one keeping her alive in her newly adopted family. Although the film avoids the gratuitous sadism and drug addiction affecting Barbara in the novel, it depicts the existence of a perversely dysfunctional order of things motivating the main characters originating from within the family as well the social world outside.

Although Ma Grissom (Irene Dailey) rules her "family" in the same manner as the historical Ma Barker (embodied by Shelley Winters in *Bloody Mama*), parallels also exist to those dangerously dysfunctional family situations of *Autumn Leaves, What Ever Happened to Baby Jane? Hush . . . Hush, Sweet Charlotte,* and *The Killing of Sister George.* The Grissom family is a much more deadly version of those families because it is explicitly based on an authoritarian violence it never attempts to conceal. Sprouting a moustache on her upper lip, Ma Grissom embodies the patriarchal appropriation of male violence seen in other Aldrich female characters such as Jane Hudson, Miriam Deering, and June Buckridge. She rules her various "sons" like a strict father, enjoying sexual pleasure from the body of downwardly mobile Doc (Don Keefer), whom she also dominates like a mother. Before she machine-guns him when the police surround their nightclub in the latter part of the film, she tells him: "Doc, I've looked after you for a long time. Now you look after yourself." She has attempted to dominate her psychopathic son Slim until he rebels against her influence. She treats Slim like a child, feeding him constantly on cookies and apple pie so that he is little better than Jane Hudson in his emotional development. When he later learns of Ma's death, he sobs to Barbara, "They killed Ma. That's the kinda people you're dealing with . . . see? They killed an old lady." He is oblivious to the fact that the "old lady" is really a tough cookie who has chosen to die like a man in a hail of police bullets.

Wesley Addy's Mr. Blandish belongs to Aldrich's gallery of cold, manipulative fathers, such as Hanson in *Autumn Leaves* and Big Sam Hollis in *Charlotte*. After paying ransom money to release his daughter, he uses Dave Fenner for "revenge" on her kidnappers. Believing her dead, Blandish is appalled to discover that Barbara is still alive, living as Slim's mistress. When he surveys their love nest, he judgmentally condemns his daughter despite Fenner's plea on her behalf: "I don't think she had much choice." When Fenner describes Slim's dangerous character, the "Father of the Year" regards death as more socially appropriate than dishonor. When he finally sees Barbara in a distraught condition before Slim's mutilated body, he callously abandons her.

The Grissom Gang is a deliberately bleak film. It chooses not to romanticize the Great Depression but, instead, depicts the ugliness it has brought on the American character. Rich and poor are equally grotesque and unfeeling. Although the film drops several of the depression references contained in the screenplay drafts, the dehumanized world of the protagonists owes much to this defining historical era. When the gang receives the ransom money, Ma plans to "go big time and legitimate," aiming to move into the nightclub business: "Long as prohibition lasts we make dough." In an addition to the film, Doc adds, "Like Mr. Hoover says, 'Prosperity is around the corner.'" After referring to a president whose callous attitude to the unemployed resulted in his removal from office, Doc sees being "in on the ground floor" as good economics.

Surrounded by a harsh existence from which no escape seems possible, none of the film's characters ever exhibits heroic or noble qualities. But although Aldrich avoids romanticizing certain characters, he never rules out the possibility of change. Dave Fenner begins as somebody out to make a buck because he has not worked for two months. He eventually turns out to be the one character who shows some sympathy for Barbara. Barbara and Slim change toward the end of the film. They exchange their various manipulative roles of victim and aggressor and become two people who genuinely reach out to each other before confronting a bleak future. This change never occurs in the original novel.

The key moment in the film involves Barbara's symbiotic reaction to the death of Eddie Hagen (Tony Musante). As Slim plunges his knife repeatedly into his rival's body, Barbara's body convulses orgasmically. This action does not occur in the various screenplay drafts or the original novel, where Eddie dies in an orgasmic manner. For Arnold and Miller, "She has for the first time responded to him in a sexual sense, with Eddie as surrogate and with sex and death impossibly mixed. She faces her own capacity for evil, for violence, and, indeed, recognizes the basic kinship she shares with the people she has so hated."[62]

Later, by emotionally reacting to Slim's murder Barbara becomes not a "secret sharer" but a person who breaks social and behavioral boundaries, experiencing feelings that her previous class insulation from the effects of the depression protected her against. If Barbara understands the darkness existing inside her, Slim now becomes more caring and loving in the last hours he shares with his captive princess. Despite his murderous deeds, he is a character capable of redemption. But society will not allow this. Neither will it permit any mitigating circumstances to influence its judgment of Barbara. Like Slim, she is as good as dead in the climax.

Aldrich could easily have fallen back on familiar cinematic stereotypes in depicting both these characters. Like Jack La Rue in the 1948 British film version, Slim could have emerged finally as a likable character. Similarly, Barbara could have been an acceptable heroine like Faye Dunaway's Bonnie, dangerous but fun. However, Aldrich makes both these figures equally grotesque and uncongenial to any form of deceptively emotional audience identification. Instead, he wishes the audience to concentrate on the dark psychosexual feelings motivating both these characters and consider the more deadly nature of the family and historical forces that influence them. Box-office problems affecting the film reveal the gamble Aldrich took in departing from established conventions. But he also deserves credit for again breaking the rules.

Seeing his chances of survival as negligible, Slim exhibits a fond nostalgia for the home that will supposedly welcome Barbara back. Barbara pleads that she is "not worth dying for" and that "nobody's worth that." Slim becomes touched when he recognizes that she now really cares for him. The sequence ends when Barbara touches his hand before a fade-out suggests that their lovemaking has now become genuine.

But despite Slim's parting words, "You're going home. It doesn't matter now," Barbara can never return there. Shocking her father before a crowd of police, bystanders, and newsmen by weeping over the body of a man who could not give her "anything but love," she becomes a social outcast. After Barbara traumatically pleads to her father, "He wouldn't let me go . . . he loved me. . . . Can't you understand?" Blandish refuses to recognize her emotional condition and rejects her: "No . . . and I never will. Mister Fenner here will look after you." As Blandish walks to his car, Fenner moves Barbara away from the surrounding media, avariciously hungry for the "real" story, who resemble the carnivorous dogs in the final image of *The Legend of Lylah Clare*. Blandish never looks back. He slams the door of his car on an impoverished farmer asking about reward money. The final image ends on a freeze-frame of Barbara traumatically looking back at her father and a callous media world that will pursue her to the bitter end. Rather than concluding with a final scene of Barbara jumping into a nearby river aided by Fenner's complicity, Aldrich chooses instead to end the film with this devastating image. As credits roll to DeVol's musical rendition of "I Can't Give You Anything but Love," the camera slowly zooms in to a close-up of Barbara as the image gradually darkens. It is a bleak, but honest, ending, reaffirming the nihilistic philosophy of noir at its best whenever it contradicts misleading ideological optimism. The original screenplay and first version of *The Grissom Gang* ended with Dave Fenner's defensive wisecrack.[63] But the theatrical version more appropriately concludes with an image documenting Barbara's social damnation at the hands of a society that will not recognize its responsibility for the events that have condemned her both psychologically and socially.

Hustle is another of Aldrich's bleakest and most uncompromising films. As one of the earliest neo-noirs, it not only complements his contributions to classical film noir but is also a companion piece to *Force of Evil*. As with *The Grissom Gang*, Aldrich presents a world in which everyone is contaminated in one way or another. It is a world in which a brief victory may be achieved by bending the rules. But it is also one whose premises cannot be fundamentally altered under present social conditions. Like *The Garment Jungle, Hustle* begins and ends in a circular manner. But this time it also involves a specific sound effect evoking both *Kiss Me Deadly* and *Twilight's Last Gleaming*. Before changing to an overhead shot of a bus on the highway, the opening shot of the film pans over a Californian landscape accompanied by the dehumanizing sound of wind. This sound returns in the final credits accompanying an overhead shot of the airport where Louis Belgrave (Paul Winfield) moves the bereaved Nicole Bretton (Catherine Deneuve) toward the red sports car belonging to Phil Gaines (Burt Reynolds). The sound of the wind returns to the soundtrack following the end of Frank DeVol's melancholy, romantic trumpet theme associated with Phil. *Hustle* belongs to that group of early pessimistic neo-noirs such as *Chinatown*, which anticipated, accompanied, and followed the devastating national traumas of Vietnam and Watergate.[64] But it is also a Robert Aldrich film, giving mature expression to themes occurring throughout his career.

The following shots take the audience inside the bus, where the driver (played by James Hampton, Aldrich's "Caretaker" from *The Longest Yard*) listens to the progress of the Philadelphia Rockets on loudspeakers and instills the value of team sports playing into his young charges. It is an unusual opening for an Aldrich film and strikingly reminiscent of the climactic scene in *Dirty Harry* (1971) involving the school bus. At any moment, the audience would expect a Scorpio figure to hijack the bus and begin the action. However, this type of audience expectation is temporarily suspended. The driver takes his charges safely to a Malibu beach. But before they begin swimming, they discover the dead body of Gloria Hollinger (Sharon Kelly) at the shore. The camera zooms in to her body before ending in an overhead freeze-frame with Aldrich's director/producer credits. This character will initiate *Hustle*'s narrative. *Hustle* never employs the expected good cop/bad guy scenario of so many thrillers like *Dirty Harry*. Although Eileen McGarry argues for including Don Siegel's film in the noir canon, its structure does follow the usual *film policier* trajectory leading to the anticipated conflict between its two major protagonists.[65] *Hustle* operates in a more sophisticated manner. It refuses to allow its audience to experience the expected resolution by employing darker imagery in which boundaries are more blurred than usual. But a similarity does exist between both films whereby the discovery of the female corpse triggers off repressed aspects within the psyche of an emotionally tarnished hero.[66]

The next sequence reveals an entirely different geographical location from the one where schoolchildren can play freely on a public beach, although we later learn that the area has been "rezoned" to keep out undesirables. Another overheard shot begins, this time taken from a helicopter, showing the glamorous residence shared by Phil and Nicole. As Nicole walks onto the balcony on a Sunday morning, with church bells prominently ringing on the soundtrack, the camera zooms in to her in a manner recalling the introduction to Gloria's body. The next two shots pull back from Nicole's face, as if signifying her class difference from the murdered girl, before the camera zooms in to her face in the next shot. These introductory shots visually articulate the dualistic aspects structuring *Hustle*'s narrative. When Nicole enters the darkened interior of the apartment, Aldrich introduces Phil in close-up. But this typical star introduction becomes undermined by his first line. Although spoken humorously, it reveals much about his hidden regressive nature. He asks for a glass of milk as if Nicole were his mother.

Such an introductory line is not accidental, for *Hustle* also employs the dysfunctional family themes Aldrich saw in the plays of Clifford Odets. If not as infantile in his behavior as Jerry from *Clash by Night*, Phil Gaines bears as many emotional scars from a past family trauma as the other characters in the film, both major and minor. He lives in an illusionary past world similar to his "secret sharer," Marty Hollinger (Ben Johnson). Already traumatized by the Korean War, Marty has suffered the same adulterous betrayal as Phil. He has also acted more like a mother to Gloria than his wife, as we see in his memories of her growing up, scenes in which Paula Hollinger (Eileen Brennan) is conspicuously absent. As Paula tells Phil later, "The only thing in the world my husband lived for was Gloria." His obsessive feelings toward his daughter represent not only the result of his war trauma but also overcompensation for feelings of personal inadequacy. They resemble the disastrous paternal care that ruins the lives of Jane Hudson and Charlotte Hollis. All these fathers have tried to give their daughters everything, whether celebrity status, a plantation, or material goods. But they all fail in providing the important emotional sustenance necessary to any child's growth. As Marty says of Gloria, "She chased the things she didn't have and they killed her." His statement also applies to Jane and Charlotte as well as a daughter whom Phil later describes as "an ambitious loser who gave up." When Paula criticizes Marty as being "obsessed," he responds, "She saw what we didn't have. You can't hide what you don't have." These lines suggest that Marty's intense feelings about being a nobody within an affluent American dream may have contaminated Gloria to the extent that she decided to follow another path, which eventually polluted her body and soul. As Leo Sellers (Eddie Albert) later tells Phil, Gloria "wanted things so she balled and had tried to get a bright light" and also mentions that she had "suffered severe psychic damage long before I met her." Although Phil recognizes Leo's duplicity by commenting, "You never helped the girl," his version may not be entirely far from the truth in a film where no clear-cut boundaries actually exist.

Two key sequences in *Hustle* cinematically identify Phil and Marty as alter egos. After we view Marty reliving memories of his daughter, Paula enters his room. Their positions echo the first scenes between Phil and Nicole when he lies on the bed and she walks toward him. Despite Paula's statement of the real situation, "We lost her long ago," a statement repeated later before the ineffectual minister (Peter Brandon) when she says, "We failed her. You failed her. You chased Gloria out of this house," Marty remains adamant in searching for another cause for his loss by blaming others. During the next sequence, Phil walks outside on the balcony overlooking the night landscape of Los Angeles as Nicole talks to her client on the phone. She begins her erotic conversation with the lines, "This is mother with a bedtime story," evoking Phil's memories of his past bedtime story when he found his wife in bed with another man. His fragmentary past memories conclude with an enigmatic shot of a dark-suited man seen against the background of a cemetery. The man's face is in shadow. Although depicting Phil's 1930s radical uncle in the original screenplay, this shot now functions to represent an older version of Phil whose discovery of his wife's adultery leads him to bury his deep emotions within the graveyard of a death-in-life relationship with Nicole. Both Phil and Nicole are emotional hustlers engaging in a perverse arrangement that represses their real emotional needs for each other. Because of his betrayal, Phil cannot commit himself to a romantic union with Nicole. He achieves sexual pleasure according to a deal in which each partner is free to pursue his or her own independent life. Marty and Paula have not lived as man and wife from the very beginning of their marital relationship. Nicole recognizes the contradictory nature of her involvement with Phil: "I'm a whore so I'm all right. But she's your wife." Phil still feels guilty over his justified abandonment of his adulterous wife. He refers to his last meeting with her to Belgrave: "She has a wonderful way of making me feel I deserted her." Belgrave replies, "But you did." His partner may discern deep irrational masochistic tendencies affecting Phil similar to those motivating Marty Hollinger over his adulterous betrayal. Finally, when Leo asks Phil, "Why single me out?" over questions concerning Gloria's death, Phil replies, "I can't get everyone." Later, during Marty's final confrontation with Leo (who abruptly ceases speaking about the relationship *he* has with *his* daughter upon seeing Marty's dark expression), the latter repeats again the same question he earlier asked Phil, "Why single me out?" This time he receives a reply from Marty, "Because I can't kill everyone."

The family battleground of *What Ever Happened to Baby Jane? Hush . . . Hush, Sweet Charlotte,* and *The Killing of Sister George* also occurs in *Hustle.* When Phil confronts George Bellamy (David Spielberg), who has killed two women in the Garment District and threatens to murder another, the latter insanely comments, "They took my friend away. They gave me electric shocks. She tried to strangle me." As if aware of some maternal damage to Bellamy as a helpless child, Phil replies, "That's wrong. Your mother strangled you. That lady doesn't even know you." Bellamy's history of violence originated from some past moment of traumatic child abuse causing him psychic damage. His other lines concerning his "friend" and "electric shocks" evoke not only an earlier scene when Phil encountered a drug-addicted gay murder suspect in an elevator who had cut his friend into little pieces but also the treatment Marty suffered in the mental hospital he entered following the trauma caused by his Korean War experiences.

Toward the climax, Marty is in danger of suffering further electric shocks in an institution where Phil tells him he will "play Juliet to some faggot's Romeo." Although some gay critics accuse Aldrich of homophobia, he is also aware of the dark side of existence within alternative communities, as *The Killing of Sister George* shows. He never provides false ideals in any of his films, especially in *Hustle,* where everything is interconnected through a (noir) glass darkly.

As the film progresses, the audience becomes more aware of Phil Gaines as a character exhibiting not only the naive romanticism of figures such as Mike Callahan in *World for Ransom* but also the male immaturity seen in such characters as *Attack!*'s Captain Cooney who have been psychologically scarred by some past traumatic incident. Like Barbara and Slim in *The Grissom Gang*, Phil and Nicole are trapped individuals, psychologically and historically. Phil's father died in the Spanish Civil War. His last letter to his family warned of the destructive American fascination with "enthusiasm," as opposed to the more sophisticated national demises of the French by alcoholism and the Spanish by heartbreak. Phil also has naive idealism in mind when he tells his partner Belgrave about his family history. Nicole's father died in an explosion as a right-wing opponent of Algerian independence, leaving her alone to fend for herself, a situation she again encounters at the film's conclusion. She speaks of her father as being "obsessed about being right . . . and he was killed for it." Similarly, Paula criticizes Marty in similar terms: "You've always been obsessed." Phil, too, is obsessed in his own way. Gloria compares him with Marty in believing in a "right and wrong world." Marty obsessively believes that murder, rather than suicide, caused the death of his daughter. He acts the anachronistic role of a Warner Bros. hero from a 1930s social consciousness studio movie starring Humphrey Bogart or John Garfield. But both era and stars are now dead and only appear on *The Late Show* watched by Belgrave. Belgrave does a bad impersonation of Bogart's romantic hero Rick from *Casablanca* (1943), leading Phil to comment, "Don't make fun of my heroes." Belgrave also mentions Paul Robeson, another forgotten social hero of that time, who, like John Garfield, suffered from the blacklist. Seeing Marty almost like Joseph Conrad's *The Secret Sharer*, Phil attempts to educate him in the realities of living "in Guatemala with color television." But it has disastrous results.

After murdering Leo Sellers, Marty still clings to his illusions, wanting his day in court like a Warner Bros. social justice hero. But, after informing him about his likely fate involving homosexual use and abuse, which ironically echoes his daughter's last hours, Phil finally enacts the role of one of his cherished 1930s cinematic role models but in a manner that would never be depicted in any Warner Bros. film. This tormented 1970s version of John Garfield attempts to reintegrate body and soul by faking evidence. It is technically illegal but justifiable in terms of the old social consciousness philosophy of now-redundant Warner Bros. films. As he tells Belgrave, "There's got to be a little charity in the system for the Martys, the albinos, and the Glorias because they ain't got no juice." As well as being a metaphorical term, *juice* also evokes the carrot juice consumed by those blood brothers on opposite sides of the fence—Sellers and Santoro (Ernest Borgnine). Although Belgrave accuses Phil of using Marty "just like a hit man," Phil responds, "There comes a time when you've got to try to turn the wheel around." Both factors probably motivate Phil. But after faking the evidence and phoning Nicole, Phil loses his life in a heroic gesture in a holdup. On one level, he is acting his role as an honest cop whose integrity will not allow him to just stand by. But his redundant heroism contains masochistic overtones, suggesting that he really does not want to commit himself fully to Nicole in the last resort.

Duality affects virtually every character in the entire film. After Phil speaks of his desire to take Nicole to a Rams–Vikings game and exhibit her as his prized possession to the spectators, the sequence ends with a line from Charles Aznavour's "When I Was Young." The image significantly changes to an overhead shot of the actual game as loudspeakers call for Marty Hollinger during a sequence of shots before the concluding shot shows his face. Aznavour's line "foolish game" also undercuts any false idea of a world structured on rules involving right and wrong.

Hustle is another Aldrich film ruthlessly breaking down the false illusions of American society and showing a world in which the real rules of the game operate behind the scenes. Aldrich's previous film with Burt Reynolds, *The Longest Yard,* already depicted an American society little different from the dictatorships it usually condemns in the name of democracy and freedom. As a traumatized Korean War veteran (who may have undergone a lobotomy), Marty Hollinger shares several characteristics with Phil. Although Phil hides his yearning for the supposedly clean-cut world of the 1930s involving "Cole Porter, Dizzy Dean, clean air, clean weather, when young girls were treated with respect" and constantly plays classics from that era on his record player, Marty is a "war-wounded nobody," obsessively believing in values of right and wrong no longer relevant to the society in which he lives. While Marty reacts aggressively against what he sees as the uncaring nature of his social order, Phil buries his discontent in Cole Porter and a sexual relationship with Nicole, which he can control by preserving his vulnerable personality from being hurt again. Despite the loving nature of their liaison, it is a mechanical business type of relationship lacking the real emotional commitment that Nicole seeks from Phil.

As Silver and Ursini note, several scenes reveal Phil's relationship to earlier flawed heroes such as Mike Callahan and Charlie Castle in *The Big Knife*.[67] A symbiotic brotherhood exists between Phil and Marty that will become actual at the climax of the film. Similarly, Nicole and Gloria are hustlers at different ends of the social scale in a world in which, as Nicole recognizes, "everybody hustles."

The dark, claustrophobic environments of the residences of Phil and Marty as well as Phil's own office evoke this imagery. But the domains of crooked lawyer Leo Sellers and police chief Santoro are deceptively brightly lit and spacious. Phil is a tormented character more in control of his emotions than Marty. But he is eager to find an excuse to exercise violence legally, as shown by his confrontation with Bellamy, whom he shoots several times after one fatal bullet has entered him. This scene parallels Belgrave's earlier brutal interrogation of a suspect, a red-eyed black albino, whom he uses as a surrogate victim to take out his anger against Hollinger. A reverse-shot sequence shows Marty and Belgrave looking at each other in a manner similar to the silent, hostile exchange of looks between Reisman and Breed in *The Dirty Dozen*. Like Breed's hostility toward Reisman, Marty's racist glance and Belgrave's equally aggressive posture need no lines of dialogue. Frustrated in his attempt to arrest Marty after he assaults Phil, Belgrave takes it out on the albino until Phil intervenes. When Belgrave comments, "There's something wrong with that albino," Gaines replies, "Nothing, absolutely nothing," and urges his partner to show some compassion. Virtually all the characters in *Hustle* seek their version of the "great whatzit," whether in a search for a convenient scapegoat to release their frustrated, emotionally violent tendencies against or a false quest for the American dream of affluence whose downside is use and abuse—a factor uniting both Gloria and Nicole.

Significantly, Phil's favorite film is John Huston's *Moby Dick* (1956), which we see once on a television screen and hear again in a later scene emanating from an offscreen television set. In a line relevant to himself as much as Marty, Phil tells Louis: "Every man is in search of the white whale and when he finds him he usually kills him." Silver and Ursini note that if Gaines sees himself as Captain Ahab, then he has many doubles "reflected in the felons and psychopaths who wage their own war against society and the system."[68] This is also true of both Santoro and Sellers in their scenes with Phil, which also reinforce *Hustle*'s duality. During the first Santoro scene, Phil's chief (played by an actor usually cast by Aldrich in dominant authoritarian roles) receives the report of Gloria's suicide and then inquires, "The girl's father. Is he anyone?" When Phil accompanies Leo to the plush L.A. restaurant modeled on "Harry's in Florence," the latter also asks, "That kid's father. Was he anybody?" Visual and verbal parallels between the chief of police and mob attorney Sellers occur throughout the film. During the second scene between Phil and Santoro, the latter makes a crude threat about arresting Nicole on Christmas Eve and giving her as a present to the "bull-dyke" lesbians. Like Leo, he knows that Phil and Nicole are living together. Although his threat is a crude jest, he has the authority to exercise this, as Phil well knows. When Phil's meeting with Leo draws toward its conclusion, the lawyer makes a veiled, but nonetheless authoritarian, threat to Phil of a similar nature. Without employing Santoro's vulgarity, Leo suggestively hints at the economic resources he possesses to take Nicole away from Phil: "Brilliant whores become courtesans. I think Nicole loves it. Ciao Phil." Leo's employment of the Italian farewell punctures Phil's romantic ideals of an untarnished Rome in more than one way. He has not only experienced the fact that the corrupt world he inhabits has appropriated one of his cherished dreams of escape, symbolized by his favorite Italian restaurant, but he also sees Leo giving the head waiter some money on his way out. Phil sees that money talks in more ways than one, a fact that may explain his eventual decision to commit himself to Nicole.

But it is too late. When Phil phones Nicole on his way to the fatal liquor store, the opening overhead shot of a canopy blocking her from view suggests the impossibility of its culmination. It is as ironic as the televised episode of *Mission Impossible* in the dingy bar Phil took Nicole to after viewing Claude Lelouch's *A Man and a Woman* (1966). The tacky nature of the television production counterpoints the film's impossible dream of romanticism embodied in the Lelouch film. The dark urban jungle of Los Angeles and its material trap tarnish any naive dreams of romanticism, whether foreign or national. When Marty visits the nightclub where his daughter once performed, manager Herbie Dalitz (Jack Carter) watches a western on television with his bodyguard, the very genre with which Ben Johnson himself is identified.[69] But the westerner finds himself outmatched by the mob.

When Phil enters the nightclub, both men are watching a television quiz show, *The Dating Game*, whose title ironically evokes the other dating game that has destroyed Gloria. Marty experienced a brutal beating by the mob. His battered face forms a grim contrast to the bruise on Phil's forehead following his violent fight with Nicole. Both Marty and Phil physically abuse their ladies during certain points of the film. Although Phil succeeds where Marty fails, both men are trapped within a corrupting nihilistic world. Whether it involves economics, sex, or television (*Mission Impossible, The Dating Game*), it is a world in which the old values are now useless and heading immediately for apocalypse, whether personal or global. Aldrich's noir films embody this grim vision. But it is also one that appears in his westerns, another major Hollywood genre he would use for his own purposes.

NOTES

1. See David Cochran, *America Noir: Underground Writers and Filmmakers of the Postwar Era* (Washington, D.C.: Smithsonian Institution Press, 2000), 1–16.

2. For the neo-noir movement, see Todd Erickson, "Kill Me Again: Movement Becomes Genre," in *Film Noir Reader*, vol. 2, ed. Alain Silver and James Ursini (New York: Limelight Editions, 1996), 307–30; Alain Silver, "Son of *Noir*: Neo–Film Noir and the Neo–B Picture," in *Film Noir Reader*, vol. 2, ed. Alain Silver and James Ursini (New York: Limelight Editions, 1996), 331–38; and Foster Hirsch, *Detours and Lost Highways: A Map of Neo Noir* (New York: Limelight Editions, 1999). It should be noted that John Alton had already pioneered the use of Technicolor noir in Allan Dwan's *Slightly Scarlet* (1956).

3. See Francois Truffaut, "Rencontre avec Robert Aldrich," *Cahiers du Cinema* 64 (1956): 4. See also Martin C. Myrick, "John Lewis and the Film Score for *Odds against Tomorrow*," in *Odds against Tomorrow: The Critical Edition*, ed. John Schultheiss (Northridge: California State University Press, 1999), 299–307.

4. Cochran, *America Noir*, 7.

5. Cochran, *America Noir*, 13–14, quoting Geoffrey O'Brien, *Hardboiled America: Lurid Paperbacks and the Masters of Noir* (New York: Da Capo, 1997), 16.

6. See Cochran, *America Noir*, 223n6. He also names other talents who belong to this "underground culture."

7. Cochran, *America Noir*, 14.

8. See Michael Denning, *The Cultural Front: The Laboring of American Culture in the Twentieth-Century* (London: Verso, 1997), 118–24.

9. Denning, *The Cultural Front*, 122.

10. Denning, *The Cultural Front*, 123. This feature may explain the origins of those grotesque and visual attributes that several critics note in the films of Robert Aldrich. See Adrian Martin, who cites Dave Sanjek's reference to the "purposeful avalanche of deformation" animating Aldrich's films: "As a form, specifically, of bodily or corporeal figuration, the grotesque is an exaggerated, expressionistic form, akin to caricature. Aldrich used it often, in grand and small ways alike: think of how, for instance, he condenses the whole character and style of Lancaster in *Vera Cruz* down to the recurrent flashing of those amazing, gleaming white teeth of his" ("The Body Has No Head: Corporeal Figuration in Aldrich," available at www.latrobe.edu.au/screeningthepast/firstrelease/fr0600/rmfr10e.htm, 30 June 2000). The same can be said of Shack's grotesque close-ups in *Emperor of the North*. Adrian Danks notices that Aldrich's ironic Hollywood citations contain "a bizarre, grotesque almost inhuman, human geography" ("The Hunter Gets Captured by the Game: Robert Aldrich's Hollywood," available at www.latrobe.edu.au/screeningthepast/firstrelease/fr0600/adfr10h.htm, 30 June 2000). See also David Sanjek, "Fear Is a Man's Best Friend: Deformation and Aggression in the Films of Robert Aldrich," available at www.latrobe.edu.au/screeningthepast/firstrelease/fr0600/dsfr10b.htm, 30 June 2000.

11. Denning, *The Cultural Front*, 122–23.

12. Cochran, *America Noir*, 14. The reference to "untrained in irony" comes from Paul Fussell, *Wartime: Understanding and Behavior during the Second World War* (New York: Oxford University Press, 1989), 83. Such a feature was absent from best-selling authors of the time such as Herman Wouk, James Michener, and James Gould Cozzens. Cochran further comments that Jim Thompson "insisted on seeing the grotesque as central to postwar culture" (*America Noir*, 28).

13. Cochran, *America Noir*, 14.

14. Cochran, *America Noir*, 20.

15. Cochran, *America Noir*, 32. The reference to God in the "Pledge of Allegiance" was only introduced during the Cold War era by President Eisenhower in 1954. For the conformist role of religion in this period, see Stephen Whitfield, *The Culture of the Cold War* (Baltimore: Johns Hopkins University Press, 1991), 77–100.

16. Cochran, *America Noir*, 34.

17. Cochran, *America Noir*, 32. For a key analysis of contemporary thought, see Elaine Tyler May, *Homeward Bound: American Families in the Cold War Era* (New York: Basic Books, 1988).

18. Cochran, *America Noir*, 35–36.

19. Cochran, *America Noir*, 38.

20. Marshall Berman, *All that Is Solid Melts into Air: The Experience of Modernity* (New York: Simon & Schuster, 1982), 121. Although critics such as Richard Maltby and James Naremore emphasize the French influence in

elevating *Kiss Me Deadly* to its present position, the American underground cultural connections should not be underestimated. Despite Maltby's interesting analysis of the film as a contemporary discursive product, this should not overwhelm the rich dimensions contained in the text. See Richard Maltby, "'The Problem of Interpretation . . .': Authorial and Institutional Intentions in and around *Kiss Me Deadly*," available at www.latrobe.edu.au/ screeningthepast/firstrelease/fr0600/rmfr10e.htm, 30 June 2000; and James Naremore, *More than Night: Film Noir in Its Contexts* (Berkeley: University of California Press, 1998).

21. Quoted in Richard Combs, ed., *Robert Aldrich* (London: British Film Institute, 1978), 51. On the critical reception and its aftermath, see Edwin T. Arnold and Eugene I. Miller, *The Films and Career of Robert Aldrich* (Knoxville: University of Tennessee Press, 1986), 21.

22. According to most authorities such as Alain Silver and James Ursini (*What Ever Happened to Robert Aldrich? His Life and His Films* [New York: Limelight Editions, 1995], 323), Aldrich directed four episodes of the first season. I have only been able to verify and trace two (see chap. 3).

23. See Silver and Ursini, *What Ever Happened to Robert Aldrich?* 74–77; and Michael Grost, "*Kiss Me Deadly* and *World for Ransom*," Classic Film and Television Home Page, available at www.members.aol.com/MGM4273/ a.6/23/2001, 23 June 2001, 4–8.

24. Robin Wood, "Ideology, Genre, Auteur," *Film Comment* 13, no. 1 (1977): 47.

25. Robert Aldrich, "The High Price of Independence," *Films and Filming* 4, no. 9 (1958): 7.

26. Grost notices that a ceiling appears over the staircase and that the length of the shot is "claustrophobic and unusual" ("*Kiss Me Deadly* and *World for Ransom*"), whereas Silver and Ursini comment on an implied notion of predestination contained in this sequence (*What Ever Happened to Robert Aldrich?* 73). The use of deep focus and prominent ceiling shots are reminiscent of the techniques employed by Orson Welles. Richard Combs also notes the significance of this scene and remarks that Callahan "is pinned in place like some translucent insect by both the harsh lighting and the quick cut to a reverse angle from the position of the hoodlum looking down on him at the top of the stairs" (*Robert Aldrich,* 7).

27. Although uncredited because of the blacklist, Hugo Butler wrote the screenplay that Aldrich revised. See Jean Rouverol, *Refugees from Hollywood: A Journal of the Blacklist Years* (Albuquerque: University of New Mexico Press, 2000), 51.

28. See Silver and Ursini, *What Ever Happened to Robert Aldrich?* 75, as well as their meticulous visual analysis of other scenes between "hero" and "heroine" in this film (*What Ever Happened to Robert Aldrich?* 76–77).

29 Again, Silver and Ursini concisely note how "the identification factors which propel the audience in towards Callahan's point of view are contro-

verted or at least neutralized by the staging" (*What Ever Happened to Robert Aldrich?* 76).

30. Grost, "*Kiss Me Deadly* and *World for Ransom*," 6. Combs suggests that the alliance between Callahan and Bone "might be taken as a wish-fulfillment revision" of the relationship between Callahan and March (*Robert Aldrich,* 8).

31. See Loren Baritz, *Backfire: A History of How American Culture Led Us into Vietnam and Made Us Fight the Way We Did* (Baltimore: Johns Hopkins University Press, 1998).

32. Silver and Ursini, *What Ever Happened to Robert Aldrich?* 77.

33. The sexual subtext of *World for Ransom* is remarkable in many ways. Combs notes at least one anticipation of *Kiss Me Deadly*'s conjunction of sex, apocalypticism, and death in a scene "when the belly-dancer at the Golden Poppy night-club initiates her act by rising from a steel vat incongruously tricked out like a military silo" (*Robert Aldrich,* 6). The Chinese dancer is one of Julian's girlfriends. Her performance precedes Frennessey's, thus giving an ominous overtone to his remark to Mike in their first scene together, "Do you want to share all my girls?"

34. Berman, *All that Is Solid Melts into Air,* 13.

35. Berman, *All that Is Solid Melts into Air,* 15.

36. Berman, *All that Is Solid Melts into Air,* 345. Antoine de Baecque also notes that Aldrich has perverted the genre of film noir by making *Kiss Me Deadly* a "film blanc" in the concluding scenes where whiteness symbol-izes universal destruction ("La boîte atomique," *Cahiers du Cinema* 425 [1989]: 51).

37. See Denning, *The Cultural Front,* 323–28, 342–48.

38. Denning, *The Cultural Front,* 344.

39. Denning, *The Cultural Front,* 347.

40. See Carol Flinn, "Sound, Woman, and the Bomb," *Wide Angle* 8, nos. 3–4 (1988): 115–27; Michael Rogin, *Ronald Reagan, the Movie and Other Episodes in Political Demonology* (Berkeley: University of California Press, 1987), 236–71; and Elaine Tyler May, "Explosive Images: Sex, Woman, and the Bomb," in *Recasting America: Culture and Politics in the Age of Cold War,* ed. Lary May (Chicago: University of Chicago Press, 1989), 154–71.

41. See Alain Silver, "*Kiss Me Deadly*: Evidence of a Style," in *Film Noir Reader,* vol. 2., ed. Alain Silver and James Ursini (New York: Limelight Edi-tions, 1996), 209–36.

42. Cochran, *America Noir,* 40.

43. As one critic has brilliantly noted, Hammer misreads the actual mes-sage of the poem. Rather than giving up the quest and saving the world by his inaction, his selfish actions result in world destruction. See Rodney Hill, "Remembrance, Communication, and *Kiss Me Deadly*," *Literature/Film Quar-terly* 23, no. 2 (1995): 146–49.

44. Silver and Ursini, *What Ever Happened to Robert Aldrich?* 233.

45. Flinn, "Sound, Woman, and the Bomb," 122. *Kiss Me Deadly* begins with the halting breath of Christina and concludes with the roaring breath of the "great whatzit." It is an ironic parallel to theoretical work on film narrative concerning the end of the film answering its opening scene. See here Thierry Kuntzel, "The Film Work, 2," *Camera Obscura* 5 (1980): 7–69.

46. See Truffaut, "Rencontre avec Robert Aldrich," 5. Peculiarly, when Truffaut asked about the duration of the scene involving the attack on Mike, Aldrich replied that it created a very advantageous effect *"pour le rhythm du film"* ("Rencontre avec Robert Aldrich," 5, emphasis added). As far back as 1977, Jack Shadoian had recognized several key stylistic features of *Kiss Me Deadly*: "The film's look is surreal, the world is carefully and fastidiously distorted. *Kiss Me Deadly* has the cold design of a modernist painting in black and white" (*Dreams and Dead Ends: The American Gangster Film*, 2d ed. [New York: Oxford University Press, 2003], 221–22). The author also hints at the fact that Hammer could have been a very different type of person in another society: "Hammer's instinct leads him to be with people, depend on them. His manner of dealing with them—unresponsive, reticent, brutal, coldly direct—is determined by the nature of the society, which he has perceived and taken to a philosophical position" (*Dreams and Dead Ends*, 226).

47. Cochran, *America Noir*, 46.

48. See Jonathan Rosenbaum, *Placing Movies: The Practice of Film Criticism* (Berkeley: University of California Press, 1997), 125, 128.

49. Grost, "*Kiss Me Deadly* and *World for Ransom*," 2.

50. G. Cabrera Infante, *A Twentieth Century Job*, trans. Kenneth Hall and G. Cabrera Infante (London: Faber and Faber, 1991), 60. Infante's review is aptly titled "Spillane Macabre."

51. Infante, *A Twentieth Century Job*, 60. For the definitive solution to the question of the "two endings," see Silver and Ursini, *What Ever Happened to Robert Aldrich?* 240–41.

52. According to Silver and Ursini, Sherman replaced Aldrich five days before the scheduled completion of shooting and sixteen days before the actual completion (*What Ever Happened to Robert Aldrich?* 249). Any analysis of this film is tentative at best.

53. See George N. Fenin, "An Interview with Robert Aldrich," *Film Culture* 2, no. 4 (1956): 9.

54. Aldrich, "The High Price of Independence," 35.

55. See Paul Buhle and Dave Wagner, *A Very Dangerous Citizen: Abraham Lincoln Polonsky and the Hollywood Left* (Berkeley: University of California Press, 2001), 146–55; and Mark Rappaport, "Abraham Polonsky's *I Can Get It for You Wholesale* (1951) Reconsidered," *Senses of Cinema*, available at www.sensesofcinema.com/contents/02/20/polonsky.html, 2002.

56. See Silver and Ursini, *What Ever Happened to Robert Aldrich?* 186–88; Arnold and Miller, *The Films and Career of Robert Aldrich*, 76–79.

57. Arnold and Miller, *The Films and Career of Robert Aldrich*, 77.

58. Sigmund Freud, "A Child Is Being Beaten," in *On Psychopathology: The Pelican Freud Library*, vol. 10 (London: Penguin, 1979), 159–94.

59. Silver and Ursini, *What Ever Happened to Robert Aldrich?* 188. Any attempts at guessing which scenes belong to Robert Aldrich rather than Vincent Sherman are hypothetical. In addition to the scenes mentioned above, the shots involving Wesley Addy, a perennial member of his stock company, certainly belong to Aldrich. An enigmatic shot involving Addy's Mr. Paul and Adam Williams's Mr. Ox occurs just before Walter's murder. Both are having their shoes shined outside Walter's business. Mr. Paul notices a paper descending in the air that looks like a signal for them to begin their work. Nothing further is made of this in the film. Is there a "plant" inside the business such as Tony? Or does Alan subconsciously want his father out of the way to take his place? These ideas are purely speculative, of course. Vincent Sherman's autobiography is notoriously unhelpful in this matter. See Sherman, *Studio Affairs: My Life as a Film Director* (Lexington: University Press of Kentucky, 1996), 252–56. He claims that he reshot in thirteen days "almost 70 percent of what Aldrich had shot in thirty-one days" (*Studio Affairs,* 255).

60. After the first appearance of Hadley's novel in 1939, a stage version preceded the British film production with Jack LaRue and Linden Travers. This version waters down the book considerably but also exhibits a characteristic classical film noir style.

61. In both versions he has his way with Barbara and curses her before she dies.

62. Arnold and Miller, *The Films and Career of Robert Aldrich,* 161.

63. Both the first and the final drafts of Leon Griffiths's screenplay conclude with Fenner allowing Barbara to jump into a dangerous Missouri river. When Chief McLaine asks why Fenner did not rescue her, he replies, "I guess I don't swim so good." The present version affirms Aldrich's correct sensibility here. Aldrich's unproduced *Rage of Honor,* from Denne Bart Petticlere's screenplay based on his 1966 novel, also reveals the human devastation caused by the economic effects of the Great Depression. This fascinating work complements *The Grissom Gang* in many ways and would have made a really interesting film had Aldrich managed to acquire the right cast and appropriate backing.

64. For an intelligent survey of neo-noir, see Alain Silver and Elizabeth Ward, eds., *Film Noir: An Encyclopedic Reference to the American Style,* 3d ed. (New York: Overlook Press, 1992), 398–443.

65. Eileen McGarry, "Dirty Harry," in *Film Noir: An Encyclopedic Reference to the American Style,* 3d ed., ed. Alain Silver and Elizabeth Ward (New York: Overlook Press, 1992), 91–92.

66. Anthony Chase, "The Strange Romance of 'Dirty Harry' and Mary Ann Deacon," *The Velvet Light Trap* 17 (1977): 13–18.

67. Silver and Ursini, *What Ever Happened to Robert Aldrich?* 189.
68. Silver and Ursini, *What Ever Happened to Robert Aldrich?* 189.
69. One wonders whether the casting of B western actor Don "Red" Barry as the barman in the airport scene may represent more than Aldrich helping out a former star.

FIVE

THE WESTERN ODYSSEY

Like many Hollywood studio directors who began their careers within the classical Hollywood system, Robert Aldrich directed his share of westerns, which reflected the different social circumstances surrounding their production. Now almost virtually extinct as a cinematic genre, westerns in the 1950s offered many directors the opportunity of not only expanding generic horizons but also making contemporary social comment. This was also true of succeeding decades. Westerns such as *The Wild Bunch* (1969), *Soldier Blue* (1970), and *Ulzana's Raid* afforded the opportunity for directors to make allegorical parallels between the dark side of the frontier ethos and the contemporary American involvement in Vietnam. Apart from two unfortunate comedy westerns, which represent low points in Aldrich's career—*4 for Texas* (1963) and *The Frisco Kid* (1979)— Aldrich significantly explored several dimensions of the American western in *Apache* (1954), *Vera Cruz* (1954), *The Last Sunset* (1961), and *Ulzana's Raid* (1972).

During the 1950s, westerns such as Charles Marquis Warren's *Arrowhead* (1953) and Fred Zinnemann's *High Noon* (1952) made several comments on particular aspects of American foreign policy and internal security, the former being pro-McCarthyite and the latter following the strategy of allowing itself to be read in different ways by audiences. Other examples interrogate internal problems in American society.[1] The early 1950s saw the emergence of liberal pro-Indian westerns such as *Broken Arrow* (1950), *Devil's Doorway* (1950), *Drum Beat* (1954), *Taza, Son of Cochise* (1954), *White Feather* (1955), and *Run of the Arrow* (1957). These films attempt to break away from one-dimensional cinematic stereotypes of Native Americans as violent savages. However, a return to that other ideologically misleading "noble savage" archetype, which had coexisted with its opposite since the beginnings of American history, contained certain difficulties.[2] It presented the Native American as an object viewed through white liberal eyes, which often blinded audiences to the complexities of the actual culture. However, as Richard Slotkin points out, the genre provided certain opportunities for directors to explore social problems that were not available in mainstream cinema. The days of *Crossfire* and *Gentleman's Agreement* (both 1947) were long past. Such films would be judged "unpatriotic" in the Cold War climate of the 1950s. But as an entertainment genre safely located in the past, the Hollywood western offered other avenues for those willing to take the risk:

> The Western was a safe haven for liberals, because its identification with the heroic fable of American progress covered its practitioners with a presumption of patriotism that was essential in Hollywood during the years of the "Red Scare." Because it was safely "in the past," the tale of White–Indian conflict and peace-making allowed filmmakers to raise questions of war and peace and to entertain the possibility of co-existence without the kind of scrutiny to which a film set in or near the present would have drawn. Moreover, the same setting would allow them to address the race question without offending southern sensibilities.[3]

Yet the difficulties of casting led directors to select Caucasian actors and actresses for leading roles such as Burt Lancaster in *Apache*, Debra Paget and Jeff Chandler in *Broken Arrow*, Robert Taylor in *Devil's Doorway*, and Jeffrey Hunter in *White Feather* and *Seven Cities of Gold* (1955). Foreign actresses such as Elsa Martinelli and Sarita Montiel could portray dusky female "others" in films such as *The Indian Hunter* (1955) and *Run of the Arrow* (though dubbed by Angie Dickinson in the latter film), as could American stars such as Barbara Rush in *Taza, Son of Cochise*. The same custom also applied to character actors. While still surnamed Buchinsky, Charles Bronson played an Indian role in *Apache* before going on the warpath under his "new Cold War sensibility" surname in *Drum Beat*, *Run of the Arrow*, and *Chato's Land* (1972). Brooklyn-born Jewish actor Jeff Chandler received an Oscar nomination for his role as Cochise in *Broken Arrow*, a performance he briefly repeated in the prologue of *Taza, Son of Cochise*, whereas Rock Hudson could portray examples of a symbolic icon of gay culture within the safe confines of the celluloid closet, playing Young Bull in *Winchester 73* (1950) and the "name of the father" in *Taza, Son of Cochise*.

However, Aldrich used the genre and its contemporary conventions in his own distinctive way. *Apache* illustrates this concisely. Rather than falling into the trap of depicting his Indian hero as a one-dimensional wronged "noble savage," Aldrich depicts a character torn by both his own psychological torments and the contradictions he encounters in a now changing society. In many ways, the character of Massai is a descendant of not only those disturbed characters facing the challenges of the depression and postdepression era in the plays of Clifford Odets but also the complex figures of Charley Davis and Joe Morse. All these figures are not entirely positive characters with whom the audience may comfortably identify. Massai is certainly no typical Hollywood hero. He is as far removed from Jeff Chandler's Cochise and Rock Hudson's Taza as possible, making his ideological incorporation into the status quo both absurd and impossible.

Brought to the attention of the Hecht-Lancaster Co. because of his association with Charlie Chaplin on *Limelight* (1952), Aldrich had also worked as assistant to Harold Hecht on his production of the foreign legion adventure film *Ten Tall Men* (1951), starring Burt Lancaster. Aldrich's efficiency in directing *World for Ransom* (1954) on a low budget during a short shooting schedule also worked in his favor. However, despite the opportunity of advancing his career, Aldrich would find (as he did later) that not all stars were as supportive to directors and screenwriters as John Garfield had been at Enterprise.

Apache was based on a novel published in 1936. It deals with a real-life figure who refused to accept Geronimo's surrender in summer 1886. He escaped from a train taking him to a reservation in Florida at some point before it reached St. Louis, walked back to his New Mexico homeland across America, and lived an outlaw existence before his brutal capture and ignominious death at the hands of white pursuers.[4] The actual novel ends with Massai's escape. Conscious of the significance of location shooting he acquired from Jean Renoir when working on *The Southerner*, Aldrich chose Massai's actual home territory to shoot the film.

The credits open with a shot of a high mountain, a location representing Massai's revered homeland. It is an image that the film returns to on two other occasions. It appears when Massai takes a final look at his ancestral land before boarding the train taking defeated Apache warriors to a Florida reservation. When Massai finally returns home, it is the first thing he sees before noticing the

Apache chain gang that Weddle (John Dehner) has introduced into his homeland. This contrast between the nobility represented by Massai's holy mountain and the humiliation experienced by his people in a changing society represents the contradiction between an ideal and a grim reality characterizing most of Aldrich's cinema. Massai encounters several contradictions during the film, both psychologically and geographically, making his story a physical and psychological odyssey. A film fully employing Burt Lancaster's acrobatic physical perfection, *Apache* contrasts bodily warrior heroism and the soul's confrontation with different forms of social reality that it must come to terms with. The film employs elements from *Body and Soul* but takes them in a new direction.

As the credits close, the image of the mountain changes to a shot showing three shadows moving on the ground in a rightward direction. The camera moves and follows them before tilting up to reveal three men, Geronimo (Monte Blue) and two Apache warriors, one of whom carries a white flag. Two other shots follow, revealing divisions between opposing sides. The camera tracks left along a line of Apache warriors watching the action. Then the image changes to the other side, the camera moving right along a line of white soldiers, scout Al Sieber (John McIntire), Weddle, and Apache soldiers. These diverging camera movements illustrate two opposing sides ready to begin fighting once more. But the opening camera movement showing Geronimo and his men walking in a rightward direction reveals not only their surrender but also their reconciliation to a powerful new world they cannot oppose. However, this movement toward compromise becomes disrupted in two ways, first by Massai shooting the flag bearer and, second, by the high-angle overhead shot that disrupts the complementary movements of the formerly mobile camera. Such a strategy is not accidental. Although Massai believes that he is performing a heroic action as the last real Apache warrior, the overhead camera diminishes the effectiveness of his heroic role, seeing him as a mere dot on the New Mexico desert landscape. It reduces him into insignificance, making him little better than the Wall Street population in the opening shot of *Force of Evil*, who are little better than ants. The director already undermines Massai's heroic role. He may see himself as such, but Aldrich's use of landscape reveals the real picture to the audience as early as the fourth shot of the film. Geronimo's diplomatic movement involving surrender is more important than any futile individual heroism.

Despite Massai's action, the next shot shows Geronimo grasping the white flag from his fallen compatriot and clearly gesturing that he wishes the peace process to continue. Before Sieber shoots Massai's horse, he notices Weddle's desire for more bloodshed rather than reconciliation: "Mr. Weddle. Maybe, you'll get your name in the paper." This remark is more than satirical because it parallels Massai's desire for a heroic public death with the avaricious motivations of his white antagonist.[5]

Furthermore, as Silver and Ursini note, when we finally see Massai with Nalinle (Jean Peters), the sequence of shots again undermines his heroic status. Although we see Massai through her perspective in a high-angle shot while he looks down on Nalinle, who is filmed in a deceptively subordinate position, "the cheated angle, as if he were somehow above the ground looking down, could only be the point of view of a man whose adrenalin rush makes him feel as if he has been lifted off the ground."[6] Massai is totally egotistic. He acts alone and wishes to die alone. But solipsistic individualism is no answer for either the changing world that will follow the bloody Indian wars or a twentieth century producing a western such as *Apache.*

Despite her subordinate position in the cinematic frame and in a male-dominated culture, it is Nalinle who often articulates a more rational approach in contrast to Massai's male warrior hubris throughout the film. She also echoes the affirmative roles of Peg in *Body and Soul* and Doris in *Force of Evil*. Although shot in a low angle from Massai's perspective, Nalinle states the actual reality of the situation: "You saw the peace pipe in Geronimo's hands." She suggests compromise: "But at least you would be alive, Massai." However, the last Apache warrior refuses any alternative to a desired heroic death: "If an Apache cannot live in his home mountains like his fathers before him he is already dead." The image of the mountain in the opening credits dominates his entire perspective. But it infrequently appears throughout the film, suggesting that there are other ways of living and surviving that he should consider. Before Massai can die his warrior's death and provide a legendary example to other young Apaches who would fall in equally futile rebellions against a powerful system, Sieber captures him. Although his comments appear sarcastic, they echo the reality of the situation facing Massai: "To die in battle would be a sweet death, a warrior's death. . . . But you're not a warrior anymore. You're just a whipped

Indian. And nobody sings about handcuffs." These remarks come from a man who respects and understands his adversary. Although they appear callous, they also suggest that Massai accept the reality of a changed situation and cease living in the past. When Sieber sees Massai and other Apache warriors boarding the train to Florida, he comments sincerely, "I'll miss him." Like Massai, Sieber loves his profession. But at the climax of the film he mentions that he will also face an uncertain future like his adversary: "It's the only war we had and we ain't likely to find another."

During the next scene Aldrich shows that black soldiers have the job of guarding the Indians on their way to Florida. This subtly reveals not only the allegorical aspects of *Apache* as a 1950s western in terms of the *Brown v. Board of Education* decision but also a sympathy that one minority group has for another. Although the task is not pleasant, this group appears in a more positive light than those Apaches who have sold out to the establishment such as Hondo (Charles Buchinsky). They not only speak kindly to their charges but also give reasons why the blinds of the train are drawn during the journey—in contrast to the white captors. After the train leaves St. Louis, Weddle agrees to pose for a publicity photo with Geronimo, obviously seeing himself as "the man who captured Geronimo," evoking Henry Fonda's arrogant Colonel Owen Thursday in John Ford's *Fort Apache* (1948). However, this gives Massai an opportunity to escape. One black soldier poses behind Weddle and grins at the camera, not only in a "Hi Mom" posture but satirically undermining the solemnity of the pose. These are, admittedly, brief moments in the film. But they serve to extend *Apache* well beyond its generic framework in terms of contemporary social relevance. We must remember that the 1950s was a bleak decade for civil rights, one seeing the cancellation of *The Nat King Cole Show* on American broadcast television because of its inability to find a permanent sponsor.

Massai manages to escape and hide in the back of a wagon until the sounds of a fire engine in St. Louis awake him. Jumping from the wagon, he discovers an alien environment far beyond his comprehension. As the camera follows Massai during his urban odyssey, it reveals to him the absurdities and the negative side of the developing world of white civilization. Arnold and Miller note that this moment represents "*Apache*'s most cleverly-edited and humorous sequence of shots," during which Aldrich and cameraman Ernest

Lazlo convey the nightmarish, alien, unintelligible quality of big-city life as seen through the eyes of the outsider.[7] But it is much more than this. The camera follows Massai's progress in a right-to-left direction, paralleling that earlier camera movement during Geronimo's surrender. Massai sees the absurd and wasteful aspects of white society such as a mechanical piano and large-size bustles as well as an overweight man gorging himself with food inside a restaurant. He notices a shoeshine boy performing a task that people could do for themselves. Massai also confronts the negative sides of white capitalist civilization. Affluence and poverty coexist in St. Louis. Massai confronts a white beggar on the streets. He also passes an impoverished black man near the restaurant. The only positive contact he has is with another outsider from a minority group. A Chinese laundry owner notices him staring outside and changes from Cantonese to English, bowing slightly and wishing him, "Good evening." However, Massai soon experiences the racism of white society when a group of youths taunts him with stereotyped expressions such as "Rain in the Face" and inquire what he is doing outside the reservation. This action significantly occurs when Massai reaches a bank, symbolizing the white economic power that has resulted in the removal of Indians from their homelands into reservations according to the philosophy of Manifest Destiny.

But not all Indians suffer this fate. When Massai reaches Oklahoma he encounters a Cherokee (Morris Ankrum) who has recognized the changing face of history and compromised with the different world around him in a positive manner. Now taking a white surname, Dawson represents a balance between Massai's destructive false idealism and Hondo's opportunistic behavior. Dawson tells Massai that the "warrior's day is over" and that compromise need not necessarily involve total capitulation. Now relocated to Oklahoma from the Carolinas (and perhaps becoming a future beneficiary of the early-twentieth-century oil boom), Dawson informs Massai of the benefits of agriculture that will make Indians self-sufficient: "We can live with the white man only if we live like him." Massai also exhibits astonishment when Dawson's wife requests that he undertake a domestic task that, ironically, foreshadows his change of heart when he later ploughs for Nalinle. Although initially refusing to accept Dawson's gift of seed corn, Massai changes his mind. He returns and takes it. At this point of the film he is willing to recognize alternatives. He now decides to become the savior of his people in a different way from the path formerly envisaged.

When Massai finally reaches his home territory, he is appalled at the state of his tribesmen affected by the alcoholic leadership of Nalinle's father Santos (Paul Guilfoyle). Like Hondo, he has made his own pact with the devil and become totally compromised. Massai sees Hondo attempting to court Nalinle. But her facial expressions and comments reveal that she has nothing but contempt for a man who has sold out and gone over to the other side, similar to those who "named names" during the 1950s. Hondo speaks about his forthcoming promotion to corporal and its material benefits. Nalinle sarcastically answers the uncomprehending renegade: "I know you have worked very hard, Hondo. You keep your buttons well shined." Before he departs, he gives her the whisky he uses to bribe Santos into agreeing to sell him his daughter. Even the debilitated Santos recognizes the virtues of his future son-in-law as a result of Apache decimation: "Even a hawk is an eagle among crows."

However, Massai has now returned not for individualistic destructive heroic ideals but for the benefit of his entire community, something he never considered during his earlier attempt at a "Last Stand." Massai is even willing to forsake his desire to kill Weddle: "It is hard to be a man of peace. It would be a pleasure to kill Mr. Weddle." But despite Massai's desires to make a "warrior's peace, a peace between equals" based on seed corn representing "a new life for our tribe," he is betrayed by Santos and recaptured by Sieber. Massai's idealism is destroyed. He now becomes an avenging agent, changing from benign savior to a ruthless deity exercising his own type of apocalyptic judgment.

Massai's personal tragedy lies not only in his refusal to see the complex set of circumstances resulting in his recapture but also in his relapse into a self-destructive heroic ideal witnessed in his very first appearance in the film. He blames both Santos and Nalinle for his betrayal. But as Aldrich reveals to the audience, this is not the entire picture. After Massai is led away from Santos's tent, the next shot shows Santos walking toward the camera from a distance. As the camera angle changes, we see that he has bound and gagged Nalinle. After he releases her, the camera moves toward the right to view Massai being led away into the distance. This shot is not accidental, as Silver and Ursini note: "The net effect is to carry the viewer in one movement from a strong empathy with Massai and a subjective participation in his sense of betrayal to an objective perspective, aware of facts which Massai does not have and an apprehensive identification with Nalinle."[8] It moves the audience away from traditional identification with the hero to consider the wider set of social circumstances that he is not aware of. As a result, Massai's violent hubris becomes all the more tragic. The shot begins with Santos in the background and ends with Massai in a similar position within the frame. But it also emphasizes the significance of Nalinle, who has attempted to mediate between father and lover. Both Santos and Hondo refuse to recognize the pragmatic side of her idealism. Santos describes her as a young girl who "thinks with her heart, not with a head." Hondo later patronizes her, remarking, "A young girl believes what she wants to believe. Maybe, it's just as well." Nalinle represents the moral center of this film, resembling not only Peg and Doris from *Body and Soul* and *Force of Evil* but also Christina Bailey in *Kiss Me Deadly.*

However, like Odets and Polonsky, Aldrich also depicts the various obstacles preventing the realization of ideals in a hostile world. As Silver and Ursini note, when Nalinle visits the office of Lt. Col. Beck (Walter Sands), bringing the seed corn Massai brought from Oklahoma, twenty individual shots reveal the awkward interaction between two cultures as Nalinle attempts in vain to persuade Beck, Sieber, and Weddle that Massai's return to his people involved agricultural self-sufficiency rather than destructive violence. The camera does not move during this rapid succession of shots, expressing the different forms of tension existing within all three characters.[9] Beck expresses politeness. Sieber cannot believe that a warrior can change into a farmer. Weddle is still hostile toward Massai.

Massai eventually escapes from Weddle's custody and later kills him in the fort. His bullet symbolically penetrates his adversary's body to fragment Geronimo's peace pipe hanging on the wall of Beck's office. Massai now becomes little better than a raging bull avenging his fury on a white society that has betrayed him. Having murdered Weddle and (presumably) butchered soldiers offscreen during a daytime raid, he will never escape the consequences of his violent path. He kidnaps Nalinle because of his outraged sense of betrayal and with the knowledge that he will cut off Santos's economic supply of alcohol by her suitor Hondo. He intends to torture Santos in the same way as he does Nalinle, tying her up a few feet away from a river so that she cannot quench her thirst. Massai then follows his original goal in becoming the last real Apache warrior. By doing so, he turns away from a positive communal solution to his people's dilemma toward following a path of selfish individualistic heroism. Viewers may understand Massai's motivations. But a wider set of circumstances undercuts his actions. Silver and Ursini significantly comment that "while the viewer can share a momentary perspective with Massai, *Apache* presents no possibility for total identification either with the individual character or the embodiment of an epic hero."[10]

However, the possibility for Massai's moral regeneration does exist in *Apache.* Aldrich presents this through the figure of Jean Peters's Nalinle.[11] During her capture, Nalinle sees through the warrior facade adopted by Massai and critiques it. In her speech to Massai before he is about to shoot her, the camera emphasizes her authority as she lies in the foreground of the frame. Censuring his movement away from "thinking of your people," she condemns his selfish individualism. She reminds him of her support from the very beginning when she reluctantly gave him an ammunition belt before his earlier abortive Last Stand: "I did not betray you Massai, the day Geronimo surrendered." As she tells him, "You fight only for yourself. You kill only for yourself. You're like a dying wolf biting at his wounds." She challenges him to shoot her if it would help make him "brave and strong." When she later warns Massai about Sieber's presence in their temporary hideaway, Aldrich begins the first of a significant exchange of looks between both characters that he frequently employs throughout the film. But they privilege Nalinle more than Massai. Despite her declaration of love, Massai brutally hits her with a stick and removes her shoes so that she cannot follow him. Although Massai later explains this action as being caused by his inability to kill her as planned, the very essence of this violent gesture undercuts any doubts concerning the dubious nature of Massai's male heroism. He grudgingly decides to accept her even though he sees no future for himself, seeing his death "someday." Nalinle, however, affirms the validity of whatever short existence they will share together: "Then we will live until 'someday.'" She slowly attempts to make Massai realize the other possibilities of human existence available to him after she announces her pregnancy. Massai still thinks of himself according to a warrior mentality now becoming anachronistic: "I am the last real Apache left in the world—except for the little one." However, Nalinle voices an alternative: "A life with Massai. A life like the Cherokees. I will not stop now." She eventually returns him to Dawson's solution of finding another set of values in a changed society. Nalinle also persuades him to perform a similar type of domestic function that Massai had initially reacted against when he saw the Cherokee agree to his wife's request. He takes the place of an ox at the plough when they plant seed that Nalinle has stolen from a nearby store. She has also stolen white man's clothes similar to those Dawson wore, which Massai now wears in his new role of prospective father and farmer.

The theft of these items immediately alerts Sieber, who has been pursuing Massai with a jilted Hondo, now having achieved his dream of becoming a corporal. Hondo is not only a "hawk among crows" but a character who has sold out to the establishment. Though he has not "named names," he and his fellow renegades use native expertise to trap their fellow men. Hondo not only represents the dark aspect of that institutional Indian policeman embodied by Rock Hudson in *Taza, Son of Cochise*. He is also an informer who will never be fully accepted by the side he has joined. During the scene at the provision store, when the owner informs Sieber of the theft, Aldrich cuts away to show Hondo's impassive face at the line, "Them savages didn't get no scalps." It is a revealing cut for more than one reason. Despite Charles Bronson's usual granite expression, his eyes reveal that the message reaches Hondo. Although now a part of the system, this does not protect him from racism on the part of white society. In other words, "once a Commie, always a Commie." Had Aldrich's ending been accepted by the producers, it would have been an ingenious mark of political irony to have Hondo kill Massai.[12]

Because Nalinle is now in an advanced stage of pregnancy, she cannot move to escape the forces pursuing them. Massai then decides to fulfill his warrior destiny. However, rather than affirming Massai's decision, Nalinle criticizes him.[13] She obviously sees her husband relapsing again into the emotionally regressive aspects of his character that earlier made any form of compromise impossible. The facial expressions used by Jean Peters in her speech suggest condemnation rather than affirmation. When Massai tells her that "someday has come," he speaks in terms of the "call of kind" rather than showing any concern for her well-being and that of their future son: "But the blood I feel here. It is still warrior's blood. It has to fight." Her reply is significant: "Then die the warrior's death you've

always wanted. Don't let Sieber cheat you out of it again." When
Massai sees his death as an inspiration to their newborn son, "Will
you sing of it to the little Massai?" she replies accusingly, "Would
you have me sing to him of the plough?" We must remember that
Nalinle refused Massai's suggestion of returning to the reservation,
fearing that her son would grow up to become a drunken Indian like
her own father: "Do you want him to grow up into another Santos?"
She clearly condemns his destructive heroism.

As with Massai's earlier movement through St. Louis, the camera
follows him on his Last Stand as he kills more soldiers before Sieber
wounds him. Massai escapes into the cornfield where he is surrounded. He is about to kill Sieber when he hears the cries of his newborn son. The final shots show him going toward his dwelling. Sieber
admires Massai's achievement: "He planted corn and made it grow.
I wish the bucks on the reservation could see this." The scout also
comments that "it's the only war we had and we ain't likely to find
another." *Apache* ends with a helicopter shot dwarfing Massai into insignificance in the same manner as his first appearance in the film.

This shot represents Aldrich's compromise ending after Burt Lancaster and the producers prevailed on him to shoot another "happy
ending" rather than the one in which Hondo shoots Massai in the
back. However, it is ambiguous in nature and represents the technique used by classical Hollywood directors such as Anthony Mann
and others to undercut the veracity of this banal technique. Although audiences may have desired to see the star live, questions
obviously emerge. Even if Massai lives, he would still face trial and
execution for the murder of Weddle and other victims. Massai cannot survive in any case. He has already compromised himself by re-
verting to his old selfish individualism and fallen away from that
positive balance between body and soul that his domestic life with
Nalinle represented. Aldrich also commented that his envisaged
ending would have been more important in terms of the film's structure: "You make a picture about one thing, the inevitability of Massai's death. His courage is measured against the inevitable. The
whole preceding two hours becomes redundant if at the end he can
just walk away."[14] For a pragmatist such as Robert Aldrich, no definitive happy ending is possible. The present climax represents a
compromise solution. But it is one that may be read both "against
the grain" of the desires of Lancaster and the producers and as suggesting some different directions. For Aldrich, it is enough to show

that some alternative potential exists; no matter how temporary and utopian, Massai *did* change for a short time.

Apache also goes "against the grain" by refusing to idealize its main character in the manner of most liberal contemporary westerns. Massai is a deeply flawed and contradictory character. His self-styled significance either as the last Apache warrior seeking his Last Stand or the presumed savior of his people becomes contradicted by his personal inadequacies as well as the prevailing historical forces dwarfing him into insignificance. *Apache* is one of many Aldrich films that critique the illusionary idea of individual heroism as well as the dangerous messianic imagery that surrounds it. As Richard Combs astutely recognizes, Massai is "a thoroughly negative register of cultural change who belongs to no cause or tradition other than his own unyielding, even solipsistic individualism."[15] He anticipates the flawed messiah embodied by Mike Hammer in *Kiss Me Deadly* (1955) and Lawrence Dell in *Twilight's Last Gleaming* (1977), characters who both rise from the dead like Lazarus and threaten a terrible judgment on their various societies if they do not comply with their egotistic demands. As Nalinle notes, Massai came back to his people "weary from a journey that no warrior had made before." At that point, he had benevolent intentions for his people. But, unlike the savior, he is betrayed after, rather than before, his resurrection. As a result, as Combs notes, even though he benefits from his relationship with Nalinle, Massai remains "the self-convinced outsider, the romantic paranoiac who declares, 'Every white man, every Indian is my enemy. I cannot kill them all and some day they will kill me.'"[16] He becomes both a destructive and a self-destructive renegade savior figure embodying that dangerous and contradictory aspect of American mythology that has damned national consciousness from its very foundation. By encountering rejection, the individual savior figure becomes a living example of a Day of Judgment that would destroy not only him but the entire world that opposes him. Cultural historians Richard Slotkin and Loren Baritz have drawn attention to a dangerous schizophrenia existing within the American cultural tradition.[17] Whether symbolized by the hunter archetype, who the community feared could change from savior to destroyer at any moment, or the messianic "City on the Hill" philosophy, seeking to conquer what it could not understand, Aldrich's Massai represents another paranoid embodiment of American individuality.

Vera Cruz followed as another Hecht–Lancaster production. Although Aldrich had many opportunities for the preproduction rehearsal strategy he would follow for the rest of his career, the screenplay was changed frequently before shooting actually began. As most critics have noted, this gave the film a spontaneous quality that made *Vera Cruz* a box-office success.[18] However, despite being able to work on his most highly budgeted film to date, Aldrich found the situation much less to his liking than the controversy over the ending of *Apache*. *Vera Cruz* brought together two major stars of the American cinema: the legendary Gary Cooper and the new presence of Burt Lancaster, an actor then having producer and director ambitions. The presence of these two figures seriously hindered the film's potential. Conscious of his star status, Cooper would not permit any ambivalent or negative overtones in his character and made sure that the screenplay reflected his concerns.[19] When his character attempts to persuade Juarista Nina (Sarita Montiel) to take the money and run ("No cause is worth three million dollars"), his delivery of these lines is unconvincing. One could not expect Gary Cooper of all people to have these thoughts! It would not be until Anthony Mann's great western *Man of the West* that a darker version of the Cooper persona would finally emerge. But, as will be shown, *Vera Cruz* represents one step in this direction.

Lancaster's assertiveness on the set led to a temporary breach between him and Aldrich. Although his Joe Erin character counterpoints the more sober and older persona of Gary Cooper's Ben Trane, at several points in the film his flashing smile and acrobatic gestures appear to signify the actor's ambitions to outact Douglas Fairbanks Sr. Lancaster seems fascinated by attempting to merge the silent actor's style of acting with a western version of Stanley Kowalski. Lancaster's table manners at the palace of Emperor Maximilian make up just one such instance!

Superficially, *Vera Cruz* belongs to the contemporary western subgenre of "American adventurers" in Mexico depicted in films starring Rory Calhoun and Gilbert Roland such as *The Treasure of Pancho Villa* (1955). But as well as revealing Aldrich's fascination with the theme of dysfunctional family conflict, as seen in the Oedipal rivalry between Joe Erin and Ace Hannah, *Vera Cruz* also develops friendship and betrayal motifs seen earlier in *World for Ransom*.[20]

As Francois Truffaut and Michael Wood notice, *Vera Cruz* operates very much in terms of a "double cross" structure. It also engages in an ironic treatment of the western heroic persona, which makes it a fascinating exercise on the formal level.[21] Many situations and lines of dialogue duplicate each other throughout the course of the film. They anticipate the duality that would become a major feature of Aldrich's work, especially in *Kiss Me Deadly* and *Hustle*. Two leading characters represent opposing sides of the same persona. *Vera Cruz's* Trane–Erin conflict represents an inverse depiction of the one seen in *World for Ransom*. Although Dan Duryea's Mike Callahan is roughly the same age as Patric Knowles's Julian March, the latter is much more mature and experienced in the world he inhabits, making their relationship perversely parallel to one between father and son. March is also corrupt and thinks nothing of betraying his friend. *Vera Cruz's* Joe Erin has no friends until he meets Ben Trane, whom he cynically regards as the first friend he has ever had as well as a substitute for his former surrogate father Ace Hannah.

Ace had killed Erin's actual father but had made the one mistake of adopting him, a mistake that would rebound on him. Likewise, Joe makes the mistake of adopting Trane as a substitute Ace Hannah father figure and making him the only friend he has ever had. It is an action very much out of character and one that will rebound on him in the same way that Ace's adoption of Joe did in the past. The checkered relationship between Joe Erin and Ben Trane in *Vera Cruz* has dark, psychological, repetition-compulsion associations. After Ben saves Joe's life (an action mirroring Ace's rescue of the orphaned Joe), he tells him about his past: "Ace used to say, 'Don't take any chances you don't hafta take, don't trust anybody you don't hafta trust, and don't do no favors you don't hafta do.' Ace lived long enough to know he was right—he lived thirty seconds after I shot him." When Trane asks, "Why are you telling me all this?" Erin replies, "Why not? You're the first friend I ever had!" Had Joe gotten his way, Ben would have been his last friend. Despite Lancaster's flamboyant performance, Joe Erin is really a character traumatized by the past, a perennial outlaw, an Oedipal rebel who has fulfilled the worst scenario of the Freudian nightmare by killing the father. However, Erin's other goal is monetary acquisition. His dalliance with the sophisticated Countess Marie Duval (Denise Darcel) is simply a ploy. He ruthlessly betrays and abandons her at the end and compares her with Ben Trane. Was Joe Erin also betrayed by his mother? Does he now decide to take revenge on a surrogate figure? We do not know because the "American adventurers in Mexico" theme dominates the film. But the film does faintly echo darker elements that occur in other Aldrich films.

Betrayal is the key motif in *Vera Cruz*, whether involving friends, family, associates, or political allegiance. Emperor Maximilian (played by George Macready in a manner far removed from the saintly figure played by Brian Aherne in William Dieterle's 1939 Warner Bros. biopic *Juarez*) plans to betray the Americans who have joined his cause. Marie plans to betray everyone by sailing to France with money meant to purchase troops to save Maximilian's Mexican Empire. Joe plans to betray everyone in sight, whereas Ben harbors dreams of restoring the ruined Southern mansion where he fought his last battle during the American Civil War. As *Vera Cruz*'s opening captions denote, after one fratricidal struggle is over, the orphaned sons head south to aid whatever side makes their services profitable in the Mexican revolutionary war. The Marquis Henri (Cesar Romero) eventually betrays Marie, who plans to betray him all along. As she tells Ben and Joe in lines hinting at sexual (as well as political) betrayal, "The emperor is very fond of the marquis. So I made the marquis become fond of me." She later comments that Henri is loyal to the emperor, "but I dare say he would be willing to die for Maximilian." Her lines echo the polite conversation between Henri and Maximilian when he returns from his "successful but distasteful" trip. As both men exhibit polite high-society manners, they consider "death a handsome reward" for their American allies. Ben, Marie, and Joe form an unholy alliance in which betrayal can happen at any moment. Ben asks Marie, "How do we know we can trust you?" She replies, "How do *I* know I can trust *you*?" Joe responds, "Countess, you're beginning to talk my language." Although far removed from the 1950s by its historical setting, *Vera Cruz* foreshadows that later blacklisting era, which saw many examples of personal and political betrayals.

When Erin and Trane first meet, Erin wears an all-black outfit, one that he resumes wearing at the climax of the film. During other parts of the film he wears a white shirt with a black vest. This may signify uncertainty over what path he may actually take. Ben Trane wears Confederate gray, a color not only signifying his former status but hinting at an ambivalent nature. It is not until the end of the film that we actually know which way each character will turn. Erin is a likeable villain who could go either way, whereas Gary Cooper is normally as reliable as James Stewart.[22] However, like Joe Erin, Ben

Trane could possibly turn either way. He could decide to betray both partner and the revolution. As depicted in the screenplay, this is quite possible. But Gary Cooper's persona makes this unlikely. This would not be the first time that Aldrich would have problems with a star's previous associations that would adversely affect the production.

Yet, despite these problems, a betrayal motif stemming from some past dysfunctional family event dominates *Vera Cruz.* Although it will not be until *The Last Sunset* that Aldrich explicitly employs the contemporary psychological western elements common to Anthony Mann and other directors, *Vera Cruz* comes close to hinting at some unresolved family issue affecting Ben and Joe similar to that affecting Brendan O'Malley and Missy in *The Last Sunset.* Toward the climax of *Vera Cruz,* Ben's "soft spot" (which Joe cynically comments on throughout the film) becomes evident in his admiration for the Juarista struggle against the French and his acceptance of General Ramirez (Morris Ankrum), who believes that a man "needs something more [than monetary gain], something to believe in." As in *Apache,* Ankrum again plays another character who attempts to influence a leading character. When Joe murders the heroic black former soldier Ballard (Archie Savage) to gain possession of the gold, the final confrontation between Joe and Ben begins. Ben replies to Joe's remark about his "soft spot" with, "Even Ace had one." Joe responds, "That was his mistake." Both men fire at each other. The resolution is in doubt until Joe collapses. This time it is Ben who walks toward Joe's body rather than the situation in the earlier part of the film. As Joe dies, Ben picks up his gun and throws it away. As well as anticipating Cooper's similar gesture to the body of his "cousin" played by John Dehner in *Man of the West,* the expression on Trane's face is one recognizing loss and waste. He regrets the fact that things could have been different, or as Jane Hudson will later say, "You mean, we could have been friends?" As in most Aldrich films, this utopian solution is impossible, especially in a world characterized by betrayal and treachery as in *Vera Cruz.*

In 1957 Aldrich acted as executive producer in the Associates and Aldrich Co. production of *The Ride Back.* Although he never directed this film credited to Allen H. Miner (but codirected by Oscar Rudolph), it is worth mentioning here as illustrating the type of offbeat western that attracted Aldrich. Although Aldrich was not occupying the director's chair, many of his stock company such as cinematographer Joseph Biroc, art director William Glasgow, and composer Frank DeVol were involved in this production. Eddie Albert sang the title song over the credits and other sequences at a time when he was trying to break away from his "song-and-dance man" image. Perhaps he may have meant it as a favor to a director helping him find a new career as a serious actor? The film also stars William Conrad, another Enterprise alumnus Aldrich knew from his involvement in *Body and Soul* and *Arch of Triumph.* Although Conrad never became a major star, he appeared in the radio version of *Gunsmoke* as Matt Dillon. For a man often condemned to character roles, this was probably his first attempt at stardom. But the film's box-office failure prevented Conrad from becoming a major star.

The Ride Back involves the familiar plot device of sheriff and outlaw. But the Associates and Aldrich production attempts to give it a new twist by emphasizing character complexity. Like most western villains such as those in Anthony Mann's films, Anthony Quinn's Mexican American Kallen is far more likable than the hero. The narrative implicitly suggests that the crime he is accused of originates more from Anglo-Saxon racism than anything else. Marshall Hamish (William Conrad) is a failure as husband, lawman, and father. He envies Kallen's sexual appeal to Elena (Lita Milan), which contrasts with his own wife's hatred toward him. After losing their first child, Hamish's wife has nothing but contempt for a man who has never been successful at anything. Hamish sees Kallen as his last chance. He is able to arrest Kallen with the aid of the local priest (Victor Millan). But the priest's offer has nothing to do with following the objective paths of law and order and everything to do with avenging his lack of authority in the village. He tells Hamish that Kallen "has weakened me in the eyes of my people" by openly sleeping with his relative Elena, whom he has not married. He may tell Hamish, "We both represent the law," but his real motivations are different. Anthony Ellis's screenplay suggests that the law's institutional authority really represents a haven for weak and unfulfilled men to exercise a power they are not morally or personally equipped to perform outside. After rescuing a young girl from a farmhouse attacked by Indians, the two men continue their journey. The girl responds more to Kallen than to Hamish. Following another attack resulting in Hamish's wounding, Kallen announces his decision to return to Mexico. However, he changes his mind and decides to accompany Hamish on the ride back to "the fair trial" promised to him.

Originally printed in a sepia tint, *The Ride Back* has several interesting characterizations and contains a critique of authority common to Aldrich. However, because of problems surrounding its production, it is a flawed film. But it again reveals the interest Aldrich often showed in changing generic formulas to reflect his own personal interests. Life is complex. There are no real heroes or villains. Although Aldrich never directed the film, he was often on the set in the capacity of executive producer. His involvement may have paralleled Howard Hawks's role as producer on *The Thing from Another World* (1951) but in a less dominant manner. *The Ride Back* is an interesting footnote to the rest of his work.

Despite Aldrich's reference to *The Last Sunset* as a "very unpleasant experience" because of script problems and coping with a very temperamental star, the film is not entirely a failure.[23] It certainly could have been improved by better performances and further screenplay revisions. However, *The Last Sunset* has several associations with the cinematic world of Robert Aldrich. As in *Vera Cruz*, the dysfunctional family theme common to *What Ever Happened to Baby Jane?* and *Hush . . . Hush, Sweet Charlotte* exists but in a more deliberate manner thanks to Dalton Trumbo's screenplay.[24] Richard Combs regards *The Last Sunset* as Aldrich's "most poeticised treatment of a sexual pathology" in a work exhibiting "a strain of visual lyricism unrivaled by any of his subsequent colour productions, allied to a highly stylised approach to the genre that capitalises on the moves tentatively made by *Vera Cruz*."[25] However, the film contains other significant elements. It not only reveals dark elements existing within the type of heroic romanticism earlier personified by Mike Callahan in *World for Ransom* but also represents a generic reworking of motifs present in the plays of Tennessee Williams, which Arthur Miller regarded as not entirely irrelevant to contemporary society. Like Mike Callahan, Kirk Douglas's Brendan O'Malley is Irish. He is a disruptive version of the "gentleman caller" character Douglas portrays in the film version of *The Glass Menagerie* (1950). Like Blanche Dubois in *A Streetcar Named Desire*, O'Malley nostalgically remembers a world that existed only in his imagination. But as a male outlaw, he violently reacts in a pathological manner against anyone and anything daring to oppose cherished past fantasies he wishes to re-create in the present. Wearing a black outfit like Joe Erin in *Vera Cruz*, O'Malley is psychologically doomed to follow behavioral patterns that will lead to his destruction. Like Mike Callahan, he remembers a woman in the past who does not exist in the present. But whereas Mike suffers emotional destruction when his ideal love reveals her true nature, O'Malley ironically experiences a second chance that leads to psychic and physical destruction. Although *The Last Sunset* resembles *Vera Cruz* in not being the film that Aldrich could have made under the appropriate circumstances, it is more radical than its predecessor. *The Last Sunset* is an appropriate companion piece to melodramatic expressions of sexual pathology appearing in *What Ever Happened to Baby Jane? Hush . . . Hush, Sweet Charlotte, The Legend of Lylah Clare,* and *The Killing of Sister George.*

Like *Vera Cruz, The Last Sunset* opens with a shot of a lone rider against a distant landscape. In both instances, it features both the major star and a complementary character who will be the catalyst in the drama. After showing O'Malley ride into a Mexican town and enjoy the opening moves in a cockfight, the sequence changes to show Dana Stribling (Rock Hudson) riding into the scene in a similar manner. But unlike O'Malley, he is as remote and distant as Gary Cooper's Ben Trane. He takes no pleasure in village activities and tries in vain to gain information about the man he is pursuing. These two sequences express both similarities and differences between the two men. Both are introduced in a similar manner, but the difference lies in their behavior. O'Malley is more flamboyant, whereas Stribling is more remote. Like Erin and Trane in *Vera Cruz,* both are psychological blood brothers in many ways. O'Malley and Stribling are also obsessive characters like Alan and Tullio in *The Garment Jungle.* Whereas O'Malley wishes to re-create obsessively the past and reunite himself with the "pretty girl in a yellow dress" who is now a mature woman, Stribling wishes to bring the murderer of his brother-in-law to justice, even though he may realize that the actual facts are more complicated than he cares to admit. Like O'Malley, who consciously ignores the changes that time has brought to Belle (Dorothy Malone), Stribling suppresses the actual facts leading to his sister's suicide. When O'Malley's sarcastic remarks—"That sister of yours was just a free drink on the house and nobody went thirsty. I mean nobody"—provoke Stribling into a fight, nothing contradicts O'Malley's statement.

Stribling also idealizes his own version of the past. Similarly, O'Malley has made a career of buying drinks by inventing poetic lines embodying his past romantic loss. Both O'Malley and Stribling's deceased sister are traumatized victims of a love relationship that has gone wrong. O'Malley hopelessly idealizes the past, resembling Uncle Jacob in Odets's *Awake and Sing!* It is not accidental that both characters commit suicide and leave a dubious legacy for the younger generation. O'Malley and Stribling also play a Galahad role like Mike Callahan. But these roles conflict with the more complex circumstances of human existence, which undermine their idealistic beliefs.[26] Whereas Stribling represses his violent feelings beneath the repressive institutional control of a Texas sheriff, O'Malley releases his tensions at any time by violence. O'Malley cannot control his actions. His past violent behavior turned Belle away from him. The sequence showing his attempt to choke the Breckinridge dog reveals his psychotic nature.[27] This action occurs after he tells Missy (Carol Lynley), "When you come right down to it, all men in their hearts are killers." This also applies to Stribling. Like Hamish in *The Ride Back*, he is using the law's institutional authority for his own ends.

Belle has married psychologically scarred war veteran John Breckenridge (Joseph Cotten). He indulges in alcohol to bury his guilt over cowardice in the Civil War in a way similar to O'Malley's use of alcohol to forget his past trauma. Belle obviously wished to give Missy a father. But she chose Breckenridge because of his different personality to O'Malley. After Breckinridge's death, she defines him as a "gentle" person who would run away from conflict rather than engage in violent behavior. Belle thus preferred an older man rather than a former dashing lover who carries his own "storm clouds" wherever he goes.

O'Malley attempts to woo Belle in vain. Although he first greets her by whistling Dmitri Timomkin's song "Pretty Little Girl in the Yellow Dress" (which he will later sing to Missy when she appears in her mother's very same dress), stating, "All those years I've remembered you as you were—a pretty girl in a yellow dress," she criticizes his obsessional romantic fascination with the past. Unlike in *Casablanca* (1943) when the two separated lovers will always "have Paris," Belle wants no part of a past in which she remembers her former lover as a "jealous boy" who ripped a primrose corsage from her dress in anger. Like Frennessey in *World for Ransom*, she criticizes O'Malley's fascination with a persona that no longer exists: "You loved a 16-year-old girl in another country and another world. Don't you see I'm not that girl? That girl died a long time ago." When the poetically inclined O'Malley tells her, "I stopped time from touching you. I trapped you in my heart," Belle condemns him for not seeing her as the woman she actually is: "You don't see it because you don't want to."

Perversely, O'Malley gets a second chance when he loses Belle to Stribling. Missy appears like his dream girl in a yellow dress during the fiesta celebrating the next day's crossing of the Rio Grande. But his dream has dark consequences when Belle tells him that Missy is his actual daughter. During his final hours before that last sunset when Stribling intends to arrest him on Texas soil for the murder of his brother-in-law, O'Malley acts the role of both gentle lover and caring father in preparing Missy for her eventual loss. O'Malley walks to his death like a classical hero of Greek tragedy. He has removed bullets from his derringer so that his violent tendencies will not hinder his chosen course. But he leaves one final legacy—a primrose corsage for Missy to replace the one he tore from her mother's dress years ago. It is a romantic gesture. But as the camera zooms out in an overhead shot showing the four main protagonists in this dark Oedipal drama dwarfed into insignificance, the impression remains that the darkness will be with everyone long after the last sunset has elapsed.

Ulzana's Raid is Aldrich's last western. It illustrates his pragmatic and philosophically bleak picture of a universe that tolerates no illusions and no mistakes. As world-weary scout McIntosh (Burt Lancaster) remarks to the inexperienced Lt. DeBuin (Bruce Davison), "Remember the rules. The first to make a mistake gets to burying some people." But although Macintosh suggests that some type of rules exists in the deadly game of tracking Ulzana and his renegade band, who have escaped from the reservation, in reality no firm set of standards exists—at least in Aldrich's western landscape. *Ulzana's Raid* is a film that not only further explores Aldrich's perennial theme of survival in a hostile universe but also mercilessly undermines the false nature of idealism.

Ulzana's Raid can be read on many levels. First, as an Aldrich text, it reverses the premises of *Apache* by moving the central perspective from the Indian to the scout. Both roles are played by the same star, but the latter has now reached the age of his antagonist in the earlier film. Although billed as leading actor, Lancaster had passed his peak of stardom and moved toward his sunset years as a character actor. As Aldrich pointed out, "Burt was playing an 1870 guy who had seen *Apache*. That was his frame of reference: he respected the Indians, because he knew more about them than the soldiers did."[28] In this respect, *Ulzana's Raid* may be related to films that directors remake during their careers after dissatisfaction with the first version. Hitchcock's *The Man Who Knew Too Much* is one such example. *Ulzana's Raid* may also be read as an allegorical depiction of the Vietnam War via the western genre. This was certainly in the minds of those working on the film.[29] With the exception of *The Green Berets* (1968), no explicit representation of the Vietnam War appeared in Hollywood until well after the conflict. This did not prevent indirect depictions from appearing in several genres such as science fiction, biker movies, gangster films, and many others.[30] Both these readings are correct and complement each other. The film represents variants of themes Aldrich dealt with throughout his career, namely, pragmatism and survival. *Ulzana's Raid* is a brilliant summing up of these elements but characteristically provides no easy answers.

The film begins with a bleak night shot of Ulzana and his braves leaving the reservation to begin the raid.[31] It complements the equally barren nature of the following shot showing the barren landscape by day and the mundane nature of Fort Lowell. A baseball game is in progress. But tension already occurs, as seen by the men's frustration at Lt. DeBuin's incompetence as umpire. As well as evoking the frustration of his sergeant (Richard Jaeckel) by inaccurately calling, "Strike!" he allows his attention to be distracted by the distant presence of a rider announcing Ulzana's raid. The scene appears to be set for another replay of *Attack!*'s scenario as well as those numerous Vietnam War narratives dealing with the fragging of incompetent officers. But *Ulzana's Raid* is much more complex.

The following scenes introduce McIntosh (Burt Lancaster), who is justifiably contemptuous of a Washington-connected Captain Gates (Lloyd Bochner), who will escape commanding a cavalry detachment in pursuit of Ulzana by passing the buck to an inexperienced DeBuin. The British version of the film reveals that Gates uses his political connections to blackmail his superior officer into giving the assignment to the junior officer. As the film progresses, DeBuin undergoes several conversions from unpragmatic idealist, to irrational Indian hunter, and finally to a more experienced commanding officer. The respective ages of actors Lancaster and Davison present father–son imagery on more than one level. As well as contrasting experience with innocence, *Ulzana's Raid* engages in the same ironic appropriation of Christian values as *The Dirty Dozen*'s "Last Supper" scene. As a walking embodiment of the hymn "Onward Christian

Soldiers," DeBuin believes that it is possible to combine the cross and the sword according to familiar values of Manifest Destiny. When Major Cartwright (Douglass Watson) questions whether De-Buin's Philadelphian minister father harbors doubts concerning his son's different vocation, DeBuin naively replies that father and son both believe that the Indian problem is caused by "a lack of Christian feeling." When the major hears that DeBuin's father believes that the Indian is a "human being," he ironically replies that "from a pulpit in Philadelphia, it's easy to make that mistake."

Ulzana's Raid undermines American missionary zeal in many ways, not least of which by showing that the Indian culture operates by values that are opposite to Western culture but values that Indian scout Ke-Ni-Tay (Jorge Luke) states are rational for that culture no matter how horrendous they may appear to the invading forces. Ulzana's culture is also one that knows Western strategies and uses them to defeat "the enemy." Several scenes show Ulzana (Joaquin Martinez) planning his campaigns like a seasoned General Patton and using binoculars in a manner seen in World War II movies. Like the Vietcong, they use American technology against their enemy, as seen in the ironic use of the bugle that concludes the sequence dealing with the siege of Rukeyser (Karl Swenson). Reminiscent of Lorne Greene's performance as God-fearing Ben Cartwright in early episodes of *Bonanza,* Rukeyser places his trust in the Lord when Ulzana attacks his ranch. When he hears the bugle (that familiar Hollywood symbol of the cavalry riding to the rescue), he lays down his rifle and goes outside to meet his saviors, raising his voice in thanks, "God, you take all the praise and all the glory." But, in ironic Aldrich terms, the savior is a destroyer, and when we next see Rukeyser it is as a mutilated body destroyed by fire torture with his dog's tail in his mouth. The sequence is as deliberately subversive as the earlier one showing Trooper Horowitz (Dean Smith) riding to the rescue of Mrs. Rukeyser (Gladys Holland). But unlike in D. W. Griffith's *The Battle at Elderbush Gulch* (1914) and *Birth of a Nation* (1915), Horowitz literally saves her from a fate worse than death by firing a bullet through her brain. Then he commits suicide, "breaking the rules" of Ulzana's game by dying before the Indians can capture him and gain his "power" by torturing him to death. The Indians express contempt at his action in a manner recalling the sergeant's earlier dismay at Lt. DeBuin disregarding the rules during their baseball game. They mutilate Horowitz's body, dig out his heart, and play ball with it in a manner recalling that earlier game. Later, DeBuin's men will attempt the same thing with the dead body of Ulzana's son.

Like Nathan Slaughter in Robert Montgomery Bird's *Nick of the Woods* (1837), DeBuin moves from being naive Christian to Indian hater, an archetypal American cultural figure also depicted in Herman Melville's *The Confidence Man* (1857).[32] Appalled at what he has witnessed, he cannot comprehend Ke-Ni-Tay's explanation of an Indian philosophy that makes sense on its own terms. DeBuin then unfairly projects his anger on the Indian scout, who is also Ulzana's brother-in-law. This occurs following the discovery of Rukeyser's body. The sergeant notes DeBuin reading from the Bible his father gave to him on his last visit to Philadelphia, wishing he "could ask him about Apaches." DeBuin misses the advice of his actual father. He is hesitant about listening to McIntosh, who suggested earlier (after closing Rukeyser's family Bible in his ruined shack) the futility of hating the Apaches: "Be like hatin' the desert cause there ain't no water in it. I can get by just bein' plenty scared of them." The sergeant suggests that his superior officer forget the New Testament and follow the precepts of the Old in a manner reminiscent of the Puritan captivity narratives. An "eye for an eye" is the only way De-Buin is going to "get the Apaches": "Christ never fetched an infant out of a cactus tree and watched him two hours before it died so he could bury it. Well, I did. Ain't no one going to teach me to turn the other cheek." However, as in the earlier scene showing McIntosh closing a Bible that had been of no use to Rukeyser, the Old Testament philosophy of vengeance is as irrelevant to the situation as the New. Instead, some pragmatic strategy for integrating opposites and accepting the world as hostile and irreducible to human conceptions appears the only way.

This strategy is seen in the characters of McIntosh and Ke-Ni-Tay. McIntosh is the hunter figure from the Puritan captivity narrative who represents its worst nightmare. He is the white man who has "gone Indian" and married into the alien community. However, McIntosh is no renegade Simon Girty but, rather, a person who has recognized the dangerous nature of idealistic solutions and decides to adopt a pragmatic course of survival. Because of editing cuts affecting the film, we see little of the relationship he has with his Indian wife (Aimee Eccles). However, before the cavalry sets off in pursuit of Ulzana we also see Ke-Ni-Tay stooping down in the foreground of the frame with his wife in the background. The only major shot of McIntosh's wife shows her concealing her face. But her eyes suggest that she is as attractive as Ke-Ni-Tay's wife, who is also Ulzana's sister, symbolically making both McIntosh and Ke-Ni-Tay members of Ulzana's own family. McIntosh and Ke-Ni-Tay have accommodated themselves to the new rules of the game in the Arizona of the 1880s. Instead of blindly pursuing an impossible goal leading to their destruction, they have adapted to a new situation as best as possible.

It may not be too far-fetched to see in these figures echoes of the former New Deal idealists attempting to find some form of different existence during the Cold War era but not by compromising themselves too much. Ke-Ni-Tay is obviously a new version of Hondo from *Apache.* But instead of regarding him with contempt, *Ulzana's Raid* sees him as a figure who has decided to make a difficult transition from one society to another. Although he is still a part of his culture, he has signed papers that represent his word of honor to the U.S. Cavalry. Both McIntosh and Ke-Ni-Tay understand each other without speaking any words. When DeBuin humiliates Ke-Ni-Tay by making him walk instead of riding by ordering McIntosh to take his horse, the scout reduces the sense of disgrace by presenting Ke-Ni-Tay with his own rifle in exchange for the horse. At the end of the film, the two men again silently exchange glances as the remnants of the decimated troop leave McIntosh alone at his own request to die in the desert. By this time DeBuin has learned important lessons that his own culture never gave him and makes a tentative gesture of apology and acceptance to Ke-Ni-Tay by calling him "Scout" and appointing him McIntosh's successor. Perhaps DeBuin's education may continue further after the death of a father figure who has appointed a younger man in his place? When DeBuin objects to McIntosh's request to be left to die, he remarks, "It's not Christian." McIntosh subtly replies, "That's right, Lt. It's not." The young lieutenant offers no further comment and decides to accept.

Ulzana's Raid is very much a "bildungsroman western according to Robert Aldrich." But instead of following the traditional status quo formulas of many Hollywood World War II narratives concerning the education of a young man by the baptism of fire, Aldrich suggests that the process is both complex and contradictory, with no final resolution. DeBuin has learned from one bloody conflict. But there is no guarantee that he will survive the next day. As McIntosh states when DeBuin begins to agonize over the men he has lost on his mission, "Don't start 'if'-ing man. You made your pick. Live with it. Hell, Lt., there ain't none of us right." He then adds, "Never mind, you'll learn." DeBuin makes several mistakes during the mission, such as sending two men on a suicidal mission to track a wounded Indian (from which only one returns), humiliating an Indian scout whose services are essential to him, and splitting his force to trap Ulzana. Although the last appears as a plausible strategy on paper, DeBuin arrives too late and makes the mistake of announcing his arrival by blowing a bugle. As Combs points out, by "precipitating a showdown on ground chosen by Ulzana, he is indirectly responsible for the deaths of half his troop, including Lancaster."[33] Furthermore, he breaks his promise to Mrs. Riordan concerning safe conduct back to the fort by using her as bait to trap Ulzana. Although his decision is based on objective grounds of strategy, his late arrival nearly ruins this plan. Mrs. Riordan's last appearance sees her as traumatized as her earlier scenes. It is unlikely that she will ever regain her sanity. Ulzana uses her as bait. So does DeBuin. His action reinforces the comment McIntosh made to him when he earlier reacted in horror at his men's mutilation of the body of Ulzana's son: "What bothers you is that you don't like to think of white men acting like Indians. Kind of confuses the issue, don't it?"

Alan Sharp regards *Ulzana's Raid* as a sincere homage to John Ford's *The Searchers*, with McIntosh as a more humane version of Ethan Edwards.[34] However, McIntosh is far removed from Ford's original conception. DeBuin better represents the Ethan Edwards parallel in the middle part of the film. However, the young lieutenant does learn from experience, unlike Ford's tormented protagonist. But from this perspective, as Arnold and Miller point out, *Ulzana's Raid* represents a "bleak and severe" initiation story.[35] It is also a film without any illusions, presenting the nature of survival in a hostile universe as tentative, temporary, and uncertain. By presenting this dark image, Aldrich directed a more mature version of the themes touched on in *Apache* as well as a film fully in tune with the temporary sensibilities of some sections of the audience in the period it appeared. The old formulas did not work. Whether they involved the Hollywood western or the contemporary Vietnam War, it was important to voice objections while at the same time not replacing one tarnished set of illusions with others that would also become equally redundant. The post-Watergate experience leading to the Reagan presidency and the American symptomatic "denial" tendency would soon demolish the expectations of the 1960s, just as the Cold War era did the idealism of the 1930s. To his credit, Aldrich presented his audiences with many grim realities that needed confrontation rather than rejection. *Ulzana's Raid* is a western of its time, but it speaks beyond its era. Aldrich's genre movies involve the same set of problems that he and the post–New Deal generation faced in their era and which continue to exist today. There would be no easy answers or solutions.

NOTES

1. The allegorical aspect of Hollywood westerns in this era could form a separate study of its own encompassing such examples as Allan Dwan's *Silver Lode* (1954), dealing with a town's paranoia and suspicion fed upon by the villainous McCarty(!) played by Dan Duryea.

2. See Richard Slotkin, *Regeneration through Violence: The Mythology of the American Frontier, 1600–1860* (Middletown, Conn.: Wesleyan University Press, 1973), 59–62, 202–5.

3. Richard Slotkin, *Gunfighter Nation: The Myth of the Frontier in Twentieth-Century America* (New York: Athenaeum, 1992), 367. See also George N. Fenin and William K. Everson, *The Western: From the Silents to the Seventies* (New York: Penguin, 1973); Brian Henderson, "*The Searchers*: An American Dilemma," *Film Quarterly* 34, no. 2 (1980–81): 19–34; and Edwin T. Arnold and Eugene I. Miller, *The Films and Career of Robert Aldrich* (Knoxville: University of Tennessee Press, 1986), 22–23.

4. James Webb's screenplay was based on Paul I. Wellman's novel, *Broncho Apache*. For historical information concerning the real Massai, see Jason Betinez, *I Fought with Geronimo* (Harrisburg, Pa.: Stockpole Co., 1959), 142–45; and Eve Ball with Norma Henn and Lynda Sánchez, eds., *Indeh: An Apache Odyssey* (Salt Lake City: Brigham Young University Press, 1980), 260.

5. Weddle's status clearly echoes that of the figure of the corrupt reservation sutler held responsible for Indian rebellion in films as diverse as *They Died with Their Boots On* (1941), *Fort Apache* (1948), and, of course, *Ulzana's Raid*.

6. Alain Silver and James Ursini, *What Ever Happened to Robert Aldrich? His Life and His Films* (New York: Limelight Editions, 1995), 150.

7. Arnold and Miller, *The Films and Career of Robert Aldrich*, 25–26. Sound also plays a prominent role in beginning this sequence, representing the assault on Massai's perceptions when encountering this new environment. See Silver and Ursini, *What Ever Happened to Robert Aldrich?* 152. However, the days were now over when the type of aural experimentation begun by Polonsky in *Force of Evil* could continue. *Apache*'s score is by the same composer who worked on *Force of Evil*. But this time David Raksin's score is

more traditional. Aldrich expressed displeasure with a score imposed on him by the studio. He preferred the counterpoint aspect of modern music as employed by his regular soundtrack composer and collaborator, Frank De-Vol. See Francois Truffaut, "Rencontre avec Robert Aldrich," *Cahiers du Cinema* 64 (1956): 4.

8. Silver and Ursini, *What Ever Happened to Robert Aldrich?* 152.

9. Silver and Ursini, *What Ever Happened to Robert Aldrich?* 151.

10. Silver and Ursini, *What Ever Happened to Robert Aldrich?* 153.

11. Aldrich described Peters as an "extraordinarily gifted woman who was marvelous to work with." He applauded the dedication she gave to her performance. In the same interview, he mentions that Joseph Losey once attempted to buy *Broncho Apache* and that they "had talked about it three or four years before it was made." Losey never directed a western, but this reference might explain several factors involving the figure of Hondo in this film. See Ian Cameron and Mark Shivas, "Interview with Robert Aldrich," *Movie* 9 (1963): 9.

12. On Aldrich's preferred ending, see Truffaut, "Rencontre avec Robert Aldrich," 4; Arnold and Miller, *The Films and Career of Robert Aldrich,* 24–25; and Silver and Ursini, *What Ever Happened to Robert Aldrich?* 11. Having Hondo shoot Massai in the back would have complemented Massai's earlier shooting of Weddle through the back. In both cases, the possibilities of peace and compromise now definitively end.

13. For Arnold and Miller, Nalinle "reminds Massai of the imperishability of his dream" (*The Films and Career of Robert Aldrich,* 28). But they also comment that "it is an illusion."

14. Joel Greenberg, "Interview with Robert Aldrich," *Sight and Sound* 38, no. 1 (1968–69): 9.

15. Richard Combs, ed., *Robert Aldrich* (London: British Film Institute, 1978), 9.

16. Combs, *Robert Aldrich,* 10.

17. Slotkin, *Regeneration through Violence*; Loren Baritz, *Backfire: A History of How American Culture Led Us into Vietnam and Made Us Fight the Way We Did* (Baltimore: Johns Hopkins University Press, 1998).

18. See Arnold and Miller, *The Films and Career of Robert Aldrich,* 31.

19. See Arnold and Miller, *The Films and Career of Robert Aldrich,* 34. They quote Burt Lancaster on this point.

20. Arnold and Miller, *The Films and Career of Robert Aldrich,* 35. For a visual analysis of the significance of both characters within the frame, see also Silver and Ursini, *What Ever Happened to Robert Aldrich?* 78–82.

21. See Francois Truffaut, "Le Derby du Psaumes," *Cahiers du Cinema* 48 (1955): 42–45; and Michael Wood, *America in the Movies* (New York: Dell, 1970), 85–86. Truffaut sees the film as a dazzling exercise in narrative construction, an intellectual western involving both humor and duplicity. For a

perceptive article dealing with *Vera Cruz*'s influence on the Italian westerns of Sergio Leone, see Rolando Caputo, "Aldrich, Leone, and *Vera Cruz*: Style and Substance over the Border," available at www.latrobe.edu.au/screeningthe past/firstrelease/fr0600/rcfr10g.htm, 30 June 2000. Caputo comments that Aldrich deliberately counterpoints "Cooper's classical poise in contrast with Lancaster's baroque excess" in a film that reworks the classical western's generic conventions toward a different type of style. Theodore Apstein's screenplay for *Rebellion* based on original material by Apstein and Aldrich reveals that *Vera Cruz*'s structure was by no means an isolated conception. Adapted from Nelson and Shirley Woolford's post–American Civil War novel *West of Appomattox* (1961), the screenplay also deals with American mercenaries in Mexico but extends *Vera Cruz*'s themes of betrayal, duplicity, and game playing in a fascinating manner.

22. Significantly, Anthony Mann would undermine Stewart's star persona in his "westerns" as Hitchcock did in his "thrillers."

23. For Aldrich's comments on the production, see Greenberg, "Interview with Robert Aldrich," 12. T. J. Ross sees certain virtues in Aldrich's use of the star: "Douglas is the screen's leading hysteric: he is flappable as a windmill and as set to start up at the first flurries of the weather. Aldrich likes to push things to a point where they are made shockingly clear. What suddenly hits us as we watch the screen's perennial wound-up man throttling a dog, is the perfect—naked—aptness of the action to the *persona* of the actor" ("Dark Legend," *December* 13 [1971]: 198). This is a really informative article intuitively recognizing not only the hero's relationship to other Aldrich figures who wish to stop time, such as Mike Callahan, Jane Hudson, and Lewis Zarkan, but also the director's involvement in a particular type of Hollywood action movie combining "populist with older avant-garde twists and turns" (Ross, "Dark Legend," 198n1). Furthermore, Ross notices that "perhaps in no film of his has Aldrich developed a more ruthless and more brilliant critique of the lust for innocence (a topic to which Americans continue to be bitterly sensitive) than in this Western (a film which includes in its targets the cliche, still spun out by ignorant critics, of the 'refreshing' innocence of the Western genre)" ("Dark Legend," 197). Both O'Malley and Joe Erin will resurface in the similarly black-clad figure of Henry Fonda's Frank in Sergio Leone's *Once upon a Time in the West* (1967). Like Frank's alter ego antagonist Harmonica (Charles Bronson), all these men are stuck in the past and have "something to do with death."

24. Aldrich credits the emphatic use of the incest theme to Trumbo. See Arnold and Miller, *The Films and Career of Robert Aldrich*, 92. It does not occur in the original novel, which is merely perfunctory in nature. Missy does not exist. Her place is taken by a son, and Breckenridge dies a heroic death on the range.

25. Combs, *Robert Aldrich*, 19.

26. For the visual parallels between both men, see Silver and Ursini, *What Ever Happened to Robert Aldrich?* 156–59.

27. Arnold and Miller comment: "He seizes the dog by his throat and begins to choke it to death. After several agonizing seconds—man and beast locked head-to-head in close profile, mirror images of one another—O'Malley's rage subsides, and he releases his grip on the cowering animal" (*The Films and Career of Robert Aldrich,* 94). Marcel Ophuls also sees O'Malley as a "killer-poet, a man who does not know how to live, and really in love with death." His description evokes the tortured Jack Palance persona seen in *Attack!* and *Ten Seconds to Hell,* especially the "poet of pain" in the latter film. Ophuls also regards *The Last Sunset* as a rare vision of a cursed human condition, though also involving a powerful poetic touch. See Ophuls, "De Noir Vertu," *Cahiers du Cinema* 130 (1962): 58–60.

28. Harry Ringel, "Up to Date with Robert Aldrich," *Sight and Sound* 53, no. 3 (1974): 168.

29. See Combs, *Robert Aldrich,* 34, Arnold and Miller, *The Films and Career of Robert Aldrich,* 173; Silver and Ursini, *What Ever Happened to Robert Aldrich?* 163.

30. See, e.g., the numerous representations in Tony Williams and Jean-Jacques Malo, eds., *Vietnam War Films: Over 600 Feature, Made-for-TV, Pilot and Short Movies, 1939–1992, from the United States, Vietnam, France, Belgium, Australia, Hong Kong, South Africa, Great Britain and Other Countries* (Jefferson, N.C.: McFarland, 1994). For *Ulzana's Raid,* see Williams and Malo, *Vietnam War Films,* 449–50.

31. *Ulzana's Raid* was heavily cut and reedited for British release. I refer to the American version currently available on 16-mm, VHS, and DVD formats. However, a definitive text may not exist. On this issue, see Brad Stevens, "Variant Versions of Robert Aldrich's Films: A Case Study," available at www.latrobe.edu.au/screeningthepast/firstrelease/fr0600/bsfr10c .htm, 30 June 2000. For a stimulating examination of *Ulzana's Raid* in terms of Aldrich's other films and experiences in Hollywood, see David Sanjek, "Fear Is a Man's Best Friend: Deformation and Aggression in the Films of Robert Aldrich," available at www.latrobe.edu.au/screeningthepast/firstrelease/ fr0600/dsfr10b.htm, 30 June 2000.

32. For the importance of these two works to the American cultural tradition, see Slotkin, *Regeneration through Violence,* 509–15.

33. Combs, *Robert Aldrich,* 33.

34. Arnold and Miller, *The Films and Career of Robert Aldrich,* 171.

35. Arnold and Miller, *The Films and Career of Robert Aldrich,* 167.

SIX

MELODRAMA, AUTHORITARIANISM, AND HYSTERIA

Ian Jarvie ends his 1961 study of the films of Robert Aldrich by noting the presence of hysteria and authoritarianism in the director's films. He concludes that Aldrich had made some "remarkable studies of the stresses on the individual in modern society—what Popper has called the 'strain of civilization'—and he treats his subjects with a style that is both appropriate and persuasive."[1] Jarvie begins the article by emphasizing his anxiety "to capture just what it is that projects itself from the screen and its impact when seeing an Aldrich film; and especially, why its impact is so strong."[2] He also recognizes that Aldrich's fascination with studies of individual entrapment in authoritarian situations evoked an aggressive formalism that depended heavily on the technical advances developed by Gregg Toland and others. This resulted in a hysterical mode of filmmaking.[3] Films such as *Kiss Me Deadly, Attack!* and *Ten Seconds to Hell* exhibit these qualities. But there are also others the director would make later in his career. Aldrich's cinematic vision depicts individuals struggling against restrictive social institutions and the psychological pitfalls such struggles involve. It is a tension that exists within melodrama, a genre that Aldrich also contributed to.

Despite the popular image of Robert Aldrich as a "macho director," several of his films deal with female issues within contemporary society. However, rather than reproduce classical Hollywood versions of female entrapment, the director delivered certain inflections to the genre. Films such as *Autumn Leaves, What Ever Happened to Baby Jane? Hush . . . Hush, Sweet Charlotte, The Killing of Sister George,* and *What Ever Happened to Aunt Alice?* focus on the plight of the aging female in modern society. Although they all interrogate the dangers of American fascination with youth and condemn neglect of those who can no longer compete within various arenas of glamorized commodification, they also depict a specific "Hollywood imaginary." Aldrich was well aware of the "use and abuse" nature of the system he worked in, particularly in its ruthless discarding of former stars once they no longer fit into Hollywood's fetishistic fascination with youth.

The presence of once attractive stars who appeared in Aldrich films in their mature years, such as Bette Davis, Joan Crawford, Olivia de Havilland, and Geraldine Page, evokes a Hollywood industry relegating its former icons to either obscurity or genres they had avoided throughout their former illustrious careers. Although these stars appear as social victims and victimizers within the various cinematic worlds they inhabit, audiences would remember them in their heyday and naturally compare their present and past images. *Autumn Leaves, Baby Jane, Charlotte,* and *Aunt Alice* do not belong to the "Hollywood on Hollywood" melodramatic subgenre like Vincente Minelli's *The Bad and the Beautiful* (1953) and *Two Weeks in Another Town* (1962). But they do evoke the industry itself by virtue of casting. They form companion pieces to Aldrich's own "Hollywood on Hollywood" explorations represented by *The Big Knife* and *The Legend of Lylah Clare.* These films characterize the ruthless nature of an industry psychologically destroying its children, in a manner akin to Kronos of Greek mythology, by consuming their talents and casting them aside once they become "redundant." Although *The Killing of Sister George* is not specifically a "Hollywood on Hollywood" film, it also reveals the ruthless nature of a commercial industry indirectly responsible for the personal downfall of its title character. Despite featuring a British comedy actress unknown to Hollywood who had made her name in the stage production, Aldrich originally envisaged Bette Davis in the title role.

Aldrich's melodramas exhibit the same types of hysterical traits that characterize his other films. But they differ by focusing on issues of infantilism and sexuality, which appear as marginal elements elsewhere. *Attack!*'s Captain Cooney exhibits classic regressive hysterical symptoms when he collapses on his bed sucking his slipper like a fetish object, fully aware of the fact that he will never become either a man or a World War II hero. He has also suffered from child abuse in his formative years. Cooney grovels before the powerful Colonel Bartlett and takes infantile sexual pleasure by grinning during the last moments of the dying Lieutenant Costa.

Aldrich also intuitively recognized that the traditional American family was a highly flawed institution. He knew of the existence of other minority groups in society confronting personal and social dilemmas. . . . *All the Marbles* and *World for Ransom* originally contained lesbian themes, which producers removed from release prints. But *The Legend of Lylah Clare* and *The Killing of Sister George* appeared at a time when Hollywood taboos were in retreat, allowing Aldrich some latitude in treating such themes. However, he never fell into the trap of creating false utopian "positive images." Instead, he revealed that these minorities also faced as dangerous a world as his heterosexual characters. In *The Choirboys,* young homosexual Alexander Blaney may briefly encounter an understanding cop. But he exists in a world of rampant homophobia and male violence, the latter element causing his death. A certain lifestyle may also contain problematic pitfalls.

Autumn Leaves, Baby Jane, and *Charlotte* also indict the damning nature of a patriarchal family system that has prevented young women from realizing their true potential and has blighted their lives, resulting in a grotesque maturity. In the Aldrich production of *What Ever Happened to Aunt Alice?* Claire Venable (Geraldine Page) believes that her deceased husband has left her to face an impoverished old age. She embarks on murdering lonely middle-aged women who share her personal dilemma of loneliness and acquiring their savings. While Jane and Charlotte suffer from the sins of their fathers, Millicent in *Autumn Leaves* masochistically sacrifices herself as a dutiful daughter in her younger days. But years later the maternal spinster falls for the aberrant charms of a man young enough to be her own son.

The Big Knife and *The Legend of Lylah Clare* are complementary works. Although the first film is an adaptation of Clifford Odets's 1949 Broadway play and the second is a reworking of an original teleplay, both reflect the psychological entrapment of individuals caught in authoritarian institutions. Both Charlie and Elsa supposedly obtain material success in that most glamorous of American industries—Hollywood. But they become personally contaminated by the malignant aspects of that "genius of the system" hailed by Andre Bazin, which eventually destroys them.

Like *Attack! The Big Knife* is an Aldrich film haunted by the ghost of John Garfield, who would presumably have repeated his stage performance had he survived brutal persecution by the House Un-American Activities Committee. After a vain attempt to interest several Hollywood stars such as Burt Lancaster to play the leading role, it finally went to Jack Palance and became the first of three collaborations between actor and director.[4] As the first official Associates and Aldrich Co. independent production, *The Big Knife* was shot at a cost of $425,000, which was a considerable drop in comparison to the million-dollar budgets of *Apache* and *Vera Cruz*.[5] Although it was viewed as an attack on the Hollywood studio system, Aldrich commented that the dilemma of Charlie Castle "can apply to any sphere of business, or the arts, where man's natural liberty or expression is squelched by unworthy, incompetent, tyrannical leaders or bosses, many of whom are not deserving of their powers."[6] Nevertheless, it is a "Hollywood on Hollywood" film inextricably linked with Clifford Odets and John Garfield, who experienced creative frustrations with Hollywood and wished to do something better. Garfield's desire to break away from his Warner Bros. contract and achieve more significant work—as his involvement in Enterprise Studios shows—lies behind the trapped image of Charlie Castle. Jack Palance achieved a relatively brief period of stardom during the 1950s. His emotionally tormented performance naturally differs from what Garfield could have delivered. But it must also be remembered that Palance was one of the actors who played Stanley Kowalski on stage, a role Garfield had turned down, after Marlon Brando left the production. Aldrich also belonged to the same type of cultural movement influencing the works of Odets's theatrical successors such as Tennessee Williams and Arthur Miller, both of whom criticized the inhumane values of Cold War America in their own specific ways.

The Big Knife opens as the credits roll with an image of the tormented Charlie Castle. It resembles a modernist noir version of that well-known expressionistic painting *The Silent Scream*—an association that cannot be entirely coincidental in terms of Aldrich's associations with contemporary underground noir movements. Finally, the screen fragments like a broken mirror, abstractly illustrating psychological crisis. Saul Bass's title design superbly evokes not only Charlie's existential dilemma but also the modernist crisis imagery appearing in *Kiss Me Deadly*. This excessive opening imagery reveals Aldrich's understanding of *The Big Knife* as an exercise in male hysteria, the dilemma of a trapped man caught within the confines of materialist success but lacking artistic and personal freedom. The film is definitely a male melodrama. It is a genre associated with elements of excess such as horror and film noir. Like *Kiss Me Deadly*, *The*

Big Knife is also a film noir set almost exclusively within the "play-room" of Charlie's Bel Air mansion, whose walls exhibit modern art paintings. Unlike scenes showing Charlie at the studio where camera mobility is possible, his movement is much more circumscribed inside his "playroom." The interior of his house reflects emotional entrapment. Aldrich depicts this by the use of relevant camera angles, cutting, and deep-focus photography and the employment of shots showing the ceiling overhead, symbolically limiting any possibility of human agency. Aldrich had used overhead shots in *World for Ransom* and his television work, but these scenes appear indebted to the RKO collaboration of Welles and Toland in *Citizen Kane*. Furthermore, Everett Sloane's casting as Nat represents another Aldrich use of a *Citizen Kane* alumnus, whereas Shelley Winters's appearance may also represent another indirect John Garfield reference, for she starred in the actor's last film, *He Ran All the Way* (1951). After the credits, the film opens with a voice-over commentary by Richard Boone (an actor whom both Aldrich and Odets would work with in the future), describing the plush exterior of Bel Air in a world where "failure is not permitted" and finishing with a line that would become the major signature of Robert Aldrich in his later films: "Our story has to do with a twentieth-century phenomenon. Name—Charlie Castle. Profession—Movie Star. Problem—Survival."

The presence of canted angle shots introducing the audience to Charlie's mansion, though shot in daylight, contradicts the deceptive tourist guide images presented on the screen. They suggest instability existing side by side with these illustrations of material success. The canted angle is a familiar film noir technique (used ad nauseam in Carol Reed's 1949 film *The Third Man*). These unusually filmed daylight scenes suggest that Charlie's success in the American dream involves aberrant undertones. His mansion also represents a modern version of Charles Foster Kane's Xanadu. If not as Gothic as its predecessor, it is still a domain containing its own particular heart of darkness. As the image changes to a helicopter shot moving in to show Charlie sparring with his trainer, Nickey Feeney (Nick Dennis), Boone's voice-over concludes with the ominous lines, "Charlie Castle has sold out his dreams but he has not forgotten them."

The next image shows the arrival of gossip columnist Patty Benedict (Ilka Chase). She is ushered into Charlie's playroom by his publicity agent, Buddy Bliss (Paul Langton). As Patty walks to the window, she is conspicuously framed by the window bars, which signify not her symbolic imprisonment but that of the man she watches outside. This use of framing also appears in Aldrich's two *Four Star Playhouse* "Dante's Inferno" episodes, "The Squeeze" and "The Hard Way," where the person outside the bars, rather than the one inside, is most under threat. The boxing references are not in Odets's actual play, but they immediately evoke John Garfield's performance in *Body and Soul*. The film was Enterprise Studio's biggest financial success, establishing Garfield's image for the new postwar generation. Charlie has also become his own type of "Golden Boy" by enjoying the American dream of affluence and success.

Although lacking much of the information concerning Charlie's original socialist background contained in the original play, James Poe's screenplay contains several clues to its hero's past. Like Garfield, Charlie is a product of the 1930s. Once part of an idealistic movement, he achieved success on the stage before moving to Hollywood and signing a contract with studio boss Stanley Hoff (Rod Steiger). Scattered dialogue references to the "New Deal" and the "Group" contain enough clues as to the dreams this person has "not forgotten." When Charlie first met Patty (a monstrous amalgamation of Hedda Hopper and Louella Parsons) in 1945 all he could talk about was the New Deal. Now he exists in a world in which the "unhappy endings" of Mercury and Group Theatre productions are, in Stanley Hoff's own words, "uncommercial." Evading Patty's questions concerning his marriage and un-American tastes in art when she notices a modernist Roualt painting of an old clown, Charlie acts like a boxer in another type of ring. He reacts against Patty's artistic parochialism concerning his taste for modernist European art, "Is it impossible to be *democratic*?" but evades her other questions by uttering platitudes such as his change from belief in the New Deal to faith in "health, hard work, and rare roast beef." But Patty is on the hunt for her own special brand of meat. She caustically attacks her prey when he refuses to answer probing questions. Like Charley Davis in *Body and Soul*, he is also trapped between the worlds of business and personal integrity, succinctly summarized by his later remark to his wife Marian (Ida Lupino), "I'm in the movie business. I can't afford your attacks of integrity." She acts as his moral conscience in the same way as Peg in *Body and Soul*, Doris in *Force of Evil*, and Nalinle in *Apache*. Like Peg, Marian evokes Charlie's former creative self. The parallels between the two films become explicit when she evokes the title of

William Blake's famous poem: "He was a tiger. He liked to argue. . . . I want you to tear Stanley Hoff apart, tiger."

Irritated at Charlie refusing to confirm a divorce rumor, Patty departs from his mansion, leaving him to muse in self-pity at Roualt's modernist painting of an "old clown waiting in the wings to go on. . . . Don't mean anything, anymore." Deep-focus photography and low-angle shots of the ceiling emphasize his creative imprisonment and emotional isolation. His Hollywood dream of material success has become a living nightmare. Also, as in *Kiss Me Deadly*, the presence of several modernist paintings in Charlie's playroom evokes the crisis aspects of postwar popular culture underground movements. Such discordant modernist overtones also characterize the work of Abraham Polonsky, especially in *Odds against Tomorrow* (1959).

When his agent Nat (Everett Sloane) arrives to discuss Charlie's future prospects, an unusual low-angle shot, showing Charlie leaning on the table for his daily massage with Nat towering above him, visually demonstrates another form of entrapment. Although Nat sympathizes with his client, he is another cog in the Hollywood machine. Although supposedly looking after his client's best interests, he cannot prevent Charlie from appearing in bad movies such as the musical project they refer to later. Nat warns Charlie that his New Deal idealism is now over: "Business and idealism do not mix, like oil and water. A movie is not a movie. To you, it's like a gospel." When Charlie responds, "Every way is a way to die," Nat replies, "I'm old. Every way is a way to live." Nat here articulates Aldrich's philosophy of struggling against overpowering circumstances no matter what the outcome. However, Charlie now has to face a major battle when studio boss Stanley Hoff and his associate, Smiley Coy (Wendell Corey), suddenly turn up on his doorstep.

Charlie arrives for the confrontation clad in a boxing robe resembling Charley Davis's in his final encounter with Roberts in *Body and Soul*. Introduced by military drumrolls, Hoff embodies a dangerous patriarchal system seeking constantly to devour its children. He is the first monstrous father figure in the world of Robert Aldrich, anticipating similar types in *Autumn Leaves, What Ever Happened to Baby Jane?* and *Hush . . . Hush, Sweet Charlotte*. He also incarnates the fascist tendencies inherent within the militaristic persona of General Douglas MacArthur (one of whose pens, supposedly used during the Japanese surrender, he possesses) as well as bullying studio bosses such as Harry Cohn and Louis B. Mayer, who attempted to control the lives of those under contract to them. Playing a gentle father to Charlie (who may have correctly guessed its homosexual overtones) as in the past, Hoff wishes to seduce his star into signing another seven-year contract. He begins to tell a story. Several revealing cutaways to a bemused Smiley reveal that he has heard it often before. Stanley's tale articulates misogynistic feelings against his former wife who, supposedly, attempted to destroy his career. In reality, Stanley obviously drove her away. He uses this narrative to undermine the influence that Marian Castle has on her husband. She wishes to persuade Charlie to refuse to sign another contract so that they can both regain creative and emotional security. As Stanley's story begins to take a more aggressive line, he puts on his dark glasses, evoking a menacing mob boss more than a paternally benevolent studio head. He finally plays his trump card in mentioning a drunken driving accident involving the death of a small child that the studio had hushed up. Charlie eventually capitulates. He kneels down in a position resembling that of an execution victim (or a small child before a stern parental figure) and signs the contract.

During Stanley's melodramatic legalistic cross-examination of his submissive client, Charlie relinquishes any attempt to speak up for himself. He cringes on the sofa, clinging to the cushions like an infant before a punitive father. Charlie's gestures resemble Captain Cooney's infantile behavior in *Attack!* If *Attack!* combines war movie with film noir, *The Big Knife* similarly amalgamates film noir and Hollywood melodrama. The acting styles of Palance and Steiger counterpoint each other in significant ways. Although Steiger's performance appears excessive, it complements the hysterical melodramatic tones of a film dealing with male crisis, as well as the different type of isometric performance embodied in Jack Palance.[7] Charlie is a man struggling with internal tensions. Stanley can openly display authoritarian anger by cathartically projecting his pain over a past he was responsible for onto others. He acts like a manipulative melodramatic father figure eager to instill guilt feelings into his son using techniques similar to those used by Raymond Massey against James Dean in *East of Eden* (1954). Charlie can only internally fume against his entrapment over a past event he was responsible for. Submissive once more, Charlie requests the pen he used to sign the contract to keep as his "only proof that the war was over or it was ever fought." When Marian phones and learns of Charlie's surrender, she hangs up, leaving her husband alone in the image. After showing Charlie framed by shelves in his cabinet, a lap dissolve begins the next scene, illustrating another form of entrapment.

Charlie listens to classical music alone, a taste he has learned from Marian. But the arrival of Connie Bliss (Jean Hagen) disrupts his temporary haven of cultural salvation. The music changes to a banal pop song as Connie plays on the sadomasochistic sexual tendencies that Hollywood has nurtured within him. He desperately wishes that Marian will drop divorce proceedings and return to him with his young son. However, Charlie finds himself dragged further into the dark realms of the Hollywood machine. Smiley Coy subtly attempts to enlist his help in silencing Dixie Evans (Shelley Winters), a young starlet who accompanied Charlie on the night of the fatal crash and is using this knowledge to upset the studio.

As played by Shelley Winters, Dixie represents another female muse figure in Charlie's life. She is also a female version of Charlie's former self. Dixie is a girl from the wrong side of the tracks who rejects the material temptation that has destroyed Charlie and fights against it in her own way. Dixie also resembles Cleo's muse figure from Odets's *Rocket to the Moon*. Both women stumble blindly toward some utopian goal of their own and reject existence in an environment that offers little hope. As Odets critics note, within the context of the play's Shakespearean associations, Dixie represents Charlie's "Banquo's ghost." She evokes the dreams Charlie abandoned in his current state of half-idealism, one that his writer friend Hank (Wesley Addy) later describes as "peritonitis of the soul." Dixie also explicitly understands her role as a commodified object within the Hollywood system, something that Charlie would prefer to forget: "I'm a deductible item. They write me off." The line echoes Stanley's earlier comment to Charlie, "I need your body, not your good-will." It succinctly defines him as an objectified commodity within a Hollywood whorehouse.

Dixie temporarily raises Charlie's spirits after he has succumbed to Smiley's cynicism. Charlie behaves like a naive child before Smiley's powerful father figure, who often calls him "kid" or "doll" as if recognizing the insecurity behind the star's masculine facade: "The warrior minstrel with the forlorn hope. That's you, doll." Dixie also recognizes the nature of Charlie's psychosexual problems when she calls him a "masochist," as if perceiving that part of his problem arises from unresolved sexual tensions. Charlie is a passive figure unable to act on his own. His final lines to Marian reveal this: "All my life I've yearned for people to bring out the best in me." He is a submissive son easily manipulated by positive (Marian) as well as negative (Stanley/Smiley) influences. Smiley supposedly operates independently from Stanley when he counsels Charlie. But Stanley and Smiley are opposite sides of the same coin who play on their victims in different, but equal, complementary ways. Like movie actors, they attempt to manipulate their audiences by controlling emotions. Charlie recognizes this when he tells Smiley, "You'd make a great actor," as if remembering Stanley's earlier performance.[8] Smiley then leaves with the final comment: "Ideals, kid? Nowadays? A lost crusade. . . . Don't study life. Get used to it."

Charlie can never accept this solution. When he learns of Smiley's plan to involve him in Dixie's murder, he decides to confront his monstrous Hollywood father for the last time. Facing exposure, Charlie decides to commit suicide. Aldrich initially affirmed the nature of Charlie's act, regarding it as a "gesture of revolt" as did Clifford Odets.[9] But he later changed his mind, believing that Charlie should have listened to the advice of his Horatio alter ego Hank: "Struggle, you may still win a blessing."[10] Charlie clearly fails. But he fails because of negative psychological components existing within his own persona, which destroy him just like the internal demons affecting several Clifford Odets characters. Aldrich would attempt to move away from certain themes he encountered in Odets toward more positive solutions. But they would be ones that still recognize the bleak nature of a hostile universe affecting various characters. However, Aldrich's later characters would neither passively "study life" nor "get used to it" in Smiley's words. In an article significantly titled "Life Is Worth Living," Aldrich commented: "Why not struggle and maximize the victories. They may not come, probably *won't* come, but they might come, and if they come you're one victory ahead of total defeat."[11]

Charlie's act is certainly no positive gesture of revolt. He has blighted the lives of his wife and son forever. Despite Hank's "Good-night, sweet prince" attempt to redeem Charlie's deed as a sacrificial act—"He killed himself out of the pain and anguish and love he had for others"—it is clearly one of selfish escapism, as the final scene shows. Marian collapses into insanity, calling for help to a husband who can no longer answer. The camera tracks up into an overhead shot revealing the artificial nature of the studio set, as if inviting audiences to consider the diverse implications of the final scene. For Silver and Ursini, "As the camera moves back and back creating the imaginary fourth wall and ceiling of the set, it creates a sardonic afterthought: 'Hollywood life' is not figuratively or literally, a real life. It is not lived but only acted out in an empty search for stage center with darkness surrounding."[12] At the same time, it evokes a comparison between the fictional image and its relationship to problems affecting everyday life. Could these problems be surmounted in a different way? No matter how powerful the forces of oppression are, Charlie Castle's solution represents no positive alternative.

The Legend of Lylah Clare is one of Aldrich's most flawed productions. Despite interesting moments and superb performances by Peter Finch, Ernest Borgnine, Coral Browne, and Valentina Cortese, the film is incohesive and disjointed, as several critics note.[13] Yet, even with its manifold faults, the film is not as dismissible as *4 for Texas, The Choirboys,* and *The Frisco Kid.* It exhibits a fascinating perversity, not only in terms of being a project the director should have avoided but also in relation to other Aldrich family melodramas. Based on a 1963 NBC *Du Pont Show of the Week* featuring Tuesday Weld and Alfred Drake, *The Legend of Lylah Clare* was purchased by Aldrich, who engaged Hugo Butler, Jean Rouverol, and (uncredited) Lukas Heller to work on the screenplay.[14] Obviously viewing this as a companion piece to *The Big Knife,* Aldrich attempted another self-reflexive examination of a movie industry he both loathed and understood. After searching for a star to play the title character and her successor, he signed up Kim Novak.[15] The Butler–Rouverol screenplay contains many Hollywood references, even featuring James Wong Howe as a cameraman filming the doomed star's last appearance. The veteran cameraman uses techniques associated with *Body and Soul.*[16] Had Aldrich developed a more cohesive film less dependent on its original source material, the project could have worked. *The Legend of Lylah Clare* is broken-backed and incohesive. But it is not without interest.

Dying Viennese agent Bart Langner (Milton Zelzer) elicits the interest of retired director Lewis Zarkan (Peter Finch) by presenting to him a reincarnation of his former star, Lylah Clare, who died in a mysterious accident at their home many years before. Living in a mansion with Lylah's former companion, Rosella (Rosella Falk), Zarkan becomes attracted by the resemblance Elsa Brinkman (Kim

Novak) has to his former wife and star. He engages in a project to return Lylah to life and star her in a biographical re-creation of the last days of his former wife. Zarkan lives in a peculiar platonic, antagonistic relationship with the drug-addicted Rosella. He also engages in masochistic games, presenting himself as a target in a home shooting gallery for any guest who wishes to participate. Eventually, Zarkan not only gets to relive the past but also makes the same mistakes as before. He again psychologically destroys and murders his former star Lylah, now re-created as Elsa Campbell. In *The Legend of Lylah Clare*, a star has been not only born but reborn to die once more as a sacrificial victim to her creator's egotistic ambitions.

During the film's penultimate sequence, a television announcer interviews Zarkan following the success of Elsa's last film. The normally egotistic director is now fully conscious of the guilt he bears in both past and present. Instead of contributing to the myth of Hollywood, Zarkan confesses to the television audience, "You make a terrible mistake, and your consolation is the thought that you've learned something. You gather up the courage to start over and learn that you make the mistake all over again." Zarkan's comments apply not only to the film's melodramatic tragedy within the film but also to those socially reproduced destructive repetitive-compulsive mechanisms ingrained within the human personality, which continually cause the personal tragedies. The film concludes with a frightening image of a dog commercial on television. Aldrich substituted this more powerful sequence for the screenplay's original ending, when Zarkan returns home to be shot by a grieving Rosella for his role in killing Lylah once again.

The commercial begins harmlessly enough with a woman presenting a dish to a cute poodle. But a pack of growling, angry mongrels follows the poodle to the consternation of its owner, even though the commercial voice-over pretends that nothing is really going wrong. The final image is a close-up freeze-frame of the bared teeth of one of the dogs. This frightening climax metaphorically represents the savagery within the human condition often denied by a Hollywood industry indulging in glamorized fabrications and denial of what really lies beneath the surface of everyday existence. It is a powerful image reminiscent of certain aspects of Stanley Kubrick's dark satire on the human condition. But it is also as apocalyptic as the climax of *Kiss Me Deadly*. Aldrich made some astute remarks in relation to the previous Fellini-type scene in *The Legend of*

Lylah Clare showing clowns weeping over the dying Elsa: "It was not a joke. It was that if anybody didn't realize before the fact that it's all dog meat, and you're all going to get destroyed. If you haven't figured that out by now, here's the commercial that's going to let you know that."[17]

A world of difference exists between George Eliot's *Daniel Deronda* and *The Legend of Lylah Clare*. But both have something in common. If, as F. R. Leavis has recognized, Gwendolyn Harleth represents the real core of Eliot's novel, Lewis Zarkan performs a similar role in Aldrich's film.[18] Unfortunately, Kim Novak's casting immediately evokes associations with her role in Alfred Hitchcock's *Vertigo* (1958) that cloud the potential strengths of Aldrich's film. Similarly, the story of Daniel Deronda also distracts readers away from the interesting dilemma experienced by Gwendolyn Harleth. Perhaps the film may have worked had Aldrich successfully managed to cast Jeanne Moreau? However, despite better performances Novak achieved in her Hollywood career, she is seriously miscast in the film. Also, Lylah's narrative moves audience attention away from the central character of *The Legend of Lylah Clare*, Lewis Zarkan. As Aldrich pointed out to John Calendo, Peter Finch's concluding scene embodies the tragic dilemma of a man who now really understood what he had done. The savage nature of the dog food commercial symbolically represents not only his consciousness at turning another human being into "dead meat" but also viewer awareness of his impending fate: "The inevitability of the dog ad is the inevitability that he's going to face that she's going to kill him."[19] Victim and victimizer share the same fate in the Hollywood machine.

Novak's casting and campish, self-reflexive "Hollywood on Hollywood" elements lead to a highly confusing film. *The Legend of Lylah Clare* is no *Vertigo*. Nor is Kim Novak's performance up to the level of her dual persona as Madeleine/Judy in the earlier film. The film evokes many references, as well as parallels to the Marlene Dietrich/Josef von Sternberg collaboration and the enigmatic persona of Greta Garbo (seen in the re-creation of a scene from the 1930 film version of *Anna Christie*), which eventually overwhelm its real core. In addition to Billy Wilder's *Sunset Boulevard* (1950), the ghost of Alfred Hitchcock's *Rebecca* (1940) haunts the production. As Zarkan's housekeeper, Rosella is the film's Mrs. Danvers, reverently guarding the memory of her former mistress. Instead of discovering an untouched bedroom in a house dominated by the portrait of its dead mistress as in *Rebecca,* Elsa finds a bridal suite violated by Lewis Zarkan on his fatal wedding night. Zarkan has dominated his star on the studio set. She was originally discovered by Langner in a German brothel specializing in "some pretty unusual fantasies."[20] The director makes similar use of her talents within the Hollywood machine. Like a Hollywood Maxim De Winter, Zarkan attempts to dominate Lylah within marriage so that she will continue her career as well as further his own. However, like Dietrich and Garbo, Lylah had an identity of her own, as revealed in the three flashback sequences providing different versions of her death. The first sanitized official version presents her death as being caused by the violent intrusion of a crazy male fan. But the second version, related to Elsa by Zarkan, reveals a different gender perspective. Lylah enjoyed a lesbian flirtation until Zarkan's sudden appearance caused her accidental death. The final version occurs during Elsa's fatal trapeze scene. Zarkan commands her to look down from a height as he once did to Lylah in their final moments together. The final flashback reveals that Zarkan decided to avenge his affronted sense of masculinity because Lylah refused to curb her polymorphous sexuality and submit to his patriarchal control. Knowing her fear of heights, he commanded her to look down from the top of the staircase. The command resulted in her death. Now Zarkan tells Elsa to look down in a scene where fact and fiction finally merge. Zarkan's commanding words have the same effect. Lylah died in the past after rebelling against Zarkan's patriarchal control. After Lylah's lover has fallen down from the top of the staircase, Zarkan decides to dispose of his wife in the same way. But this time he blames the victim for his own patriarchal violence: "Look down at your friend, Lylah. It's your fault. See what you've done." However, as Lylah's successor, Elsa is now envisaged as a celluloid sacrifice for the cinema audience: "Your audience is down here. Look down. Smile at them. Wave—!" Zarkan controls Elsa for the last time. After she falls, he keeps the cameras rolling so that his screen surrogate can speak those "lying words" that Lily Carver wished Mike to speak before she shot him: "I love you."

However, any sense of definitive narrative closure conflicts with a constantly changing world where everything solid "melts into air" and nothing is certain. The sexual preferences of the main characters are constantly changing. Lylah wished to retire and have children with Zarkan, who is horrified at the very suggestion. Zarkan may be a repressed homosexual with a fear of femininity that he conceals within an authoritarian posture. He seeks to dominate a bisexual female in the same manner as Callahan attempts to do in *World for Ransom*. Lylah engages in a lesbian affair on her final day similar to her earlier one with Rosella, repeating one of her "undisclosed" former duties in the German brothel where she was discovered. Zarkan perversely keeps Rosella in his presence rather than dismiss her. Their platonic relationship has perverse masochistic overtones. When Rosella offers herself to Zarkan to save Elsa from Lylah's eventual fate, she receives the sarcastic comment, "Don't tell me your talents are changing after all these years!" Zarkan and Rosella have lived in his old-style Hollywood mansion for twenty years like an odd couple. They cannibalistically live on the memory of a woman they have both slept with. Like the animals that appear in the film's closing dog food commercial, they consume her memory after death. Zarkan masochistically punishes himself by living daily with a woman embodying the lesbianism of his former star. Rosella also has perverse overtones in her own character. She actually witnessed Zarkan's responsibility for the death of Lylah. But she still remains in his presence, perhaps perversely desiring to take her former lover's place and become her surrogate. Both wish to live in the past in a dangerously dysfunctional manner reminiscent of characters in the plays of Clifford Odets and other Aldrich melodramas. *The Legend of Lylah Clare* is a film deliberately dealing with gender confusion. During the flashbacks, masculine and female voices alternate on the soundtrack; Lylah's husky male-accented tones often dominate it. Zarkan's voice appears feminized and humiliated, especially during the second flashback. He regains the masculine control of his voice in the third flashback when he commands Lylah to fall to her death using deep patriarchal intonations. Secondary characters such as Valentina Cortese's Countess "Bozo" Bedoni speak in "husky, almost male tones," often matching those of Lylah, Elsa (when possessed by her predecessor), and Rosella.[21]

The film also evokes themes in Hugo Butler's first collaboration with Aldrich, *World for Ransom*. Frennessey prefers Julian March to the idealistic romanticism of Mike Callahan. Callahan puts her on a pedestal in the same way Zarkan does with Lylah. But Zarkan is a much more complex personality. He refuses to acknowledge self-destructive oppressive desires. He also refuses to recognize not only the real personalities of both Lylah and Elsa but also the complex psychology motivating his own feelings. When Elsa confesses her love for him in a manner recalling Lylah's profession of love many years before, Zarkan reacts against her with horror. He fears threats to his masculinity: "You don't own me, control me." Like Norma Desmond in *Sunset Boulevard*, he becomes a virtual recluse in his mansion. But unlike Norma, Zarkan also knows that he was nothing without Lylah Clare. Unlike Norma, Zarkan knows that the movies have not gotten smaller. But his own creativity, which was exclusively dependent on Lylah, has now ceased to exist. His masochistic shooting contests contrast with his sadistic treatment of Lylah when they were both together. But Zarkan never learns from past mistakes. He repeats them in the present. When he returns home, Rosella waits for him with a gun to play another game. But this time Zarkan will not live to repeat any further replays. In Hollywood terms, he has already had his opportunity for a sequel but abused it in more than one sense.

The Legend of Lylah Clare is a melodramatic mirror image of many themes found in Aldrich's film noirs, especially *Kiss Me Deadly*. Arnold and Miller comment that *Lylah Clare* "combines his scathing criticism of the Hollywood studio system with his most boldly experimental visual style since *Kiss Me Deadly* thirteen years earlier, and, while the combination does not always work, *Lylah Clare* remains a challenging provocative film."[22] Although no film noir, *The Legend of Lylah Clare* shares the dark vision of *Kiss Me Deadly*. Zarkan achieves his great "whatzit," but it turns out to be illusory and destructive.

The film's reverse appropriation of *Sunset Boulevard* now becomes apparent. During one scene Elsa descends the stairs in a manner evoking the last exit of Norma Desmond in Billy Wilder's film. But she is merely a puppet in the hands of Lewis Zarkan, who desperately needs her to reverse his insecure masculinity and creative failure. He directs Elsa in the same manner as von Stroheim finally directs Swanson in *Sunset Boulevard*. But the insanity is not within the star but, rather, inside the director. To the outside world Zarkan may appear as masculine as Charlie Castle. But inside he exhibits similar insecurities, as revealed in masochistic games involving firearms, narcissistic attitudes, and his Christlike posture of martyrdom when he humorously (but revealingly) announces the second coming of Lewis Zarkan. Like Mike Hammer in *Kiss Me Deadly*, he will face his own version of apocalyptic self-destruction by using and abusing a female body. In the original screenplay, Bart warns him before the final shoot, "I told you once. The story's a Pandora's box. I knew if you opened it you'd be ruined. I prayed to God that would happen. (soft, deadly) You've got your hand on the lid."[23] Ignoring the warning he goes ahead like Lily Carver in *Kiss Me Deadly*. Like Orson Welles's Charles Foster Kane, Zarkan destroys himself and others. He knows his reputation is really due to a woman he has created out of his own inner being. Lewis Zarkan is as much a creation as Lylah. He later tells Elsa, "You're an illusion. Without me you don't exist." She responds, "Lewis, you're God. I'm created in your own image." But she also thrusts a mirror into his face as if challenging him to recognize the feminine component of his own personality he has consistently denied.[24] Elsa also delivers the greatest insult she can to Zarkan's professional role by directing her last scene herself. She challenges Zarkan's masculinity by arguing that he is really economically dependent on her: "You 'created' me. . . . You can't earn a dollar without me. We'll see who's Number One! Afraid? *Pensioner!*" Zarkan regains control in a deadly manner by destroying Elsa in the same way he did Lylah by using her Achilles heel, her fear of heights.

Lewis Zarkan was also a creation of studio boss Barney Sheean (Ernest Borgnine). Before being "born again" in Hollywood, his real name was "Flack." As Zarkan states, "We make the legend. The legend becomes the truth"—a fact relevant to both Hollywood and the everyday nature of human existence whereby people follow sexually and socially mandated roles violating their inner selves. For Aldrich, the Hollywood industry is based on lies and fabrications that are economic in nature. The film also cynically refers to the concession stands of popcorn, percentages, and popsicles that now dominate the industry rather than artistic and creative concerns. Hollywood is the appropriate environment for the dissemination of lies and fabrications. However, most Aldrich films attempt to break this celluloid ceiling by presenting other more realistic visions. These involve bleak depictions of the destruction of human beings caused by their worst instincts and the savage nature of the surrounding social structure.

Autumn Leaves was not an unusual choice for Aldrich. He was not just a director of male action movies. The director once commented that he chose the film to break prevailing critical stereotypes applied to his work.[25] For Arnold and Miller, *Autumn Leaves* is less of a digression and more a restatement of motifs in his earlier films and an anticipation of future ones such as *What Ever Happened to Baby Jane? Hush . . . Hush, Sweet Charlotte, The Killing of Sister George,* and *The Grissom Gang.*[26] *Autumn Leaves* is a melodrama but one in which the social elements characterizing the director's other films are by no means absent. During another interview, Aldrich commented that he saw the film as a study of American socially induced psychological immaturity, which he hoped to explore further.[27] *Autumn Leaves* also involves another attack on American patriarchy. As Arnold and Miller concisely comment, the film is "another example of father-as-terrorist."[28] However, a key aspect involves the role of human responsibility. The real emphasis is on its leading character, Millicent Weatherby (Joan Crawford), and the struggle she engages in to overcome certain aberrant psychological features within her own persona. The conclusion of *Autumn Leaves* tentatively suggests that she, unlike Charlie Castle in *The Big Knife,* may have won her "blessing" by engaging in her own form of struggle.

Scripted by Jean Rouverol from one of her own stories, *Autumn Leaves* is a composite generic work fusing melodrama, film noir, and psychological Gothic horror genres. The introductory scenes have certain similarities to the opening of *The Big Knife.* Richard Combs sees the opening shots introducing viewers to the apartment area where Millie lives as resembling both the introduction to *The Big Knife* and Hitchcock's *Psycho.*[29] In many ways, Millie resembles a character from one of Clifford Odets's plays trapped by both past family circumstances and psychological failure. She and Burt Hanson (Cliff Robertson) are symbiotic soul mates.

After the introduction to Cedar Courts, the first image we see of Millie shows her seated at her typewriter working at home. Although she appears to be an independent working woman preferring the freedom of her own apartment to an office, the frenzied nature of her typing and the shadow bars cast on the wall behind her suggest deep insecurities beneath her professional appearance to the outside world. Millie's friend and apartment manager Liz (Ruth Donnelly) comments on her workaholic nature: "I've been working day and night—just like you." When her client, Mr. Ramsey (Frank Gerstile), arrives to pick up his manuscript, Millie's face expresses fear when he offers her two tickets for a concert until she learns that his girlfriend dislikes classical music. After he leaves, the two women discuss Millie's lost opportunities. Although Millie believes, "Maybe,

I'm just too choosy," Liz replies, "Maybe, you're just plain scared."
Millie is a lonely woman who fears commitment, as illustrated by a
revealing shot of a diagonal shadow cast over her face by the desk
lamp. Although she appears to regret being alone, as seen in her reply to Liz's complaints about her quarreling family—"Well, at least
you have a family. That's something you can't win in a lottery"—her
fear of commitment has left her alone at middle age.

During the concert Millie's mind returns to a past event when she
refused a suitor to look after her ailing father, who had also urged
her to continue the relationship: "Now, Milly. I want you to go out.
I don't want to be the reason for you breaking up with Paul." Despite her reassurance, "Don't worry about me. I've got plenty of
time. There's plenty of time," the discordant sound echo of the last
line, coupled with Frank DeVol's dissonant reproduction of the classical sonata beginning and concluding Millie's flashback, reveals the
emotional torment she feels over her lost chances. However, once
she reaches a restaurant she encounters the youthful Burt, who appears very much like a monster from her own id. Millie has repressed her fears of sexual involvement by psychologically overin-
vesting in a maternal role by caring for her father. She later transfers
her energies into work. Smiling and talking in a manner very reminiscent of Eddie Albert's Captain Cooney from *Attack!* Burt appears
in her life and charms her with his vulnerable childlike personality.

Millie's fate was sealed the moment she walked into the restaurant, symbolized by her image framed through the kitchen's oval
glass door as the waitress (Marjorie Bennett) walks to the entrance
to find Millie a seat. When Burt learns that Millie is from New England and has family there, he utters a line very similar to Millie's earlier remark to Liz: "I can't imagine anyone leaving their family—if
they're lucky enough to have one." Both remarks are evasive because we learn that neither Burt nor Millie experienced positive family relationships. Whereas Burt was victimized by his father from an
early age like Cooney, Millie is the victim of personal insecurities.
Both become symbiotically attracted to each other. They recognize
mutual loneliness but deny their own psychological malfunctions.
Burt sees in Millie the mother he never had. He tells her, "I never
knew my mother. My father died when I was so high." Affected by
his father's symbolic castration of his manhood, he wishes to be reborn as a little child seeking a lost mother. Millie falls into a maternal role, seeing in Burt both a romantic lover and the child she never

had. Eventually, they get married despite Millie's recognition of contradictions in the stories Burt tells her about his past. Aldrich depicts
the problematic nature of their eventual reunion in several shots by
using shadows. One scene shows them both walking down a dark
noirish street outside a cinema in one of Aldrich's deliberately ob-
trusive high-angle shots.

Millie eventually discovers the darkness existing in the soul of
Burt when she meets his ex-wife, Virginia (Vera Miles), and his father (Lorne Greene). They both tell Millie that her husband is a
pathological liar. Mr. Hanson's verbal delivery echoes that of Albert
Dekker's Dr. Soberin from *Kiss Me Deadly*. It reveals a sophisticated
manner and the use of a classical world Aldrich finds both dangerous and irrelevant in a modernist postwar era. Hanson attempts to
seduce Millie by making a subtle pass at the end of their meeting. He
also poses as a classically educated gentleman, using phrases like
weapons in a manner similar to his predecessor in *Kiss Me Deadly*:
"To do or not to do? That is the question." He speaks of his desire to
"spend the whole night reading the classics." Hanson also deceptively frames issues in a devious moralistic narrative structure concealing the dark realities behind his own responsibility for his son's
insanity: "Like in the story book we have a hero and a villain. But
I'm not a villain. We'll let the gods decide." However, when Millie
asks him direct questions such as *when* Burt began to lie, Hanson remains conspicuously silent. He later emphasizes that his son is beyond redemption and that "no one is going to save him, *not anyone*."
Millie leaves after Hanson's seductive remark, "I hope to see you
again while I'm here." She pauses outside the hotel corridor, expressing uncertainty over what she has heard.

However, before she learns the truth, Aldrich reveals the incestuous affair between father and former daughter-in-law in a striking
shot. As Hanson phones for a bucket of ice, his bedroom door opens
to reveal Virginia entering. The camera then pans left, reversing the
movement in the scene where Mike watched Velda practice ballet in
Kiss Me Deadly, showing that what we took for reality was something else. This scene not only symbolically depicts the secret incestuous relationship between Hanson and Virginia. It also subtly suggests the dark nature of the attraction between Burt and Millie. A
father sleeps with a wife. The son goes to the mother for comfort.
The father has symbolically castrated his son by sleeping with his
wife. After discovering them in a perverse reenactment of Freud's

primal scene scenario, Burt turns to Millie, who embodies the nurturing maternal figure he never knew as a child. He showers her with presents, expecting approval and gratification from a mother rather than a wife.

After mistaking Millie's defense of him before Hanson and Virginia outside their Cedar Courts apartment for conspiracy, Burt becomes "born again" into a parody of monstrous masculinity. He beats Millie and injures her hand by throwing a typewriter on it. Framed in a low-angle shot with the ceiling prominently appearing above him, Burt looks like a violent Mike Hammer relishing his power over a mother figure he feels has betrayed him. He also resembles a grinning Captain Cooney gloating over the body of his dying adversary in *Attack!* But he then realizes what he has done and collapses like a guilty child. By throwing the typewriter onto her hand, Burt violently reenacts a line he had earlier spoken during the visit of Colonel Hillyer (Leonard Mudie) about not wanting a wife to work. His action represents an insecure masculine wish to remove the threat of a working wife as well as make her dependent on him. Burt's regression becomes permanent the evening after he relives his incestuous discovery when Millie has made him visit his father. As Millie comforts Burt in a pietà position, she looks up at the ceiling. A shadow bar horizontally crosses her chest, embodying her realization of the relevant words she once spoke to her infantile spouse: "The present is built up of little bits of the past. You can't just pick and choose."

Millie's meeting with Dr. Couzzens (Sheppard Strudwick) brings this home to her. Couzzens responds to her assessment of Burt as resembling a child, "Yes. Like a child with his mother. But a child has to grow up." Millie realizes that she has to accept the challenge of mature responsibility even though it may result in the eventual recovery of a husband who may not accept her when cured. When Millie asks him, "Am I a neurotic need?" Couzzens remains silent. He can offer no guarantees for the future. Burt's eventual six-month incarceration in an insane asylum parallels the period of his marriage to Virginia. Alternating shots of Burt's treatment and Millie waiting use low-canted angles. They suggest that both husband and wife undergo a healing process having no secure guarantee. During these scenes, Millie obviously recalls the words she once spoke to a young husband who showered her with gifts like an adoring child: "The present is made up of little bits of the past. You can't throw it away as useless and worthless." She tells Liz of her own need for a cure: "Why can't I get my turn? Everybody needs help. I need help, too!" When Millie eventually sees Burt, he kneels before a flower garden tending it like a nurturing mother, a role implied by the suggestive remark of Nurse Evans (Maxine Cooper), "How does your garden grow?" Delivered by the same actress who appeared as the supportive Velda in *Kiss Me Deadly,* the comment has positive overtones. It suggests that Burt has now conquered his personal demons and become a gentle person no longer needing to resort to lies and violence as a means to prove his masculinity. He has already decided to break from his traumatic past by signing away the property that once belonged to his mother. This issue of property, desired by Mr. Hanson and Virginia, led to Burt's psychological collapse, one that may have been engineered deliberately by those family members close to him.

Millie now offers Burt his freedom and walks away. However, Burt follows her and reveals not just his recovery into real adulthood but also that he has decided not to pick and choose from little bits of the past. He asks about her injured hand, the "one I hurt with the typewriter," and kisses it. He notices that the "scars have almost gone." The comment also refers to their psychological scars. In an earlier scene, Millie recognized that any cure must be twofold in nature: "To live again. That's like being born again, isn't it, Doctor?" The words "born again" reverse those identical lines earlier spoken in uglier tones by Burt when he threatened Millie. In one of the most affirmative conclusions to a Robert Aldrich film, the camera moves right to left as Millie and Burt walk away into daylight. The movement reverses that earlier scene when the camera remained immobile in a high-angle shot as they walked into the darkness. No guarantee exists as to their future relationship. However, the ending appears positive. Burt and Millie overcome traumatic obstacles and may remain together. But not everything ends in such a tentatively positive manner, as *What Ever Happened to Baby Jane?* and *Hush . . . Hush, Sweet Charlotte* both show.

What Ever Happened to Baby Jane? represents Aldrich's return to the Hollywood card table. Its box-office success must have represented tinsel town's equivalent of a royal flush for Aldrich. Marketed as both a Gothic horror film and a melodramatic, campish "Hollywood on Hollywood" movie starring two legendary screen queens who had never acted together before but hated each other, the film was sure to attract attention. Although the director regarded its unofficial sequel, *Hush . . . Hush, Sweet Charlotte,* as a more realized film, the "bludgeoning close-ups, lurid angles, and shock cuts" represent a visual style appropriate to the hysterical text of a film dealing with the psychological wasteland of family trauma.[30]

What Ever Happened to Baby Jane? belongs to the horror of personality genre of the 1960s and anticipates the family horror film of the following decade.[31] The film does trade on an audience's lurid satisfaction in seeing two former Hollywood stars reduced to appearing in a genre they would have disdained during their heyday. However, despite the camp sensibility often greeting revivals of this film, the theme is more tragic and universal. *Baby Jane* represents another Aldrich appropriation and restructuring of a familiar Hollywood genre. It also evokes themes in his earlier films. During 1963 Aldrich referred to *Baby Jane* as a return to "the old days of *Attack!* and *The Big Knife.*"[32] But Aldrich denied the fact that the film was a specific attack on the Hollywood industry like *The Big Knife*: "It's not a story about films. It's a story about people. It's about the demise of a child prodigy who just didn't mature emotionally or intellectually. It's not against the industry, it's against her family."[33] Although D. H. Lawrence's axiom of trusting the text rather than the author holds good for most situations, a director may often supply certain comments that help the audience to focus on the key elements of the text rather than other distracting avenues. As Richard J. Evans points out in another context,

> As historians we clearly cannot recover a single, unalterably "true" meaning of the dispatch simply by reading it; on the other hand, we cannot impose any meaning we wish to on such a text either. We are limited by the words it contains, words which are not capable of an infinity of meanings as the postmodernists suggest. Moreover, the limits which the words of the text impose on the possibilities of interpretation are set to a large extent by the author who wrote them.[34]

Hollywood associations are not negligible, as seen by the film's use of extracts from old movies starring Bette Davis and Joan Crawford as well as the contemporary audience's knowledge of their loss of prestige thirty years later. However, other more dominant meanings are active. Aldrich saw the message of *The Big Knife* as resonating beyond its Hollywood context. Similarly, critics such as Arnold and Miller see *Baby Jane* as a tragedy of the waste of human potential and arrested development in which people who could have once been friends are now opposed to each other because of a situation resulting from family oppression. As in many other films, Aldrich never engages in simplistic definitions of good and evil. Arnold and Miller further note that "a variation of [the] 'who is the enemy' theme found in his war films also occurs in this film which asks 'who is the monster.' We can never take absolute sides either for or against Blanche or Jane. They are both villains, both victims. By the film's end, to condemn either would be an act of supreme hypocrisy."[35] This film also belongs to that popular modernist movement that influenced Aldrich and others in the postwar era. Rather than seeing the "plot as a model of duplicity with which scriptwriters seek to please," it is more appropriate to see it as playing on the false nature of typical audience identification.[36] Audiences may possibly identify with a helpless heroine and condemn an ugly sister (although the poignancy of Bette Davis's performance blunts this). But the film finally undermines normal audience expectations. On a second viewing it becomes possible to detect ironic intonations contained in the lines spoken by Joan Crawford and see that the "victim" is really playing passive-aggressive, sadomasochistic games contributing to a false sense of guilt on the part of a supposed "victimizer." Jane is eventually proved right about recognizing her sister as a pathological liar. As Arnold and Miller note, during the final beach scene when the camera focuses on the jeering audience members who laugh at Jane's regressive spectacular performance, "we see ourselves, the audience, who have also gawked, laughed, and pointed at the misfits on the screen. Thus it is also a moment of reevaluation, for now we understand Jane and Blanche and feel sympathy for their plight."[37]

What Ever Happened to Baby Jane? is indebted to two key components of the American horror film: the Gothic genre and the more modern "horror of personality" theme. Like Coral Courts in *Autumn Leaves,* the Hudson mansion looks normal on the outside. But it harbors a grim Gothic interior, symbolically representing the dark symbiotic relationship between the Hudson sisters. The glamorized portrait of Blanche Hudson in her room and the photographs of Baby Jane below represent contemporary equivalents of the ancestral portrait of Judge Pyncheon dominating the Gothic house in Nathaniel Hawthorne's *The House of the Seven Gables.* Both images and the house itself represent variants of the horror film's "claustrophobic family dominance, that is, the past's hold upon the present. *Curse of the Cat People, Meet Me in St. Louis,* and *Psycho* all feature Gothic houses."[38] The casting of Anna Lee, another aging Hollywood actress, as Mrs. Bates represents not only Aldrich's humorous reference to *Psycho* but also evokes her role in Val Lewton's *Bedlam* (1946), an early horror of personality movie. Following Aldrich's practice of inverting genres and Hollywood character types, Mrs. Bates represents a normal version of what Blanche and Jane could have become: a married woman whose daughter is played by none other than Bette Davis's adopted daughter, Barbara Merrill. This is just one of many ironic self-referential dualities structuring the text of *What Ever Happened to Baby Jane?*

As the title suggests, the film is about nostalgia and loss. But these features are by no means sentimental. They are inextricably connected to a dysfunctional family situation involving the removal of a normal childhood from a young daughter who is thrust into the role of family breadwinner. After her years of fame as "Baby Jane," the title character can only mourn her lost youth and retrogressively attempt to recapture an impossible past within the changed world of the present. Jane's dilemma represents not only those former Hollywood stars and child actors who cannot psychologically adjust to a different life but everyone traumatized by a dysfunctional family situation contaminating all caught in its trap, whether as victims or victimizers. Jane and Blanche represent two sides of the same dysfunctional family coin.

Baby Jane is certainly a hysterical text. But it is one reacting against the ruthless authoritarian mechanisms of family oppression. Audience escapism into laughter and camp interpretations may be as evasive as typical reactions to the implications of radical horror films by those not wishing to take the subject matter seriously. *Baby Jane* has many points of contact with Aldrich's other films. It is both a film noir and a melodrama. Its formally excessive nature and the grotesque elements contained within Bette Davis's performance also represent Aldrich's fascination with postwar modernist grotesque that formed so central a part of the contemporary popular culture.[39] Furthermore, as with *Autumn Leaves,* the film contains another parallel to the world of *Kiss Me Deadly,* as well as anticipating the climax of *The Legend of Lylah Clare,* by employing a significant line of dialogue not in the original screenplay. As Mrs. Bates and her daughter watch an old movie of Blanche's on television, an announcer (played by the ubiquitous Michael Fox, who reprises this role in *Lylah Clare*) interrupts the film with a dog food commercial. However, although Liza turns the volume down, Aldrich satirically inserts the name of the brand, "Iliad, the classical dog food."[40] Eighteenth-century miniature portraits also appear in Blanche's room, signifying her relationship with the authoritarian classical world of *Kiss Me Deadly*'s Dr. Soberin and Mr. Hanson of *Autumn Leaves*. Such features again demonstrate Aldrich's dark modernist sensibilities. The classical Hollywood world represented by Bette Davis and Joan Crawford no longer exists. Like *Kiss Me Deadly*'s high culture references, it is now redundant and little better than a convenient excuse for allowing dog meat television commercials to interrupt the program.

Aldrich never cheats the viewer throughout the entire film. The credit sequence begins and ends with a Baby Jane doll. The credits open with titles emerging from the dark, broken head of the doll, symbolizing the devastated psychological state of the heroine. They end by showing the same scene. But this time, Aldrich's personal credits as producer and director accompany the shattered image. Aldrich shows where his sympathies actually lie. He challenges the audience to read the film in a more critical manner than most Hollywood productions. As Arnold and Miller point out, both sisters are crippled. Blanche is paraplegic because of a car accident in 1935 for which Jane was held responsible. However, "of the two, Jane is the more seriously wounded victim. Because of her father's profound influence over her during their vaudeville years and because she associates success and self-esteem solely with childhood and her father's approval of her performance on stage, Jane lives literally in, and for, the past, rummaging often through dated clippings from *Variety* and fondling 'Baby Jane' dolls symbolic of her faded stardom."[41] It does not seem accidental that Aldrich requested Jane's favorite song, "I've Written a Letter to Daddy," and the title theme from *Hush . . . Hush, Sweet Charlotte* for his memorial service.[42] He identified strongly with traumatized family victims who suffered at the hands of both their parents. But he also condemned those siblings and other relatives who continued to torment their victims with authoritarian psychological control mechanisms originating from within the nuclear family.

The opening image of *Baby Jane* suggests that the situation of the Hudson sisters is by no means unique. We hear an adult male voice against a darkened screen perversely suggesting sexual molestation as a child cries: "Want to see it again, little girl? It shouldn't frighten you." However, the next shot shows a camera lens opening up in a disjunctive modernist fashion to show a sinister jack-in-the-box doll emerge to frighten a young girl with her mother. She clings to her mother's dress for comfort. The next scene shows the 1917 marquee announcing Baby Jane's performance. After Jane's "family values" performance of "I've Written a Letter to Daddy," watched resentfully by her older sister, Blanche, accompanied by their passive mother, a dysfunctional family situation erupts with Jane now dominating her father. The spectators may regard this as an act of bad manners caused by a lack of parental control. But Jane may also wish to avenge herself on a figure who has controlled her young life and made her the family breadwinner. After successfully demanding an ice cream for herself and her sister (who refuses the offer, to her father's chagrin), Jane walks away. Mrs. Hudson then attempts to comfort her eldest daughter, who coldly affirms that she will never forget the treatment she receives from her father and younger sister. During this scene Aldrich shows a man with a satanic dark beard wearing a black costume directly behind Blanche, as if prompting the audience to consider who is the real "bad seed" in the Hudson family. An offscreen voice from the crowd watching Jane's tantrums emphasizes the real origins of the film's future violent tensions: "I always say that it's the parents' fault in cases like this." But parental fault may involve questions other than lack of discipline. It may also encompass a manipulative father who forces his child into a situation she does not want in the first place, which distorts her personality for the rest of her life. Jane's passive mother who just stands by represents another culpable family member.

The scene changes to 1935. A producer (Wesley Addy) and director (Bert Freed, who wears his tie in a Robert Aldrich fashion) groan over the adult Jane's bad performances and Blanche's contractual demand that her sister make one film for each of hers before the night of the fatal accident that cripples Blanche and makes her dependent on Jane's services. As they go outside, they pass Blanche's monstrously gigantic car, another element Aldrich supplies as a clue to his viewers. When one enquires, "Who do they make monsters like this for?" the other replies, "For Blanche Hudson."

Several decades later, the audience sees the changes the years have brought to the two sisters. Whereas Blanche retains her star mannerisms, deliberately evoking "Joan Crawford" as she watches one of her old films, *Sadie McKee* (1934), on television, Jane has degenerated into a bloated drunken hag whose "childishly fussy clothes" and "heavy, unfashionable make-up" reveal the futility of her attempts to arrest the progress of time. Jane is in a sad state of arrested development. As Blanche tells her cleaning woman Elvira (Maidie Norman), Jane was not like that once: "You didn't know her then, when she was young. It wasn't that she was pretty—she was different. . . . She was . . . alive." Although a first viewing of the film usually places the audience against Jane, the climactic revelation and later viewing reveal that Blanche has manipulated her sister into ugliness and child-like dependence as an act of revenge. She felt antagonism toward her in 1917 and attempted to humiliate her publicly on screen during her Hollywood years in the 1930s. Despite her disability, Blanche plays devastating manipulative psychological games on her sister, contributing to already deeply ingrained feelings of guilt and infantile dependence. We learn later than Jane is correct when she tells her sister, "You're a liar, you're just a liar. You always were," as she reacts angrily against Blanche's plan to sell the house that their father bought for them from Jane's own earnings. Blanche has always used "the accident" as a passive-aggressive psychological weapon against her sister, to whom she allots "pocket money" as she would a dependent child. Although Elvira later tells Jane, "You've got to act like a grown woman like anybody else," both she and the audience are oblivious of the fact that Blanche is responsible for this arrested development.

When Jane attracts the attentions of a gentleman caller, Edwin Flagg (Victor Buono), whose arrested development parallels her own, she reacts angrily against her sister, who "always tried to stop me having friends—anything I ever wanted."[43] After physically making Blanche more dependant on her in revenge for her treatment over the years and killing Elvira, Jane decides to escape again to the Santa Monica shore where she had rehearsed long ago as a young girl with her father and sister. She desperately yearns for the friends she once had whom Blanche deprived her of during their Hollywood days. At this point, the dying Blanche relinquishes control over her sister and tells the truth about an accident she caused herself. Additional material contained in the original screenplay fully reveals the nature of Blanche's guilt:

We're sisters . . . I should have looked after you—but . . . I lied to you— cheated you. Spent my whole life trying to make you suffer. . . . I hated

you when we were children. You had everything, and I hated you. . . .
When Father died and I started making the money I tried to get even—
I kept you working—ran your life, stopped you marrying or even having friends—just to make you dependent on me. But you fought
back—wouldn't give in. So in the end I had to make you waste your
whole life thinking you'd crippled me.

Blanche thus admits that she has taken over the role of an oppressive patriarch. When Jane hears her confession, she poignantly says,
"All this time, we could have been friends?" It is one of the most
touching lines in the cinema of Robert Aldrich. After Blanche mentions that she continued to make Jane believe that she was responsible for the accident, she concludes, "You weren't even ugly then—I
made you that way. . . . I even did that." As she speaks these lines,
the screech of seagulls appears prominently on the soundtrack in a
manner evocative of those winged creatures symbolizing psychological tensions in Alfred Hitchcock's *The Birds* (1963). Jane then
goes to fetch the ice cream she wanted to give to her sister many
years ago. But this time she offers it in a spirit of generosity. Although the scene when she appears rejuvenated seems awkward in
terms of realistic conventions, it is symbolically justified. Like Millie
in *Autumn Leaves,* Jane has been "born again." But this time the revelation leads to the comforting realms of insanity and a return to the
past. She can no longer live in a callous world of the present. Although the climax is tragic and poignant, it represents a blessed release for Jane Hudson, who has suffered the torments of a hellish authoritarian control for most of her adolescent and adult life.[44]
However, as in *Autumn Leaves,* this particular tragedy of a dysfunctional family is not really isolated from economic circumstances, as
two key scenes show. When Edwin phones his mother after Jane refuses to let him into the house following the murder of Elvira, a bill-
board appears prominently in the background: "FOR UNDERTAK-
ING UTTER MCKINLY UNDERSTANDS—FOR $100." Earlier,
when Elvira waited at a bus stop following her dismissal by Jane,
the sign on her seat advertised a company called "American Mon-
eymakers." These two billboards are certainly not accidental within
the context of the film.

Aldrich aptly described *Hush . . . Hush, Sweet Charlotte* as "cannibal-
time in Dixie!!!"[45] Despite this humorous aside, the film represents a
companion piece to *Baby Jane.* It again deals with emotional cannibalism within an authoritarian family. As in *Baby Jane,* others will con-

tinue the process begun by a ruthless father. The film opens with individual shots of the Hollis mansion in 1927, resembling introductory shots in *The Big Knife* and *Autumn Leaves*. But this time the voice of an angry father fills the soundtrack. After zooming in to an exterior shot, the image changes to show Sam Hollis (Victor Buono) in his study. The camera then zooms back to reveal him confronting John Mayhew (Bruce Dern). Sam expresses anger not only at a married man's seduction of his daughter but also at the appropriation of his "property" by a lower-class person: "This mansion belonged to my father before you *people* stepped off the cattle boat!" In a room containing antique furniture, nineteenth-century portraits, and a classical bust, Sam speaks reverently about his father to an intruder he regards as "Jewel Mayhew's husband," not an individual in his own right. John Mayhew is also regarded as the property of his Southern-bred wife as much as Charlotte is Sam's: "I fought to build this house and aim to keep it. I don't have a son to give it to, only Charlotte. You're not going to get my house and my daughter. I'm going to see to that. I created both and I'm going to keep them." John challenges Sam's incestuous possessiveness: "Your daughter is not a little girl anymore and she's going to have other men in her life besides you." Sam then ceases his violent movements and temporarily sees the truth in his rival's statement. However, he orders the end of the relationship. The scene concludes with the defeated suitor framed in a diagonal low-angle shot dominated by Sam's huge portrait towering above him on the wall.

As Silver and Ursini note, the Hollis mansion bears an "uncanny resemblance to the *Baby Jane* house," evoking not only traditional Gothic fiction but also a primal battleground where individuals struggle with inner conflicts.[46] Family trauma, class barriers, thwarted sexuality, and incestuous possessiveness pervert the lives of the major characters as much as they do in *Baby Jane*. Aldrich metaphorically represents the inner tensions in the Hollis mansion during the party scene when a young Southern belle (Alida Aldrich) searches for Charlotte to tell her a secret. Informed by a beau (William Aldrich) that Charlotte was last seen dancing with John Mayhew, the belle passes a scowling Sam Hollis. The camera then reverses its direction to follow the progress of a phallic champagne bottle thrust into an ice bucket. It passes a portrait in the ballroom. Like verbal and visual clues in *Baby Jane*, this briefly glimpsed portrait supplies the alert viewer with information relevant to the rest of the film. The portrait shows Sam seated between his two "daughters." Charlotte is on his left illuminated by bright colors. But her cousin, Miriam Deering (whom will we meet later in the film), appears in shadow on Sam's right. This portrait does not feature in the revised final screenplay that Lukas Heller and Robert Aldrich collaborated on. It is most likely Aldrich's addition to the film. When Charlotte discovers her lover's mutilated body, the guests naturally assume that she is guilty of the crime. Thirty-seven years later Charlotte still inhabits the Hollis mansion and is regarded as the Lizzie Borden of Louisiana. Like Jane Hudson, she lapses into madness until the truth is finally revealed.

Hush . . . Hush, Sweet Charlotte was conceived as an informal sequel to *What Ever Happened to Baby Jane?* after Aldrich worked on the disastrous *4 for Texas* (1963). Originally intended to reunite key figures involved in the earlier film such as Bette Davis, Joan Crawford, and Henry Farrell (author of the original *Baby Jane* novel), the project fell apart in May because of Crawford's illness and Farrell's departure from the set. After Aldrich persuaded Olivia de Havilland to replace Crawford and Lukas Heller to redraft the screenplay, production began again and finished in October. Unfortunately, because of adverse circumstances affecting the production, the film is not as successful as its predecessor and appears contrived in many ways. However, the poignancy of Davis's performance and the supporting roles of Hollywood veterans like de Havilland, Joseph Cotten, Cecil Kellaway, Mary Astor, Agnes Moorehead, and Aldrich's own repertory company, including Wesley Addy, George Kennedy, Percy Helton, and William Campbell, often compensate for the plot's artificial nature. The casting of Cotten and Moorehead again evokes the director's fondness for casting former members of Orson Welles's Mercury Theatre in his films. And despite the flaws, the film's reworking of the traumatic family territory of *Baby Jane* is not without interest. Arnold and Miller note that

> in both films, the central characters are made to suffer intolerably for crimes they never committed, with the surprising and liberating truth being revealed only at the end. In both films, intense rivalry between two young girls for the approval and affection of a father figure produces in these adult females, serious identity problems and warped value systems. In both, a father's too possessive love for his daughter leaves her with permanent psychic damage.[47]

Like its predecessor, *Charlotte* also operates as a metacommentary on Hollywood itself. The film is a dark Gothic version of a twentieth-century *Gone with the Wind,* revealing the toll on the human personality that property and patriarchal traditions demand. Although Olivia de Havilland is well known for her role in the earlier film, Bette Davis was also one of the contenders for the prized role of Scarlett O'Hara. She now plays this character later in life in a 1960s Gothic noir rather than a 1930s Technicolor film. Charlotte refuses to move out of her condemned mansion because of its significance as a morbid living shrine to the memory of a father she believes responsible for the murder of her suitor and whose guilt she bears as penance for her own adulterous sin over the decades. Sam refused to relinquish Charlotte and his mansion to John Mayhew. John obediently complied with the law of the father. Both men contributed to Charlotte's psychic incestuous dilemma, a fact made clear in the fantasy ballroom sequence later in the film when both appear with their heads significantly tilted in the same direction.[48]

Drew Bayliss (Joseph Cotten) jilted Miriam after the family scandal in 1927. Miriam has worked in "public relations" (an Aldrich joke?) since she left Louisiana. But she has been blackmailing Jewell Mayhew (Mary Astor) for many decades after discovering that she is the real murderer. Before the audience discovers Miriam's true character, Aldrich films her with revealing horizontal shadow bars across her chest, a technique he used to suggest ambiguous motivations for characters in *Autumn Leaves* and *Attack!* Even before Miriam actually appears, Aldrich opens and closes a sequence with an overhead shot of a staircase reminiscent of imagery seen in *Kiss Me Deadly.* It begins with a representative of the outside world (Luke Standish [Wesley Addy]) leaving the Hollis mansion and concludes with Charlotte's hopes for Miriam's return: "She's the only one who can help. She's got to come." Introduced by DeVol's lush Hollywood theme (reminiscent of musical leitmotifs used to introduce well-known actresses as in *The Loretta Young Show*), Miriam returns. But her initial lines appear more evocative of a lady of the manor out to claim her rightful inheritance: "It's just as I left it." Finally, Charlotte takes revenge on her two tormentors, Miriam and Drew, when she discovers their plot, as well as finding out that both her beloved daddy and her devoted suitor John Mayhew were actually philanderers. Big Sam was not the morally upright figure Charlotte supposed him to be. She finally learns the irony involving the waste of her life for many decades.

The next morning a crowd of gossips arrives to see Charlotte taken away to the mental asylum, which is now her only sanctuary.

Stripped of illusions concerning father and lover and denied the possibility of a late romance with British insurance agent Willis (Cecil Kellaway), who saw her briefly many years ago, Charlotte exhibits a dignity contrasting with the vulgar behavior of the spectators and tabloid crime reporter Paul Marchand (William Campbell). She puts down the music box that John had given her many years before and gallantly moves toward an uncertain future in the dignified Southern tradition she attempted to maintain throughout her life. Again, this is another scene that does not occur in the revised final screenplay and probably originates with Aldrich, who saw his heroine poignantly rejecting an illusionary past that has dominated her for most of her life. As Sheriff Standish earlier remarked, "She's not really sick. She just acts that way because people expect it." Earlier in the film, a black woman responded to her friend's comment about Charlotte, "She sure acts crazy," with, "I wouldn't bet on it. I wouldn't bet on it at all." Before presenting her with Jewell's letter of confession, Wills comments to Marchand, "Charlotte Hollis suffered all her life for a murder she never committed." As Charlotte drives away looking at her family home for the last time, she leaves free and unburdened of her past demons. Although it is too late for her to start a new life, she can finally leave the scene of her family torment behind her. She now possesses attributes of dignity and sanity that may enable her to struggle against the adversities she will encounter during her remaining years.

Lukas Heller's screenplay for *The Killing of Sister George* followed closely the original Frank Marcus play in which British comedian Beryl Reid had revealed her talents as a serious actress. Combs regards Aldrich's attraction to a project that seems to have little to offer—apart from the commercial possibilities of its lesbian theme—as "shrouded in mystery."[49] But the film does contain parallels to his other work. Other more qualified critics may explore issues of lesbian spectatorship, production history, and the problematic question of positive images of minority groups.[50] But the key issue here involves the question of Aldrich's authorship.

The Killing of Sister George complements the director's treatments of the tragic plight of individuals and their relationship to an increasingly hostile environment. We must also remember Aldrich's treatment of lesbians in *World for Ransom* and *The Legend of Lylah Clare* as well as his sympathy for those individuals who have psychologically suffered from entrapment within a negative family situation. Although we know virtually nothing about the past histories of Sister George's characters apart from Childie's (Susannah York) abandonment of her illegitimate child at the age of fifteen and the fact that Mrs. Mercy Croft's (Coral Browne) deceased husband was a mountain climber (perhaps seeking escape from his marriage?), the film's main characters are all trapped in a hostile world. It is sometimes one of their own making. Despite Aldrich's sympathetic view of the tragic dilemma of Sister George, he depicts the self-destructive elements in her character that finally end her relationship with Childie. Furthermore, despite the director's sympathetic and nonprurient treatment of the lesbian community in the London Gateways club, he also shows that even membership in an alternative community does not provide a utopian escape from personal and social problems. Beryl Reid's Sister George adopts the butch mannerisms of the lesbian stereotype, playing an oppressive father to Childie's femme figure, while Mrs. Mercy Croft "comes out" as the predatory vampire icon.[51] Like Charlotte Hollis, these characters may behave in ways society expects them to and not according to their actual personal desires.

The Killing of Sister George is not one of Aldrich's major cinematic achievements. It operates on a theatrical performance level, recording for posterity Beryl Reid's great performance in the title role. However, as Arnold and Miller note, it is not "a work to be ashamed of" and "remained one of Aldrich's favorites."[52] As in *The Big Knife,* *What Ever Happened to Baby Jane?* and *The Legend of Lylah Clare,* the entertainment industry plays a major role in destroying the relationship between June Buckridge/George and Childie. Also, like Clifford Odets, Aldrich recognized that tragic flaws in the individual persona could prevent personal and social liberation. Although this feature remains in the background of *The Killing of Sister George,* it influences its structure and may provide the reason why Aldrich became attracted to this very unusual property.

Like Jane Hudson and Charlotte Hollis, June is an older woman facing the onset of aging and insecurity. She takes out her tormented feelings on Childie in an abusive manner. This not only echoes Captain Cooney's and Burt's treatment at the hands of their respective fathers but also evokes the aggressive sibling treatment that Jane and Miriam mete out to Blanche and Charlotte. Like Charlie Castle and Lylah Clare, June is trapped within by the arbitrary performance requirements of the entertainment industry. She plays a stereotypical role in a BBC soap opera and definitely knows more about television performance than her snobbish ratings-winning rival, Leo Lockhart (Ronald Fraser). She is as much a "dog food" product as those other entertainers Jane Hudson and Lylah Clare. Although more honest about the type of weekly performance she grinds out than most of her fellow artists, George also knows that she has nowhere else to go once her contract runs out. As the patient and sympathetic Freddie (played by gay actor Hugh Paddick) says to the television writers after George's exit from the series, "What sort of job is she going to get when she leaves us?" It is a line that does not occur in the original play. The character of Sister George is based on Ellis Powell, the original Mrs. Dale on the long-running BBC radio soap opera *Mrs. Dale's Diary*, who was arbitrarily dismissed from the series and committed suicide after working in the uncongenial job of a nightclub hostess. This would have been very much in the mind of British audiences when they heard Freddie's remark.[53] As a result, George becomes alcoholic (a typical pitfall affecting certain individuals working in the entertainment industry) and engages in a series of incidents giving the austere BBC corporation bad publicity, which eventually leads to the elimination of her character from a long-running television series. Like Jane Hudson, George becomes so identified with her fictional character that she is in danger of losing her own identity.

Her aberrant behavior has much in common with that of Charlotte Hollis, of whom Sheriff Standish remarks that she "just acts that way because people expect it." Also, George's on-set behavior provides welcome entertainment to veteran actors such as Ted Baker (Cyril Delavanti) who harbor no illusions about the only type of production they can work on during their declining years. Freddie and his friends secretly enjoy George's subversive behavior toward snobbish BBC executives and pretentious actors such as Leo. However, like Jane Hudson's "Baby Jane," "George" has taken over the identity of June Buckridge. Thus, Childie and Mrs. Croft address her as such rather than by her actual name. Like several Aldrich characters, George is trapped by a false identity. Like Jane and Charlotte, she is now too old to change her routine. An illusionary fantasy identity created by the entertainment industry destroys her opportunity of moving on to more satisfactory roles or finding other more satisfying forms of existence.

Although lesbian, the alternative nature of her lifestyle cannot provide her with salvation. She is wracked by personal insecurities and will soon face betrayal. Aldrich never believed in easy answers for any dilemma, and his depiction of lesbian characters here illustrates the same concerns. Like Stanley Kubrick, he never engaged in the illusionary depiction of positive characters and escapist solutions. What Mario Falsetto states about Kubrick's depiction of women has much in common with Aldrich's view of heterosexual and lesbian characters: "Kubrick's male characters are generally as negative, weak, flawed, monstrous or victimized as his female characters. If Kubrick's view of humankind—male and female—is negative, it is not a selective view; everyone is in trouble. Everyone bears some responsibility for arriving at this point in evolution. Kubrick's world indicts good and bad, male and female alike."[54]

Whereas June plays the role of Sister George, the thirty-two-year-old Alice McNaught engages in the retrogressive performance of "Childie," a character she escapes into to disavow guilt for abandoning an illegitimate daughter conceived at the age of fifteen. Rather than helping her develop toward maturity, George encourages Childie's regressive behavior. Like Blanche Hudson and Miriam Deering, she uses the past as a weapon to control her victim. But both George and Childie perform roles that harm whatever potential directions exist in their personalities. They are little better than warring factions within a traditional patriarchal family structure. Both women retreat into a world of fantasy rather than face the realities of their actual situation. Reality and fantasy merge in dangerous ways.

Aldrich depicts the negative aspects of that merger. For Sally Hussey, the notorious seduction scene 176 contains elements of lesbian pleasure in shoring up "the collapse of gender and sexuality while soliciting its collapse to formally represent the female orgasm."[55] The mother-daughter imagery involving Mercy and Childie does contain a maternal metaphor that allows for the possibility of lesbian pleasure within this scene. Hussey provides an extremely interesting reading here. But it must be seen within a specific context. Childie and Mercy betray George at this point in the film. If George's masculine-butch stereotype is problematic, then so, too, is Mercy's assumption of the maternal role George never acted out with Childie. Childie moves from being dominated by one regressive family model to another. She transfers her affections from the "masculine-paternal" role typified by the phallic cigar–smoking and hard liquor–drinking aspects of George's male-influenced persona to Mercy's "caring mother" figure. Mercy thus manipulatively adopts a different type of role than George. She caresses Childie's favorite doll as she moves toward seducing her adopted daughter. Before Mercy moves into Childie's room, she clutches the doll Emmeline to her chest and laments, "Oh what a shame, are you really so lonely?" Hussey's comments are as follows: "Transferring the object loss (Childie's daughter) into an ego loss (Mercy's loneliness) in the scene (as we aren't aware at this stage that Childie has an abandoned daughter), Aldrich presents a narcissistic lesbian fantasy through scene 176."[56] However, despite whatever positive aspects this narcissistic fantasy may have for its two protagonists, it is still one influenced by a patriarchal system. Despite the fact that Childie initiates Mercy's movements, the relationship is as false and artificial as that romantic meeting between Edwin Flagg and Jane Hudson in *What Ever Happened to Baby Jane?* There, both partners indulge in narcissistic performances and conceal their real natures. The encounter between Mercy and Childie is little different.

Aldrich may not have been conscious of the implications of this scene. But it does have several associations with the negative role of the family in society that he acquired from the plays of Clifford Odets and transformed in his own way. The collapse of the boundaries between reality and fantasy is often dangerous in Aldrich films, though sometimes it may provide a final blessed release for victims such as Jane Hudson. Hussey notes such a collapse in scene 176:

> The collapse of unconscious and conscious representation, or fantasy and representation, is however previously suggested through Mercy's extending Childie's fantasy with the dolls. As she talks to Emmeline, Aldrich literalizes the merging between reality and fantasy (In point of fact, the principal theme of the film is that George is unable to separate her character from her life, exemplified by the mise en scene by the television that frames her persona, Sister George. For, in that empty studio at the film's conclusion, George opens Sister George's coffin, which falls apart as she yells, "Even the bloody coffin's a fake").[57]

Like *The Big Knife* and *Attack!* the film ends with an overhead shot surrounding the character with a prevailing darkness that will soon engulf her. Realizing that she has nowhere else to go, George begins to practice the sounds of her new character Clarabelle, the cow for an animated series offered to her earlier by Mercy Croft. Like Marian Castle, she has probably relapsed into insanity. But here it is not entirely caused by others but may also result from her own personal demons. After destroying the studio set, she begins to perform her new role. As Silver and Ursini eloquently remark, "In a series of cuts which echo the craning at the end of *The Big Knife*, the camera moves to a high angle and the screen darkens to a small square in which the broken George sits reembracing the refuge of make-believe while mooing pathetically."[58]

Aldrich produced but did not direct *What Ever Happened to Aunt Alice?* (1969). However, the film is worth considering because of its affinity to other Aldrich melodramas dealing with the psychotic consequences of female aging in a materialistic society. Probably deciding not to repeat himself, Aldrich assigned the director's role to Bernard Girard, who was replaced by Lee H. Katzin after four weeks.[59] Based on *The Forbidden Garden* by Ursula Curtis, a property Aldrich purchased in 1967, the film represents another bleak indictment of the havoc caused by capitalism on the human situation. Hearing from her lawyer that her recently deceased husband left "no assets, only liabilities," Clare Marrable (Geraldine Page) moves to the desert community outside Tucson, Arizona, at the invitation of her nephew, George Lawson (Peter Brandon). His greedy and adulterous wife, Julia (Joan Harrington), articulates the real reason at a party where Clare performs the role of a wheelchair-bound rich aunt: "Aunt Clare. She's got so much money. That's why you invited her to live in Arizona." However, both Clare and her relatives are engaged in playing false roles because they are not as affluent as she believes. Theodore Apstein's screenplay contains several key lines that also relate to Aldrich's dark universe in *Baby Jane* and *Charlotte* where human beings are valued solely in terms of economic value. Replying to George's comment concerning Clare's belief that she has wealthy relatives, Julia replies, "We've failed her. But she may be playing the same game."

After discovering that her husband has left her little except a few personal possessions and an old stamp album, Clare moves to Arizona and begins murdering a series of housekeepers after she has persuaded them to invest their savings in the stock market. She buries the bodies in deep pits intended for saplings and becomes paranoid each time an adopted dog of her new neighbors begins sniffing the evidence. Possessively affirming the status of both her property and her boundary, Clare eventually finishes off her latest housekeeper Alice Dimmock (Ruth Gordon), who has come to investigate the disappearance of her former employee Edith Tinsley (Mildred Dunnock). After disposing of Alice's body in a car, Clare plays at expressing shock at the discovery of the body for the benefit of George and Julia. But they are more concerned about the condition of their lost car than anything else. This leads Clare's neighbor, Harriet Vaughan (Rosemary Forsyth), to act as the film's moral conscience in expressing the line, "Nobody seems to care," condemning the inhumane materialism embodied in the characters of Clare, George, and Julia. It parallels June's Sidney Greenstreet imitation—"There's not enough kindness in the world"—in *The Killing of Sister George* as well as Edwin Flagg's self-serving (yet ironically correct) comment concerning money in *What Ever Happened to Baby Jane?*—"I mean to say, it's not that important is it? Not like relationships between people and that kind of thing."

After attempting to murder Harriet and her nephew, Clare wakes up the next morning to find her beloved garden in ruins. She now faces the consequences of her actions. Seeing her garden torn up to exhume the bodies of her victims, she envisages her enchanted realm as being more alive than those humans she has used and abused in the past: "They've torn you up by your roots." Before she relapses into insanity, she learns that her late husband had invested all his money into his stamp collection. Her final lines affirm the dark nature of a capitalist ethos that has motivated her murderous activities: "This is my garden. This is my house. This is my land. You're trespassing." Earlier, Alice had worked on Clare's capitalist greed by announcing an economic insecurity common to most Americans: "I'm not a greedy woman but it irks me how little my money earns in the bank." Clare now sees irony not only behind her murderous activities, which have now been revealed to be entirely unnecessary, but also concerning a husband who has played a posthumous joke on her: "He must have hated me more than I hated him."

Aldrich never persuaded potential investors into financing *The Greatest Mother of 'Em All*, even after filming a twenty-minute promotion reel.[60] He attributed lack of interest to the inadequacies of Alexandra Hay's performance as a fifteen-year-old victim of her mother's callous ambitions as well as the fact that the cycle of "Hollywood on Hollywood" films had passed. Another factor may have been the addition of sexually explicit scenes to the screenplay, originally written by A. I. Bezzerides, by Leon Griffiths. Although it is problematic to comment on a project Aldrich never completed, the actual Bezzerides screenplay contains many Aldrich elements that may one day appear in finished form similar to Steven Spielberg's completion of Stanley Kubrick's *A-1* project. The screenplay contains an indictment of the callous nature of the family reminiscent of *Attack!* and other Aldrich melodramas as well as reworking the major theme of *The Legend of Lylah Clare* concerning the obsession of a burnt-out director, Sean Howard (played by Peter Finch in the promotional reel), with a young adolescent. As performed by Ann Sothern, Dolly Murdoch is a monstrous parent, pushing her young daughter into an entertainment career she lacks the talent for. Like Jane Hudson's father, she uses and abuses her child, making her work as a cocktail waitress and stripper and encouraging her to sleep her way to success. The screenplay represents a dark version of *Gypsy* cast in Aldrich's dark terms, revealing the director as one continuing the family horror legacy begun in the 1960s by Alfred Hitchcock in *Psycho* and William Castle in *Homicidal* (1961).[61] Several lines in the Bezzerides screenplay echo the emotional damage caused by parents to their children in *Baby Jane* and *Charlotte*. At one point, Gina Murdoch criticizes her mother: "You filled my head with dreams. Impossible dreams. And suddenly sitting here, watching myself, I woke up. No more dreams!"[62] In a later scene, after Dolly has urged Gina to claim that she is pregnant by Howard, her boyfriend, Jack, urges her to become independent of her mother. Gina speaks fondly of her deceased lover: "He kept asking over and over: Whose little girl are you? I always gave him the right answer. I'm my *own* girl (whispers) But all the time, inside, I kept saying . . . (through gritted teeth) I'm Mummy-mummy-mummy. . . ." When Jack's friend, Moxie, tells him that he is glad he hasn't got a mother, Jack replies, "You're just lucky, that's all. Not *everybody* can be lucky." Eventually Dolly not only indirectly causes her daughter's suicide by her oppressive control but also relapses into insanity in the Bezzerides version.

As Arnold and Miller comment, the finished screenplay would have probably caused Aldrich more of the same censorship problems that he faced with *The Killing of Sister George* as well as the *Lolita* aspect of both screenplay versions.[63] Another collaboration between Aldrich and Bezzerides might have resulted in the director finally achieving his desired aim of critically condemning the industry he worked in for the promotion of false illusions that echoed oppressive family mechanisms. This was not to be. However, Aldrich left an important melodramatic legacy, not only one relevant to the family horror film genre but also one as critical of the status quo as his other work would be. Perhaps it is now time to reevaluate the director's melodramatic legacy and see another example of his work that tends to usually be regarded as exclusively masculine in nature.

NOTES

1. Ian Jarvie, "Hysteria and Authoritarianism in the Films of Robert Aldrich," *Film Culture* 22–23 (1961): 111.

2. Jarvie, "Hysteria and Authoritarianism in the Films of Robert Aldrich," 96.

3. Jarvie, "Hysteria and Authoritarianism in the Films of Robert Aldrich," 108–9.

4. For the differences between the stage and film versions of *The Big Knife,* see Tony Williams, "*The Big Knife,*" in *Video Versions: Film Adaptations of Plays on Video,* ed. Thomas L. Erskine and James M. Welsh (Westport, Conn.: Greenwood Press, 2001), 29–30; and Tony Williams, "*The Big Knife,*" in *The Encyclopedia of Stage Plays into Film,* ed. John C. Tibbetts and James M. Welsh (New York: Facts on File, Inc., 2001), 31–32. Aldrich explicitly recognized Jack Palance as embodying similarities to the late John Garfield. See Francois Truffaut, "Rencontre avec Robert Aldrich," *Cahiers du Cinema* 64 (1956): 7.

5. See Alain Silver and Elizabeth Ward, *Robert Aldrich: A Guide to References and Resources* (Boston: G. K. Hall, 1979), 25.

6. Charles Higham and Joel Greenberg, *The Celluloid Muse: Hollywood Directors Speak* (London: Angus and Robertson, 1969), 26.

7. John Belton writes, "By 'isometric' I mean actual stress against one's self, strained and restrained gestures. Each character becomes trapped between the inevitability of his situation and profession and his own personal feelings" (*Cinema Stylists* [Metuchen, N.J.: Scarecrow Press, 1983], 237). Belton's comments about the performance style seen in Howard Hawks's *The Dawn Patrol* (1930) can equally apply to Palance's acting in this film.

8. Smiley earlier remarks to Charlie, "In my end of the business you have to know types," thus equating his role with the Mafioso boss performance of Stanley Hoff in his first confrontation with Charlie. Wendell Corey's character anticipates the role of Robert Duvall in *The Godfather* (1972).

9. See Truffaut, "Rencontre avec Robert Aldrich," 10. Roger Tailleur aptly describes Charlie as the "messiah of the New Deal broken by the Hollywood Inquisition" ("Avènement du Cinema Americain," *Positif* 11 [1956]: 23).

10. The Shakespearean references obviously derive from Odets's original play, with Charlie combining the indecisiveness of Hamlet with the persona of Macbeth, as one of his lines shows: "You murdered Cass. I was there. I saw him do it." Marian later emerges in the final scenes of the film with her dress covered with blood, vainly attempting to wipe stains from a cigarette case very much in the manner of Lady Macbeth. She had earlier evoked a line from *The Merchant of Venice* with her remark to Charlie, "You've given the studio their pound of flesh." When Smiley leaves after Charlie's final meeting with Stanley, he tells him, "You threw away a kingdom today."

11. See John Calendo, "Robert Aldrich Says 'Life Is Worth Living,'" *Andy Warhol's Interview* 3 (1973): 30.

12. Alain Silver and James Ursini, *What Ever Happened to Robert Aldrich? His Life and His Films* (New York: Limelight Editions, 1995), 207. For a pessimistic interpretation of the ending, see also Edwin T. Arnold and Eugene I. Miller, *The Films and Career of Robert Aldrich* (Knoxville: University of Tennessee Press, 1986), 51.

13. See Arnold and Miller, *The Films and Career of Robert Aldrich*, 138–39.

14. See *"Du Pont Show of the Week,* May 22, 1963," *Variety Television Reviews 8, 1963–1965* (New York: Garland, 1987). This negative review of a production originally directed by Franklin Schaffner should have warned Aldrich away from a project attempting "to put the legendary tale of the dybbuk into show biz terms," described as "notable for its corn, melodramatics, and sheer absurdity." Self-reflexivity, akin to *The Big Knife*'s name-dropping, also appeared in references to actual stars such as Elizabeth Taylor and Kim Novak!

15. According to William Aldrich (telephone conversation, 18 September 2002), Novak was the third choice after a very meticulous search. The television Lylah was based on Marilyn Monroe. Jean Rouverol (telephone conversation, 17 September 2002) has also confirmed that Novak was not Aldrich's original choice.

16. Hugo Butler and Jean Rouverol, *The Legend of Lylah Clare*, screenplay, 1 May 1967, 116–17, 124.

17. Calendo, "Robert Aldrich Says 'Life Is Worth Living,'" 33.

18. See F. R. Leavis, *The Great Tradition* (New York: Doubleday, 1954), 101–54.

19. Calendo, "Robert Aldrich Says 'Life Is Worth Living,'" 33.

20. The original screenplay also mentions that Langner discovered Lylah working in a butcher's shop according to the official studio biography, a point mentioned in the film along with her real origins. A later scene in Zarkan's biopic of Elsa re-creates his meeting with her in a brothel, which is now possible because of a relaxed production code, rather than the butcher's shop meeting within the original screenplay.

21. This description occurs in the original character sketch in Butler and Rouverol, *The Legend of Lylah Clare*, 2.

22. Arnold and Miller, *The Films and Career of Robert Aldrich*, 132. The film does contain some striking shots and modernist imagery characteristic of Aldrich's noirs a decade ago. See also Silver and Ursini, *What Ever Happened to Robert Aldrich?* 219.

23. Butler and Rouverol, *The Legend of Lylah Clare*, 118.

24. Several critics such as Robin Wood and Robert Lang have drawn attention to a homosexual subtext within Aldrich's films. Wood notes that "an interest in the ambiguities of gender and sexuality recurs spasmodically throughout Aldrich's work," which he sees as "partly responsible for the distinctive quality of his work" ("Creativity and Evaluation: Two Film Noirs of the 1950s," in *Film Noir Reader*, vol. 2, ed. Alan Silver and James Ursini [New York: Limelight Editions, 1999], 104). Lang notices repressed homosexual tendencies in Mike Hammer of *Kiss Me Deadly* (see "Looking for the 'Great Whatzit': *Kiss Me Deadly* and Film Noir," *Cinema Journal* 27, no. 3 [1988]: 33). These features are what Wood once termed signifiers of an "incoherent text." They are not fully developed in Aldrich's films but do provide evidence of other elements existing beneath the surface of the text that contribute to its hysterical nature. Zarkan may very well be in this category. According to the 26 April 1978 American Film Institute seminar, Aldrich mentioned that even Zarkan could fit into the concept he borrowed from Abraham Polonsky of a "man struggling to redeem his self esteem" ("The American Film Institute Seminar," transcript, Center for Advanced Film Studies, 26 April 1978 [Beverly Hills: American Film Institute, 1979], 36). Unfortunately, Zarkan fails as badly as Charlie Castle.

25. Higham and Greenberg, *The Celluloid Muse*, 30.

26. Arnold and Miller, *The Films and Career of Robert Aldrich*, 60.

27. George N. Fenin, "An Interview with Robert Aldrich," *Film Culture* 2, no. 4 (1956): 8.

28. Arnold and Miller, *The Films and Career of Robert Aldrich*, 58.

29. Richard Combs, ed., *Robert Aldrich* (London: British Film Institute, 1978), 19. For Jean Rouverol's reminiscences over her work on *Autumn Leaves*, see Paul Buhle and Dave Wagner, "Jean Rouverol Butler," in *Tender Comrades: A Backstory of the Hollywood Blacklist*, ed. Patrick McGilligan and Paul Buhle (New York: St. Martin's Press, 1999), 169–70.

30. Combs, *Robert Aldrich*, 23.

31. See here Charles Derry, "The Horror of Personality," *Cinefantastique* 3, no. 4 (1974): 15–19; Charles Derry, *Dark Dreams: A Psychological History of the Modern Horror Film* (London: Thomas Yoseloff, 1977); and Tony Williams, *Hearths of Darkness: The Family in the American Horror Film* (Cranbury, N.J.: Fairleigh Dickinson University Press, 1996).

32. Ian Cameron and Mark Shivas, "Interview with Robert Aldrich," *Movie* 9 (1963): 10.

33. Cameron and Shivas, "Interview with Robert Aldrich," 9.

34. Richard J. Evans, *In Defense of History* (New York: W. W. Norton, 1997), 91.

35. Arnold and Miller, *The Films and Career of Robert Aldrich,* 108.

36. Combs, *Robert Aldrich,* 24.

37. Arnold and Miller, *The Films and Career of Robert Aldrich,* 107. This scene is not in the actual screenplay and was obviously added by Aldrich. In terms of Aldrich's knowledge of how Hollywood generally discards those who have not succeeded, his frequent use of actors such as Maxine Cooper (*Kiss Me Deadly, Autumn Leaves, What Ever Happened to Baby Jane?*), Michael Fox (*Baby Jane, The Legend of Lylah Clare*), James Goodwin (*Attack! Ten Seconds to Hell, Emperor of the North*), and, of course, Nick ("Va-va-voom") Dennis (*Kiss Me Deadly, The Big Knife, Attack! 4 for Texas, The Legend of Lylah Clare*) may represent not only a Robert Aldrich repertory company along the lines of John Ford but also the director's generosity to actors who found it difficult to find work in Hollywood. For example, the bank clerk played by Maxine Cooper in *Baby Jane* is male in the original screenplay. Not every actor and actress in Aldrich films achieved the type of career illustrated by the examples of others who had worked with him, such as Ernest Borgnine, Charles Bronson, Jack Elam, and Strother Martin. Aldrich actually recommended Borgnine for the film version of *Marty* and employed John Cassavetes when he was taboo in Hollywood, casting him as one of the Dirty Dozen.

38. Williams, *Hearths of Darkness,* 27.

39. See here David Cochran, *America Noir: Underground Writers and Filmmakers of the Postwar Era* (Washington, D.C.: Smithsonian Institution Press, 2000), 14.

40. Lukas Heller wrote: "An unspeakably cheerful ANNOUNCER comes on bearing aloft a tin of dog food between two fingers as if it were some rare jewel" (*What Ever Happened to Baby Jane?* screenplay, 7 August 1962, 18). All subsequent screenplay quotations are from this edition.

41. Arnold and Miller, *The Films and Career of Robert Aldrich,* 104–5, 238. Brooks has also recognized the irony behind Blanche's revelation in the closing moments of the film. Blanche has psychologically tortured Jane for the past thirty years and "has blackmailed Jane into relinquishing her own life and will to look after her. In the light of this most horrific of acts, Jane's physical torturing of Blanche—which makes up the bulk of the film—starving her, dragging her down the stairs, tying her to the bed and gagging her until near death in the final moments of the film is mere child's play. Moreover it seems totally just—a relatively speedy suffering compared to the long drawn out torments of Jane, of which we see only the end product" (Jodi Brooks, "Fascination and the Grotesque: *What Ever Happened to Baby Jane?*" *Continuum* 5, no. 2 (1992): 230.

42. Arnold and Miller, *The Films and Career of Robert Aldrich,* 238.

43. Ironically, in this the role Aldrich originally cast Peter Lawford, an actor with a dark history of mother domination and bisexual tendencies. After shooting some scenes he left the film for several undisclosed reasons. See James Spada, *Peter Lawford: The Man Who Kept the Secrets* (New York: Bantam Books, 1991), 337. After his falling out with the "Chairman of the Board," Lawford never appeared in any Rat Pack films after *Sergeant's Three* (1963). It appears that Victor Buono filled his roles, perhaps because of a perverse sense of humor on the part of "Ol' Blue Eyes," who referred to Lawford as "fat boy" on the set of *Sergeant's Three*. See Spada, *Peter Lawford*, 266; and Shawn Levy, *Rat Pack Confidential* (New York: Doubleday, 1998), 181. Buono thus played the roles originally designated for Lawford in *4 for Texas* (1963) and *Robin and the Seven Hoods* (1964).

Significantly, Edwin also represents another example of the manipulative use of classical traditions in Western society. Edwin conceals his disdain toward Mr. Hudson's musical expertise on the piano and banjo by commenting in a supposedly positive manner: "Banjo! A very *native* American *instrument*." His British father worked in the "classical tradition, Shakespeare, you know." We later learn that he is an illegitimate child of uncertain parentage!

44. The original screenplay contains the reason for Blanche's lie about the accident: "I just let them go on thinking it was you—let you go on thinking it and paying for it, because that way I could hold on to you." As Arnold and Miller note, the "final horror of *Baby Jane,* then, is the horror of loss, lost youth, lost identity, lost love" (*The Films and Career of Robert Aldrich*, 107).

45. Calendo, "Robert Aldrich Says 'Life Is Worth Living,'" 33.

46. Silver and Ursini, *What Ever Happened to Robert Aldrich?* 199.

47. Arnold and Miller, *The Films and Career of Robert Aldrich,* 114.

48. Silver and Ursini mention that during this scene, "the camera angle adjusts to reveal that Big Sam is headless and missing a hand mutilated just like Mayhew was" (*What Ever Happened to Robert Aldrich?* 202). This scene does not occur in the film, but the authors are correct in seeing an "incestuous transposition" between both characters. Also, Arnold and Miller are incorrect when they state that a policeman nearly sees Drew's body (*The Films and Career of Robert Aldrich,* 115) when it is actually Willis who arrives. A similar error occurs earlier when they mention that Jane has a ride on Edwin's lap in Blanche's wheelchair in *Baby Jane* (*The Films and Career of Robert Aldrich*, 105) when it is actually a Baby Jane doll!

49. Combs, *Robert Aldrich*, 28.

50. See, e.g., Vito Russo, *The Celluloid Closet: Homosexuality in the Movies,* rev. ed. (New York: Harper and Row, 1987), 173; Andrea Weiss, *Vampires and Violets: Lesbians in the Cinema* (London: Jonathan Cape, 1992), 64; Chris Straayer, *Deviant Eyes, Deviant Bodies: Sexual Re-orientation in Film and Video* (New York: Columbia University Press, 1996), 276; Claire Whatling,

Screen Dreams: Fantasying Lesbians in Film (Manchester: Manchester University Press, 1997), 83–84; Judith Halberstam, *Female Masculinity* (Durham: Duke University Press, 1998), 197–98; Sally Hussey, "Scene 176: Recasting the Lesbian in Robert Aldrich's *The Killing of Sister George*," available at www.latrobe.edu.au/screeningthepast/firstrelease/fr0600/ shfr10d.htm, 30 June 2000, 21–27; and Kelly Hankin, "Lesbian Locations: The Production of Lesbian Bar Space in *The Killing of Sister George*," *Cinema Journal* 41, no. 4 (2001): 3–27. On Aldrich's sympathy for the title character, see Arnold and Miller, *The Films and Career of Robert Aldrich,* 149. Russo also describes her as "the only multifaceted woman in the film" (*The Celluloid Closet*, 172).

51. According to Hussey's progressive reading of the notorious seduction scene, "Mercy is presented as a novitiate, unknowledgeable in the ways of lesbianism" ("Scene 176," 21). This article also contains extracts from contemporary reviews of the film. Childie actually turns Mercy on, but both are equally guilty for betraying George.

52. Arnold and Miller, *The Films and Career of Robert Aldrich,* 149.

53. See Tony Williams, "*The Killing of Sister George*," in *The Encyclopedia of Stage Plays into Film,* ed. John C. Tibbetts and James M. Welsh (New York: Facts on File, Inc., 2001), 169–70.

54. Mario Falsetto, *Stanley Kubrick. A Narrative and Stylistic Analysis,* 2d ed. (Westport, Conn.: Praeger, 2001), 177. Susannah York's comments on her role are also very revealing. She regarded her character as being the victim of maternal abandonment and several unhappy love affairs. As a basically weak heterosexual female, "George represented a sort of rock to her, resulting in a sexual relationship." Affected by a traumatic family life, Alice "had a horror of violence and rows; and since the bullying side of George was very strong, in her own little and rather weak way she revolted and just simply lied, because she couldn't really face up to it. One has to take into account that this was the equivalent of a seven-year marriage, when you *are* irritated by your partner, frequently, they *do* bore you sometimes, you know, you could just scream at them. And when Alice saw that her rock, which was George, was foundering—was not the strong rock—that was a shock." See Derek Elley, "Experiences: An Interview with Susannah York," *Focus on Film* 9 (1972): 29. York also commented that she was very proud of her work on the film and agreed with Aldrich's feeling that the lesbian seduction scene is a necessary part of the film.

55. Hussey, "Scene 176," 27.

56. Hussey, "Scene 176," 26.

57. Hussey, "Scene 176," 24. My reading of this scene naturally differs from Hussey's.

58. Silver and Ursini, *What Ever Happened to Robert Aldrich?* 225.

59. Silver and Ursini, *What Ever Happened to Robert Aldrich?* 319.

SEVEN

THE PRIVATE WAR OF ROBERT ALDRICH

Like Robert Aldrich's other generic explorations, his war films reflect antiauthoritarian concerns as well as elements derived from other cultural traditions. *Attack!* (1956), *Ten Seconds to Hell* (1959), *The Dirty Dozen* (1967), and *Too Late the Hero* (1970) all reflect in different ways not only Aldrich's subversion of the traditional Hollywood war movie but also features occurring within his other generic appropriations. As well as condemning a corrupt institutional authority, *Attack!* contains a melodramatic male hysteria component that Aldrich also utilizes in *Autumn Leaves*. Furthermore, *Attack!* is both a war film and film noir. Style and genre significantly merge. Lt. Costa's failure to control his emotions and employ a more rational type of strategy against his adversary, Captain Cooney, not only resembles the psychological flaws affecting characters in the plays of Clifford Odets but also illustrates Aldrich's own philosophy of calmly remaining at the card table to fight against the odds. *Attack!* also radically destabilizes the iconic role of the hero in the traditional war film, a feature Aldrich later developed in *Too Late the Hero*. *The Dirty Dozen* reflects the antiauthoritarian mood of the Vietnam era. But despite its misleading status as a macho war film, it contains many discordant elements contradicting this reading. *Ten Seconds to Hell* appears incongruous among this group. It is not traditionally a war film. But it indirectly relates to other films in this group by raising the question of postwar survival in terms of psychological dilemmas derived from wartime conditions.

Like Aldrich's noir films and melodramas, the war films represent a heterogeneous group, more often than not relating to the director's other generic explorations. This hybridity is not exceptional in terms of a flexible understanding of the classical Hollywood system's generic operations. As Robin Wood has pointed out, one of the "greatest obstacles to any fruitful theory of genre has been the tendency to treat the genres as discrete. An ideological approach might suggest why they can't be, however hard they may appear to try; at best, they represent different strategies for dealing with the same ideological tensions."[1] Wood also notes that classical Hollywood cinema often contains motifs that cross repeatedly from genre to genre. The same may also be said for a director's fascination, conscious or not, with certain predominant themes that occur in his work. Aldrich's antagonism toward all forms of authority, whether military, business, or family, is another predominant trait. Finally, *Attack!* is an example of the influence of Enterprise Studios on the director. It is not only a war film designed to raise questions in the audience's mind but also one representing another version of that lost cinematic vision embodied by Enterprise Studios, which confronted the harsh realities of Cold War America.

Attack! is based on a five-act play, *Fragile Fox,* by Norman A. Brooks. It opened at New York's Belasco Theatre on 12 October 1954 and closed on 27 November of that year after only fifty-five performances. Featuring John Garfield clone Dane Clark in the role of Lt. Costa, future director Don Taylor as Lt. Woodruff, Andrew Duggan as Captain Cooney, and James Gregory as Col. Bartlett, the play presented a grim vision of military corruption during the Battle of the Bulge as well as a "fragging" motif that supposedly did not happen until the Vietnam War.[2] Appearing during the Cold War a year after the Korean War stalemate, the vision of *Fragile Fox* certainly did not appeal to patriotic audiences and would be an unlikely subject for Pentagon approval for any future film version. However, Aldrich's attraction to this property not only represented his antiauthoritarian instincts but also exhibited the influences of both Clifford Odets and John Garfield.

According to Larry Swindell, Odets informed Garfield in 1951 that *Fragile Fox* would make an ideal theatrical property for a star who wanted to return to the New York theater. Garfield became fascinated by the character of Lt. Costa, took out an option on the play, and began to search for a producer. Should one prove unavailable, he would both produce and star in the play, which he hoped Lee Strasberg would direct. If the play proved to be a success, then Garfield intended to both direct and star in a film version produced by his own company. However, because of Garfield's increasing problems with the House Un-American Activities Committee, the project collapsed.[3]

Although a different actor in both physical stature and performance, Jack Palance continued the tradition begun by John Garfield in
both *The Big Knife* and *Attack!* In the first film, he played the role pioneered by Garfield on the stage. He would now portray a character that Garfield would have played had he lived. As the second of
two collaborations by director and star, *Attack!* represents another
work Aldrich attempted to direct in the spirit of the radical system
of inquiry represented by Abraham Polonsky in his two Enterprise
films, which also question the American status quo.

Fragile Fox's action occurs in winter 1944.[4] It contains five scenes
set in a town hall, a cellar, and a farmhouse. The film basically follows the play, with a few notable exceptions. It opens in the city hall
of Belgian village Planviex, with Captain Cooney complaining to his
orderly, Corporal Jackson, about the army's supposed inefficiency:
"Damn army. If I tried to run my business back home the way *they*
do things, I'd go bankrupt in a month. . . . I'd be a break for the tax-
payers if they'd let some business men take over for a change."[5] He
prepares for a card game with his Georgia associate Colonel Shehan,
Lt. Woodruff, and Lt. Sidney Joseph (later Costa in the stage and film
versions). Joseph expresses anger to Woodruff concerning Cooney's
incompetence during an incident at Aachen that cost the lives of
some of his men. Woodruff counsels Joseph to accept the reality of a
situation in which Shehan will always protect Cooney. As Cooney
stated earlier to Jackson, back home he used to say that "Erskine
Cooney's gonna own this State and Clyde Shehan'll be Governor."
When Shehan arrives he speaks reverently of Erskine's father, the
judge, who "couldn't have treated me better if I'd been his own son"
and who expressed disappointment when Erskine flunked law
school. The judge also forced his son into a loveless marriage. Now
a company commander thanks to Shehan, Cooney is hoping for a
"little ribbon" that would redeem him in the eyes of his father. The
card game begins with Joseph unable to conceal his contempt for
Cooney. He also accuses him of responsibility for the death of
Sergeant Ingersoll during the Aachen incident. Tensions rise, leading to the end of the card game. Both Joseph and Cooney leave. Shehan questions Woodruff about the Aachen incident. He refuses to replace Cooney but assures Woodruff that there is little likelihood the
unit will see combat again. The film version ignores the dialogue
among Woodruff, Jackson, and Bernstein concerning women in the
play. But it does include the "fragging" threat made by Joseph to

Woodruff, who takes a moralistic stance over this matter. Sergeant Tolliver then enters to inform both men that the Battle of the Bulge has commenced.

Act 1, scene 2, occurs in the command center where Woodruff attempts to persuade battalion surgeon Captain Gerstad to declare the alcoholic Cooney physically unfit to command. After some dialogue with Private Ricks, Woodruff sees Cooney and Shehan enter. The colonel places an infiltration operation into Cooney's hands. Joseph utters his suspicions as to whether Cooney will offer infantry support on this mission. Rather than take Cooney's, he asks Woodruff to give his word over this matter. Woodruff agrees. Before leaving, Joseph threatens Cooney: "If I ever lose another man because of you, just one, you'll never see the States again." The scene ends with Cooney refusing Joseph's request.

Act 2, scene 1, opens in a country house abandoned by the Germans. Joseph's platoon arrives after suffering severe casualties because of Cooney's failure to offer them support. Trapped in a town by a reinforced German company, the men grimly consider their situation. Ricks utters a line that also occurs in the film. He cannot understand why the enemy should hate him. When Bernstein tells him, "You're the enemy," Ricks replies, "What do you mean I'm the enemy? I'm an American, for Christ sake, *they're* the enemy." After using a dummy to draw enemy fire, the men discover two concealed German soldiers in the cellar. One is a sergeant who hits his smaller companion for revealing their presence. Snowden remarks, "That big one's a sergeant. It's the same in every Army, huh?" The rank would be changed in the film for obvious reasons. When the sergeant threatens his subordinate, Joseph shoots him on the spot. Obtaining information that panzers are in the town, Joseph requests artillery support from Woodruff so that his men can withdraw. He also asks him to tell "Cooney I'm coming back." Before they leave Tolliver mentions the danger of friendly fire. His line would never appear in any pre–Vietnam War movie: "It's not that I mind the war so much, Lieutenant. But I sure would like to know which side's trying to kill me."

Act 2, scene 2, returns to the same set as act 1, scene 2. Cooney reacts in fear over Joseph's expected return and claims that he suffers from a fever. He assaults the captured German soldier Tolliver has brought before him, an act resulting in the sergeant's expression of contempt for his superior officer. A military interpreter enters and learns from the prisoner that their adversaries are SS. Cooney retreats into alcoholic oblivion. Shehan arrives and expresses anger at his incompetence. He orders him to hold the company position. After Woodruff smashes his last bottle, Cooney silently settles back into a chair. Brooks's comments over Cooney's mental condition provide material that Aldrich would develop: "All defense is gone now. There are no more exits, not even the bottle. What's on his mind at this moment? Maybe his Mother, perhaps a desire to re-enter the womb. He suddenly starts to cry. Not like a man, but like a little boy." When Cooney's speech returns, he first speaks about his mother: "She was a beautiful woman, beautiful. Long hair, long yellow hair." His following lines intimate that his real persona has no place in either his traditional Southern culture or a homophobic Cold War America: "How'd you like to be me? No, you'd rather stop one. You'd rather be dead, that'd be easier. Well, I've got no choice, I've got to be me. I've got to live in a world of men that despise me. A world that spits on me. Coward, they say. My own Father, he'd be the first. Yes, my own Father'd spit on me."

Cooney is a male hysteric clearly adrift in a hostile American culture of masculinity. His inability to live up to the Law of the Father places him in the same category as Dave Waggomann in Anthony Mann's *The Man from Laramie* (1955) and Kyle Hadley in Douglas Sirk's *Written on the Wind* (1956). But he is in a much worse condition than these figures because he also bears responsibility for the lives of the men under his command. Lt. Joseph enters the room. He is silent at this point. Woodruff appeals to Joseph to return to his own men rather than kill a pathetic drunk who is little better than "a lump of sod." He also admits that he betrayed Joseph by giving him his word earlier and not following up on his promise. The scene ends as Jackson enters to inform Joseph that his men are pinned down by a big tank. All leave except Woodruff and Cooney, the latter collapsing on his knees praying.

Act 3 opens in the same location some hours later, when Ricks and Snowden carry in an injured Bernstein. Captain Gerstad attends to his broken leg. Tolliver enters and informs Bernstein that their adversaries are SS, whose wartime behavior the latter is fully aware of: "Jesus, Tolliver, those bastards don't take prisoners. 'Specially a guy named Bernstein what can't walk." Woodruff appears and intends to carry Bernstein out. Cooney also emerges into the scene. All then hide. They hear voices of the SS, who decide not to investigate any further. Because of Cooney's incompetence, the men are now cut off from their own lines. Cooney decides to surrender despite the fact that it will mean certain death for Bernstein. Woodruff understands the real reason: "You'd like a chance to sweat out the war in P.O.W. camp, wouldn't you? Six months behind wire and you're still a hero—well, forget it." Joseph's avenging appearance forestalls Cooney's action. Although wishing to kill his nemesis, Joseph collapses to the floor, drops his tommy gun, and dies. Cooney decides to continue with his plan to spend a few months in a camp. According to Woodruff, he wishes to "waltz home with a lot of pretty ribbons." But Woodruff prevents this by shooting his superior officer. Although Woodruff asks Tolliver to place him under arrest, the sergeant fires a shot into Cooney's corpse along with Bernstein. Tolliver then speaks a line that does not appear in the film version emphasizing Woodruff's hidden motivations behind doing the right thing: "Way I see it, a piece of dung's been swept out the door. Now, there just ain't no point in putting thorns on our head, sir, 'caus this aint no world for playing Christ in, Lieutenant." Tolliver's speech also echoes Aldrich's own postwar modernist philosophy whereby classical values no longer apply, whether to art, literature, morality, or religion. A different ball game is now playing. So different rules must operate in terms of personal survival.

The Fifth Armored Division arrives, forcing the Germans to retreat. Shehan enters. He immediately suspects what has actually happened after listening to Tolliver's story. He pressures Woodruff into agreeing to a scheme to make Cooney a posthumous hero for a father who had to lose a son to gain one. Despite Woodruff's threats to reveal the whole story, Shehan suggests that he consider his options. Rather than risking his own court-martial and possibly those of his men who collaborated in the incident, Woodruff should realize that he has "got the high card" and ought to "scoop up his chips." Shehan departs uttering lines that also appear in the film: "I'm betting now that you keep your mouth shut. I've lost hands, but never two in a row." The mortuary detail arrives to pick up Cooney's corpse. They speak about future American wars. As he watches them leave, Woodruff breaks into convulsive and uncontrolled weeping. The play ends leaving the audience with no real indication as to how Woodruff will act.

This plot synopsis of *Fragile Fox* is necessary to show how much Aldrich took from the original play. Aldrich naturally employed cinematic techniques in his version. But he also made certain changes in the screenplay with James Poe. Both men had already collaborated on the film version of *The Big Knife* with Jack Palance. *Attack!* lacks those affirmative messages contained within contemporary Hollywood war films such as *To Hell and Back*, *Mr. Roberts*, *Battle Cry*, and *Strategic Air Command* (all from 1955). After unsuccessfully attempting to option Irwin Shaw's *The Young Lions* and Norman Mailer's *The Naked and the Dead*, Aldrich finally purchased a property that had once interested his former Enterprise Studio mentor, John Garfield. Aldrich's approach would be as iconoclastic as Samuel Fuller's. It would also represent his own type of philosophy.

Aldrich regarded *Attack!* not so much as a traditional antiwar film as a work dealing with "the terribly corrupting influence that war can have on the most normal, average human beings, and what terrible things it makes them capable of that they wouldn't be capable of otherwise."[6] As various critics have noted, the film's visual style appropriately complements the radical nature of the content.[7] Aldrich employed the film noir techniques used in *Kiss Me Deadly* and *The Big Knife* to destabilize the traditional war movie's generic formulas and lead audiences to question rather than accept. Issues of honor and integrity occupied his mind. But these concepts now had to adapt to a different era. A new code of honor was necessary for a changed era in which neither Costa's irrational messianic beliefs nor Woodruff's compromising mediation with a corrupt status quo would result in any worthwhile survival, whether individual or collective.

Aldrich shot the film on the RKO back lot he had once worked on as an assistant director on William Wellman's *The Story of G.I. Joe* (1945). He opens *Attack!* with a pre-credits sequence showing the unnecessary slaughter of Sergeant Ingersoll (Strother Martin) and his men. It results from the unseen Captain Cooney's refusal to order backup, despite the anguished pleas of Lt. Costa (Jack Palance). All we see of Cooney is an anonymous figure in a uniform wringing his hands. As one of Ingersoll's men attempts in vain to flee up a hill, he is downed by German fire. The image then abruptly changes to a diagonal tracking shot as the camera moves left to right as the soldier's helmet falls down the hill to stop near a flower. If we change helmet and flower to hand and butterfly, then this scene obviously evokes the final shot of *All Quiet on the Western Front* (1930), directed by one of Aldrich's mentors, Lewis Milestone. The credit sequence begins. The music changes from a somber score to contemporary "swing" jazz played from a loudspeaker as the Fragile Fox men line up for coffee. They express irritation when Cooney's orderly, Corporal Jackson (Jon Sheppod), cuts in line. When Jackson returns to the manor house Cooney uses for his headquarters, our view of the captain is obscured both by the chiaroscuro lighting and by the mailroom pigeonholes covering his face. Once Cooney appears, Frank DeVol changes the music once more. But this time the composer uses discordant notes from nursery rhymes. This type of score represents not only Cooney's regressive infantilism but also Aldrich's interest in modernist musical thematic counterpoint. It acoustically complements the visual style of *Attack!* making the film easily recognizable as the work of "a director whose worlds are always in turmoil, his characters *in extremis,* and his intense, battering style productive of more *angst* than the narratives can comfortably contain."[8]

Attack! not only employs film noir–style shadow bars and claustrophobic imagery symbolizing character entrapment. It also interrogates different strategies concerning survival. *Attack!* certainly condemns the incompetence of Captain Cooney (Eddie Albert), put into a position of authority by the corrupt Colonel Bartlett (Lee Marvin). But it also contrasts two types of oppositions and finds that both lack any relevant strategy necessary to overcome a deadly system. Lt. Costa represents the first alternative. He is a character whom most films would ordinarily privilege. But Aldrich condemns the dangerous emotional streak of self-righteous anger in Costa that hinders the justice of his cause.

When first seen at the 500-year-old blacksmith's forge inside a ruined church, Costa appears as a man of the people and potential messiah. He is also a blacksmith and carpenter, employing the latter trade by making a wooden handle for his bazooka. Like the original Messiah, he is an artisan. But he is also a warrior. Costa represents an early version of the contradictory figure of the warrior-messiah embodied by General Lawrence Dell in *Twilight's Last Gleaming.* Costa speaks about his experiences working on the Pittsburgh railroad with a Belgian blacksmith. Persuaded by Lt. Harry Woodruff (William Smithers) against his better judgment to participate in the card game with Cooney and Bartlett, Costa remarks that "one crack out of Cooney" will cause him to explode. But when we later see the card game in progress, it is Costa who makes the "one crack" that enrages Cooney and disrupts the game.

Upon receiving from Cooney the deadly mission to infiltrate the village, Costa threatens him with fragging. Although angered by the loss of his men, Costa lacks a cool head to deal with a dangerous situation. He gives in to his emotions and makes a verbal threat that results in his later abandonment by Cooney, who certainly would not want him to return. Costa does not rationally consider any other effective strategy. Instead, he hates his antagonist and displays the irrational type of behavior McIntosh warns against in *Ulzana's Raid*. When Costa later "rises from the dead" like Mike Hammer in *Kiss Me Deadly*, bleeding to death from the injuries he has suffered from a panzer, this potential messiah now becomes a blasphemer anguished at his own failing strength: "Father. May I go to hell before I. . . ." These lines do not appear in *Fragile Fox*. Costa's savior status also appears in earlier scenes. He speaks the "Hail Mary" before Abramowitz's body prior to leaving the farmhouse. He also utters a prayer before the dead body of Ricks (Jimmy Goodwin), whom he has attempted to carry to safety despite previous orders to his men before leaving the farmhouse to leave the wounded behind. A low-angle image of Costa before Ricks significantly lap dissolves from Costa looking left of camera into a space in which the figures of his two betrayers—Cooney and Woodruff—will appear. Costa's face exhibits righteous indignation and anguish. But it is also evident that his emotions will dominate the sanity he needs to survive this dangerous situation.

By contrast, William Smithers's Woodruff is an organization man who believes in the system. He cautions Costa several times about his threats to eliminate Cooney. But Woodruff turns out to be ineffective. He breaks his promise to Costa concerning reinforcements and deserves the epithet "mealy-mouthed" that Costa justifiably applies to him. Although he attempts to act as mediator between Costa and Cooney, he is really ineffective, as the scene of him going to the blacksmith's forge shows. The camera follows his minuscule figure framed by the jagged edges of a broken stained-glass window as he walks toward the forge. Before Woodruff tells Costa his plan of getting Cooney transferred, a goat bleats in the background, undermining his very character. At the card game, Woodruff also triggers off Costa's sarcastic remark to Cooney by accidentally mentioning the last game they played with Bartlett and an officer who died because of Cooney's neglect. After several appeals to Colonel Bartlett, Woodruff finally finds himself in Costa's role by fragging Cooney, preventing him from surrendering and leaving them to the tender mercies of the SS. Woodruff then tells Tolliver (Buddy Ebsen) to place him under arrest, falling back again into his acquiescence of following the "proper channels." As Eric Kreuger points out, "If he couldn't apply the laws of society to Cooney, he can at least apply them to himself. Harry is not an Aldrich code-hero, for his rules are not of his making; they come from without, from an alien institution that had indirectly forced him into a position where he had no choice but to break the laws of that institution."[9]

However, another interpretation is possible. Woodruff also falls back into a regressive position like Cooney. It involves a redundant savior complex, which leads to his martyrdom within an unjust institution that will follow the "proper channels" rather than investigate the complex set of circumstances that caused the problem in the first place. Any institution will always seek out a convenient scapegoat rather than undergo radical change. As Tolliver tells Woodruff, his court-martial will never involve any investigation dealing with relevant issues of justice and truth but, rather, will display careerism by a prosecuting attorney out for promotion and concealment of the actual facts.

The film ends with Woodruff finally deciding to phone the general and reveal the truth. But this climax was forced on Aldrich by the Hays Code. However, the director undercuts its supposedly positive nature by using the same subversive visual device he chooses to conclude both *The Big Knife* and *The Killing of Sister George*. The camera changes to an overhead shot, framing Woodruff against a dark background as he makes a phone call that could lead to his court-martial. Although not as ambiguous as the actual ending of *Fragile Fox*, the visual composition emphasizes the futility of his actions. But Woodruff has decided not to play the "high card" according to Bartlett's rules. Woodruff accuses him of engineering Cooney's death: "I may have pulled the trigger but you aimed the gun. You planned it this way." It is a bleak climax embodying a vision that occurs throughout many Aldrich films. As Arnold and Miller succinctly state: "If you stand against the system, you will be crushed. If you compromise with the system, you will pay with your self-respect. If you step outside the system, you forfeit your self-determination by default."[10] Woodruff will not compromise, as the ending of *Fragile Fox* suggests. Neither will he stand against the system. Instead, he puts himself in a situation where he will lose his "self-determination" by facing a court-martial and a prosecuting attorney "bucking for his majority," as Tolliver states.

It is a situation where former standards and codes of morality no longer apply. Costa changes from being savior-messiah of his men to being a thwarted avenging blasphemer. After Costa dies, the Jewish Private Bernstein (Robert Strauss) appeals to a Catholic deity to understand that the tormented man did not really mean what he said. The religious connotations of the blacksmith's shrine where we first see Costa form a contrast to the manor house Cooney uses as his headquarters. Although the house is ruined, a prominent coat of arms appears above the fireplace, with a chandelier dominating the ceiling. It is very reminiscent of the chateau in Stanley Kubrick's *Paths of Glory* (1958) as well as the equally deceptive civilized surroundings where Major Reisman first meets his superior officers in *The Dirty Dozen*. Religion and Western civilization are irrelevant against the corruptions of a changed world. They are also as ineffective as they are in *Kiss Me Deadly*. Before being killed by Tolliver, a German sniper uses the top of a church to fire at his victims trapped in a farmhouse. The interior of the farmhouse resembles a cluttered cubist, modernist painting. A portrait of the Sacred Heart briefly appears above the Jewish Bernstein before he seeks refuge in the cellar. It is the sad sack Bernstein who utters prayers in Hebrew over the body of the Catholic Costa, praying to another God to forgive Costa his blasphemy. After Costa dies, Tolliver cradles him in a pietà position.

Although Costa never gets to kill Cooney, he indirectly causes the death of a German captain (Peter Van Eyck) by his own men. The captain is a surrogate victim for Cooney, as his changed rank in the film denotes: "The mean one's a Captain, Lt. It's the same in any Army." Even Cooney emerges as a pathetic victim, a product of child abuse by his brutal father. He is a regressive figure who woke up at the age of thirty to find that he had still not reached adulthood. Clutching a slipper as a fetish replacement for his lost mother, Cooney weeps as he tells Woodruff that he fears both his father and his surrogate father, Bartlett: "I'm different, Woodruff." He acts like a malicious child, kicking away Costa's gun on the floor as the man dies in agony trying to reach it. When Woodruff finally shoots Cooney, a look of relief briefly appears on his face. It is almost as if he now realizes that he has been relieved from continuing to live up to a masculine ideal that torments him daily. The rules of existence have changed drastically, as the confused lines of Ricks reveal: "What do you mean I'm the enemy? I'm an American." *Attack!* is the first Aldrich war film to acknowledge a postwar dilemma in which no secure values exist any longer, a dilemma visually articulated by Aldrich's critical use of modernist noir imagery.

Ten Seconds to Hell is a flawed and truncated work. It was a project resulting in the end of Aldrich's collaboration with Jack Palance as well as disappointing the expectations of its European producers. The film was extensively reedited, resulting in the loss of some forty minutes of footage.[11] As it stands, it is difficult to analyze in terms of Aldrich's work. However, traces still exist exhibiting certain key elements of his vision. Although set in the immediate postwar era, it has equal claims to be regarded as a war film. Like *The Dirty Dozen,* *Ten Seconds to Hell* begins with a group of characters who agree to a suicidal mission in clearing the rubble of unexploded bombs from a defeated Germany, a mission from which only a few will return. As critics have noted, the conflict between Eric Koertner (Jack Palance) and Karl Wirtz (Jeff Chandler) echoes that earlier symbiotic relationship between Ben Trane and Joe Erin in *Vera Cruz.* However, *Ten Seconds to Hell* also deals with Aldrich war film themes of survival and its accompanying costs.

The film opens with documentary footage of Allied planes dropping bombs over Germany in the last days of the war. After an explosion, appropriately following Aldrich's director credit, the voice-over begins. It not only speaks about the unexploded bomb problem in both Allied and former Axis cities but also poses the question, "What was to rise from these ashes?" It is a question relevant to the devastated landscape of Berlin and to the human remnants who also emerged in the postwar era. The image then changes to show six men emerging from a train, all of whom had been in disfavor with the Nazis and given the onerous task of deactivating bombs in wartime. Because of the privations of the postwar era, these men have little opportunity to pursue their peacetime professions. Instead, they have to return to their deadly wartime occupations. Ironically, the victorious Allies use these men in the same way as their defeated opponents did, thus blurring traditional generic boundaries between the two sides. This theme also anticipates the critique of the military establishment in *The Dirty Dozen.*

The group comprises a youthful Globke (Jimmy Goodwin), "who, despite all, had held on to the fragments of his youth and innocence"; animal-loving, gentle Loeffler (Robert Cornthwaite); the resigned Salke (Wesley Addy), trying to provide for his family; and two other significant opposing figures. They are "Karl Wirtz, with one big idea in mind—his own survival—and one way to assure it— play for high stakes and deal from the bottom of the deck"; and alter ego Eric Koertner, "another big man . . . a man whom other men followed instinctively. A strange, brooding mixture of passion and compassion. Passion for the promise of words like 'right' and 'justice'; compassion for other confused and lost souls."

Whereas Wirtz easily fits into the Joe Erin pattern, Koertner is a tormented version of Ben Trane, having also the disturbed psychological traits of Charlie Castle of *The Big Knife*. Whereas Trane has lost his plantation and seeks to rebuild his former life by becoming a mercenary, Koertner believes that returning to his former life as an architect is impossible. Described by Wirtz as "the poet of pain," Koertner wallows in brooding self-imposed isolation, passively following the new circumstances of his existence and preserving his own private self. These two opposing characters represent the key conflict of *Ten Seconds to Hell*. The future of a city is at stake. Like a phoenix, it will rise from the ashes by choosing between different alternatives embodied in two men: the mercenary, calculating Wirtz or the conscientious but psychologically debilitated Koertner. It is a contrast Aldrich treats with some degree of ambivalence. The opening voice-over parallels the concluding comments in the film. It begins stating that these six men coming home were destined to share "in the gigantic challenge of converting the rubble of war into the makings of a new and lasting peace." The film ends with a reprise of the faces of the six, ending with the sole survivor Koertner, as the final voice-over comments that "they had breathed new life into the phoenix which rose from the ashes." Although Aldrich rejected *Ten Seconds to Hell*, an irony occurs in the concluding comments also characterizing the supposedly uplifting voice-over concluding *The Dirty Dozen*.[12]

The group members decide to make a pact to set half their money aside for whoever survives a three-month period of defusing unexploded bombs. As Salke significantly comments, "I'm not so sure about this betting against death. Maybe, it's a way of staying together." The men remain together until their numbers are diminished by the hazards of the job. Despite Wirtz's attempt to take over the group by opposing his calculated-risk methodology to Koertner's "emotional" judgment, the men decide on the latter candidate. However, Koertner offers Wirtz the job of assistant. But it is not on the basis of "fair play," as his rival insinuates. It has more to do with the fact that they are both expendable in having the "least to live for." Wirtz and Koertner are nihilistic figures. The former lives by the epithet "Kismet" and gleefully speaks about disposing of his Uncle Oscar, who had taught him the hard facts of Darwinian survival of the fittest. As Koertner later comments, the whole game is a "battle of survival between the Karls of this world and the me's of this world." However, it is a battle that Koertner is in danger of losing because he wallows in a masochistic isolation also affecting Charlie Castle in *The Big Knife.*

Ten Seconds to Hell is really about the development of Eric Koertner, a development resulting from his interaction with his French landlady, Margot Hofer (Martine Carol). She survives by black market activities, living in an environment where she is as isolated as Koertner. Like him, she cannot go home again: "I'm French, married to an enemy soldier during wartime. It's considered a crime to fall in love, especially with the enemy." As she tells Koertner, "Here, I'm still the enemy. I can see in their eyes that I remind them of something dead in themselves." Her comments evoke Koertner's self-awareness of his own debilitating emotional isolation. He had once been a successful architect before speaking out against the Nazis, who sent him on deadly missions to defuse bombs. Now he has returned to see the devastation of his formerly creative work. But rather than follow Wirtz's individualist philosophy, he eventually reaches out to Margot. Unlike Mike Hammer in *Kiss Me Deadly,* he "becomes one of Aldrich's few self-realized heroes" by breaking away from his masochistic desires.[13] During an earlier scene between Koertner and Margot, her image appears in a mirror as she confesses her own emotional isolation and tries to convince him to "try to live" rather than "try to die" in expressing his warped sense of superiority.

Ten Seconds to Hell leads to a climactic confrontation between the two survivors. After realizing that certain bombs have double fuses, which caused the deaths of their companions, Wirtz and Koertner decide to collaborate. However, Wirtz cheats and attempts to kill Koertner. He fails, and Koertner walks away, leaving his partner to defuse the bomb by himself. Wirtz accepts the consequences of his actions and dies alone. However, the look on Koertner's face after he hears the explosion amid the devastated rubble reveals conflicting emotions. After Wirtz's behavior, Koertner had little alternative but to walk away. Wirtz agrees that he has responsibility for defusing the bomb, despite the fact that he cannot defuse it alone. By walking away, Koertner acts in a manner paralleling the actions Wirtz took against his Uncle Oscar. But his face does not reveal the cynicism typical of Wirtz once he hears the explosion. Koertner is clearly aware of the consequences of his actions, which will haunt him forever. Wirtz dealt from "the bottom of the deck." But Koertner also realizes the destructive waste of human life in a manner similar to Ben Trane's regret over the death of Joe Erin in *Vera Cruz*. Survival comes with a cost.

The Dirty Dozen was the most financially successful film Aldrich directed. It allowed him to realize his dream of purchasing his own studio. Based on the novel by E. M. Nathanson and coscripted by Nunnally Johnson and Lukas Heller, the film captured the antiauthoritarian mood in American society fueled by Vietnam War demonstrations when it first appeared. It also gained the reputation of being a gratuitous macho war movie, resulting in Aldrich being stereotyped as an emotional primitive in the eyes of most critics.[14] Three years later, a different reaction led to the financial failure of *Too Late the Hero*, when many of the youthful audience members who accepted the antiauthoritarianism in *The Dirty Dozen* failed to understand the later film's complexities, particularly because of the Kent State shootings, leading to condemnation of any film dealing with war. On closer analysis, *The Dirty Dozen* is a much more complex film. Although most male audiences may have unwittingly cheered the testosterone nature of the action, the entire film is different. *The Dirty Dozen* complements the radical visions in Aldrich's other films, which often transcend convenient generic boundaries and interpretations.

After finding that Nunnally Johnson's screenplay reflected the anachronistic elements of classical Hollywood World War II films, Aldrich hired Lukas Heller to rework the script to make it more in line with the spirit of the original novel. Although Heller changed the original text drastically, the novel's overwhelming cynical attack on an uncaring military bureaucracy remains the central focus of the film. Following a tense incident when MGM offered the role of Major Reisman to John Wayne rather than Aldrich's original choice, Lee Marvin, the director breathed a sigh of relief when the Duke rejected the screenplay as unpatriotic and communist inspired.[15]

In the film, the novel's Jewish Captain Reisman becomes Lee Marvin's ethnically indistinct major. Reisman receives a suicidal mission order from his superior officer involving leading twelve condemned prisoners in a pre-D-Day attack on a German chateau containing the cream of the military high command. As with his other generic explorations, Aldrich took the framework of the typical World War II movie and subverted it. *The Dirty Dozen* became a film that explodes the popular archetype of World War II as "the Good War." At the same time, the film also merges the premises of the Vietnam War into its context, especially in the final sequence when Reisman orders gasoline poured into the wine cellars where the German high command and innocent civilians are hiding. It is also an implicit comment on what the Nazis themselves were doing to others at the time as well as containing the radical suggestion that American soldiers were equally capable of the same inhumane acts. As Aldrich later pointed out,

> What I was trying to do was say that under the circumstances, it's not only the Germans who do unkind and hideous, horrible things in the name of war, but that the Americans do it and anybody does it. The whole nature of war is dehumanizing. There's no such thing as a nice war. Now American critics completely missed that, so they attacked the picture because of its violence, and for indulgence in violent heroics. Now, fascinatingly, European critics all picked up on the parallel between burning people alive and the use of napalm, whether they liked the picture or not. They got the significance of what was being said.[16]

Aldrich begins his comment by referring to the scene where Jim Brown's Jefferson runs across the forecourt and drops grenades into the ventilation system, already saturated with gasoline. Jefferson is one of the victimized members of the Dozen with whom the audience might have some degree of sympathy, unlike John Cassavetes's Franko and Telly Savalas's Maggott. At the time, Brown was also well known as a football player at the height of his prowess. During this particular scene, Aldrich complicates the nature of the spectator's response, which, on reflection, may be seen as a guilty pleasure. We see Brown performing his well-known routine cheered on by the survivors of the Dozen (and, presumably, most of the contemporary audience). But he is also performing a vicious act. Most spectators would not reflect on the complexity of this action. But it is definitely inserted here by a director who never didactically manipulates his audiences but, rather, presents them with contradictory facts that they may investigate further or reject entirely.

The pre-credit sequence introduces the audience to Reisman and his mission. But several disturbing overtones appear. Reisman has been ordered by his superiors to witness the execution of a soldier. It is a lesson for both Reisman and the audience. The prisoner is scared. His commanding officer (Lionel Murton) exhibits embarrassment toward this inhumane performance. Reisman exhibits disdain as the chaplain reads an irrelevant religious text to the condemned man. At the release of the trapdoor lever, Aldrich cuts to a low-angle shot as the prisoner's feet hit the audience. It is a blatant act of audience aggression. Like Reisman, audiences become involved in a civilized ritual many would not ordinarily attend. Although filmed in Aldrich's particular manner, the shot parallels Kubrick's shot placing his audiences behind the firing squad in *Paths of Glory* (1957), making them also complicit with an institutional procedure sanctioned on their behalf. Like Kirk Douglas's Colonel Dax, Reisman has to confront a military high command structure whose members inhabit a large room containing many of the classical artifacts that Kubrick associates with two corrupt generals in his earlier film. A classical bust and a suit of armor appear in the room, representing another indication of Aldrich's view of the redundancy of classical civilization in the brutalized world of the twentieth century. As Reisman is about to enter, his friend, Major Armbruster (George Kennedy), cautions him: "Be nice. Take it easy. This time, it's serious, John. You've got to cooperate."

After passing Col. Everett Dasher-Breed (Robert Ryan), whose expression reveals his immediate memory of a past confrontation, Reisman enters the main room where members of the American high command (and others such as Army psychologist Captain Kinder, played by Ralph Meeker) sit around a large green table very reminiscent of a gambling table. The analogy is not incorrect, for Reisman is in a game where General Worden (Ernest Borgnine), like Colonel Bartlett in *Attack!*, holds the "high card." As Reisman enters, an overhead shot frames him into insignificance at the same time as it symbolizes the authority of the high command. The angle also recalls those overhead shots showing Colonel Bartlett at the card game in *Attack!* where he wins every game. Worden deliberately withholds his response to Reisman's salute, making the major feel his authority from the very beginning. During the briefing for the mission, which Reisman cynically understands he has "volunteered" for, it becomes clear that another (unstated) purpose involves the convenient elimination of a maverick officer along with the condemned criminals he will command. After eliciting a compromise by which survivors will be granted amnesty, Reisman begins his onerous task. The credits begin as he returns to the scene of execution, a prison that was formerly a castle. Despite the twentieth-century setting of *The Dirty Dozen*, these opening scenes reveal that the supposedly civilized Allied world still retains vestiges of feudalism. Reisman and the Dozen are little better than serfs allotted dangerous tasks by medieval barons.

Arnold and Miller complain that "Aldrich does not play entirely fair with us in this film" because the Dozen are not all bad "and they are treated with differing amounts of respect, allowed differing degrees of redemption."[17] Admittedly, characters such as Wladislaw (Charles Bronson) and Jefferson are far removed from others such as Franko and Maggott, who deserve their punishment. But they ignore the fact that both Wladislaw and Jefferson have been unjustifiably railroaded. As Sergeant Tolliver tells Woodruff in *Attack!* any prosecuting attorney in a military court-martial could easily twist the facts to turn justifiable homicide into the actions of a "bloodthirsty maniac." Audiences familiar with the trial sequence in *Paths of Glory* already understand this. *The Dirty Dozen* operates in a different world from the one envisaged by Arnold and Miller.

Unlike Woodruff, Reisman is on his own and has no means of support. He has been dealt a hand from the bottom of the deck, and his survival depends on both his calm resilience and his effective use of strategy. Unlike Costa, Reisman cannot indulge in overemotional behavior that will destroy both him and his men. Furthermore, because of the circumstances of his mission, he finds himself one of Aldrich's savior-destroyer figures. Less opportunistic than Mike Hammer in *Kiss Me Deadly* and more streetwise than Costa, he plays the cards passed to him by a group of crooked dealers and tries to survive in the best way he can. During Aldrich's famous "Last Supper" scene before the mission, which may be a satirical reference to Bunuel's similar scene in *Viridiana* (1961), Reisman informs his men that not all of them will return. As "Redeemer" figure in this tableau, he has saved his men from their respective sentences. But, at the same time, he will lead them into an apocalyptic situation as destructive to them as the final infernoesque scenes of *Kiss Me Deadly*.

Surrounded by figures such as Samson Posey's (Clint Walker) "Beloved Disciple," Franko's "Doubting Thomas" and Maggott's "Judas," Reisman perversely reenacts one of the poignant scenes in Western Christian tradition. However, it is now as contaminated as an outside world where little difference exists between the opposing sides of Allies and Nazis. During the mission, the Dozen find themselves performing actions little different from those of the enemy they have been forced to defeat. Aldrich wished to deal with certain issues in the film, namely, "to show the necessity for collective action in circumstances that would make collective cowardice more likely, and to show that almost anybody can be redeemed if certain circumstances and pressures are sufficient."[18] At the same time, the actions the Dozen perform are mandated by a civilization that has condemned them for crimes that ironically will appear much less horrendous than those the system requires of them.

During an earlier scene Aldrich suggests that a thin line exists between the opposing forces. When Reisman interviews Wladislaw, who represents a fusion of Costa and Woodruff in *Attack!* a copy of *Yank* magazine appears in the frame. The Slavic Silesian coal miner's son has just been reading an article titled "What It Means to Be a Jewish Girl." The presence of this article not only informs the reader about the enemy's anti-Semitic practices. It also suggests the real reasons behind Wladislaw's death sentence for committing an act of justifiable homicide by shooting a cowardly officer who attempted to run off with much needed medical supplies. Unlike Woodruff, Wladislaw belongs to the wrong race. Jefferson's justifiable homicide of some "cracker bastards" attempting to castrate him means little to a military establishment as racist as its supposed enemy, despite Reisman's reference to the "Krauts" being "the real master race bastards."

As Reisman informs Captain Kinder, the Dozen are at war with the U.S. Army: "These guys think the United States Army is their enemy. But the Krauts haven't done anything to them yet. But, at least, they know the United States Army." He aims to transfer resentment against the military establishment toward the Germans in the same way that Costa sublimates his murderous rage at Captain Cooney by using his German counterpart in *Attack!* as a surrogate victim. The idea is to get the Dozen to function like a sports team individually and collectively. This analogy occurs in two scenes. When Maggott provokes a fight with Jefferson, Sergeant Bowren

(Richard Jaeckel) speaks to his fellow MPs outside about baseball, as if comparing the fight inside to a necessary ritual of team practice. Later, during the humorous word-association scene between Wladislaw and Kinder, the former's supposedly aberrant connections reveal subconscious associations that will aid his later survival. When Kinder calls "weapon," Wladislaw repeats "baseball." He also does this when he connects "Dodger" to "knife." When Reisman provokes Posey into attacking him with a knife, he teaches him a lesson that Costa never learned in *Attack!* "You've got to learn to take care of your temper. Then no one will be able to take that knife from you."

The Dirty Dozen deliberately undermines certain spurious ethics of the traditional Hollywood World War II film that sees the officer classes as having the best interests of their men at heart. The military brass regard Reisman and the Dozen as expendable pawns. The Dozen cheat against Col. Breed's men in the military exercise, granting them a reprieve from the execution of their original sentences. But Breed also cheated by getting his men to beat up Wladislaw for information. Spurred on by Franko's taunts, "Three wise men! [another ironic biblical reference] Trust your major! I'd rather trust Adolf Hitler," the Dozen initially blame Reisman until Breed's illegal invasion of their camp reveals the true story. During Reisman's second meeting with General Worden, the dominating overhead shot again appears. But this time a chandelier shows up in the scene, reminiscent of the one in the opening interior scene of *Attack!* It follows the Dozen's humiliation of Breed and his men when they invaded their camp. The mission appears in doubt. Aldrich frames the serious consequences of this by using familiar devices from his film and television work to express uncertainty. Reisman persuades the general to allow his men to participate in the training exercise and prove themselves. Once successful, the Dozen meet for a Last Supper before the mission. In an obvious reference to Clifford Odets's *Golden Boy,* Reisman informs them, "If you guys foul up on this one, none of us will play the violin again." He leads them in a ritualized rehearsal of their task, which they all articulate like a chorus repeating the various stages that will lead to D-Day. The penultimate lines of the "turkey shoot" chorus assert both the Satanic nature of their future roles and their gleeful anticipation at finding surrogates to vent their anger on: "We all call out, 'It's Halloween.' And kill every officer in sight."

The German high command inhabits a chateau similar to its Allied counterpart. Its exterior resembles the castle used as a prison and execution site for condemned American military prisoners in the film's opening sequences. Worden's conference room contained a classical bust and portrait of Franklin Delano Roosevelt. The German chateau contains similar classical objects as well as a bust of Adolf Hitler. Masquerading as German officers, Reisman and Wladislaw briefly pause before it in an ironic shot. Wladislaw is again probably conscious of his own status as a member of what is considered an inferior race on both sides. Before Maggott penetrates the German woman (Dora Reisser) with his knife in a parody of an orgasmic embrace, he and his victim pass a genteel figurine showing an eighteenth-century couple dancing. This figurine not only symbolically depicts the macabre dance of death involving Maggott and the woman but also represents another ironic Aldrich reference contrasting different forms of "civilized" behavior.

After Maggott nearly betrays the mission by pronouncing Judgment Day, all hell literally breaks loose, with the audience soon becoming fully aware of the brutal implications behind the mission. Members of the German high command and their ladies seek refuge in an underground cellar that contains high explosives. Although Combs correctly notes that many actions in this sequence occur with "dazzling speed and skill," three scenes in the film attempt to counter the spectacular, exciting dynamics that sway most audiences.[19] First, after Reisman and Wladislaw change uniforms, they order Gilpin (Ben Carruthers) to shoot the Germans and feed the French before they leave. Gilpin lines up German soldiers and French servants, the latter of whom speak no English and are afraid of their "liberators." Although Reisman's remark usually evokes laughter from audiences, he orders Gilpin to kill unarmed soldiers, an act usually associated with Germans in most World War II narratives prior to *Saving Private Ryan* (1998). In the eyes of the French servants, no difference exists between the two sides.[20] Second, when Reisman orders Sergeant Bowren to pour gasoline down the air vents, he questions the order of his superior officer for the first time in the film, asking him, "Are you sure?" Bowren has a shocked expression on his face. He now fully realizes the consequences of his actions and the nature of the actual mission. Reisman does not reply but instead stares at him with a deadly look on his face. Bowren immediately gets the message as he belatedly replies, "Yes, sir." Although this scene is brief, it suggests that Aldrich envisaged Bowren to represent certain audience members who were now critically understanding the ugly nature of the dynamic violence employed in the final third of the film. Finally, a long shot shows the French servants escaping from the chateau. But a panning shot, rather than showing them running away, follows them moving right back inside the chateau, which soon explodes in a fiery inferno reminiscent of the fate of Soberin's beach house in *Kiss Me Deadly*. It is a brief scene but one containing significant implications. But, as well as the irony of these people seeking refuge in a place that will soon explode into flames, other questions exist: Why they are doing this? Have they witnessed a brutal execution on the part of Gilpin that has sent them running back to their former masters for protection?

With the exception of Wladislaw, the Dozen "die in the line of duty." Reisman and Bowren also survive. All three coldly receive the congratulations of their superiors, Generals Worden and Denton (Robert Webber), on achieving their mission. The three figures ironically echo Christ on the cross accompanied by the penitent thief—Bowren, whose one moment of doubt qualifies him for this role—and his unrepentant counterpart—Wladislaw, who cynically remarks after the pompous Denton's departure that killing officers "could get to become a habit." The film ends with an overpowering overhead shot showing the three men associated with the dominant colors of the American flag—red, white, and blue. All three wear white hospital gowns. Bowren wears a blue dressing gown. Red blankets are on the bed. The music ironically reprises the military tune that greeted the Dozen's humorous arrival at Breed's training camp. It also heralded their victory over him at the maneuvers. The image then changes to show shots of the individual members of the Dozen matched to the official story heard on the soundtrack: "They lost their lives in the line of duty." However, as in the concluding voice-over of *Ten Seconds to Hell*, there is no easy resolution. The audience now knows the whole story behind the mission. Whether they will draw the appropriate implications is another matter.

Too Late the Hero was based on an earlier property Aldrich had acquired several years before the film became one of his studio projects. So far, his previous films had not achieved the financial success of *The Dirty Dozen*, and his production deal with ABC Palomar was in jeopardy. Possibly believing that another war film would repeat the success that enabled him to fulfill the dream of purchasing his own studio, he retrieved a story he had cowritten in 1959. Collaborating once more with Lukas Heller, Aldrich cowrote the screenplay, which the latter viewed as a "tremendously self-conscious examination of heroism" rather than another treatment of the ambiguous nature of human courage seen in the director's other films.[21] *Too Late the Hero* was both a critical and commercial failure, especially among the youth audience who appreciated *The Dirty Dozen* and possibly expected a less ambiguous treatment of militarism. As with Aldrich's other studio projects, such as *The Legend of Lylah Clare, The Killing of Sister George,* and *The Grissom Gang,* its failure to capture audience imagination led to the collapse of his attempt to recapture the Enterprise Studio dream.

However, *Too Late the Hero* is a complex film. Like *The Dirty Dozen,* it also undermines the conventions of the classical Hollywood war movie, though in a manner avoiding the macho identification characteristics of the earlier film. The mission in this film also succeeds at the cost of many lives. But the nature of the achievement is characterized by an ambiguity missing from the earlier film. As Aldrich would learn, most audiences reject narrative ambiguity unless that element appears in a framework that may superficially appear to confirm their attraction to a genre in the first instance. Very few directors in this era had the artistic freedom and studio support of a Stanley Kubrick to develop these themes.

The opening credits of *Too Late the Hero* foreshadow the unconventional nature of this film. Three new flags of America, Britain, and Japan appear in the left-hand side of the frame, accompanied by what first appears to be a rousing militaristic score by Gerald Fried. But as the images of the flags gradually change to show them worn-out, bullet-ridden, and ragged, the score also winds down to express fatigue and lassitude rather than the deceptively suggestive gung ho militarism of the opening minutes. The first sequence introduces Lt. Lawson (Cliff Robertson) lounging on a beach before he is summoned into the presence of Captain Nolan (Henry Fonda). Although less of a threat to the military bureaucracy than Major Reisman, he is another thorn in the side of the establishment. Lawson is clearly a manipulator and slacker, exhibiting little of Reisman's pragmatic qualities of survival except for his own gratuitous self-interest. Threatened with demotion unless he undertakes a mission as interpreter with an Argyle and Sutherland Highlander force on a New Hebrides island partially controlled by the Japanese, he begins his

journey as the credits continue. Although Nolan exhibits little of the
sadistic glee associated with General Worden in the earlier film, he
is also an authoritarian figure, though one less successful in his military career. Played by Henry Fonda, an actor generally associated
with leadership roles in American cinema, Nolan appears too old for
the rank of captain. His age raises questions in the mind of the audience as to why he is in that particular position rather than occupying another higher up in the military bureaucracy. He is clearly resentful toward Lawson for trying to fix him up with a date at a party.
Some sexual jealously against the younger man clearly exists, and he
uses the mission to get rid of a nuisance for more than one reason.

The next sequence follows Lawson's arrival at the British base and
introduces the audience to a group of soldiers betting on a game
with cockroaches eventually disrupted by Corporal Thornton (Ian
Bannen), who squashes the "competitors" in the same manner as
Private Ferol (Timothy Carey) does the cockroach in *Paths of Glory.*
These men have the edge over the cockroaches by living. But they
will also be in a similar situation once they begin their mission. The
soldiers leave their base and march through a perilous no-man's-
land resembling a football field, one involving a deadly game between the British and the Japanese, where the players are cheered on
by military spectators resembling those in a football stadium. Lawson soon witnesses this deadly game. It is one that will ironically involve his later participation. Sergeant Johnstone (Percy Herbert)
threatens another slacker, Campbell (Ronald Fraser), with a court-
martial should he attempt another "accidental" wound to remove
himself from combat. Although specifically a Scottish regiment, it is
composed of different groups of soldiers whom their commanding
officer describes as "anxious to escape the Army as well as the
Japanese." Medical orderly Private "Tosh" Hearne (Michael Caine)
cynically presides over this new version of *The Dirty Dozen,* expressing contempt against whatever new national version of the hated officer class may appear: "That's not a Yank. That's Snow White and
very pretty too."

Lawson's initial interview with Captain Nolan began with an introductory high-angle shot paralleling one used for Reisman's appearance before General Worden and the high command in *The
Dirty Dozen.* The reluctant lieutenant now introduces himself to
Colonel Thompson, whose office is an abandoned church complete
with a stained-glass window: "Rather an imaginative location for a

military headquarters." But the comment evokes no surprises for an audience familiar with Aldrich's view of the redundant nature of Western civilization and the cynical manipulation of its sacred artifacts. Ironically, the church bell will ring from the headquarters once the deadly sport between the Japanese and the British players begins.

Led by the incompetent Captain Hornsby (Denholm Elliot) and Lt. Lawson, the men begin their deadly mission to disable Japanese communications and send a false message in Japanese to aid the war effort. Despite Hearne's question concerning the expedition's viability should Lawson become accidentally killed (or fragged), Thompson orders it to begin. The men set off. When Lawson notices Thornton's aberrant behavior as they begin moving across the playing field, Hearn cynically replies, "They wouldn't let him in the Army if he's cuckoo, would they, sir?" It is an onerous mission complicated both by Hornsby's dismal leadership, resulting in the deaths of half the men by friendly fire, and by his murder of wounded Japanese prisoners, an action normally reserved for the "enemy" in the classical Hollywood war movie. Lawson reluctantly participates in the mission, rejecting the bravado of comments made to him by Hornsby with contempt. However, Hornsby's encouraging remarks such as, "You'll be one of the first over the top," and his emphasis on responsibility toward those who "depend on you" will later have ironic reverberations. When the group reaches the Japanese transmission station following the loss of the radio on which Lawson was to send misleading information, Hornsby suddenly proves himself a hero by deciding to use the Japanese radio and continue the mission. He tells Lawson, "I haven't got time to argue. You know what you have to do." Hornsby and another soldier overpower a Japanese radio officer and await Lawson's arrival. Despite this action, Lawson refuses. His face is shown in shadow, revealing the negative nature of his personality at this point. Although the plans have changed, Hornsby is technically the superior officer in charge whom Lawson should follow. His hesitation results in not only Hornsby's death but those of more British soldiers. Before dying, Hornsby crawls toward Lawson and gazes at him critically, causing the slacker to feel traumatic guilt. Ironically, the incompetent Hornsby has proved himself too late a hero, and Lawson's behavior causes the deaths of more men on the mission, similar to the deceased officer's previous actions.

By another stroke of irony, the survivors accidentally discover the presence of a Japanese airfield that would have nullified their original mission even if it had been successful. As Hearne comments, "Three rousing cheers for our air reconnaissance." However, this time they have to deal with Major Yamaguchi (Takakura Ken), a Japanese officer who offers them survival if they all temporarily surrender because of their knowledge of the airfield, whose planes will attack the American fleet. While the treacherous Campbell and two other soldiers decide to accept the offer, Hearne and Lawson express distrust. Colored by his experience of Japanese atrocities in Singapore, Hearne is reluctant to take up Yamaguchi's offer and cynically suggests his own plan for survival: "In six months time, the Japanese will be sitting on their side of the jungle and we on our part. And none of this will make any difference." Ironically, Lawson sees no difference between the sides and comments, "That Jap major would be lying like I would." However, in a portrayal deliberately subverting stereotypical Hollywood World War II movie images of the Japanese, Takakura Ken's Yamaguchi turns out to be the most honorable and moral person in the entire film. He is not lying and, in fact, keeps his word even though the full conditions of his offer have not been technically met. He does not execute the two surviving soldiers but is powerless to prevent his men from taking revenge on Campbell for his mutilation and robbery of a respected officer. As Yamaguchi says on the microphone, "It has been an incident that none of us can take any pride in." After his strategy of a fake execution, he looks at the two British soldiers with sadness after commenting, "Do you really find it so easy to believe I would shoot you?" As he had earlier commented to the surviving members of the mission, "The medals they give to dead heroes are made of blood. All they do is add weight to your coffins."

By this time, Lawson has become a hero by refusing to agree to Hearne's request that they go into hiding. Hearne correctly recognizes that Lawson's real motivation is guilt for his involvement in the death of Hornsby. Despite this, Lawson decides to make one more effort to return to their base and inform the Allies of their accidentally acquired information by causing a diversion. Their chosen target is Yamaguchi, whose death will cause temporary confusion among the Japanese, allowing them a head start across the playing field. Although Hearne speaks from his limited perspective as the hunted quarry, stating that Yamaguchi "has been asking for it for some time," the audience knows that the Japanese officer is simply doing his job in the most humane manner possible. Although a character like Yamaguchi would never have existed in the real-life situation of the Pacific campaign, his role in the film represents another example of Aldrich again destabilizing accepted generic conventions. Takakura Ken's performance deliberately departs from John Wayne's definition of the enemy as "Tojo and his bug-eyed monsters" in *The Fighting Seebees* (1944).

By killing the one moral character in the film (and, by implication, leaving their surrendered colleagues to the tender mercies of the Japanese, who may dispose of them in the same manner as Campbell after the death of another beloved officer), Hearne and Lawson begin the run across the playing field. As several critics point out, this is not only the most exciting sequence in the film but one resembling a football game as the two survivors run for their lives across the deadly terrain.[22] The sequence begins with eye-level medium shots clearly identifying the two men before the camera angle changes to high-angle long shots, making both impossible to identify. The audience shares the perspective of the Scottish regiment seeing one man falling in a rain of bullets and another appearing to die. However, like Lazarus rising from the dead in *Kiss Me Deadly*, a resurrected hero emerges and reaches the safety of his home base before collapsing once more. Aldrich cuts to an overhead shot of the soldiers moving toward the body and then changes to a close-up of Thompson as he recognizes the survivor. Hearne finally rises in mid shot. He answers his commanding officer with a parody of the heroic ideal, "Out there is a hero . . . killed fifteen bloody Japs single-handed . . . thirty if you like." His remarks are ironic and sarcastic, not only criticizing the false ideals of heroism but also presenting a perspective that the audience knows is entirely false. However, Lawson has died a hero but "too late." In a film echoing the ironic nature of contingencies in the universe of Stanley Kubrick, various character transformations have occurred that would have been unthinkable to those who began the mission.[23] Both the incompetent Hornsby and slacker Lawson have died as heroes. The opportunistic Hearne has become one in spite of himself. As Silver and Ursini comment, "The pragmatist survives but for no reason other than chance. The cynic who becomes a team player dies. Like the image of Costa and Cooney lying side by side in death, the capriciousness of war is underscored in the staging of the entire final scene."[24]

Aldrich eliminates the traditional mechanisms of audience identification and generic certainties from *Too Late the Hero*. It is a grim film that would please neither pro-war nor antiwar audiences, a film that is radically ambiguous at its core. However, what remains is a profound antiauthoritarian attitude. It motivated a director who accepted no easy solutions but, instead, recognized the arbitrary nature of human existence in a world devoid of meaning. Aldrich's war films echo the bleak pessimism of both his noir films and those that use sport as a metaphor for the dilemma human beings encounter in whatever game they may find themselves. These are often games in which they may not hold the "high card" in the words of Colonel Bartlett but ones in which an opportunity sometimes presents itself to either win temporary victory (*The Longest Yard*) or achieve an impossible goal of survival (*The Flight of the Phoenix*).

NOTES

1. Robin Wood, "Ideology, Genre, Auteur," *Film Comment* 13, no. 1 (1977): 47.

2. See Daniel Blum, *Theatre World: Season 1954–1956* (New York: Greenburg, 1955), 23.

3. See Larry Swindell, *Body and Soul: The Life of John Garfield* (New York: Morrow, 1975), 126. Aldrich had also hoped to collaborate with John Garfield in the future. During 1950, he cowrote the original story of *The Gamma People* with Louis Pollack. When Garfield became taboo, the project was shelved, but it was later acquired by producer John Gossage and director John Gilling, who made an appalling film version in 1955. Aldrich sued for disputed rights and credits. See Alain Silver and James Ursini, *What Ever Happened to Robert Aldrich? His Life and His Films* (New York: Limelight Editions, 1995), 320. Viewing the film again some forty-eight years after first seeing it confirmed my memories of its appalling nature. Aldrich would certainly have done a much a better job.

4. For a comparison between play and film, see Tony Williams, "*Fragile Fox*," in *The Encyclopedia of Stage Plays into Film*, ed. John C. Tibbetts and James M. Welsh (New York: Facts on File, 2001), 117–18.

5. Norman Brooks, *Fragile Fox* (New York: Dramatists Play Service, 1955), 1. All subsequent quotations are from this edition.

6. Pierre Sauvage, "Aldrich Interview," *Movie* 23 (1976–77): 59.

7. For viewing *Attack!* as a film noir, see Raymond Durgnat, "Paint It Black: The Family Tree of Film Noir," *Cinema* 6–7 (1970): 50.

8. Richard Combs, ed., *Robert Aldrich* (London: British Film Institute, 1978), 15. For other examinations of *Attack!*'s visual style, see Eric Kreuger, "Robert Aldrich's *Attack!*" *Journal of Popular Film* 2, no. 3 (1973): 262–76; and George Robinson, "Three by Aldrich," *The Velvet Light Trap* 9 (1974): 46–49.

9. Kreuger, "Robert Aldrich's *Attack!*" 274.

10. Edwin T. Arnold and Eugene I. Miller, *The Films and Career of Robert Aldrich* (Knoxville: University of Tennessee Press, 1986), 75. Aldrich disliked the conventional ending of *Attack!* stating that he would have preferred Woodruff to have accepted Bartlett's proposal. When Truffaut disagreed, Aldrich said that he believed that a compromise ending could have occurred when Woodruff stood before the corpses of Costa and Cooney. The audience could then assume that Woodruff would make the phone call later. This is a really interesting indication of Aldrich leaving the actual conclusion up to the audience. His own perspective represents a cynical, but unfortunately realistic, observation of the ways things happen in everyday life. See Francois Truffaut, "Rencontre avec Robert Aldrich," *Cahiers du Cinema* 64 (1956): 8.

11. See Arnold and Miller, *The Films and Career of Robert Aldrich,* 81; Silver and Ursini, *What Ever Happened to Robert Aldrich?* 99; and Denis Meikle, *A History of Horrors: The Rise and Fall of the House of Hammer* (Lanham, Md.: Scarecrow Press, Inc., 1996), 82–83.

12. Charles Higham and Joel Greenberg, *The Celluloid Muse: Hollywood Directors Speak* (London: Angus and Robertson, 1969), 33. Despite the lost footage, Luc Moullet believes that *Ten Seconds to Hell* has suffered less drastically than *The Garment Jungle*. Although many scenes explaining the psychological characteristics of the two leading characters ended up on the cutting-room floor, Moullet argues that the final film reflects an aesthetic form of geometric beauty, resulting in a better form of visual clarity reinforcing the theme without the baroque overtones seen in *Kiss Me Deadly*. The critic also applauds the combination of poetic and realistic dialogue in certain scenes that combine the best virtues of both literature and cinema in terms of a psychological lyricism. Although Moullet never mentions either Odets or Polonsky, the parallels to their work appear inescapable. See Moullet, "Le Poète et le Géometre," *Cahiers du Cinema* 101 (1959): 53–54.

13. Arnold and Miller, *The Films and Career of Robert Aldrich*, 82.

14. See particularly Robin Wood, *Hollywood: From Vietnam to Reagan* (New York: Columbia University Press, 1986), 32. To be fair, Wood's postscript regrets his disparaging reference to both Aldrich and Samuel Fuller as "emotional barbarians" (*Hollywood,* 45). Although he has not written in depth on Robert Aldrich, Jonathan Rosenbaum appears to share this attitude, as his humorous aside on *The Dirty Dozen* shows. See Rosenbaum, *Movies as Politics* (Berkeley: University of California Press, 1997), 93. The description has stuck over the years.

15. See Arnold and Miller, *The Films and Career of Robert Aldrich*, 125.

16. Sauvage, "Aldrich Interview," 59.

17. Arnold and Miller, *The Films and Career of Robert Aldrich*, 129.

18. See Robert Windeler, "Aldrich: To Shut Up and Take Your Lumps," *New York Times*, 3 September 1967: II, X9, quoted in Arnold and Miller, *The Films and Career of Robert Aldrich*, 129. For problems concerning the morality of the film, see Combs, *Robert Aldrich*, 27.

19. Combs, *Robert Aldrich*, 27.

20. Because of length many scenes were cut from the final print of *The Dirty Dozen*. Among these must have been Gilpin's execution of the Germans in front of the French servants. This would have given an added irony to the last time we actually see the servants in the film. The death of Samson Posey probably ended up on the cutting-room floor also.

21. Arnold and Miller, *The Films and Career of Robert Aldrich*, 152.

22. Arnold and Miller, *The Films and Career of Robert Aldrich*, 154; Silver and Ursini, *What Ever Happened to Robert Aldrich?* 136.

23. For the most thorough discussion of this concept, see, e.g., Thomas Allan Nelson, *Kubrick: Through a Film Artist's Maze* (Bloomington: Indiana University Press, 2000).

24. Silver and Ursini, *What Ever Happened to Robert Aldrich?* 136.

EIGHT

THE GAME OF SELF-RESPECT

At the climax of Robert Aldrich's *The Dirty Dozen* a hospitalized Major Reisman begins the process of his recovery by squeezing a rubber ball. Although he utilizes a familiar medical physiotherapy practice, it is also a familiar baseball practice routine. Not only has Reisman coached the Dozen into becoming a team, he also has to get back into shape for the next deadly game his superiors order him to play. Teamwork is a central issue in the war films, which often use sporting metaphors to symbolize complex goals of personal survival and the rational necessity of cooperative strategy. The baseball game played in the second sequence of *Ulzana's Raid* also illustrates Aldrich's lifelong interest in sport. Power politics rather than adherence to objective rules often dominate the game. In *Ulzana's Raid*, the sergeant can only express frustration when Lt. DeBuin inaccurately calls, "Strike." He dare not question the authority of his superior officer, even though he is incorrect. Also, in *Sodom and Gomorrah*, Astaroth and his associates deceive Queen Bera by pretending to play a game in her father's tomb while they are really plotting against her. Aldrich often uses such parallels in his films. For example, as assistant director on the boxing melodrama *Body and Soul*, he witnessed a drama where the central protagonist makes an important decision to regain his self-respect no matter how much it may cost him in the future. Personal integrity and teamwork become essential concepts in his films. Neither could exist without the other.

Despite their diversity, *Big Leaguer* (1953), *The Flight of the Phoenix* (1965), *Emperor of the North* (1973), *The Longest Yard* (1974), and . . . *All the Marbles* (1981) share many common themes. *The Flight of the Phoenix* initially appears the most incongruous among this group. Although resembling contemporary airplane survivalist dramas such as *Sands of the Kalahari* (1965), Aldrich's version of this dilemma eschews Cy Endfield's Social Darwinist "survival of the fittest" premises to emphasize instead cooperation and teamwork. A nominal hero must recognize the superior qualifications of a character he detests and follow his guidance. He must also overcome destructive self-pity and work with others toward achieving both individual and collective survival. *Emperor of the North* is a depression drama involving a deadly contest between two rugged individualists. Although the contest does not involve collective team spirit, the secondary plot involving Cigaret casts doubt on the younger generation's ability to learn from the mistakes of the past and form viable collective alternatives. *The Longest Yard* combines the prison movie with sports film. . . . *All the Marbles* pursues Aldrich themes of teamwork and adversity against overwhelming odds using a very different type of team.

Aldrich tended to dismiss his first film. But *Big Leaguer* is not devoid of interest. Although an apprentice work, it foreshadows themes the director develops in his later work. In many ways, it parallels the relationship Howard Hawks's aviation drama *Ceiling Zero* (1936) has to his more mature *Only Angels Have Wings* (1939).[1] Like *Ceiling Zero*, *Big Leaguer* provides a structural framework that Aldrich later refined. Aldrich's involvement in Enterprise Studios indirectly led to his first film as director. He had worked with Herbert Baker at the time. Baker was now writing a screenplay for a baseball film for an MGM unit engaged in producing low-budget second features. He enthusiastically recommended Aldrich as director on the basis of his track record in film and television as well as his former role as an athlete in college.[2]

Shot on location at the New York Giants training camp in Melbourne, Florida, on a fourteen-day schedule, *Big Leaguer* opens unpromisingly with sportswriter character Brian McLennon (Paul Langton) addressing the camera directly. Documentary footage of baseball stars and kids playing the game follows. These opening shots prime the audience for what appears to be a minor routine production of interest only to baseball fans featuring two stars fallen from their former glory, "graylisted" Edward G. Robinson and MGM musical heroine Vera-Ellen. Although Robinson escaped the fate of stars such as John Garfield, his artistic, ethnic, and 1930s liberal associations rendered him suspect during the blacklist era. Vera-Ellen became a star casualty of a genre MGM now began to discard. This would be her last film for the studio. McLennon's voice-over primes the viewer for a B movie dealing with life at the bottom of the baseball game. Young men arrive at a training camp to pursue their chance at the big time. The winners will achieve a $150-a-month contract with the Giant's farm club as the first step in their tentative careers. As Silver and Ursini note, Aldrich's equation of sports and combat already appears in a narration comparing the time before the tryouts as "zero hour" and the big day on the field as "D-Day."[3]

Coach John Lobert (Edward G. Robinson) tells his young charges that their grandfathers may have seen him playing third base. He also instills in them an important motto, namely, that doing their best, rather than aiming for a contract that only a few of them will gain, represents "the three important words" in his personal philosophy. Like Aldrich, the important thing is to "give it all you got."

As played by Edward G. Robinson (who was not in peak physical condition at the time), Lobert appears a gruff but benevolent father figure, lacking the complex characteristics of later Aldrich heroes. The actor's health and brief shooting schedule probably affected his depiction of a character who is not entirely noble. But Aldrich provides certain visual and thematic clues to reveal that not everything is ideal in Lobert's world. He is an older man nearing retirement. But he wishes to remain in the game for as long as he can. Lobert asserts that he is the one who will know when it is time to leave the game. However, his niece Christy (Vera-Ellen), on vacation from the New York Giants headquarters, informs him that he may not have a choice in the matter. Certain bureaucrats have criticized the past few training sessions. She describes them as "a couple of people, not even baseball players, giving the office a beating." Christy has heard front office gossip about "a replacement" for her uncle. These lines would have a particular resonance for a director often struggling with an industry emphasizing the exclusive values of box-office returns. Aldrich would also find himself replaced during the shooting of *The Garment Jungle*.

Lobert is an idealist. He enthusiastically informs his niece that his real pleasure occurs at the beginning of the training session by "opening the Cracker Jack box" and, maybe, finding "a real diamond inside." However, Christy warns him: "That's fine. But baseball is a business." So is cinema. Lobert later expresses regret when he has to begin rejecting several recruits. He understands that his decisions may not all be objective. Although Bobby Bronson (Richard Jaeckel) proves himself as a pitcher in the exhibition game concluding the tryout season, Lobert drops him from the team. He decides to retain the more mediocre Tippy Mitchell (Bill Crandall), the son of a friend and celebrated player who has now retired. Lobert wishes to make an old friend happy. Wally Mitchell (Frank Ferguson) hopes that Tippy will follow in his footsteps. Lobert's decision also reflects the cronyism and nepotism occurring in a Hollywood industry when a more talented newcomer loses out to a less talented competitor. As Combs and Silver and Ursini note, when Bobby leaves the camp, a specific camera angle emphasizes Lobert's guilt when he remarks, "I may have just booted one." As Bobby departs and walks away into the background, the camera moves around Lobert.[4] The coach obviously fears that his mistake will come home to haunt him. It does in the final game when Bobby returns as key pitcher with the Dodger farm team. His prowess nearly causes another dent in Lobert's record by threatening his removal from a game he loves. Lobert makes a wrong decision, one that would lead to his "retirement." As he recognizes, "This camp is lousy with fathers." Lobert makes another wrong decision toward the end of *Big Leaguer.* He persuades an angry father to agree to his son's participation in the final game by promising him that he will later (illegally) reject him from the team.

Adam Polachuk (Jeff Richards) has sneaked away from college to pursue his dream of becoming a baseball player. He defies the wishes of his immigrant father that he follow a more secure version of the American dream. As Adam tells the understanding Christy, his father is "tough to understand." His mother deserted the family when he was fourteen. As a product from the industrial mining town of Piston, Adam is another version of Joe Bonaparte of *Golden Boy.* The screenplay suggests this in both its opening narration referring to the "little people" and Christy's humorous remark to Adam: "Your family are ashamed of you. They always wanted you to be a concert violinist."

Like certain Clifford Odets characters, Adam has psychological conflicts involving his own motivations. He expresses self-doubt. After his photo appears in a sports magazine, Adam decides to submit to his father's plans for his future. But Christy criticizes his decision and warns him of its future consequences: "If you quit tonight, it'll follow you through every law book you ever open." Adam's angry father (Mario Siletti) arrives in time for the final game and attempts to make his son return to law school. However, Lobert achieves a temporary respite that will allow Adam to fulfill his dream during the baseball game. During the game Mr. Polachuk sits next to Wally Mitchell, who recognizes his own son's lack of promise and also acclaims Adam a "born player." However, Polachuk finally agrees to allow his son to follow his dream when he learns of the economic rewards. Money rules his final decision rather than altruism to allow a son to follow his own creative directions. By informing him that the next phase of training will result in a $150-a-month contract, Mitchell educates Mr. Polachuk toward the fact that his son may find fame *and* fortune in an American dream seen in the film's opening documentary footage featuring baseball heroes such as Joe DiMaggio and Billy Thompson. Mr. Polachuk also represents an ironic depiction of Odets's father, who wished for his son's material success in the New World. These wishes never involved understanding any type of creative aspirations.[5] By pursuing a different career from his own father, Aldrich probably faced similar problems.

Big Leaguer concludes with Lobert saying farewell to his successful "sons." Three voice-overs state that others will strive for different "big leaguer" goals in law, business, and marriage. However, as Combs points out, *Big Leaguer* concludes with a sequence that suggests the kind of symmetry and unruliness anticipating Aldrich's later films. As "the sportswriter/commentator intones 'this story ends where it began, with the kids,' the film returns to a sequence of children playing a makeshift game of baseball, whose final image is of an argument with the umpire dissolving into a mass of flailing limbs."[6] *Big Leaguer* is a minor film but prophetic. As Arnold and Miller note, Aldrich has begun an initial sketch for the motifs of group solidarity and the contradictory nature of decisions made under pressure occurring in works such as *The Flight of the Phoenix, The Dirty Dozen,* and *The Longest Yard.*[7] This first film echoes the director's own personal philosophy.

The Flight of the Phoenix is based on a novel by Elleston Trevor adapted by Lukas Heller. Unlike *The Dirty Dozen,* the film attracted critical acclaim but did not achieve box-office success. However, it is one of Aldrich's most accomplished films, in that his pragmatic adaptation of the message of Clifford Odets achieves full cinematic realization. Despite Aldrich's definition of the film as a "patrol picture" along the lines of *Too Late the Hero,* the spirit of Odets is not too far away in terms of the film's emphasis on the most appropriate form of personal and communal survival.[8] Instead of showing the Great Depression affecting an already dysfunctional American family, *The*

Flight of the Phoenix envisages the deadly environment of an Arabian desert causing as much psychological tension to the survivors as that earlier devastating blow did to those members of a 1930s generation who once believed in a false American dream. A motley group of individuals travels together in an old aeroplane leaving the Arabco oilfields. An arbitrary sandstorm causes the plane to crash in the desert. Two men are killed, and another is fatally injured. Confronted with the possibility that no rescue mission will arrive in time, the survivors decide to follow the seemingly insane idea of building another aeroplane from the "ashes" of the permanently damaged plane. It is a goal affected by personal antagonisms that threaten the success of the entire enterprise. Although the frailty of human hope wins against overwhelming odds, it is not achieved without personal loss and conflict. But the survivors learn the necessity of putting aside individual dissension to work toward a common enterprise.

The Flight of the Phoenix shows that cooperation among conflicting individuals can succeed. But it involves a pragmatic approach that involves the rejection of all deceptive illusions hindering that goal. Much like *Ten Seconds to Hell,* based on a novel significantly titled *The Phoenix, The Flight of the Phoenix* is Aldrich's most optimistic film in terms of critiquing human alienation and emphasizing the goal of collective action. As Silver and Ursini note, the film has an existentialist dimension in which "hope lies only in action, and that the only thing that allows a man to live is action."[9]

Another key influence haunts the film very much like Marx's metaphor of the spirit haunting Europe in the opening lines of *The Communist Manifesto.* It is, namely, the ghost of a Great Depression that shattered the illusions of those living in the past and emphasized another goal of collective action, one opposed by the ruling elite both then and now. Odets's understanding of the dangerous psychological effects of the depression and the importance of striving toward a common goal allowing the survivors to "awake and sing" also haunts *The Flight of the Phoenix.* During the 1930s, the Popular Front movement attempted to unify disparate groups in an artistic and political vision to combat the worst effects of the American depression. Although *The Flight of the Phoenix* articulates "the necessity for cooperation for human survival" and never mentions this historical context,[10] a line occurs in the film anticipating Major Reisman's concluding words to the Dozen about following the guidelines or "none of us will play the violin again." After the return of Captain Harris (Peter Finch) from the dead, the obnoxious Crow (Ian Bannen) remarks to Bellamy (George Kennedy), "Sisters of Mercy. Our brother will play the violin again." It does not occur in the final draft of the screenplay and obviously originates from Aldrich. Harris receives that second chance granted to fallen heroes in the world of Howard Hawks. But he will fail again in the more arbitrary universe of Robert Aldrich.

Odets's philosophy acts as an important influence on *The Flight of the Phoenix*. Like Jacob in *Awake and Sing!* and many other Odets figures, several characters in the film cling to illusions that are no longer relevant to their plight. Cobb (Ernest Borgnine) dies clinging to the last remnant of his masculinity by writing his name in the sand after being refused the opportunity of accompanying Harris on his journey. He looked on this as his last chance to reclaim a self-respect demolished by his nervous breakdown, which would eliminate him from future employment as a foreman. Captain Harris is a "by-the-book" British officer whose two heroic decisions lead to disaster. Gabriele (Gabriele Tinti) clings to the illusion that his wife is waiting for him until he admits to Standish (Dan Duryea) that she is actually dead. Once he loses this last fragile grip on reality, the already dying man commits suicide. Standish clings to his religious beliefs, which are of no practical use to the survivors. The humanitarian Dr. Renaud (Christian Marquand) loses his life for a good cause that proves deadly by accompanying Harris to the Bedouin camp. Frank Towns (James Stewart) lives in a past no longer relevant to his present position piloting an old aeroplane, presumably the only flying job he can get at his age. Lew Moran (Richard Attenborough) is an alcoholic. The unpleasant Heinrich Dorfman (Hardy Kruger) is an idealist. But he succeeds against all possible odds by constructing a new aeroplane and saving the survivors. These men have to work as a team or perish. Frank Towns relinquishes leadership to Dorfman. Lew Moran achieves his own form of heroic status by acting as mediator between Towns and Dorfman. These men have to reject regressive patterns of behavior. Those who remain trapped by old patterns of behavior die. Yet the question of survival is arbitrary. Noble characters die, whereas unlikable ones such as Crow and Sergeant Watson (Ronald Fraser) survive.

The Flight of the Phoenix opens with a telephoto shot of the blazing sun before tilting down to the ground as an old Arabco passenger airliner takes off. Two shots show the ominous shadow the plane casts

on the ground before revealing pilot Frank Towns, navigator Lew
Moran, and their diverse group of passengers. Lew notes that the
plane's radio is nonfunctional and the regulators appear faulty. He
moves into the passenger area to reassure a mixed group including
British military officer Captain Harris, Sergeant Watson, and Heinrich
Dorfman; oil workers "Trucker" Cobb, Crow, and Bellamy; and
Arabco company doctor Renaud, accountant Standish, Carlos (Alex
Montoya), Gabriele, Tasso (Peter Bravos), and Bill (William Aldrich).
The casting of the last two represent Aldrich's ironic sense of humor.
As a director often employing friends and family before and behind
the camera, he will eliminate his son-in-law (then married to daughter
Adell working behind the scenes) and son after the opening credits.

Other casting choices are significant. James Stewart's star persona
evokes his familiar presence in the comforting depression-era cinema of Frank Capra, *You Can't Take It with You* (1938) and *Mr. Smith
Goes to Washington* (1939). But he is much older. Stewart now finds
himself cast adrift from the world of Frank Capra and rudderless in
the very different universe of Robert Aldrich. Stewart's Hollywood
stardom was beginning its slow decline. His Frank Towns character
bears several similarities to Stewart. Both men have seen better days.
Aldrich also cast Dan Duryea from *China Smith* and *World for Ransom* in a different role from his usual stereotyped villain performance, a religious-minded bookkeeper. Aldrich pokes some fun at his
character, making Duryea even more ineffective than he had been in
the climax of *World for Ransom*. Standish worries about missing his
deadline to deliver the company annual report. Although receiving
reassurance that a rescue party will soon arrive, Standish comments,
"Insurance companies move in mysterious ways. Like God but not
so generous." Before the plane crashes Crow makes a sarcastic remark as Standish moves toward the restroom. He later teases him
about eating their only food supply of "preserved dates." Captain
Harris earlier mentioned that dates ensure "regularity" in another
line added to the revised draft of the final screenplay. However, despite Aldrich's familiar satire of religion as an outmoded convention, he does give Standish some respect. When the *Phoenix* finally
rises, a close-up reveals a rosary behind Standish's back. Standish
hides his prayer from Crow. It is a very private moment that Aldrich
allows the audience to share despite the fact that it has no practical
value. Furthermore, Standish understands what the new plane really means to the survivors, and he gives it the name of *Phoenix*.

Before the plane crash, Moran exhibits surprise at Cobb's redundant offer to loan him a transistor radio to replace the plane's defunct equipment. Cobb also makes the irrelevant remark, "Record players are nice. They're reliable." Dr. Renaud looks at Cobb with concern, while Crow questions his sanity by making a recognizable gesture. Cobb represents an extreme version of the film's dilemma involving the various struggles between illusion and reality affecting all the characters. When Cobb notices Bill attentively reading *Playboy,* he offers him a flask of whiskey so that he can "read the picture better." Cobb also comments that alcohol will result in illusion becoming reality: "It comes out of the picture and bites you." This comment foreshadows two later scenes in the film. Gabriele clings to an image of a wife who is actually dead. Sergeant Watson experiences a desert fantasy mirage involving dancer Farida (Barrie Chase). Rather than being imposed on the director by a front office wishing a female presence in a male action film, this latter sequence actually reinforces a key theme in *The Flight of the Phoenix.*[11] It emphasizes the necessity of confronting dangerous realities and discarding all illusions, no matter how comforting they may be. Farida's presence in the film also evokes Odets's frequent condemnation of a Hollywood industry manufacturing false romantic illusions. In addition, the scene may represent Aldrich's satirical dig at Hollywood conventions demanding a female presence in the most inappropriate generic context. She appears after Watson feels guilt over the death of Captain Harris. But her illusionary lures and arbitrary intrusion into the narrative offer no real comfort for Watson. Her appearance is merely a tease, and Dorfman brings him back to reality by calling him back to work on the plane.

Although Aldrich referred to *The Flight of the Phoenix* as a patrol picture, alluding to another faded Hollywood genre along the lines of John Ford's *The Lost Patrol* (1934), this version differs radically from its predecessors. Although it contains stock characters such as by-the-book officer, cowardly soldier, religious-minded figure, and eventual survivor (who may or may not become insane because of the ordeal), it subverts the genre in several ways. *The Flight of the Phoenix* is a film where *all* actors work as a team, whether they are major stars or not.

Audiences would expect James Stewart's character to be the heroic leader figure they could identify with, similar to his Frank Capra persona. But Aldrich evokes another side of the star's image.

During the 1950s, directors such as Anthony Mann and Alfred Hitchcock explored the dark side of the Stewart persona in films such as *Winchester 73* (1950), *Bend of the River* (1952), *The Naked Spur* (1953), *The Far Country* (1955), *The Man from Laramie* (1955), *The Man Who Knew Too Much* (1956), and *Vertigo* (1958), revealing features of male hysteria and dangerous authoritarian dominance. As Frank Towns, Stewart exhibits both features in the film. He reacts angrily against Dorfman's ambitions to construct a new plane and take over his former commanding role as pilot. Although condemning Sergeant Watson's behavior toward his superior officer, he often uses him as a convenient surrogate victim for his own frustrations. When Towns discovers that someone has stolen from the water ration, Aldrich cuts from a close-up of the pilot's angry face to Watson. Towns believes that he is the guilty party until Dorfman admits his guilt. During the opening scenes in the film, Towns dismisses ominous weather signs as a "local sandstorm." He then waxes nostalgically about the glory days of aviation: "A pilot is supposed to use his own judgement, don't you think? I suppose pilots now are just as good as they used to be. But they don't live the way we did when you used to take pride in just getting there. Flying used to be fun. It used to be." When Dorfman looks at Towns, he comments, "That pilot. I would have thought he's a little too elderly to be flying without a co-pilot."

Dorfman's remarks could also apply to the lack of a leading costar in the film. Although Richard Attenborough is billed second in the cast, the British actor was just starting to attempt a Hollywood career. Apart from *The Great Escape* (1963), he was not well known to American audiences. His alcoholic Lew Moran evokes the untrustworthy figures Attenborough often played in films such as *The Ship that Died of Shame* (1955), *The Man Upstairs* (1958), *Jet Storm* (1959), *I'm All Right Jack* (1959), *S.O.S Pacific* (1959), and *The League of Gentlemen* (1960). But his character is much more complex. Towns later accuses Moran of not checking equipment before takeoff. But Towns bears full responsibility himself. Were this a formula film, Towns would heroically rally the survivors into working toward a common goal, making "Kraut" Heinrich follow American leadership in collaboration with Captain Harris. Flawed figures such as Moran, Cobb, Watson, Crow, and Standish would all perish. A formulaic Hollywood narrative could have Standish following Boris Karloff's example in *The Lost Patrol* in trying to convert the Arab outlaws and dying instead of the heroic Renaud. But *The Flight of the Phoenix* defies such expectations. It insists on following its own particular patterns.

After the crash causes the deaths of Bill and Tasso, the survivors bury the bodies. When Standish asks Towns, "Do you want to say something?" the guilt-ridden pilot replies, "Like what? 'I'm sorry.'" As pilot, Towns bears a certain responsibility for the plane crash. But he masochistically indulges in an overpowering sense of guilt as crippling as that affecting Charlie Castle in *The Big Knife* and Eric Koertner in *Ten Seconds to Hell.* Unlike the more mature and resilient Geoff Carter of Howard Hawks's *Only Angels Have Wings* (1939), who tells Bonnie Lee that a multiple number of circumstances caused the death of Joe, Towns chooses to nurture his own masochism by unduly blaming himself for the disaster. But Lew's negligence and an oil company supplying a defective old plane for passenger transportation are also relevant factors. Survival in the film involves overcoming personal problems as well as the dangerous nature of a hostile environment. All must work toward a common goal that not everyone will reach. The question of survival is as arbitrary as the set of cards received at the gaming table. It does not involve neat civilized moral distinctions because both good and bad characters may survive. Crow and Watson are two characters who would not ordinarily survive in a typical Hollywood film.

After the funeral service, Crow comments about Watson's superior officer: "He's a right little organizer, your captain." Watson replies, "They're all the same, toffee-nosed little gits." He then reveals his past to Crow. A parent betrayed him years ago, making him similar to Burt Hanson, Jane Hudson, and Charlotte Hollis. His father suddenly enlisted him into the Army as a boy soldier during the Great Depression, probably for economic reasons. Watson speaks of a mother, who made him a sponge cake for his birthday on 20 November 1934. His father deserted him at the recruiting office the next day. Like Captain Cooney in *Attack!* Watson is also a family victim, though less dangerous to the group. He refuses to obey orders involving suicidal missions. Watson also expresses resentment against Captain Harris, whom he obviously regards as a hated surrogate father figure by *deserting him* on two occasions. During his final act of disobedience, Watson denies that he is afraid and rejects his superior's commanding status by referring to him as "*Mr.* Harris." Although Watson's behavior appears cowardly in Towns's eyes, it also represents an act of revolt against a father figure whose actions would lead to his own death. As the screenplay notes, although Harris never verbally bullies Watson, "his tone always assumes unquestioning obedience, so that the effect is that of a father addressing a slightly retarded child."

Moran recognizes that Captain Harris "goes by the book. You can't rewrite it for him. " He is as trapped within a fixed code of behavior as Frank Towns. During two occasions in the film he makes decisions that are both heroic and foolish. He ignores advice concerning the hazards of marching in the desert by trusting the "absolute precision" of his now useless military training. After surviving his first attempt, he finally perishes on his second mission by trying to contact a group of renegade Arab tribesmen. On both occasions, Harris indirectly causes the deaths of those who chose to accompany him on these missions: the sympathetic Carlos and the humanitarian Dr. Renaud. Like Henry Fonda in *Too Late the Hero,* he appears incongruously too old for his actual rank. The screenplay recognizes this as well. It also refers to a lack of imagination that causes not only his death but others as well: "Harris is a good officer, but as one who earnestly believes that there must be a military solution to every problem, he is inclined to lack imagination which may be emphasized by the fact that he seems to have passed the age at which he might have expected to be promoted to major."

Despite these conflicting factors, Towns never sees the entire picture. Affected by Harris's foolhardy resolution, he sees in him the heroic figure he wishes to be. Already blaming himself for the plane crash, which he ascribes in the log to "pilot's error," Towns masochistically wishes to die for his sins like a fallen savior. When Cobb deserts the group, Towns sets out in pursuit, blaming himself for another incident he could not fully control: "It was my fault. I should have watched him." He conveniently ignores the fact that he is the only pilot among the group and thus essential for Dorfman's plan of survival. By the time Towns finds him it is too late. Cobb has died. His last physical act was writing his name in the sand, as if attempting to reaffirm his fragile identity as a man for the last time. The action also symbolizes the futile nature of Towns's action. He is "too late the hero." A scene edited from the film showed a sandstorm obliterating Cobb's last desperate attempt to assert his insecure sense of identity in the sand. When Towns returns, Dorfman justly criticizes Towns's "romantic search" for someone who was already as good as dead. Like Charlie Castle and Eric Koertner, he harbors a death wish. His cynical attitude toward Dorfman's attempt to build another plane from the ruins of the old one really conceals self-destructive motivations. Towns really wishes to "go down with his ship" like a sea captain in a storm.

Trucker Cobb represents the dark side of Towns. His male hysteria also evokes parallels to Captain Cooney in *Attack!* and Burt from *Autumn Leaves*. When we first see him on the plane, Cobb exhibits regressive behavioral patterns immediately noticed by Towns, Moran, and Crow. After Cobb collapses into hysteria following his rejection from Harris's trek into the desert, we learn that Dr. Renaud (who has obviously accompanied him on the trip to Benghazi) diagnosed him as emotionally unstable. Suffering from agoraphobia because of his exposure to the desert, Cobb hoped to return home as a chief oil rigger supervising seven men. However, despite Renaud's assurances that his medical condition will not last, Cobb knows he has no future: "I can't understand those fancy words and I don't think the guys who do the hiring do anyway. They won't let no headcase run a drilling operation." Cobb symbolically embodies the dangerous male hysteria hidden inside Frank Towns, who indulges in heroic memories of the "good old days." But Towns has to understand the nature of his own character before he can help himself and others.

Despite differences, Dorfman has several similarities to Towns. As Lew later comments to a friend he recognizes as "living in the past," Dorfman always "has to be right." Towns believes that the new plane that Dorfman expects to rise from the ashes of the old plane will never fly. He angrily counters Lew's attempt at mediation with the guilt-ridden answer: "Are you asking me to kill the rest of them getting this death trap off the ground?" Lew and Renaud assert the importance of taking action rather than sitting around and watching everyone die. Whereas Towns prefers to wallow in guilt, Dorfman wishes to build another plane and give the survivors hope. However, like Towns, Dorfman exhibits negative behavior. When Towns first rejects his plan, Dorfman temporarily isolates himself from the group by sitting alone in the desert. After the second confrontation with Towns, Dorfman sulks on his bed in a manner reminiscent of Captain Cooney in *Attack!* until Lew acts as mediator.[13] Unlike Lt. Woodruff in *Attack!* he brings both sides together by both criticizing their weaknesses and appealing to the responsibility they have to the rest of the survivors. After Towns reveals his guilt-ridden feelings to Moran concerning his exaggerated sense of responsibility for the deaths of Tasso, Bill, Cobb, Harris, and Renaud—"I've done my share of killing. My score is five"—Moran recognizes that his friend is not only wallowing in self-pity but also resenting Dorfman's assumption of leadership: "That's what gets you about him. He always has to be right." Lew then criticizes Towns: "But if you mean, it's all your fault then it's up to you to get us out of it."

Moran also criticizes Dorfman later in the film. After attempting to make him understand Towns's feelings—"He needs to feel he's doing something. You don't leave him anything"—he condemns Dorfman's own selfish behavior: "If he's making stupidity a virtue, you're making it a bloody science." When Towns later relinquishes authority at Dorfman's request, he does admit his own personal failings to Moran: "I guess old Frank Towns could never stand being told what to do." Moran forms the link between Dorfman and Towns. Although Dorfman admits that a "model plane has to fly itself," the *Phoenix* needs a pilot to give it much "greater stability." Towns is the only possible candidate for this mission. The concluding scenes of the film resolve the conflicts between the two men. Towns decides to act as a member of a team rather than hinder the survival effort. When the survivors attempt to launch the plane, Dorfman orders Towns to use the seven starter devices frugally. But Towns not only disobeys his new leader by using a precious starter to clean out the engine so that it can finally operate but also keeps the engines running despite Dorfman's reservations. Towns has now returned to "doing something" by using his own experience and powers of imagination. Unlike Harris, he will not do things by the book. He acts spontaneously in a more positive manner by allowing his energies to move in more constructive rather than self-destructive directions. Towns returns again to being a hero. And, unlike other Aldrich characters, he is not "too late the hero." But his action now becomes a key link in a common group effort rather than emerging from individual assertiveness.

Justly described as "one of Aldrich's most hopeful and affirming films," *The Flight of the Phoenix* moves to an optimistic conclusion showing all survivors unified by the joy of success.[14] As the *Phoenix* takes off, Towns finally glances at the graves of Bill, Tasso, and Gabriele (who has committed suicide). He will always remember them. But he will no longer allow crippling guilt feelings to destroy his personality. When they finally land near a waterhole, no antagonisms or old grudges emerge. Towns even accepts Crow's salute. When the plane lands, Moran humorously remarks, "I never knew water looked so good. You know, I feel I might become an addict." Towns finally affirms Dorfman's vision. He not only quotes historical information he learned about model planes earlier but accepts a final correction from his former antagonist: "Meters or yards?" Dorfman replies, good-naturedly, "Meters. Mr. Towns." Rather than regarding this as an unfortunate "conventional ending," we should value this conclusion.[15] Survival is sometimes possible. Former enemies may become friends. The goal is not just surviving a difficult situation but also overcoming negative personal qualities that hinder the very nature of that survival. Sometimes the old values of the past may work in a different way. Dorfman builds a new plane from the wreckage of the old. But although his *Phoenix* rises from the ashes like that classical mythological creature, it does so in a unique manner. Dorfman has never built an actual plane. He constructs model planes. But his idealism results in survival. It is not false idealism but, indeed, involves a harsh look at reality leading to the practical teamwork arriving at a new method of collective survival.

Originally titled *Emperor of the North Pole,* Aldrich's second depression film also aimed to recover the audience he had lost since the failure of his studio and the limited success of *Ulzana's Raid.* The film depicts the conflict of two allegorical characters, the legendary King of the Hobos, A No. 1 (Lee Marvin), also known as the Emperor of the North Pole, and Railroad Man Shack (Ernest Borgnine), who identifies with his train No. 19 and basks in his reputation for not allowing anyone a free ride. Abbreviating the title to *Emperor of the North* (so audiences would not expect something set in the frozen North!), Aldrich released the film to critical and commercial indifference. He found this response difficult to comprehend. But, as several critics note, the film is flawed in many ways, most notably in attempting a schematic allegory involving a battle between establishment and antiestablishment forces that simply does not work.[16]

In his third and final role for Robert Aldrich, Lee Marvin seems less dynamic than in his previous performances in *Attack!* and *The Dirty Dozen.* He appears "tired," playing certain scenes in a manner resembling Jack Palance in *Ten Seconds to Hell* and Robert Mitchum in *The Angry Hills.* The film's most intense performance comes from

Ernest Borgnine as the demonic Shack, a character Aldrich recognized as having a particular integrity in terms of understanding what he actually was and gloating in his own murderous corruption. In many ways, Shack is as individualistic as his antagonist A No. 1. But their eventual climactic fight is individualistic rather than political. *Emperor of the North* really works as a competitive game between two opposing forces with personal systems of honor rather than as an overt political allegory. Both characters are involved in a deadly contest that operates outside their different social worlds. The other railroad workers detest Shack, whereas A No. 1 is a law unto himself. The British movie posters stressed this personal dimension with the caption, "If you ride Shack's Train you'll be Emperor of the North." However, the political issues are not entirely absent from the text, as seen in the case of one supporting character.

Aldrich initially changed the character of Cigaret (Keith Carradine) from a youth figure the audience could identify with to one representing a contemporary generation that had sold out politically. He saw Cigaret as representing the youth culture of the "post-Vietnam era, when everyone went back to sleep and said, 'I don't care. It's over. I'm gonna play melody.'"[17] In this light, Aldrich made a correct assessment of the younger generation. But he alienated this segment of the audience in the same way he did an older generation that may not have wished to be reminded of the Great Depression. The film appeared at the time of the 1970s oil crisis, which adversely affected the spirit of an American public that had so far benefited from postwar affluence. Hence, it would serve as a grim reminder that "happy times" may not be here again. In retrospect, history proved Aldrich correct. Cigaret embodies the worst aspects of an apolitical, postmodernist "me" generation that would soon emerge in the next decade. Keith Carradine would later become a supporting player in Madonna's music video for "Material Girl," and Aldrich would live to see the effects of the recession on the heavy industry locations he would use in . . . *All the Marbles.*

Carradine's Cigaret is corrupt, devious, and opportunistic, fully deserving his eventual fate after refusing tuition into the ways of the road offered by A No. 1. His character aptly symbolized a 1960s generation that flirted with the Left and later made its bed with the Right in the Reagan era and beyond. Even Shack has his own code of personal integrity, which he follows to the end. *Emperor of the North* represents another Aldrich recognition of changing times. The clear political divisions of the American depression are now becoming blurred. Despite the film's opening caption promising a life-and-death struggle between the oppressed hobos and the railroad man in which trains represent "the only source of survival," what eventually emerges is a battle between two individual dinosaurs who have no relevance to either their own time or the future. As Lee Marvin astutely noted concerning the change of the film's original title, "Because you're *Emperor of the North Pole,* that means you're an 'emperor' of nothing, and *Emperor of the North* doesn't say that to me."[18] Yet this may illuminate the very point of the film. It is a depression film made in the Vietnam era but containing none of the political clarity of earlier films such as *Wild Boys of the Road* (1931) and *Heroes for Sale* (1933). It instead reflects a "don't mean nothing" attitude indicative of American disillusion with the Vietnam War and the era's failure to form any viable alternatives to a corrupt system. The epic battle between A No. 1 and Shack means nothing unless a collective sense of community occurs. *Emperor of the North* lacks this in contrast to *The Flight of the Phoenix, The Longest Yard,* and . . . *All the Marbles.*

Despite the rigors of the depression, some potential for change is in the air. When A No. 1 visits Smile (Liam Dunn), who has retired from the road and runs a hobo jungle camp, he hears FDR. on the radio promising new deals and fair shares for all. But both men do not listen. It is almost as if they know that these promises will never materialize. Christopher Knopf's final-draft screenplay sets the period in the last year of the Hoover administration, the same period setting of *The Grissom Gang.* Although omitting the radio address, it contains a revealing description of the hobo camp that merges past, present, and future: "Everywhere are the men, or what remains of men. Most come from better times, better places, but they are not without their own style, their own humor and have a ritual and social structure as rich and colorful as the first church. Others are ahead of their time, have dropped out of the normal world for reasons not yet understood."[19]

An alternative community is possible. But Aldrich is also conscious of the powerful nature of American reaction that affected these hopes in the post-1947 period and beyond, a reaction that still continues today. The failure of the younger generation to learn from the past contributed to this reaction. If they did not exhibit passivity, then they joined the forces of reaction like the "brat pack" characters suffering from midlife crisis in *St. Elmo's Fire* (1985) who work for the

Republicans because they pay more than the Democrats! Cigaret is an opportunistic character who chooses to betray A No. 1 and acquire a status he does not deserve. Rather than forming a Popular Front alliance, he chooses to humiliate his potential mentor and face an enemy whom he has no real chance of beating on his own. Shack finally confronts a figure he earlier recognized as a "tenderfoot" rather than a "bo." Cigaret faces death by Shack's hammer until A No. 1 arrives to save his unworthy partner: "Shack! Your fight's over here."

The two antagonists engage in a deadly combat resembling a modern version of a gladiator contest incongruously set in the twentieth-century context of Shack's beloved train. A No. 1 defeats his adversary and throws him over the side. But, unlike in the screenplay where Shack merely disappears over the side, A No. 1 hears the defiant shout, "You ain't seen the last of me." The contest will continue. Cigaret then hypocritically attempts to claim partnership with a man he has betrayed: "Yes, sir, me and you, if we ain't the team." But A No. 1 also throws him over the side with the significant departing words: "Kid, you ain't got no class. You could have been a meat eater, kid. But you didn't listen. . . . You'll never be Emperor of the North Pole. You had the juice, kid, but not the heart, and they both go together."

A No. 1's final lines to Cigaret represent an extension of elements in Knopf's screenplay that obviously derives from Aldrich. When A No. 1 tells Cigaret that he has "juice" but not the "heart," it represents the director's cinematic body and soul philosophy. Cigaret becomes a Charlie Castle who sells out for selfish reasons. But he lacks any sense of conscience. He has lost a golden opportunity of gaining a personal sense of honor and self-respect by the very nature of his actions. A No. 1 saved him from Shack's chain earlier in the film. But Cigaret never returns the favor. He is an opportunist whose selfish behavior shows him entirely incapable of any moral growth and regeneration.

However, A No. 1 regains his lost honor and personal self-respect in his battle against Shack. Rather than waiting for Shack to tire himself by finishing Cigaret off, he chooses to return to the conflict. But the battle represents one between two individuals whose time has passed. They will probably meet again to engage in what Silver and Ursini describe as "a dangerous, repetitive, and ultimately pointless scenario of survival of the fittest."[20] But the country is changing around them. As A No. 1 rummages through one of several garbage heaps he encounters in his travels, he mutters, "Trash in this country has gone to hell!" Although he refers to the fact that nothing worthwhile exists for his use, his statement also applies to a country that is little better than one large scrap heap, which the New Deal may be powerless to change. As a result, the contest between A No. 1 and Shack is futile. No matter how heroic the outcome, nothing will really change. Although promoted as an action film featuring one of the most exciting physical combats in cinema, *Emperor of the North* is really pessimistic. Although it concludes on an individualistic affirmative note with Shack's train carrying A No. 1 into the distance, viewers may ask, "Where do we go from here?" It is a very valid question.

Following the problematic box-office reception of *Emperor of the North* and the loss of the *Yakuza* project, Aldrich again reworked *Body and Soul* into what was to become one of his most commercially successful films.[21] Featuring another tarnished hero who loses and then regains his self-respect, the film is far more than a generic merging of prison and sports movies with a nod toward *The Dirty Dozen*. As Arnold and Miller succinctly state, "The football game in *The Longest Yard*—like the baseball game in *The Big Leaguer,* the war games in *The Dirty Dozen,* and the survival games in *The Flight of the Phoenix*—functions both as a social ritual by which men test and define themselves and also as a metaphor for teamwork and camaraderie: the working together to achieve a common goal, a common purpose."[22] Like *Attack! The Dirty Dozen,* and *Twilight's Last Gleaming,* it is fully aware of the forces that control society, the limits set on human agency making the prison context all the more relevant, and the "fear and violence philosophy" hiding behind a spurious democratic game that is actually ruled by a manipulative "power theory." Retitled *The Mean Machine* in England, *The Longest Yard* replays the conventions of its source material.[23] But it also employs a dynamic editing style for the actual game by further developing a split-screen technique begun in *Emperor of the North* that Aldrich refined in *Twilight's Last Gleaming.*

The film opens with a panning shot accompanying the sound of a football game as the camera depicts everything we need to know about the character of Paul Crewe (Burt Reynolds). As it moves across a lavishly furnished room, passing a bureau containing photos of Melissa (Anitra Ford) with her various male trophies (including Crewe), an aura of dissipation and lost opportunity clearly

emerges before we actually see Crewe himself. As he listens to the
football game, a close-up shows the shadow of the overhead fan on
his face, evoking noir imagery common to *World for Ransom*, *The Big
Knife* and *Attack!* Oblivious to the enticements offered by a mistress
wishing her stud to perform, Crewe brusquely tosses her aside.
Melissa begins verbal provocation by referring to him as a "whore"
bought by everyone from the time he played football in college.
Crewe ironically replies, "Never looked at it this way before." He is
not a positive character. After assaulting her, Crewe departs, takes
her sports car, engages in a drunken driving spree, disposes of the
car over a jetty, and assaults two policemen before beginning his
sentence at Florida's Citrus State Prison. The credits then begin. As
in *The Dirty Dozen*, *The Legend of Lylah Clare*, and *Too Late the Hero*,
Aldrich sets in motion a considerable amount of action before the
credits.

Once Crewe arrives, the camera tilts up to show an imitation classical Greek frieze above the name of the prison. The director again
alerts members of his audience to another example of a bankrupt
Western civilization. An artifact from a culture that once inspired the
Western world with noble values is now a prison banner. Crewe
next encounters Captain Knauer (Ed Lauter), whose brutality articulates another set of values contradicting the sporting trophies and
logos in his office—"Spirit of Achievement": "The game embodies
what has made our country great." Knauer warns Crewe about accepting whatever offer Warden Hazen makes to him, educating the
new arrival by using physical force.

Aldrich modeled Eddie Albert's Hazen on Richard Nixon, even
making in-joke references to the president's then-notorious Oval Office tape recordings. Like Barney Sheehan in *The Legend of Lylah
Clare*, Hazen wishes his speeches to be recorded for posterity, an action performed by one of "the president's men" (Mort Marshall). Refusing Hazen's offer of coaching the guard team, the former professional quarterback finds himself relegated to "swamp reclamation."
Treated with contempt by his fellow prisoners because he let his
public down, Crewe notes the segregation practiced in the state
prison when black convicts arrive separately. He then finds himself
chained to Granville (Harry Caesar) because of a guard's racist sense
of humor: "Did you ever work with a nigger before?" Guards and
fellow convicts regard Crewe as having the same social status, a fact
recorded by the camera showing the handcuffing in close-up. It is a

significant shot, ironic in terms of further events when a similar close-up illustrates a rare moment of interracial solidarity during the game that occurs later in the film. Both Crewe and the rest of his white team will later work with normally segregated "niggers." Division will soon lead to unity. But potential exists even in the most unrewarding circumstances. When Captain Knauer arrives to witness a fight that the guards have allowed, Crewe and his fellow combatant, Rotka (Tony Cacciotti), mock authority by joining in laughter together. The usual "divide and rule" strategy fails. Knauer sees all the prisoners now laughing together in unity and takes action against Crewe.

Caretaker (James Hampton) had previously informed Crewe that he was to blame for his earlier isolation by his fellow prisoners: "Most of these boys don't have nothing. Never had nothing at all." As someone who gained everything they never had and then deceitfully threw it away, Crewe earns their justified contempt. Caretaker also evokes the blacklisting era by his remark, "Shaving points off a football game. That's un-American." Both Caretaker and Aldrich regard letting one's team down as the real un-American act. It parallels the acts of those "patriotic Americans" who named names or betrayed others for personal gain or career ambitions. These people also betrayed their own teams in the past.

Released by Hazen from twenty-four-hour confinement in the "hot box" after assaulting Knauer, Crewe agrees to organize a team of inmates for a preseason tune-up game. Both men would ostensibly benefit. Crewe would earn a reduced sentence and early parole rather than serving five years for striking a guard. Hazen would display his team before a public audience and promote the game as part of his "progressive rehabilitation program." Aided by Caretaker, "Pop" (John Steadman), and Nate Scarboro (Michael Conrad), whom he appoints as head coach, Crewe begins to form his team. Although *The Longest Yard* appears to follow the pattern of *The Dirty Dozen*, there are some differences. As in the earlier film, Aldrich moves audience sympathy toward characters who are dangerous to society. However, figures such as Samson (Richard Kiel) and Schokner (Robert Tessier) are far removed from Wladislaw and Jefferson of *The Dirty Dozen*. They are definitely characters one would not want to encounter in everyday life and have not been "railroaded" like the other two. *The Longest Yard* chooses to emphasize more the nature of the society that has incarcerated them. Hazen runs a tight ship, even with his progressive rehabilitation. But corruption, segregation, racism, and permitted brutality by guards against the inmates rule a ship presided over by a seemingly benevolent head of state who is also a sports fan. Yet no sense of sportsmanlike "fair play" exists in his regime. The classical Greek frieze dominating the entrance to the prison conceals its real nature. However, it is also an appropriate image, for slavery represented the economic basis of that society in the first place. The original screenplay described the prison exterior as resembling a "medieval castle."

Obvious threats to society exist inside the prison. But there are others whose incarceration raises questions. We do not know the nature of Caretaker's crime. Pop has already served thirty-four years and has been sent to swamp reclamation for his remaining time, although he is physically unable to work with the other men. His relegation to this dangerous environment appears motivated by the hope that he will contract some deadly illness there. Crewe learns that the punishment has resulted from Pop hitting Hazen many years ago when the warden began his career as a prison guard. Like Caretaker, we do not know Pop's original crime. But he obviously began his original sentence during the Great Depression. Nate Scarboro was once a well-known football player, possibly in the same league as Crewe. But age, loss of professional status, and the fact that he had no other occupation to turn to may have led him to a life of crime. It is Nate who informs Crewe that a "fear and violence philosophy" dominates the institution and that the eventual game may not be played according to the rules.

Crewe eventually gets together a multiethnic team, composed of whites, Native Americans, and African Americans. They initially gloat over the opportunity the game will allow them to assault prison guards legitimately. However, the process of formation was not easy. The black prisoners initially refuse Crewe's request: "This honky Golden Boy sold out his own team, didn't he? He did it once. He'll do it again." Because *The Longest Yard* reworks a *Body and Soul* formula inspired by *Golden Boy,* the comment also reveals Aldrich's continuing debt to his past mentor. However, black prisoners do join the team. Granville's dignified and strategic behavior when he is provoked by the guards inspires them. His attitude forms a marked contrast to the one exhibited by Lt. Costa in *Attack!* He controls his emotions and does not allow them to destroy the important balance between body and soul necessary for his survival. Granville is one of Crewe's best players. He has already joined the team against the wishes of his fellow black prisoners. Knauer orders his guards to provoke him into a fight. However, Granville refuses to respond to the racist provocation he receives. By exhibiting a calm dignity under demeaning treatment, he not only reveals a quiet heroism but also gains the respect of the other black prisoners in the library. They then decide to join Crewe's team. This sequence provides a key example of Aldrich's strategy. By remaining at the card table and taking low cards, Granville survives to play another round. He also inspires others by his calm attitude toward a dangerous situation manipulated by the system designed to destroy him.

Crewe initially takes a practical approach to the whole game. As he tells Hazen, the men may not have a chance of winning the game: "I'm just trying to give you a football team, Warden. And, along the way, maybe give the men some pride and dignity—of course, only for a little while. I know it. You know it. I don't want them to know it." Crewe soon forms the team into a unified fighting unit. When Caretaker asks Crewe why he shaved points and sold out his team, the latter narrates a story that may or may not be true. Crewe's original fall resulted from his sense of responsibility to his blind father, who could not watch him play. Seeing the opportunity of making a financial gain that would enable him to care for his father for the rest of his life, Crewe lost the game for his team. But, in a stroke of irony, his father died soon afterward. Whether he died from shame or natural causes is left open. However, Aldrich again supplies his constant theme of dysfunctional family dynamics. Possibly Crewe's father died from the shame of finding his son caught out in a "scam." Crewe refuses to confirm the veracity of the story he has just told Caretaker. His manner implicitly suggests that it is actually the real reason for his fall from grace. This element may also derive from Aldrich, for it does not appear in the original screenplay.

Once the actual game begins, Aldrich changes the conventional pattern of editing that he has used throughout most of the film. He develops the split-screen technique seen in *Emperor of the North*. As with *Twilight's Last Gleaming*, this is less of a gimmick and more designed to involve audiences in both the game and the reaction of the spectators. Crewe has formed a unified multiethnic team, breaking down many of the divisive tactics practiced by the prison administration. This unity also humorously extends to the spectators, among whom are a group of Afro-American drag queens costumed as cheerleaders. They are led by a trio modeling themselves on the Supremes, revealing the director's humorous sense of community. Played by real prisoners, even drag queens need recognition as part of the diversity of everyday life. They are also a key component of the audience who will cheer the Mean Machine on to their eventual victory.[24]

By halftime, the Mean Machine has proved its worth on the playing field, angering Warden Hazen. But he has one more card to play. During the break, he threatens Crewe with life imprisonment for being an accessory to Caretaker's death if he does not throw the game. Ironically, prison informer Unger (Charles Tyner) had perpetrated this by murdering Caretaker in mistake for Crewe, who had earlier rejected him from any involvement in the training. However, Crewe gains a compromise from Hazen. He wishes to protect his players from injury after the guards gain sufficient leading points. But Hazen has no intentions of keeping such a promise. As he tells the reluctant Knauer (who now wishes to win the game fairly), "I want every prisoner in this institution to know what I mean by power and who controls it." His line also implicitly refers to the world outside the prison gates normally regarded as "free."

Unlike Charley Davis in *Body and Soul,* Crewe faces further incarceration rather than financial gain. But the final result is the same: loss of self-respect. Once Crewe sees guards injuring his respected players Granville and Nate Scarboro, he finally decides to return to the game. The key motivation here is not only team obligation but also the inspiration of Pop, a rare father figure in Aldrich's world who acts as Crewe's mentor. After learning from the older man that his unjust incarceration was worth the punch he gave Hazen years before, Crewe returns to the field. Following initial rejection by his betrayed teammates, he regains his former glory by winning crucial points not only for himself but for his fellow inmates, who all become heroes for a day. Aldrich rapidly juxtaposes freeze-frames of Crewe winning the game with various optically edited shots of the spectators, prisoners, Granville, and Nate Scarboro before returning to real edited time. It is an important moment for everyone, whether as players or spectators. The system can be beaten!

After the game, the prisoners evoke various responses from their opponents. These range from the grudging respect of guard Rassmeusen (Mike Henry), who earlier provoked Granville, to that of a "bad loser." Crewe responds to the guard's angry, "Fuck you!" with,

"Not today." He astutely recognizes that tomorrow will be another day. But for now he has gained a temporary victory that has destabilized Hazen's authority. Hazen is rejected by both his servile assistant ("Where's your damn power theory now?") and Knauer, who refuses to shoot Crewe as he goes to fetch the ball, and his authority collapses. But the final image ambiguously evokes the climax of *Body and Soul* as well as Robert Rossen's preferred ending. Although Crewe delivers the ball to the warden, telling him to "stick this in your trophy case," his future is as uncertain as that of Charley Davis. Although he does not repeat the line "Everybody dies," he may be as good as dead. The final image of *The Longest Yard* shows Crewe and Pop in long shot walking down a dark corridor on their way to the locker room before a freeze-frame leads to the credits. Both face an uncertain future. But, as Arnold and Miller note, "it is the victory itself, no matter how fleeting or ephemeral that ultimately counts."[25] It is another scene Aldrich added to the original screenplay.

. . . *All the Marbles* differs from Aldrich's previous team playing films in several ways. Rather than concentrating on a male group, the director focuses on two females working in the "unusual" sport of female wrestling. Although wrestling is usually defined as a male sport, it is as potentially gender free as any other sport. Yet the current presence of females in formerly male-exclusive games such as boxing and football is not entirely new. According to the credits, a twenty-year veteran female wrestler, Mildred Burke, acted as technical adviser. She held the title of World Champion Lady Wrestler from 1937 to 1957. Such a feature not only illustrates Aldrich's tendency to feature minorities in his cinematic world but also again reveals his recognition of diverse contributions to an entertainment industry that has largely engaged in stereotypical representation. Aldrich delivers an ironic comment against this neglect when an affluent Las Vegas customer at the MGM Grand Hotel remarks, "I've never seen lady wrestlers before."

. . . *All the Marbles* ironically evokes the director's first film. Following the commercial failure of his previous films, he was back at MGM directing a film dealing with the world of professional sports as in *Big Leaguer,* twenty-seven years earlier. However, both MGM and America had changed radically over the past three decades. The studio was no longer viable because of the decisions of Kirk Kerkorian to move into real estate and Las Vegas hotels. Hence the setting of the final sequences at the MGM Grand Hotel in Las Vegas has ironic associations, for the studio was associated with escapist glamour during the 1930s. America was now entering another economic decline euphemistically defined as a "recession" adversely affecting American heavy industry. What Aldrich saw on location deeply moved him. It stimulated him to give the film some serious undertones. As producer William Aldrich commented,

> It was not a sophisticated movie but it was what this country was going through at the time. The recession was terrible, inflation was terrible, people were out of work. It was miserable back there in Youngstown. It was devastating, all the factories shut down. And that's why he [Aldrich] kept changing little bits of the story, and that's why all that car stuff is in there to show, "This is a rough world out there, where people are trying to struggle their way through."[26]

The use of "Vesti la giubba" from Leoncavallo's *I Pagliacci* has more than one resonance for the film. If Silver and Ursini see that "the show must go on, the clown must laugh at his fate even if he feels like crying,"[27] another irony lies in the fact that America now experienced another economic downturn similar to the Great Depression, which influenced both Clifford Odets and a Robert Aldrich who grew up among the affluent Aldriches of Rhode Island.

. . . *All the Marbles* represents an ironic comic inversion on that Horatio Alger ideological formula expressed by Horace Greeley, "Go West, Young Man." In this case, two young women managed by a cynical promoter go west. They begin in Akron, Ohio, and finally end up not in Hollywood but in Las Vegas, where one of Hollywood's most glamorous studios of the depression era had moved its interests. In many ways, . . . *All the Marbles* echoes old Warner Bros. 1930s musicals about putting on a show and beating the depression, with Iris (Vicki Frederick) and Molly (Laurene Landon) as working showgirls and Harry Sears (Peter Falk) as a cynical, streetwise, Aldrich version of those earlier producers played by Warner Baxter in *42nd Street* (1933) and James Cagney in *Gold Diggers of 1933* (1933). The world of female wrestling, with dingy dressing rooms, atavistic audiences, crooked promoters, and physical punishment in the ring, is not far removed from the boxing movie genre. Aldrich admitted borrowing again from *Body and Soul* for the climax, and the presence of black manager John Stanley (John Amos) represents another link. Harry informs his girls that Stanley was the world's light heavyweight boxing champion thirty years ago. He had even coached the

Olympic boxing team. But like Nate Scarboro in *The Longest Yard*, he has fallen from grace, presumably for reasons of race like Ben in *Body and Soul*. However, John Stanley acts as a realistic, but less cynically manipulative, mentor to Diane (Tracy Reed) and June (Ursuline Bryant-King) of the Toledo Tigers. Like Granville in *The Longest Yard*, he is also a role model for his race because he will only work with African Americans.

Wrestling is far removed from the idealistic world of baseball presented to us in *Big Leaguer*. It involves showbiz entertainment and manipulated results. But so do the games depicted in *The Dirty Dozen* and *The Longest Yard*. However, the important element for participants is to understand how the game operates, know the rules, and try to emerge with some degree of self-respect, whatever the result. The characters in . . . *All the Marbles* know this and make various compromises with the world in which they exist. But a difference exists between actual cheating and manipulating the rules of an unjust system to allow some degree of self-respect and possible victory. Although manipulative, Harry's activities differ little from Major Reisman's in *The Dirty Dozen* and Paul Crewe's in *The Longest Yard*. Struggle is important even if success is not always guaranteed. Despite the director's desire to make a commercial film that would restore him to box-office favor, many significant elements appear, making . . . *All the Marbles* an elegiac swan song to Aldrich's career.

. . . *All the Marbles* opens ominously in darkness. Pagliacci's aria "Vesti la giubba," which we hear several times throughout the film, accompanies the camera as it slowly tracks forward. As we see the signs "Goodyear" and "The House that Rubber Built" before entering the Akron wrestling arena, the pounding sound of industrial machinery gradually overwhelms Leoncavallo before merging into Frank DeVol's organ rendition of "Oh, You Beautiful Doll." It is a significant introduction in many ways. A tense acoustic clash occurs between the nineteenth-century world of classical music and the modernist sound of heavy machinery, the latter associated with an American industrial heartland now experiencing another version of the Great Depression. DeVol's Jazz Age performance of "Doll" evokes not only memories of America's affluent escapist era before the Great Depression but also Ronald Reagan's contemporary illusionist "Morning in America."

But the film ironically opens in darkness. It appeared in a year when MGM began to return to films rather than concentrate its energies on real estate.[28] Certain soundtrack elements parody MGM's fall from glory. The California Dolls' theme "Oh, You Beautiful Doll" has sentimental associations with MGM escapist musicals set during the earlier "recession" in American history. However, the theme now becomes associated with the tawdry world of female wrestling, which reaches its climax in the tacky, showbiz glamour in the Las Vegas MGM Hotel. When sleazy promoter Eddie Cisco (Burt Young) reappears in Chicago after the Toledo Tigers have beaten the Dolls, Judy Garland's "Trolley Song" from *Meet Me in St. Louis* (1945) occurs in the background played on an organ. "You Are My Lucky Star" also occurs on the soundtrack as Harry and the Dolls arrive in Las Vegas. It ironically follows "Ave Maria" after Harry acquires the necessary funds for their journey by kneecapping two thugs with a baseball bat. Following their arrival in Las Vegas, the Dolls play slot machines in the MGM Grand, and "How about You?" occurs in the background. The Tigers appear in the auditorium as "That's Entertainment" plays on the organ. MGM's documentary compilations of the same name had already appeared several years before: *That's Entertainment* (1974) and *That's Entertainment 2* (1976). The Las Vegas MGM Grand Hotel evokes the studio's prestigious 1932 film of the same name. A poster of Big Mama appears outside the Ziegfeld Theater, obviously parodying past studio productions such as *The Great Ziegfeld* (1936) and *Ziegfeld Follies* (1947). When Big Mama (Faith Minton) later sees the Dolls make their showbiz entrance into the wrestling arena, she comments that they look like "virgin vampires." The Dolls parody those earlier virginal heroines of old MGM musicals. But they are also shrewd participants in a profession living on audiences as vampires live on their victims.

. . . *All the Marbles* appeared within the first year of a Republican president who aimed to restore "Morning to America" by dismantling policies associated with the New Deal and return his people to the affluent capitalist "feel-good" ideology of the 1920s. Reagan was not only a film star who gave the American public what they wanted by performing the role of a leader. He also identified himself with the aloof business-minded president of the 1920s—Calvin Coolidge. Harry and his California Dolls also give their audiences what they want, even though they know wrestling is a fixed sport.

Aldrich's various shots of the audiences express what Arnold and Miller note as a "belligerent attitude." Whether unemployed steelworkers, middle American rural conservatives, or Las Vegas high rollers, they all gratuitously and voyeuristically indulge in a spectacle they know to be false.[29] However, Harry stimulates his Dolls by affirming their abilities as entertainers, urging them to reach the top of their profession no matter what adverse odds they face. This especially involves audiences who do not appreciate their abilities. Harry may be as cynical and manipulative as Barney Sheean and Lewis Zarkan in *The Legend of Lylah Clare*. But he also has his own form of integrity and loyalty, as well as a "pragmatic survival instinct" that sees putting on a good show as a means of reaching the top. The rules of the game could always change. But if they do not, there is always a moment of victory to enjoy. It occurs in the film's climax when Harry, Iris, and Molly all stand united in the ring.

Aldrich made several changes to Mel Froman's screenplay. Harry is no longer a character dreaming of becoming a tenured professor of English literature. In the film, we learn nothing of Iris's background apart from the fact that she is a former lover of Harry. But the screenplay mentions that she has gone on the tour circuit to support her young son after leaving the stifling domestic confines of marriage. But the major loss in the film involves Molly's background. Froman depicts her as a lesbian who has suffered incestuous assault from her father since the age of nine. Had Aldrich retained her history, Molly would have become another family victim like Jane Hudson and Charlotte as well as a character like Frennessey in *World for Ransom*, attempting to find her own way in a male-dominated world.

Harry's fondness for the classical music of Leoncavallo, Verdi, and Mozart finds parallels in other Aldrich films. Although he reveres this tradition, he also knows that it is a threatened oasis in 1980s America. Whenever Iris or Molly attempts to switch channels, Harry immediately inserts one of his classical cassettes. Like Carmen Trivago in *Kiss Me Deadly*, he reveres the past. But unlike his classical music predecessor, Harry never lives in the past but, rather, regrets the contrast between the values he grew up with and an emerging Reaganite America exhibiting industrial decline and crass materialism. He uses Leoncavallo's Pagliacci as a role model, telling the Dolls that the weeping clown is a strolling player who "goes from town to town entertaining people, even though his heart is breaking. That's why you've got to keep going, keep trying." In this way, his character differs from Charlie Castle in *The Big Knife*, who masochistically identifies with Rouault's "old clown waiting in the wings to go on. . . . Don't mean anything, anymore." Harry's clown means much more to him.

He tells the Dolls about his own background as a second-generation immigrant of a father whose garment union sent him to school so that he could learn English to gain citizenship. His teachers recommended a self-education course comprising the *New York Times*, Will Rogers, and Clifford Odets. The significance of the last figure needs no further emphasis here. However, the influence of Will Rogers needs elaboration. As Lary May has recently shown, this now-forgotten, racially mixed figure in American 1930s culture represented not only a populist figure but also an embodiment of the real western hero now appropriated by white actors such as John Wayne and Clint Eastwood. Like Odets, Rogers spoke for the common people of America.[30] But, as Harry learns from his Dolls, both figures are now forgotten. When Molly asks who Rogers and Odets were, Harry sadly replies, "They were a dance team from the Catskills." His idols are as irrelevant as religion in the modern world. After the Dolls' successful performance in Akron, Harry tells a promoter, "I'll let you have the girls for Thanksgiving." The former religious festival becomes another opportunity for commercial spectacle. Iris later irreligiously remarks, "You got to walk on water to get a girl a twelve dollar raise." The climactic match with their opponents occurs during the Christmas season in that most commercial of American cities—Las Vegas.

Harry and the Dolls constantly travel through industrial cities and towns exhibiting the ravages of the recession. They also experience the changing nature of female wrestling, which is now becoming multiethnic and multinational. The Dolls fight blacks, Mexicans, and Japanese. Ironically, promoter Clyde Yamashito (Clyde Kusatsu) offers Harry a contract if the Dolls attain championship status: "Your girls would be very, very big in Japan." He offers the monolingual Harry his Japanese business card and parts from him saying, "auf Wiedersehen." His presence in the film reflects growing Japanese corporate involvement in Hollywood studios such as Sony.

Although Aldrich dropped Molly's lesbian tendencies from the final film, both Iris and Molly share moments of female solidarity. Molly fantasizes about returning to Los Angeles to work in occupations. But her lack of a high school diploma will exclude her from her chosen professions. She nearly succumbs to retreating into a false past. But the more pragmatic Iris encourages her to face their common reality: "You're dreaming Molly. It wasn't like that." Despite their irritation with Harry and intermittent bouts of despair, both women refuse to engage in those unrealistic fantasies trapping many characters in the plays of Clifford Odets. Iris wears a football T-shirt with the significant "Dirty Dozen" number twelve, parodying the fact that she and Mollie are two disciples of a dubious savior figure. She affirms not only her love for Molly but also the fact that they are all a team of three: "I love you. I can't work with anybody but you. Like it or not, the three of us are a team and we're going to make it—or die trying."

It is a philosophy keeping them together despite their lowest moments, such as the Midwestern country mud wrestling bout, the Chicago defeat at the hands of the Toledo Tigers, and Iris selling her body to Eddie Cisco to ensure the chance of competing in the Las Vegas tag wrestling contest. When Harry makes the girls undergo the humiliating mud wrestling contest, he is also conscious of other degrading aspects. The Kiwanis Club carnival contest aims to raise money for an American Legion recreation hall. Its sleazy promoter tells Harry, "You'd be surprised how much a game of ping pong could add such fun to these soldier's lives." Harry gruffly responds to a remark beneath contempt.

Although Molly wishes to retain some form of idealism in her profession—"We want to be the one tag team without a gimmick"—Harry pragmatically educates his Dolls into the harsh realities of their profession. Angry at the Dolls' use of T-shirts and posters to promote their work, Big Mama confronts her manager, Myron (Stanley Brock), "How come you never thought of selling a poster of me?" She eventually comes to admire the Dolls' performance in the ring, so much so that she asks Myron to get her a "*real* beer" rather than the "light" one she has been drinking.[31] As Lt. Woodruff discovers in *Attack!* idealism is impossible in the real world where the rules of the game are often fixed to unfair advantage. Arnold and Miller also recognize the grim realities depicted in this film: "Despite all of the girls' vocal abhorrence of gimmicks, their championship match is nothing but one vast public relations display, the epitome of tinsel glamour. In its own sneaky way, . . . *All the Marbles* becomes a parody of all the other come-from-behind, spiritually invigorating films which feed our national mythos. Once again, Aldrich undermines the very genre he seems to employ, at least to a degree."[32]

The Reno referee tells the Dolls, "It's a wrestling match, not a vaudeville show. How do you expect me to see cuts with all that crap on their faces?" However, his own particular behavior undercuts the supposedly impartial comments he makes. Departing from Froman's screenplay, Aldrich added the character of crooked referee Bill Dudley (Richard Jaeckel), who is employed by Cisco to fix the match in favor of the Toledo Tigers. His unfair decisions during the bout anger not only the crowd but John Stanley himself, who has his own sense of honor and self-respect. Stanley warns the Tigers that the Dolls have wounded pride on their side after losing the Chicago bout. As he tells his championship team, "Pride, hope, greed. They got it all." By contrast, Harry tells his Dolls, "There's only one way you are going to win. That's if, if you want it more than they want it." Whereas Stanley tells his Tigers, "We're the better team," Harry combines a genuine affection for Iris and Molly with his final advice: "I love you both. We've come too far to lose. Go get 'em." He kisses them both before sending them into the ring. The Dolls take great punishment but achieve that last-minute victory indebted to the climax of *Body and Soul*.

But everyone knows that the game will still continue. Harry and the Dolls enjoy their moment of victory. However, in a line added by Aldrich, John Stanley consoles his team: "You were the champions three months ago and you'll get to be the champions three months from now." He urges the Tigers to behave like champions and congratulate their opponents. Although they do this reluctantly, Iris holds onto Diane's hand and affirms the prowess of the opposing team: "Thank you. You're wonderful wrestlers." This parallels an earlier remark she made to the losing team in Akron at the beginning of the film: "Sorry we had to win but nice working with your guys anyway." Iris's tribute is sincere. She recognizes the opponents not only as equals but as champions who may defeat them one day. For the moment, Harry and the California Dolls have all the marbles.

As Aldrich commented, "The film is really about people striving to gain self-respect, to capture that one moment of glory. . . . If I've done my job well, audiences should understand why it is so important for these characters to feel like winners after struggling for so long. They get discouraged, they feel low sometimes, but they keep going."[33] However, despite Aldrich's optimistic comments, the mood of the film is ambivalent and bleak. It suggests that the "go-

ing will get tougher"—as it did in future decades, which the director was no longer around to comment on.

NOTES

1. See Tony Williams, "*Ceiling Zero*," in *The Encyclopedia of Stage Plays into Film,* ed. John C. Tibbetts and James M. Welsh (New York: Facts on File, 2001), 46–47.

2. Edwin T. Arnold and Eugene I. Miller, *The Films and Career of Robert Aldrich* (Knoxville: University of Tennessee Press, 1986), 15–16.

3. Alain Silver and James Ursini, *What Ever Happened to Robert Aldrich? His Life and His Films* (New York: Limelight Editions, 1995), 137.

4. Richard Combs, "*Big Leaguer,*" *Monthly Film Bulletin* 44, no. 527 (December 1977): 266; Richard Combs, ed., *Robert Aldrich* (London: British Film Institute, 1978), 6; Silver and Ursini, *What Ever Happened to Robert Aldrich?* 139. As in Combs's review, the actual title (as on the credits of the original film) is *Big Leaguer,* without a definite article. Despite the fact that Aldrich and other critics often use "The," this book follows the original title of the film.

5. See Margaret Brenman-Gibson, *Clifford Odets, American Playwright: The Years from 1906–1940* (New York: Athenaeum, 1981).

6. Combs, "*Big Leaguer,*" 266.

7. Arnold and Miller, *The Films and Career of Robert Aldrich,* 17–18.

8. Harry Ringel, "Up to Date with Robert Aldrich," *Sight and Sound* 53, no. 3 (1974): 167.

9. Silver and Ursini, *What Ever Happened to Robert Aldrich?* 85.

10. Philip French, "*The Flight of the Phoenix,*" *Sight and Sound* 35, no. 2 (1966): 94.

11. French lists this scene among the errors he believes adversely affect the film resulting from Aldrich's mistake in allowing intrusions from the outside world, such as "a slushy song heard on a transistor radio in the hands of a dying man and the silly mirage of a belly-dancer. One suspects that someone wanted to have a woman's name on the hoardings and a theme tune" ("*The Flight of the Phoenix,*" 95). This may be correct as far as studio politics goes. But Aldrich uses these possible impositions to emphasize the weak nature of both characters. Gabriele commits suicide after he confesses to Standish that his wife is really dead, and Farida's image appears to the guilt-ridden, cowardly Watson following the death of Captain Harris. Furthermore, the screenplay description represents a more ambiguous conception that never reached the screen: "The sinuous grace with which she moves her beautifully controlled body is in striking contrast to her general appearance. The soiled condition of her brief and slightly torn costume, her unkempt hair and the cheap, vulgar ornaments she wears, all

convey the sleazy tawdriness of the establishments in which Watson must have seen her. It is clear that her talents as a dancer are far greater than the erotic purposes to which others have forced her to bend them" (Lukas Heller, *The Flight of the Phoenix*, revised final screenplay, 22 April 1965, 133 [all further quotations are from this version]).

12. See Jeanine Basinger, *Anthony Mann* (Boston: Twayne, 1979); Robin Wood, *Hitchcock's Films Revisited* (New York: Columbia University Press, 1989), 364–65.

13. Both men need each other, and Lew plays an major role in bringing them together, as several critics have noted. See Arnold and Miller, *The Films and Career of Robert Aldrich*, 120–21; and Silver and Ursini, *What Ever Happened to Robert Aldrich?* 86.

14. Arnold and Miller, *The Films and Career of Robert Aldrich*, 122.

15. Combs, *Robert Aldrich*, 27.

16. See Combs, *Robert Aldrich*, 34; Arnold and Miller, *The Films and Career of Robert Aldrich*, 176–77; and Silver and Ursini, *What Ever Happened to Robert Aldrich?* 101–2.

17. See Stuart Byron, "I Can't Get Jimmy Carter to See My Movie! Robert Aldrich Talks with Stuart Byron," *Film Comment* 13 (1977): 51. The musical reference again appears to be an Odets reference.

18. Arnold and Miller, *The Films and Career of Robert Aldrich*, 174. Aldrich also commented on the ages of his two main stars: "Also Ernest Borgnine and Lee Marvin as two men fighting on a railroad were apparently too old for the youth audiences to identify with" (Charles Higham, "Robert Aldrich," *Action* 9, no. 6 [1974]: 20).

19. Christopher Knopf, *Emperor of the North Pole*, final screenplay, 16 May 1972, 21.

20. Silver and Ursini, *What Ever Happened to Robert Aldrich?* 105.

21. For relevant information, see Arnold and Miller, *The Films and Career of Robert Aldrich*, 180. One can only lament the loss of Aldrich as director of *The Yakuza*, based on a screenplay by Paul Schrader and featuring Takakura Ken, whom the director would feature to good advantage in *Too Late the Hero*.

22. Arnold and Miller, *The Films and Career of Robert Aldrich*, 185–86.

23. The film was remade in 2002 as a forgettable British "lad movie" starring ex-footballer Vinnie Jones. Produced by Guy Ritchie, it lacked the political significance of the original Aldrich film, substituting instead spurious patriotic metaphors.

24. The VHS version of *The Longest Yard* removed several of their scenes because of copyright problems involving the singing of "Born Free," which is one of the highlights of the film. Fortunately, this has been restored in the DVD version.

25. Arnold and Miller, *The Films and Career of Robert Aldrich*, 185.

26. Quoted in Arnold and Miller, *The Films and Career of Robert Aldrich*, 228.

27. Silver and Ursini, *What Ever Happened to Robert Aldrich?* 146.

28. See Bernard Drew, "Leo Roars Again," *Film Comment* 17 (1981): 34.

29. Arnold and Miller, *The Films and Career of Robert Aldrich*, 227.

30. Lary May, *The Big Tomorrow: Hollywood and the Politics of the American Way* (Chicago: University of Chicago Press, 2000), 11–53.

31. This is an obvious in-joke. Big Mama has been drinking Budweiser before. She now changes to a much more powerful beer.

32. Arnold and Miller, *The Films and Career of Robert Aldrich,* 225. As the Reagan era was one big tinsel exercise, one wonders whether Aldrich recognized this from the very beginning.

33. Jeffrey Wells, "Peter Falk and Robert Aldrich Tell It Straight re. MGM's 'All the Marbles,'" *The Film Journal* (October 1981): 10.

NINE

TWILIGHT'S LAST GLEAMING

When *Twilight's Last Gleaming* appeared it received a negative critical and commercial response that drastically affected the director's future choice over the types of films he wished to make. Although Aldrich directed three other films before he died, none of them measures up to the power and intensity of *Twilight's Last Gleaming*. The film represents his final cinematic testament to a culture that simply did not want to listen. Appearing a few years after Gerald Ford's notorious denial speech calling on Americans to put Vietnam "behind us" and a year before politically evasive Hollywood Vietnam films such as *Coming Home* (1978), *The Deer Hunter* (1978), and *Apocalypse Now* (1979), *Twilight's Last Gleaming* fell on deaf years at the American box office. It is a film containing many of the radical features of Aldrich's earlier work indebted to the cultural legacy of the New Deal. Following the ignominious defeat of an American-supported puppet state, it is natural that most American audiences sought banal escapism, which Ronald Reagan's "morning in America" soon supplied. *Twilight's Last Gleaming*'s direct condemnation of a corrupt military and political bureaucracy was too much for most audiences. They rejected the message, wishing to escape into ideologically familiar patterns of heroism and narrative structures that would soon reemerge in new forms. Although the aging heroic persona of John Wayne in *The Green Berets* (1968) represented an anachronism for a new generation, the ideological successors of Keith Carradine's Cigaret in *Emperor of the North* would soon embrace new masculine images provided by Chuck Norris and Sylvester Stallone. These figures emerged like contaminated phoenixes from the ashes of a once-discredited old order. Like *Too Late the Hero*, *Twilight's Last Gleaming* appeared at the wrong historical moment. It became trapped within two deadly cultural climates of denial: an America weary of the war and not wanting to learn the harsh political realities concerning its imperialistic ambitions and a new emerging generation wishing to return gradually to the deceptive glamour of old values. Tom Cruise would embody the values of *Strategic Air Command* (1955) in *Top Gun* (1986), whereas "material girl" Madonna would soon appeal to a new apolitical, postmodernist generation eager to embrace the next dehumanizing incarnation of an American culture of consumption. Aldrich witnessed the latter phase during the 1950s. Although McCarthyism and the Cold War did not reemerge with full power, cultural denial still ruled the American imagination. *Twilight's Last Gleaming* suffered from this factor.

Twilight's Last Gleaming is one of Aldrich's major achievements as a director. It combines familiar elements such as antiauthoritarianism, the team under pressure, sports as a metaphor for American society, the questioning of heroism, and a pessimistic (yet realistic) vision of contemporary malaise. The film explicitly reveals damning features about the Vietnam War that most cinematic representations tend to avoid. It presents the whole American government and military structure as not only irredeemably corrupt but corporately responsible for a conflict that cost millions of lives.[1] As Andrew Britton has shown, *Twilight's Last Gleaming* is the only film of its type to reveal the sordid political realities behind the Vietnam War, especially in highlighting Richard Nixon's "madman" strategy, which recently released archive material has shown to be less a performance strategy to scare the enemy and more a deadly serious intention.[2] Loren Baritz also notes that both Henry Kissinger and Richard Nixon engaged in a dangerous form of psychological warfare with the enemy, including an ideological use of a domino theory involving irrational, unbalanced American action against the enemy:

> Strategy should be aimed at victory over the perceptions of the enemy. An English journalist and scholar understood this about the new team: "The fight is more for myth than for reality, more for credibility than for territory, and the prospect of loss is therefore more disconcerting than the *limited* nature of the war might be thought to imply." The "prospect of loss" was whether or not the opponent believed us, would take our threats seriously, and understood how tough we could be. From early on, Dr. Kissinger felt that psychological manipulation was the key to statecraft: "What the potential aggressor believes is more crucial than what is objectively true."[3]

Unfortunately, as *Twilight's Last Gleaming* reveals, this cynical American realpolitik gamesmanship costs millions of lives. As Secretary of

State Renfrew (Joseph Cotten) informs President Stevens (Charles Durning): "We had to convince the Russians that we meant business no matter how unmotivated our actions appeared" in the manner "business has been conducted since '45." The term *business* is not accidental. It is another Aldrich insight into the well-known fact that capitalism kills, especially in the light of a "theatrical holocaust" scenario Stevens's predecessor envisaged.

By moving from the limited battlefield arenas of *Attack!* and *The Dirty Dozen* to encompass the corrupt practices of the military and political establishment, Aldrich delivered a devastating blow against a system that had affected him and his fellow countrymen for generations. Unfortunately, as the film shows, nobody will ever hear the entire truth or even want to listen. Once more Aldrich shows that the system is so tarnished that old values of honesty and heroism are no longer effective. As Stevens recognizes, this type of government policy is "not only immoral but homicidal to say nothing of suicidal." Renfrew brushes aside his objection with the comment: "That Mr. President is blood over the dam!" Any formulaic production would see General Dell (Burt Lancaster) finally winning against a corrupt system. But Aldrich has no time for such Capraesque illusions. Schooled by the visions of Clifford Odets and his own experiences of the late 1940s, Aldrich is more mature in his vision. He depicts the American hero as not only redundant but also psychologically disturbed. Dell resembles Lt. Costa in several ways. As with Mike Callahan and Mike Hammer, his messianic pretensions are both dangerous and irrelevant. As Secretary of Defense Guthrie (Melvyn Douglas) remarks, if the full story "were ever revealed . . . historians might consider General Dell some kind of modern messiah. He believes Judgment Day is HERE but he threatens a terrible wrath if we won't make . . . what he considers the right choice."[4]

Twilight's Last Gleaming embodies not only Aldrich's new version of a *World for Ransom* but also another apocalyptic scenario akin to the climactic scenes of *Kiss Me Deadly* and *Sodom and Gomorrah*. The film also develops the split-screen techniques used in *Emperor of the North* and *The Longest Yard* to increase audience perspective significantly geographically, spatially, and politically. For example, when Dell fires the missiles, juxtaposed images show not only the disturbing launching process and Dell's own reactions but also diverse attitudes exhibited by different members of Stevens's cabinet. Attorney-General Klinger and Chief of Staff Spencer are really scared. They are fully aware of the implications of a future nuclear holocaust not only for America but for the rest of the world. But others, such as Secretary of State Renfrew, Strategic Air Command General Crane, and CIA Director Ralph Whittaker want General MacKenzie's men to continue their suicidal mission and detonate "Solid Gold," a euphemistic term for a small nuclear device. This mission may result in the nuclear destruction of most of the State of Montana and also possibly cause a chain reaction. By detonating the rest of the nuclear missiles, they may cause the destruction not just of the rest of the United States but of the rest of the world as well! Yet, like the nuclear strategist Herman Kahn of the 1950s, certain members of the president's cabinet really do not care. These institutional figures attempt to rally Stevens to the cause like spectators cheering on their favorite team. But this time the stakes are too high. There may be nobody around to celebrate the team's victory.

Although the final version of the film begins with the credit title scratched onto a frame showing the Statue of Liberty accompanied by Billy Preston's ironical rendition of the American national anthem against a cold November wind, the original screenplay aimed at a much more ambitious historical framework. According to the initial pre-picture sequence note, credit images aimed to "juxtapose history against a Washington background with the unfair advantage of hindsight: events seen through no-longer trusting eyes, an attitude that is one-eighth Brecht, one-eighth Jacques Brel, one-quarter ironic cynicism, one-quarter controlled angry disbelief, and one-quarter confused hope."[5] This collage certainly owes much to intellectual montage techniques used by various modernist movements of the New Deal era and beyond. The images open with Ford Theatre; Lincoln's presidential box; the interruption of his Gettysburg address by a shot; the Lincoln Memorial (an ironic pointer to President Stevens's eventual fate?); the gradual diminution and erasure of Lincoln's voice; shots of President Hoover and General Douglas MacArthur; the dispersal of the Bonus Marchers; Hoover's callous denial of the Great Depression ("A chicken in every pot; a car in every garage") followed by a barely audible laugh track over a shot of men lining up at a soup kitchen; President Roosevelt's famous address concerning the depression ("The only thing we have to fear is fear itself"); Pearl Harbor; Harry Truman; the Korean War; Truman's Oval Office defense of the bombing of Hiroshima and Nagasaki; a canned laugh track over shots of a decimated Hiroshima; Eisenhower's warning against the

military-industrial complex; President John F. Kennedy's inaugural
speech ("Ask not what your country can do for you") followed by
shots of military involvement in Vietnam; the assassinations of John
F. Kennedy, Martin Luther King, and Robert Kennedy; President
Johnson's Gulf of Tonkin Resolution; the brutal suppression of antiwar protestors in Chicago by Mayor Daley; Spiro Agnew's attack on
free speech; Nixon and Kissinger's alliance with Egyptian President
Anwar Sadat; Watergate; the Vietnam War; implied presidential involvement in the assassinations of Belgian Congo President Patrice
Lumumba, South Vietnamese President Diem, Martin Luther King,
and Salvador Allende; the secret bombing of Cambodia; the Kent
State University massacre; and the return of American POWs from
Vietnam.

It is a very impressive opening, foreshadowing the radical theme
of Aldrich's film. But it unfortunately ended up on the cutting-room
floor. As well as being deeply indebted to the heritage of New Deal
cultural movements such as "the Living Newspaper," the sequence
aptly illustrates the manner in which American political "business
has been conducted" long before 1945.[6] Furthermore, had this original concept become juxtaposed with Billy Preston's rendition of the
American national anthem, it would have further reinforced
Aldrich's reasons for choosing song and singer, namely, to contrast
between Lincoln's ideal of freedom and the grim reality of American
business practices. Most viewers would obviously recognize the deliberate incongruity in the choice of an African American singing a
song of freedom. What hope is there for this minority group if the
American establishment acts in a certain way toward members of its
own racial group such as Dell and Stevens? Also, by juxtaposing the
assassination of President Lincoln and cutting short his Gettysburg
address with the murders of other twentieth-century figures, this
lost sequence suggests that similar corporate practices may have
motivated the act of a supposed lone assassin at Ford Theatre. The
choice of Billy Preston to vocalize an ironic version of the national
anthem also evokes historical links with earlier radical African
American cultural movements during the New Deal, such as Fed-
eral Theatre productions in Harlem as well as other musical events.[7]
These all suffered from right-wing reaction during both the late
1930s and beyond.

After the caption "Sunday November 16, 1981," the film opens
with a shot of the White House before revealing David Stevens shav-

ing in the second-story living quarters. As the camera slowly tracks in, we see Stevens confined by the frame of his window. It is an opening metaphor for his own entrapment by the system he has embraced, particularly one whose dark implications he has no real knowledge of. Like most Aldrich heroes, Stevens is a flawed character. Although he assures his former professor, James Forrest (Roscoe Lee Browne), that his reasons for not granting a political refugee asylum result from a moral refusal to condone assassination, the actual picture is entirely different. After Forrest leaves, believing that his former student is "an honest man," Stevens's aide, General O'Rourke (Gerald S. O. Laughlin), enters and knowingly remarks, "By the look on his face you must've played old Abe Lincoln . . . (chuckling) . . . obviously you didn't tell him we had to trade that kid for our air bases." As the two men turn their attention to watching the Sunday morning Rams–Vikings football game, another deadly game occurs elsewhere in Montana.

Escaped prisoners led by General Lawrence Dell (Burt Lancaster) take over the identities of missile silo personnel. This disparate group comprises the cynical Augie Garvas (Burt Young), a dangerously volatile Hoxey (William Smith), and the laid-back Willis Powell (Paul Winfield). Dell finally gains access to the control center. Before he does so, he plays a version of a game little different from the way the political establishment plays its own deadly version. After supplying the names of the two football teams (also watched by Stevens and O'Rourke on television) to the outside control gate, Dell has to play his own version of brinkmanship to gain access to the control room below. Lacking a third password, Dell decides to take a gamble by affirming that there is no third word. When faced with the statement, "I challenge you," the seasoned commander replies, "I challenge YOU." He wins the contest and gains access. This is the first of many examples in the film linking the deadly game of nuclear warfare to an infantile contest. When Hoxey shoots a soldier whom Dell has allowed to pick up a phone, the general shoots him in reprisal: "I chose the wrong man for the job." But it is a comment that also negatively reflects on the judgment Dell exercises in his self-appointed heroic role as messianic leader. Dell shoots the one man who could perform a very essential task once they have gained access to the control room. It also reveals at an early point in the film Dell's own lack of rational qualities as a leader. By performing this action, Dell reveals a disturbing kinship to the emotionally irrational messianic Lieutenant Costa of *Attack!* rather than the more rational figure of Major Reisman in *The Dirty Dozen*.

As we later learn, Dell has also been part of a military establishment involved in nuclear war gamesmanship. When the three men descend in the elevator on their way to the control room, Garvas states his admiration for Dell's strategy: "That guy's got brass balls." However, Powell immediately contradicts this statement both by criticizing Dell's impulsive action ("And a brass head too. Hoxey's the only one who can open the safe") and by implicitly recognizing Dell as the author of the codes they have to break once they gain access below. Aldrich significantly cuts to a close-up of an embarrassed Dell when Powell describes the code creator as "some one-star asshole with nothing better to do." On their way to the missile room, Garvas and Powell appear hypnotized by the sight of a Titan nuclear rocket looming toward the top of the silo. When Dell orders the men to return to duty, his comments also reveal an American infantile fascination with destruction in terms reminiscent of Kubrick's use of the Mouseketeer anthem in the climax of *Full Metal Jacket* (1987): "C'mon . . . we're not on vacation . . . this isn't Disneyland." When they finally gain entry and overpower the officers in charge of the Launch Control Center, a revealing shot from Dell's perspective emphasizes his fascination with the destructive mechanisms he created in his former role as a bureaucratic destructive messiah. As the camera pans right to the poignantly emotional sounds of Frank DeVol's musical score, the scene evokes a romantic reunion between two separated lovers.[8] It not only illustrates the deadly connection between Eros and Thanatos in twentieth-century civilization, noted by both Norman O. Brown and Stanley Kubrick, but also reveals Aldrich's recognition of the destructive aspects of masculinity:

> When Dell informs the Duty Controller he has "full launch control," Powell notes that this is the "first time I ever saw (Dell) with a hard on." When Dell threatens to launch, the missiles are shown rising out of the underground silos in a parody of an erection. Dell is obviously sexually titillated by the power he gains by controlling the Titan missiles. Not only can he control the President but can also destroy the entire world. A similar shot resembling an erection occurs when Dell raises the remote camera to view the military moving against him. The technological edge provided by the remote camera makes him an omnipotent voyeur exemplifying the relationship between power domination and sexual excitement.[9]

After Dell dismantles the circuit breaker and informs the Strategic Command duty controller of his successful infiltration of Silo Three, the scene changes to a sparsely attended military chapel. General Martin MacKenzie (Richard Widmark) listens in boredom to the Reverend Cartwright's address. MacKenzie's beeper interrupts the sermon after Cartwright comments about "lusting after PX goodies" and enquires "what our responsibilities are to our fellow man." This scene does not represent Aldrich's usual dig at the ineffective nature of religion. It is much more complex here. The Reverend Cartwright is played by Phil Brown, an American actor long resident in England who moved there to escape the blacklist. He is not entirely an ineffectual figure. Like Aldrich, he speaks a message nobody wants to hear. Although this brief sequence shows that Cartwright recognizes that his institutional flock lacks interest in his sermon, the original screenplay contained a more critical address that ended up on the cutting-room floor.

Originally, Cartwright began his sermon by mentioning that "a multitude of evasions . . . from this pulpit or any other . . . cannot hide the fact that half of humanity wakes in hunger and lies down in rags." He ended his sermon by condemning commodification as well as championing a God who "demands more than occasional attendance and scattered attention."[10] Cartwright is an isolated figure but is far more preferable to the Christian soldier figure of MacKenzie (obviously modeled on General Curtis LeMay) and Dell's apocalyptic messiah, who are really mirror images of each other.[11] Dell can read MacKenzie's mind. So he is not surprised when his alter ego launches a tactical assault: "Bring the First Team in. And it's Sunday."

Dell needs the combination to the safe that holds the keys to launch the rockets and attempts to persuade his former friend and fellow Vietnam POW Captain Towne (Richard Jaeckel) to reveal crucial information to the American public. Towne expresses astonishment at Dell's naively patriotic attitude and accuses him of not learning a thing and "still going up against a stacked deck." When Dell urges him to collaborate in telling the truth and exposing the establishment, Towne comments, "They'll crucify you." As the film proceeds, it becomes evident that Dell intends much more than merely taking over the silo and holding the government to ransom. He wishes to become a real patriot and savior of his people in a country engaging in historical denial. Traumatically affected by a nation blaming him for involvement in the Vietnam War, Towne decides to become a team player again. The idealistic Dell becomes depressed and sulks about Towne's lack of cooperation. But streetwise tactics used by Garvas and Powell supply the relevant information. Once he has the keys allowing him to launch the Titan missiles, a victorious Dell proclaims, "Gentleman. We are now a superpower."

Garvas and Powell have joined Dell merely for the economic reasons of holding the government to ransom. But the general has another agenda in mind. He wishes to play a game of military brinkmanship that differs little from his own government's political philosophy. He announces his intention of launching nine Titan missiles against the Soviet Union unless the American public learns the establishment's real reasons for the Vietnam War.

Informed of this action by MacKenzie, Stevens assembles his cabinet for an emergency meeting. Played by well-known veteran American actors, the group resembles the "Wise Men" Senior Advisory Group that President Lyndon Johnson established early in the Vietnam conflict, which he occasionally turned to for advice. It comprised former secretary of state Dean Acheson; Johnson's secretary of state Dean Rusk; McGeorge Bundy; Generals Omar C. Bradley, Matthew Ridgeway, and Maxwell Taylor; Henry Cabot Lodge; Cyrus Vance; and many others. Aldrich's Wise Men comprise Melvyn Douglas's Secretary of Defense Guthrie (modeled on Acheson and Henry Kissinger), Joseph Cotten's Secretary of State Renfrew, William Marshall's Attorney-General Klinger, Leif Erickson's CIA Director Ralph Whittaker, Charles McGraw's Air Force General Peter Crane, and Simon Scott's Chairman of the Joint Chiefs General Phil Spencer.[13] Stevens learns not only that General Dell was "railroaded" after a convenient bar-room brawl resulted in a manslaughter charge but also the real reasons for the Vietnam War. Guthrie previously informed him that past and present administrations really had no policy at all—only deceitful statesmanship. Stevens now learns the truth about the true nature of American democracy as well as the fact that the president has no real power.

Dell demands the release of the contents of NSC Document 9759, a fictional version of *The Pentagon Papers*, as well as the president's promise to appear on television to inform the American people about decades of deceit. While the group reads the document, MacKenzie awaits permission to launch an assault on Silo Three using a nuclear device ironically termed "Solid Gold," evoking Marshall Berman's text "All that Is Solid Melts into Air" as well as revealing the economic reasons behind all forms of warfare. Crane, Guthrie, and Renfrew outweigh the reservations of Klinger and Stevens concerning the "acceptable" level of radiation fallout on the population of Montana. After Stevens attempts to bribe Dell with an additional $5 million, free pardons, and safe transit to any part of the world, Dell reiterates his condition concerning the revelation of the deadly poison stemming from "the treacherous doctrine of credibility" that cost so many lives during the Vietnam War. Although impressed by Dell's patriotic rhetoric, Stevens orders the assault.

Before the attack, the Wise Men discuss the implications of NSC 9759. Whereas Crane believes that release of the document will make the "military look criminally negligent," Whittaker and Klinger (representing the offices of the CIA and attorney general), argue that public consumption "would shatter confidence forever in our government." Renfrew emphasizes that the original decision was unanimous. Only the upwardly mobile Spencer believes that his country "is great enough to survive the truth" and that it may be "our last opportunity to trust our people." However, Guthrie plays the high card at the political gaming table when he states that releasing information under pressure "would be a tragic mistake."

A diversion is created, allowing MacKenzie's men access into the underground tunnel leading to the control room. During the assault, Aldrich creatively employs multi-split-screen techniques showing the action from the contradictory perspectives of various characters as well as giving his audience the full picture of the overall sporting strategy. When armored personnel carriers move toward Silo Three, Powell criticizes Dell's belief in "presidential credibility." Dell can only see the diversionary tactics of the assault team. But Stevens's cabinet and the audience gain a broader perspective. They see MacKenzie's assault team arrive by helicopter, making its way down the tunnel leading to the control room. Those in the Oval Office view the action from the three television screens on which Stevens and O'Rourke originally watched the Rams–Vikings game. While viewing Klinger refers to the "fifty-yard line," and Whittaker remarks, "We're in the middle of this game." MacKenzie also orders his men to "stay 1,000 yards from the church," his language reflecting Aldrich's ironic attitudes toward two sacred American institutions—sport and religion. When the Montana Strategic Air Command base later watches the martyrdom of Stevens, Dell, and Powell, the events are relayed through three giant monitor screens paralleling the three television screens in the Oval Office earlier depicting the football game.

Although MacKenzie's men successfully place the nuclear device directly outside the control room, the contingent accident of a layer of grease sticking to Kopecki's foot, during his earlier descent down the shaft, results in him slipping outside the door and setting off the alarm. When Dell launches the missiles, split screens show the deadly effect of this action on all concerned. These competing dialectic images show MacKenzie's men, who are urged to remain stationary and become sacrificial victims; members of Stevens own cabinet, some exhibiting fear at a possible nuclear war, while others urge the release of Solid Gold; Dell calling countdown; and the shocked reactions of Garvas and Powell. While Guthrie and Klinger urge the president to stop the mission "before it's too late," Crane and Renfrew urge him to give the order to fire. Stevens eventually orders MacKenzie to call off the attack. Dell ominously warns him that "next time they go."

Dell has also suffered losses. While playing his own version of nuclear brinkmanship he loses Garvas during a surprise attack by Towne and Canellis. Dell kills Canellis. Both sides lose one man. However, Dell is now left with the critical presence of Powell, rather than the more mercenary Garvas, who will try to educate him into the realities of the situation he faces. While Dell blames MacKenzie for the attack and religiously affirms that "the President's not a liar" (a line evoking humor among most audiences), Powell gradually demolishes his naive beliefs in the American system's flaunted values of integrity and justice: "While you're talking justice, he's calling up armor." Dell believes that MacKenzie was totally responsible for the attack. But the audience knows that Stevens ordered it himself.

Stevens also receives his own form of political education when he reads the details of the document. Chosen as a compromise presidential candidate during a deadlocked convention, he is shocked to learn the way foreign policy was conducted during the Vietnam War. As with Nixon's "madman theory," Stevens learns that the real reason for the Vietnam War was to demonstrate to the Russians "a brutal National Will" regardless of "the cost in American blood" threatening the perpetuation of a "theatrical holocaust." The recent brinkmanship contest between Dell and Stevens ironically echoes past political actions little different from fascism. As Renfrew reveals, "Let's not forget what Hitler and Stalin did to Spain. They were both ready to fight to the last Spaniard." As CIA Director Whittaker informs Stevens, the murderous card game of "cold, calculated gamesmanship" is "the way *business* [emphasis added] has been conducted since '45. All Presidents have had to do it" in order to prove (as Renfrew euphemistically puts it) that the American government is "capable of inhuman acts." Dell, of course, threatens his own type of inhumane act on the world if his economic and political demands are not met.

Guthrie recognizes that the establishment now has an opportunity to inform its people as to the bloody realities of limited war in a nuclear age. When Stevens asks Guthrie whether Dell may be correct in "how he perceives the world," the secretary of defense ambiguously replies, "He may very well be. But I didn't come down from Princeton to either preach open government or lobby for the IMPERIAL PRESIDENCY." The casting of Melvyn Douglas (the husband of Helen Gahagan Douglas, who was smeared as a communist by Richard Nixon during the 1950 California senate campaign) suggests that Guthrie may prove to be a positive influence. However, appearances are deceptive. As a veteran character actor Douglas had played deceitful patriarchal roles in recent films such as *I Never Sang for My Father* (1970) and *The Candidate* (1972). Guthrie will also prove to be another of Aldrich's negative father figures, such as Hanson (Lorne Greene) in *Autumn Leaves* (1956), the unseen Judge Cooney in *Attack!* (1956), Walter Mitchell (Lee J. Cobb) in *The Garment Jungle* (1957), Brendon O'Malley (Kirk Douglas) in *The Last Sunset* (1961), Ray Hudson (Dave Willock) in *What Ever Happened to Baby Jane?* (1962), Lot (Stewart Granger) in *Sodom and Gomorrah* (1963), Big Sam Hollis (Victor Buono) in *Hush . . . Hush, Sweet Charlotte* (1964), and Marty Hollinger (Ben Johnson) in *Hustle* (1975). Stevens hopes that Guthrie, as the oldest member of his cabinet, will prove himself to be a father figure he can trust. But like Aldrich's other betrayed children, he will soon face bitter disappointment. Guthrie holds his cards close to his chest, awaiting the next round in the game when his fellow gamblers play the next cards.

Stevens then decides to accede to Dell's request by choosing open government rather than deceitful rule in the dark "by nameless souls who remain forever unidentified." It is a brave and heroic decision. But it is also as naive as General Dell's belief in a system that can reform itself. Infuriated by cabinet consensus involving him going to Montana as a hostage and facing possible death, Stevens retreats into

the White House sitting room. While there he looks at an unsophisti-
cated, childlike painting by the First Lady. Despite plain evidence of
its uncreative nature vouched to the viewer, Stevens believes that his
wife "might have been a really fine painter." This comment reveals
that Stevens participates in the same type of self-deception as Dell.
Both men commit acts of violence to further their goals. Stevens lies
to his former professor about the reasons for deporting a radical student to a friendly nation where he will face certain death. Dell has
obviously lied to Hoxey, Powell, and Willis concerning the real reason he involved them in his mission. Unlike the others, Dell is not in
it just for the money. Both men sulk when things do not go their way
until their associates (O'Rourke, Powell) attempt to bring them back
to reality.

Stevens and Dell also play a game of nuclear brinkmanship equivalent to the earlier code game of "I challenge you" involving Dell
and the security system. They both hope that the truth will eventually emerge. But they will both be cheated at the end of the film by
a system engaged in deception and murder to conceal its deadly secrets from the American public. Stevens now appears the most obvious sacrificial victim to cover up the American government's criminal activities by his reluctant agreement to become a hostage to
allow Dell and his men to leave the silo. Although he is initially hesitant to fly to Montana, O'Rourke persuades him to take on the full
responsibility as president by growing into the job. Misquoting
Harry Truman as "Harry Houdini" (a line that reveals the presidential role as now being little better than a conjuring act), O'Rourke
tells Stevens, "The buck stops here . . . forget right, wrong, justice, or
any of that bullshit. You're living here and you gotta go. That's it. Period!" But Stevens's growth into maturity and responsibility will
lead to his eventual death rather than fulfilling the demands of his
office. He is another Aldrich character who suddenly changes character to become too late the hero. Before he leaves he makes Guthrie
promise to reveal the truth to the American public should he die on
the mission. The inscrutable Guthrie solemnly agrees.

While Dell awaits the arrival of Air Force One, Powell begins to
work on the general's naive belief in presidential credibility. He
suggests that the authorities have set up Stevens and themselves for
assassination. Powell asserts that the Air Force may have borrowed
the assassins "from the Mafia . . . it's all the same company!" and
that they are all expendable: "We're up against the real power! Man

don't you know we're messin' with the brains of this country?" Dell sees the light. But like a frustrated child reacting against playmates who do not play by the rules, he attempts to launch the missiles once he realizes that his adversaries "have no intention of honoring their commitments." Powell replies, "Come off it General! Nobody honors nothing. Shit man that ain't no reason to blow up the world." He refuses to help Dell in his childish scheme of Armageddon. However, before he can persuade Dell to "take the money and run," Air Force One's arrival occurs, plunging Dell back again into his ingrained false illusions involving presidential honor and open government.

Stevens eventually arrives to walk his "last mile." He is transported by jeep to his destination by the corpulent Sergeant Fitzpatrick (William Hootkins), who naively reacts to "Mr. President" in a manner similar to Dell. Both men have no conception of the actual reality surrounding the office. Nor do they realize that the person occupying that position has no real power. When Stevens finally meets Dell, the latter exhibits a beatific expression like a disciple greeting the Savior. Aldrich cuts to Powell's bemused expression during this scene in a similar manner to his cutaways to Smiley (Wendell Corey) as he watches Stanley Hoff's (Rod Steiger) performance in *The Big Knife* (1955). Powell now realizes that Dell is a lost cause and the best thing he can do is to get to Air Force One where the $20 million ransom money supposedly waits for him.

Outside in a control trailer, General MacKenzie directs another performance like a studio television director (perhaps a homage to Aldrich's own work as a television director on early 1950s series such as *China Smith* and *Four Star Playhouse*?). This scene contains a deliberate reference to the three assassins conspiracy theory concerning the Kennedy assassination. MacKenzie tells one Air Force rifleman that "those clowns are not to reach Air Force One" and ignores the reservations of assassin "Robin" over the president being in their sights. As Dell, Powell, and Stevens move closer to Air Force One, MacKenzie gives the order to fire. However, unlike Harry Truman, he passes the buck in a "Harry Houdini manner" to one of the snipers: "Sparrow you are now in control." The unfortunate Sparrow will obviously be another official scapegoat in any future official inquiry, whether public or private.

The snipers fire and immediately kill Dell and Powell. Stevens is mortally wounded. As Stevens dies, Aldrich cuts to different

perspectives of the scene ranging from those of the spectators in the
Montana Air Force Control Room, who receive only incomplete official information about the events they see on a large screen, to the
more limited television monitor of MacKenzie, who has stage managed the event. But Aldrich has given *his* audience the full story.
O'Rourke tearfully rushes to his fallen leader, cradling the dying
Stevens in a pietà position. Stevens calls for Guthrie, who slowly
approaches. He asks the elder statesman if he will keep his word
and tell the people. A close-up reveals the demolition of any hopes
Stevens may have in this "last honorable man." Indecision flashes
across Guthrie's aged face. It then slowly changes to silent firm resolve. Guthrie's close-up eloquently reveals that he is unable to lie to
the dying chief executive. A matching close-up shows Stevens understanding Guthrie's reaction before he finally dies, a deeply dis-
appointed man. The final image is bleak and desolate. It begins with
an overhead shot of Guthrie leaving Stevens. The camera then
cranes up into the vast distance before the final credits appear. Billy
Preston's rendition of the national anthem then occurs before the
hostile sound of the desolate wind opening the film returns once
again. The sound also reprises the sound of the wind in the opening
and closing scenes of *Hustle* (1975), another film dealing with the redundant nature of heroism in a corrupt corporate modern world.

Twilight's Last Gleaming is Robert Aldrich's cinematic testament. Although not his last film, it is really the final coda to the radical elements characterizing his cinematic authorship. It was a vision that
never took any easy solutions and avoided illusions, choosing instead
to engage directly with the personal and political traps affecting human existence. Aldrich attempted to confront those harsh social realities normally avoided by Hollywood. Although *Twilight's Last Gleaming* ends pessimistically, its message is never cynical. Again eschewing
a false "happy ending" and providing audiences with characters they
can identify with, the film depicts the dark realities of an American
political system desperately needing change. Aldrich allows his audiences to confront the violent and destructive operations of an establishment that ruthlessly destroys any opposition, whether at home or
abroad. Dell's individual heroism is redundant in such a situation.
The man is also revealed to be insane both by his willingness to begin
World War III in a mood of childish petulance and by his stubborn belief in a system that is no longer as honorable as he thinks. Like Marty
Hollinger in *Hustle*, he longs for his day in court but is oblivious of the

fact that the status quo will never allow him to disseminate the truth. Murderous figures like General MacKenzie, who admits his lack of interest in the news between wars, remain to continue the dirty work of the system. However, viewers have seen the full story of a "world for ransom," which they cannot entirely evade. As someone who witnessed the collapse of progressive alternatives during the 1930s and beyond, Aldrich never supplied any false solutions. Instead, he chose to engage with these grim realities on their own cinematic terms. But, like several of his other films, *Twilight's Last Gleaming* reveals that collective responsibility for changing the continuing nature of the dark events depicted on the screen still remains—even if past and present audiences refuse to recognize the fact.

As Raffaele Caputo has also argued in a stimulating article, a very convincing case can be made for seeing *Twilight's Last Gleaming* as a film noir, despite the film's apparent lack of the style's characteristic qualities.[14] Dell and Stevens are both doubles, using deceitful strategies to gain control at various points of their deadly game, and naive believers in a system that has now proven to be corrupt and redundant. Dell insanely believes that the president will make things right, whereas Stevens does rise to the majesty of his office. Both men are actually impotent and disposable in the final deal at the institutional card table. *Twilight's Last Gleaming* thus complements the bleak conclusion of *Kiss Me Deadly*. Whereas in the earlier film Aldrich's cynical version of the last romantic couple gazes at the whiteness that will finally obliterate both themselves and their world from the universe, *Twilight's Last Gleaming* concludes with audience recognition that the deadly game will continue into the future, one that may lead to that devastating apocalyptic climax of *Kiss Me Deadly*. All that is gained is a temporary respite. As Caputo comments, "*Twilight's Last Gleaming* is a *film noir* in this sense of multiinflectional, symbolically fundamental levels of style tuned to the sensibility of a diseased society."[15] Aldrich's final achievement thus echoes the dark implications of his first major work as a director. The wheel has come full circle.

NOTES

1. See Tony Williams, "Narrative Patterns and Mythic Trajectories in Mid-1980s Vietnam Movies," in *Inventing Vietnam*, ed. Michael Anderegg

(Philadelphia: Temple University Press, 1991), 114, 126. The film was cut in England to remove all the political references and was marketed as a heist movie. Walter Wager's original source novel *Viper Three* and the first-draft screenplay never contained any political references. Although Ronald M. Cohen and Edward Huebsch wrote the final screenplay, when the film was under attack as being "anti-American," Aldrich disclosed at a press conference that the political elements were his idea. See William Tusher, "'Twilight's' and Controversy: They Wanted It and Got It," *Daily Variety*, 20 January 1977: 38. Aldrich also expressed apprehensions concerning the current political situation involving the withdrawal of President Carter's choice for CIA director: "That's indicative of something—I don't know what. I'm not bright or profound enough to say. It's frightening" (Tusher, "'Twilight's' and Controversy," 38).

2. See Andrew Britton, "Sideshows: Hollywood in Vietnam," *Movie* 28–29 (1981): 23; Loren Baritz, *Backfire: A History of How American Culture Led Us into Vietnam and Made Us Fight the Way We Did* (Baltimore: Johns Hopkins University Press, 1998), 187–92, 210, 213.

3. Baritz, *Backfire*, 185–86.

4. Unless otherwise noted, quotations are from Ronald M. Cohen and Edward Huebsch, *Twilight's Last Gleaming*, second-draft screenplay, 9 January 1976.

5. Cohen and Huebsch, *Twilight's Last Gleaming*, A.

6. Joseph Losey, the Group Theatre, and Nicholas Ray were involved in various aspects of the Living Newspaper tradition. See Bernard Eisenschitz, *Nicholas Ray: An American Journey*, trans. Tom Milne (London: Faber and Faber, 1993), 33–38; and Michael Denning, *The Cultural Front: The Laboring of American Culture in the Twentieth-Century* (London: Verso, 1997), 367–70.

7. See Denning, *The Cultural Front*, 338–48, 369.

8. As Chris Milazzo superbly commented in his ENGL 494 class paper, "Of Winning the American Heart and Mind: An Examination of the Cinema's (Sub)Version of Vietnam during the 70s and 80s," *Twilight's Last Gleaming* "also makes a point to demonstrate the sexual relationship Dell has with technology and weapons of mass destruction. As Baritz notes, there exists a strange psychosis in the 'Puritan middle-class mind (that gets) killing mixed up with screwing'; a similar relationship between *thanatos* (death) and *eros* (sex) that Freud discusses" (5). Milazzo also significantly notes that Dell's gaze at the launch panel "is similar to a first person perspective looking over a lover's body" ("Of Winning the American Heart and Mind," 5).

9. Milazzo, "Of Winning the American Heart and Mind," 5.

10. Cohen and Huebsch, *Twilight's Last Gleaming*, 36–37.

11. For the role of General Curtis LeMay and the relevance of the U.S. Air Force in *Twilight's Last Gleaming*, see Thomas D. Boettcher, *Vietnam: The Valor and the Sorrow* (Boston: Little, Brown, 1985), 207. Boettcher writes, "Though

the air force is a branch of the service in which hardware often overwhelms the identities of individual commanders and makes them seem nothing more than working parts of a vast machine, LeMay managed to apply his personal stamp to it. He was not just another anonymous 'businessman in blue'" (*Vietnam*, 207). Like other military commanders such as Grant, Sherman, Pershing, and Eisenhower, LeMay was a managerial figure whose strategy was based not on tactical daring and surprise but on the use of wars of attrition.

12. For the role of the Wise Men, see Boettcher, *Vietnam*, 377–82.

13. Guthrie resembles Acheson. And though not from Harvard like Kissinger, he is a Princeton professor.

Although more well known as the leading man of *Blacula* (1972) and *Scream, Blacula, Scream* (1973), William Marshall played other more dignified roles in film and television. For example, he portrayed future U.S. senator Attorney-General Edward W. Brooke in *The Boston Strangler* (1968). Marshall also had a distinguished theatrical record, having appeared in New York's Negro Theatre in 1948 as well as playing the title role in *Oedipus Rex* in Chicago during 1955 and portraying Othello in numerous New York, Dublin, L.A., and San Diego productions. Two years after *Twilight's Last Gleaming*, he appeared in the Chicago Theatre Group production of *An Enemy of the People*. According to Paul Buhle, Marshall felt that he was "graylisted" and lost patience with Hollywood after being confined to a few 1950s films whenever an out-of-control "angry African" was needed. He spent several decades abroad in Shakespearean productions before returning in the 1970s to play Blacula. See Paul Buhle and Dave Wagner, *Radical Hollywood: The Untold Story behind America's Favorite Movies* (New York: New Press, 2002), 430n55.

Formerly married to Frances Farmer, who appeared in the Group Theatre production of *Golden Boy*, Leif Erickson was also a veteran of that company. *Twilight's Last Gleaming* was his final film appearance. Charles McGraw was a veteran screen heavy whose Air Force rank in this film may ironically complement Richard Widmark if we see the latter's role in this film as an older and more dangerous version of Tommy Udo from *Kiss of Death* (1947).

Simon Scott had less distinguished credentials than most of the Wise Men. However, his journeyman record as an actor is appropriate for a chief of staff who has risen from the ranks to join his more eminent colleagues in the White House. By contrast, Gerald S. O'Laughlin (Major Rourke) received his theatrical training from figures such as Sanford Meisner at the Neighborhood Theatre and Lee Strasberg at the Actors Studio in the postwar era. He made his Broadway debut in *Golden Boy* and had appeared in several Arthur Miller and Tennessee Williams stage productions.

14. Raffaele Caputo, "*Film Noir*: You Sure Don't See All You Hear," *Continuum* 5, no. 2 (1992): 297. The writer also notes that, with the exception of

Melvyn Douglas, "the first notable feature of *Twilight's Last Gleaming* is a strong league of actors, most of whom emerged in post–World War II American cinema, who in either major or minor ways made a niche for themselves in a host of *film noir* titles" ("*Film Noir*," 297). The author lists Burt Lancaster, Richard Widmark, Joseph Cotten, Charles McGraw, Leif Erickson, and Richard Jaeckel. Cotten had played similarly untrustworthy gentleman roles in *The Last Sunset* and *Hush . . . Hush, Sweet Charlotte* as well as having being associated with Orson Welles in the Mercury Theatre (referred to in *The Big Knife*) as well as *Citizen Kane, The Magnificent Ambersons, Journey into Fear* (1942), and *Touch of Evil* (1958). Like Robert Aldrich, Alfred Hitchcock recognized the dark side of Joseph Cotten, as his casting in *Shadow of a Doubt* (1953) shows. But we should not discount the theatrical associations of some of these actors, who had links with those "fervent years" documented by Harold Clurman (*The Fervent Years: The Story of the Group Theatre and the Thirties* [New York: Hill and Wang, 1957]).

15. Caputo, "*Film Noir*," 298. Working on a more pragmatic level of an institutional history studying the symbiotic relationship between the film industry and the armed services, Lawrence H. Suid naturally finds several flaws in this analysis of *Twilight's Last Gleaming* in his exceptional study *Guts and Glory*. But he does note the film's key contradiction involving a general attempting to make the government more responsible to the people and also threatening to destroy the entire world. Suid notes that "the general comes across as a somewhat crazed victim of the Vietnam War rather than a hero trying to alert the nation to the wrongs its government has perpetrated on it" (*Guts and Glory: The Making of the American Military Image in Film*, rev. and expanded ed. [Lexington: University of Kentucky Press, 2002], 441). Certainly, according to Suid's analysis, the film has problems. But if we see Dell as the latest incarnation of Aldrich's deranged savior-messiah who threatens the world with Judgment Day if it does not suitably comply, then the difficulty vanishes. To his credit, Suid does recognize the film's merits: "For his efforts, Aldrich created a visually interesting movie. If *Twilight's Last Gleaming* did not contain the powerful warning the director and star hoped to make, they did produce a serious, sometimes stimulating movie, that reflected the nation's paranoia in the post-Vietnam, post-Watergate period" (*Guts and Glory*, 443).

TEN

CONCLUSION

Robert Aldrich died at home on 5 December 1983 from kidney failure following a gall bladder operation, just five days after he had discharged himself from hospital. During his last days, he met with many friends and associates and talked about movies he would never make, such as *Kinderspiel*. Aldrich had hoped to film J. B. Harding's 1955 screenplay about a "children's revolt" in New England against nuclear weapons ever since 1957. But the project had remained in abeyance for several decades.[1] Among Aldrich's unfilmed projects were typical subjects, such as another Spillane adaptation, *My Gun Is Quick,* as well as the 1972 screenplay *All the Marbles.* This had nothing to do with the 1981 film of the same name. It was based on a story idea by Aldrich, Robert Sherman, Edward Harper, and William Aldrich about three disillusioned middle-aged noncombatants who attempt to smuggle pearls out of Vietnam prior to the fall of Saigon in 1975. Other projects went to other directors, in both the past and the future, such as *3:10 to Yuma, Taras Bulba, Billy Two Hats,* and *The Sheltering Sky,* later to be filmed by Bernardo Bertolucci and produced by William Aldrich.[2] The last film appears quite surprising. But Aldrich was never a director of the macho films most critics tended to identify him with. Another interesting project never made was *The Human Condition,* a 1970 treatment by Robert Sherman about the moral conflicts of Japanese, English, and Americans in occupied Burma during World War II. This could have led to the development of several themes already present in *Too Late the Hero.*

This diversity is not surprising when we consider the complex ideas Aldrich brought to the Hollywood genres he attempted to transform. But, like Charlie Castle in *The Big Knife,* Aldrich was trapped within a system that often attempted to suffocate any creativity that explicitly questioned its premises. Yet, unlike Charlie Castle, Aldrich was never self-defeatist. He was a shrewd pragmatist who knew the nature of the game he played and stubbornly decided to stay at the table, no matter how unpromising were the cards he sometimes received from the Hollywood dealer's deck. On certain occasions, he was lucky. At other times, he must have been tempted to cash in his chips. But Aldrich continued to direct to the end, no matter how bad certain projects were.

One of these was *The Choirboys*. After the failure of *Twilight's Last Gleaming*, Aldrich was no longer in a position to exercise creative control. He was faced with directing a dreadful screenplay, the bulk of which came from the first draft of an author who wrote the original novel but who also managed to remove his name from the final credits of the completed film. Aldrich took the blame for the result. For the majority of its running time, *The Choirboys* is a film beyond redemption. Based on a contemporary best-selling novel by Joseph Wambaugh, the project must have seemed a sure bet after the box-office failure of *Twilight's Last Gleaming*. However, despite Wambaugh's intermittent insights into the power structure of the L.A. Police Department and the various psychological problems facing officers, the book is an interminable, vulgar catalog of despair and nihilism moving toward a pretentious Sartrean existentialist conclusion. Wambaugh's original screenplay is little different. The vulgarity he accused Aldrich of appears in both the original novel and the first-draft screenplay. However, the novel itself presented a major challenge for any cinematic adaptation in terms of its vast gallery of characters and incidents needing drastic revision. Although Wambaugh removed the novel's flashback structure from the first-draft screenplay, his version still remained a producer's nightmare. When Aldrich and his *Emperor of the North* scenarist, Christopher Knopf, began to make changes, Wambaugh sued and successfully got his name removed from the credits. Aldrich found himself in a situation in which any form of creative maneuver became impossible. He was stuck with a bad product and took the blame when negative reviews appeared.[3] However, those who blame Aldrich entirely for the final version should study Wambaugh's screenplay. All the faults within the film are already there.[4]

In many ways, history repeated itself for Aldrich. Like his mentor Lewis Milestone with the Enterprise Studio production *Arch of Triumph* (1948), he found himself removing footage that explained the motivations of several characters in the film. The final 119 minutes resulted in a truncated product. Aldrich must have been aware of problems when he viewed the original four hours of footage. But he no longer had the power to alter drastically the original source novel as he had done with *Twilight's Last Gleaming*. Aldrich again returned to Abraham Polonsky's conclusion to *Body and Soul* in trying to salvage the film's final scenes.

Aldrich and Knopf attempted to change Wambaugh's nihilistic ending when the senior member of the "choirboys," "Spermwhale" Whalen, informs on his friends after being threatened with the loss of his pension. The book ends with two cops walking through MacArthur Park, the scene of the choirboys' therapeutic practice enabling them to cope with the pressures of work. One choirboy has accidentally killed a young homosexual and collapsed into insanity, partly because of trauma he suffered in Vietnam. The other choirboys attempt to cover up the killing until they are all railroaded by an establishment seeking an excuse to punish them. As an ex-cop, Wambaugh saw them as martyrs to the system. But Aldrich considered Wambaugh's ending as depressing as Rossen's proposed conclusion to *Body and Soul*. The director decided to change it.

The last twelve minutes of *The Choirboys* (excluding the credit sequences) cannot really save the film or redeem its obnoxious characters in the eyes of the audience. But it attempts to move away from nihilistic determinism toward an ending that allows for a certain degree of agency and the temporary defeat of an oppressive bureaucracy. The final credit sequences affirm that we are again in *Dirty Dozen* territory. But eliminating it as an arbitrary concluding structure—which indeed it is—allows us to consider other implications within these last twelve minutes. It does not save the entire film. But it marks the presence of an authorial element struggling to salvage something from a worthless text.

The characters in *The Choirboys* are certainly unlikable. So were the Dirty Dozen. But Aldrich never depicted characters whom the audience could emotionally identify with. His choirboys are all complex figures and often parallel their real-life counterparts in the police. They may indulge in appalling behavior. But those in power who made them what they are actually deserve more condemnation. If the authorities cannot be entirely overthrown, the possibility may lie in a temporary victory that might lead to a permanent one in the long run. This represented the progressive nucleus of Aldrich's cinematic vision. It is not 100 percent satisfactory. But neither is life, especially when all the cards appear to be against one. When this happens, it is important to never admit defeat but, rather, to search for some unforeseen gap that may make a limited form of agency possible—even one resulting in a stalemate situation.

After the MacArthur Park shooting, the authorities interrogate Spermwhale (Charles Durning). Like the rest of the choirboys, he attempts to remain silent and protect his friends. The shooting was accidental. But the choirboys have betrayed police procedure by illegally covering up the actual incident. During the interrogation the pompous and ruthlessly authoritarian Deputy Chief of Police Riggs (Robert Webber) exerts pressure on the older man to "name names." If he refuses, then a loss of pension rights and an uncertain future at the unemployable age of fifty-three await him. Riggs tempts him: "You can slip out of town. They won't know you did it." When Riggs leaves the room, Spermwhale looks several times at the tape recorder and one-way mirror in the interrogation room. Although we never see the observers behind the glass, both the audience and Spermwhale know that he is under surveillance. This sequence evokes the blacklist era that affected so many of Aldrich's contemporaries in Enterprise Studios and elsewhere. Like Clifford Odets, Spermwhale eventually names names. Like Charley Davis in *Body and Soul*, he accepts his retirement package. But this is not the final story. Unlike Wambaugh, Aldrich adds a different type of ending.

The next sequence occurs in a Monterey wharf. Spermwhale arrives in his boat, significantly named *The Last One*, after an unsuccessful day's fishing. Meeting him at the jetty with his mail is an older man, John. He is immediately recognizable to Aldrich audiences as John Steadman, who played "Pop" in *The Longest Yard*. Like his earlier character, John delivers significant advice to Spermwhale when he learns about the unsuccessful day's fishing: "There's always hope. The next time out it'll be better." The line has a resonance beyond its immediate context. Aldrich obviously sees John Steadman's character as the spiritual successor of Canada Lee's Ben from *Body and Soul*, who inspires Charley Davis to struggle and win his blessing.[5]

Spermwhale opens the letter. It begins with an offscreen voice-over by Calvin Potts (Louis Gosset Jr.), the one choirboy not at MacArthur Park on that fatal night. Potts's voice booms on the soundtrack like a deus ex machina, causing Spermwhale to look around him. It is another Aldrich iconoclastic religious joke. Seeing neither God nor Charlton Heston in the vicinity, Spermwhale returns to the letter. He learns that his fellow victimized choirboys "don't hold it against you." They instead forgive him in a manner that is far more Christian than the institutional codes followed by their victimizers: "You did nothing wrong. . . . You beat the system. Not any of us wouldn't do what you did." This forgiveness certainly does not parallel any feelings that blacklisted victims had for their accusers. But in the context of *The Choirboys*, it expresses the understanding Spermwhale's friends have for the dilemma faced by an older man facing the loss of his pension after retirement. They express their collective delight at the fact that he has survived to enjoy his retirement against the odds, and they do not hold his decision against him. This is not a realistic attitude. It represents more of an optimistic collective utopian vision by the man's former colleagues, who express their understanding of the complex forces behind Spermwhale's decision that have resulted in his betrayal. The choirboys decide to forgive him like the Savior of a religion Aldrich found irrelevant to the modern age. They do not regard him as a Judas figure like Maggott in *The Dirty Dozen*. Instead, they forgive the older man for not really knowing what he did. This, however, is not going to be the final chapter in Aldrich's rewriting of the original conclusion of Joseph Wambaugh's *The Choirboys*.

The letter stimulates Spermwhale to face Riggs once again and force him to reinstate the other men. Despite threats of losing his pension, Spermwhale stands his ground and engages in a game of bluff that only lacks a card table. His friends face six-month suspensions because Riggs has lied to everyone concerning what actually did happen in MacArthur Park. Despite Riggs mentioning that the real story will result in criminal prosecutions against the choirboys, Spermwhale calls his bluff. When Riggs believes that Spermwhale is bluffing as an individual player and that nobody else has the guts to stand up to him, the older man produces depositions signed by the choirboys. The men have decided to play the high card. Should Riggs call their bluff, he, too, would face criminal charges. Unlike Colonel Bartlett in *Attack!* Riggs is on his own. He faces the firm resolve of a collective group rather than one person, like Woodruff, who may capitulate to a more powerful authority. A united group of men standing by each other represents a different type of ball game.

Spermwhale and Potts leave Riggs's office. They take pleasure in their minor victory, knowing that Riggs will never call their bluff.

But the victory is problematic. Spermwhale uses blackmail to achieve his ends. One choirboy has already committed suicide. Another has suffered permanent psychological damage. The remaining men are no shining examples of integrity. But life is neither fair nor clear-cut. But for Aldrich, any victory against an unjust system is important, no matter how compromised it may be.

The Choirboys proved a critical and commercial flop. It helped nobody's career, especially Aldrich's. However, by attempting to change the ending, the director may have seen himself like Charley Davis, fighting his last desperate round in *Body and Soul* and seeking that final punch that would give him victory. *The Choirboys* did not achieve this. But the last twelve minutes of the film do, at least, make the attempt. As in John Garfield's final lines in *Body and Soul*, Aldrich would soon personally confront the fact that "everybody dies." But what is important is the nature of the legacy left behind. Davis departs from *Body and Soul* displaying a powerful aura of redemption, regeneration, and resilience. No matter what the final outcome, he struggled and won his blessing, unlike his alter ego in *The Big Knife.*

Aldrich continued the legacy of *Body and Soul* in his various films. Some characters may survive and others may die. But Aldrich left audiences an important cinematic inheritance expressing many issues relevant to both the twentieth century and beyond. He saw the effects of the depression as a young man, understood the real implications behind the plays of Clifford Odets, benefited from the influence of Abraham Polonsky, and operated during the 1950s as a key contributor to that critical modernist cultural movement David Cochran labels "America Noir." As Ed Lowry recognizes, Aldrich's cinema contains several ironic and black comedy elements that also characterize the films of Stanley Kubrick. Both directors ruthlessly interrogate the self-deceptions and evasive aspects of their different characters. However, Aldrich never fled permanently to Europe. He remained to fight the system on his own terms. Sometimes he succeeded. At other times he did not. But, as Lowry mentions in his concluding paragraph, "more than any other mainstream director, Aldrich insisted on presenting the radical contradictions of American ideology."[6] Aldrich was also fully aware of his country's history, its lost opportunities, and a studio system that rejected the artistic possibilities represented by Orson Welles, another key figure of the Cultural Front. It is a link recognized by G. Cabrera Infante in his review of Louis Malle's first film, *Ascenseur pour l'Echafaud/Frantic*

(1956). Writing about the film in 1959, the critic noted "a clearly perceptible influence by Orson Welles . . . and from Welles through Aldrich and the American cinema from the fringe (through Stanley Kubrick because *Frantic* clearly resembles *Killer's Kiss* . . .)."[7] When the prodigal son returned to the Hollywood fold for the last time to direct *Touch of Evil,* Cabrera Infante associated Aldrich with many Hollywood directors indebted to his pioneering work.[8] But Aldrich was not one of Welles's "imitators."[9] He was a director influenced by the same cultural traditions as Welles and developed them in his own particular way. Unlike Welles, Aldrich had the luck and tenacity to remain in the game and continue to try to use those radical traditions within the Hollywood film industry. His struggle against the odds to maintain his vision formed an integral part of Aldrich's cinematic philosophy: "Since it's impossible to 'win' everything in life, whether you're a football player, a soldier, a politician, your interior self-esteem comes out of how hard you *try* to win—the degree of your struggle. That's the yardstick whereby effort, whether it's heroic or imaginative, is really measured. I'm concerned with man's efforts to prevail against impossible odds."[10]

Whereas Welles engaged in tiring excursions abroad to find funding for his various projects (or acting roles often beneath his creative dignity) and Kubrick retreated into cynical despair in England, Aldrich always hoped for that utopian moment of redemption when body and soul would unite to fight against the common enemy. Welles became an outsider, and Kubrick never returned to America. But Aldrich always wished to be on the inside playing the game against a powerful system. However, Aldrich's own game never involved mere entertainment. During his apprenticeship years in the late 1940s, he not only benefited from exposure to the golden age of screenwriters but also experienced a time when literature was taken seriously, before the anti-intellectual McCarthyite reaction. As Aldrich stated, "I had extraordinary exposure to important writers like Steinbeck, Faulkner, Irwin Shaw, Odets, and Remarque."[11] But after witnessing the collapse of the Enterprise Studio dream, Aldrich never underestimated the enemy or the grim realities involved in explicitly opposing the system. Like a general or football coach, he formed his own strategy, often becoming, as Donald Lyons aptly states, "the Swiftian joker at the feast of reason" who "would take an action, a *praxis,* and look at it through the prism of paradox."[12] As a young *Cahiers du Cinema* critic, Claude Chabrol admired the director's films.

Speaking several years later, he emphasized the same "discomfiting" theme structuring the director's work, namely, that "man's adventures are born out of his antagonistic relationship with the society, environment, world—call it what you will—he belongs to. The adventure of man is therefore a dialectic."[13]

Aldrich's films depict worlds of paradox and contingencies that resemble the satirical vision of Stanley Kubrick in many ways. Slackers may become heroes in *Too Late the Hero*. Barbara and Slim become the last romantic couple in *The Grissom Gang*. Murderous criminals become equally murderous heroic soldiers in *The Dirty Dozen*, trapped in a deadly scheme engineered by the military establishment during the "Good War." As Chabrol astutely recognizes, Aldrich was a wily ironic player at the Hollywood game. But his playing often led to misunderstandings on the part of most critics. *The Dirty Dozen* is one such example: "The film was so well-made and so violent that it was taken as an apologia for brutality when it was really the opposite: a virulently anti-militaristic tract (peacetime murderers make the best soldiers and vice versa). Dialectic and wiliness: the new Aldrich had arrived."[14]

Aldrich also worked at splitting audience perception in a manner demanding the application of relevant reader-reception theories to his work. R. J. Thompson's personal response to one sequence in *Twilight's Last Gleaming* may also be applied to other Aldrich films that defy the typical nature of audience expectation:

> When Lancaster sees troops approaching he says (more or less) that's it: they screwed me, now it's their turn. In all the synergy Aldrich can muster with two- and four-panel split-screen work, Lancaster does it: he presses the button. We watch the missiles slowly rise from the silos. At this point, I am simultaneously and equally registering feeling, two contradictory things: No, no, you can't do that, that's what we've been afraid of since we had bomb drills in primary school, you can't send up the atom bombs and kill people. And the other half of me, equally strongly, at the same time saying: Yes, give it to the treacherous bastards, they deserve it.
>
> The ability to evoke such responses is what Robert Aldrich, independent, has finally been marketing all these years. For me, it is the center of Robert Aldrich. And he knows it's the center of me.[15]

Donald Lyons also sees a difference between a new 1960s Aldrich and an earlier one who aimed at explicit subversion by openly destabilizing generic conventions. He notes the director's strategy in developing audience involvement in *The Dirty Dozen* until the final horrific scenes as being akin to making them walk into moral quicksand: "Aldrich is the Devil's travel agent, inviting us on what promises to be a regulated voyage up to a charted river. But we wake on the third morning and the guide is gone and the map is no good and the river is bounded by jungle on both sides."[16]

Lyons's analogy also applies to the visions contained in the plays of Clifford Odets and the changing cultural and political climate of the postwar era, which were all formative influences on the director's films. Aldrich's work reflects issues of confusion, paradox, and uncertainty. But his films also involve key issues of human survival. Characters always have to adjust to the fact that the cards dealt at the table are not always the ones they expected. Otherwise, they face destruction.

Aldrich left several important legacies for others. One of them may cause surprise. Rose Capp argues against the common denigration of Aldrich as a macho director in her analysis of *Kiss Me Deadly* in terms of its contribution to later female-centered films. Looking on the film as a "representational watershed in the American *film noir* tradition," she argues that Aldrich problematizes the overdetermined figure of the noir woman by exploring female agency in relation to image, discursive authority, and the transgressive potential of sound, "which obliquely shadows an ambitious project of feminist film theory some two decades later."[17] Such features deserve further investigation. Aldrich was never a director of "positive images." His female characters often exhibit complex feelings, unless they are deliberately stereotyped like the whores in *The Dirty Dozen* or Bernadette Peters's Nixon-type secretary in *The Longest Yard*.

The second legacy involves Aldrich's activist work within the Hollywood system, which certainly contrasts with the cynical perspectives contained in several of his films. Aldrich was a strong supporter of the Directors Guild of America throughout his career. He served as national vice president from 1971 to 1975 and two terms as president during 1975–79. During his terms of office, he reformed the Trust and Retirement Fund, overhauled the Health and Welfare System, and defined a director's right to the full version of his film. As Sanjek aptly points out, the studios would never forgive him for this and would certainly wait for the appropriate box-office returns to humiliate him later.[18] These facts may explain the disappointing nature of *The Choirboys* and *The Frisco Kid*, films over which the director had no real control. They were also ones for which a vengeful establishment would eagerly seek the opportunity to lay blame for their failure on the director alone. However, Aldrich left other important key legacies.

Twilight's Last Gleaming is certainly his masterpiece and last testament. But we should also not forget *Apache, Kiss Me Deadly, The Big Knife, Autumn Leaves, Attack! What Ever Happened to Baby Jane? The Flight of the Phoenix, The Dirty Dozen, The Grissom Gang, Too Late the Hero, Ulzana's Raid,* and *Hustle.* These films represent an important cinematic legacy for both their relevance to contemporary Hollywood cinema and their echoes of what could have been—and may even be in the future.

The final words in this book should really belong to Robert Aldrich. His endurance and resilience represent equally important inspiration for the twenty-first century as they did for the previous one. Believing that struggle was important, Aldrich felt that just sitting back and pessimistically indulging in defeat simply would not do: "Well, I don't think you can relax and enjoy it. To relax is to say, well I'm dead already. Why not struggle and maximize the victories. They may not come, probably *won't* come, but they might come, and when they come you're one victory ahead of total defeat."[19]

In 1973 Aldrich felt that Charlie Castle was wrong and that he should have listened to the Odetsian advice offered: "Struggle, you may still win a blessing." This advice is still relevant today, especially if the participants lose their innocence and understand the full relevance of the William Blake poem that Peg recites to Charley in *Body and Soul*: "Tyger! Tyger! burning bright / In the forests of the night / What immortal hand or eye / Could frame thy fearful symmetry?" When Charley asks her what *symmetry* means, she teasingly replies, "Well built." However, Charley misunderstands the real meaning of the Blake poem and sets out to achieve material success by the commercial use of his body. But symmetry involves balance and correspondence. Until Charley finally understands that body and soul complement each other, he is an alienated figure. Similarly, according to the cinematic vision of Robert Aldrich, this type of symmetry is equally important if any major victories are to be achieved in the future.

NOTES

1. See Edwin T. Arnold and Eugene I. Miller, *The Films and Career of Robert Aldrich* (Knoxville: University of Tennessee Press, 1986), 234; and Alain Silver and James Ursini, *What Ever Happened to Robert Aldrich? His Life and His Films* (New York: Limelight Editions, 1995), 332. According to Paul Buhle and Dave Wagner, many survivors of the blacklist "wanted badly to treat the threat of nuclear war and the first hints of irreversible environmental damage" (*Radical Hollywood: The Untold Story behind America's Favorite Movies* [New York: New Press, 2002], 376). This may have also appeared in Aldrich's original treatment for *The Gamma People* (1956).

2. For a detailed list of projects, see Silver and Ursini, *What Ever Happened to Robert Aldrich?* 331–40.

3. For the background history to *The Choirboys,* see Arnold and Miller, *The Films and Career of Robert Aldrich,* 206–13.

4. Joseph Wambaugh, *The Choirboys,* first-draft screenplay, 8 July 1975.

5. Aldrich's direction of favorite actors is often remarkable. Although not an official choirboy, Burt Young's Sergeant Dominic Scuzzi is allowed to join the roll call during the final credits. He deserves this honor. During an earlier scene in the film, he expresses a fatherly sympathy toward the arrested young homosexual, Alexander Blaney (Michael Wills), who will later die accidentally in MacArthur Park by the bullets of traumatized Vietnam veteran Sam Lyles (Don Stroud). Scuzzi's advice to Blaney appears in the first draft of Wambaugh's screenplay. He warns him about going to the park at night. In the final version of the film, Burt Young delivers his (thankfully) abbreviated lines in a sympathetic manner. It is another example of a supposedly macho director's recognition that many outcasts exist in society, whether they are like those in *World for Ransom* or *The Killing of Sister George.*

6. Ed Lowry, "Robert Aldrich," in *International Directory of Films and Filmmakers,* vol. 2: *Directors,* 4th ed., ed. Tom Prendergast and Sara Prendergast (New York: St. James Press, 2000), 8. Abraham Polonsky's comments about the postwar period also apply to Aldrich's 1950s films: "You can't understand those times unless you realize that radical politics, the beginnings of the cold war, the bomb, and for me the new world of making movies were in a boiling mix. I think my films reflect this in one way or another" (see Judith Spiegelman, "Interview with Abraham Polonsky," in *Contemporary Authors 104* [Detroit: Gale Research Co., 1982], 373).

7. G. Cabrera Infante, *A Twentieth Century Job,* trans. Kenneth Hall and G. Cabrera Infante (London: Faber and Faber, 1991), 322.

8. Cabrera Infante, *A Twentieth Century Job,* 242.

9. Cabrera Infante, *A Twentieth Century Job,* 244. Aldrich himself admitted this in his first interview with Francois Truffaut. When questioned about the Welles influence, Aldrich admitted the possibility but also defined it as

an unconscious one. Also, Aldrich had seen all Welles's films up to the date of the interview but disliked both *Macbeth* and the films made outside Hollywood. He saw the director's genius indissolubly linked with the financial benefits of the Hollywood system: "Orson Welles sans argent perd l'essential de son génie" (see Truffaut, "Rencontre avec Robert Aldrich," *Cahiers du Cinema* 64 [1956]: 9). Aldrich mentioned *Citizen Kane* and *The Magnificent Ambersons* as his favorite Welles films. Although no record exists of any personal encounter between Aldrich and Welles, R. J. Thompson's essay contains the most appropriate perspective on this relationship. Noting that Aldrich began working in RKO at the same time *Citizen Kane* emerged, Thompson comments that the "co-incidence establishes Aldrich's credentials as a member of the generation of directors who came up through the Hollywood system and who made their feature debuts post-*Kane,* and very much aware of it" ("Robert Aldrich: An Independent Career," available at www.latrobe.edu.au/screeningthepast/firstrelease/fr0600/rtfr10a.htm, 30 June 2000).

10. Charles Higham, "Robert Aldrich," *Action* 9, no. 6 (1974): 16. See also Gilbert Cates, "Robert Aldrich 1918–1983," *Directors Guild of America News* 8, no. 1 (1984): 1–3. This extract from Cates's remarks at Aldrich's memorial service mentions that the director used the game analogy often: "When he became a director, he assembled a strong team and kept it together for decades: two cinematographers photographed 22 of his 29 features, one editor cut 19, one composer scored 16, one art director designed 11" ("Robert Aldrich 1918–1983," 1). See also Thompson ("Robert Aldrich"), who notices the resemblances of Associates and Aldrich Co. to the earlier repertory companies set up by John Ford and Preston Sturges.

11. Higham, "Robert Aldrich," 18. Odets always remained a key influence on Aldrich, as he mentioned during many interviews. See John Calendo, "Robert Aldrich Says 'Life Is Worth Living,'" *Andy Warhol's Interview* 3 (1973): 32; and Ray Loynd, "Director Robert Aldrich: Emperor of an Empty Studio," *Los Angeles Herald Examiner,* 1 July 1973: D6.

12. Donald Lyons, "Dances with Aldrich," *Film Comment* 27 (1991): 72.

13. Claude Chabrol, "B.A., or A Dialectic of Survival," in *Projections* 4 ½, ed. John Boorman and Walter Donahue (London: Faber and Faber, 1995), 37.

14. Chabrol, "B.A., or A Dialectic of Survival," 38. Aldrich himself compared the antiwar genre with Shirley Temple speaking to the Republicans: "You don't convert anyone. I think that 'The Dirty Dozen' has some reasonably harsh things to say about the military. It's hardly a recruiting poster. I made a strong anti-war film in 'Attack,' it won the top award at Venice and nobody saw it." Aldrich went on to mention that the establishment attacked *The Dirty Dozen* as portraying an ugly picture of the military: "I think that the early anti-military feeling of the first part of the film tempers and de-

tracts from the violence later . . . and besides I can't imagine an American director going into a studio and asking for $1,200,000 to make an anti-war pic-
ture" (see Rick Setlowe, "Bob Aldrich and Dick Lester Have Differing Views
of War Films," *Daily Variety*, 25 October 1967: 6).

15. Thompson, "Robert Aldrich." See also David Sanjek, who notes that
Aldrich "routinely withholds the accepted defense mechanisms of genre convention and audiences expectation," often leaving audiences "*in medias res,*
without directorial assistance to accommodate all that the narrative has torn
asunder" ("Fear Is a Man's Best Friend: Deformation and Aggression in the
Films of Robert Aldrich," available at www.latrobe.edu.au/screeningthepast/
firstrelease/fr0600/dsfr10b.htm, 30 June 2000).

16. Lyons, "Dances with Aldrich," 72.

17. See Rose Capp, "B-Girls, Dykes and Doubles: *Kiss Me Deadly* and the
Legacy of 'Late *Noir,*'" available at www.latrobe.edu.au/screeningthepast/
firstrelease/fr0600/rc1fr10m.htm, 30 June 2002. Her article takes a much
more objective approach than the mean-spirited article by Kelly Hankin on
The Killing of Sister George ("Lesbian Locations: The Production of Lesbian
Bar Space in *The Killing of Sister George*," *Cinema Journal* 41, no. 4 [2001]:
3–27). R. J. Thompson recalls that his first experience of seeing *The Dirty
Dozen* in a 70-mm print introduced him to "different levels and layers of the
soundtrack or what we now call sound design," allowing him to experience
"the manipulation of levels, volumes, registers, and apparent spatial relationships" ("Robert Aldrich"). None of this survives in current versions of
the film. This represents another important avenue for study that necessi-
tates access to the original material, if possible.

18. Sanjek, "Fear Is a Man's Best Friend."

19. Calendo, "Robert Aldrich Says 'Life Is Worth Living,'" 30.

APPENDIX

THE LAST DAYS OF
SODOM AND GOMORRAH

Robert Aldrich always regarded *Sodom and Gomorrah* as a "terrible film."[1] But he also felt it was a "marvelous experience" in many ways.[2] Although the film belongs to the plethora of unmemorable biblical epics common to Hollywood and European cinema during the 1950s and 1960s, it allowed Aldrich the opportunity of working on a major big-budget epic as well as affording him the extended use of multicamera shooting, which characterizes his succeeding films.[3] However, a biblical epic seems as foreign to the director's nature as his comedic excursions in *4 for Texas* and *The Frisco Kid*. Yet, although *Sodom and Gomorrah* appears to be a footnote in the director's work, it does contain several significant features.[4] Aldrich commented, "I think every director wants to make one biblical spectacle. I think he's probably unwise if he wants to make more than one, but I think it's something that you should do . . . to see if you can make a picture that is not repetitive or imitative"; he also noted parallels between the "social-moral decay of Sodom" and contemporary society and so inserted these references "without being too obvious."[5] Aldrich brought his iconoclastic approach to established religion into the very genre supposedly affirming one of the major ideological tenets of Cold War America. *Sodom and Gomorrah* would certainly not follow the ideological patterns of films such as *The Robe* (1953) and *Sign of the Pagan* (1954).

Aldrich employed his friend Hugo Butler—a writer he first met while working on Jean Renoir's *The Southerner* (1945)—to work on the screenplay. He had also used Butler during the dark days of the blacklist on *World for Ransom*. Aldrich would collaborate with him again on *The Legend of Lylah Clare*. *Sodom and Gomorrah* thus became, as Arnold and Miller note, "the least religious of biblical epics" by concentrating on power politics and economics, themes also common to the director's cinematic vision.[6] *Sodom and Gomorrah* is a biblical epic directed

335

by one of the most iconoclastic and irreligious directors in the Hollywood system from a screenplay by a blacklisted Marxist. Although the film cannot be defended on any artistic level, it deserves analysis as a collaborative production by two talents often at odds with the studio system. When *Sodom and Gomorrah* first appeared, most audiences criticized a film that appeared to have very little to say about the actual nature of those sinful activities that incurred divine wrath. These cinematic Sodomites seemed to be engaged in other things rather than that well-known sin that was illegal in most Western societies. But Aldrich and Butler had other concerns.

Despite the status Stanley Kubrick's *Spartacus* has today as a biblical epic that never mentions Christianity, having now a certain notoriety for the restoration of that salacious "oysters and snails" sequence between Laurence Olivier and Tony Curtis, *Sodom and Gomorrah* is more daring in several ways. It does refer to God. But it also articulates oppositional elements that cannot be edited out as easily as Kubrick's "oysters and snails" were. As Howard Fast comments on the audio track of the DVD *Spartacus* Criterion version, the scene represents Hollywood's version of decadence. Fast regarded real decadence as involving an economic system based on human slavery. Aldrich and Butler emphasize this in their irreverent version of a biblical epic. Perverse sexuality clearly exists in the film for those who have eyes to see and ears to hear revealing references in the dialogue. But the film's sexual decadence is a minor ideological superstructural element determined by the economic basis of a corrupt social structure represented by those two sinful cities.

Like its contemporaries, *Sodom and Gomorrah* has all the drawbacks of a genre Bill Krohn sees as influenced by Steven Spielberg's cultural mentor Cecil B. DeMille:

> Wall-to-wall "history-speak," without slang or contractions; big scenes reduced to the level of a high-school halftime performance by battalions of lumbering non-pro extras that stretch as far as the eye can see; idiotic costumes (the nomad warriors sport shields covered with fur); pretty Italian actors playing Jews and Sodomites alike; special effects out of a Mothra movie; and a score by Miklos Rosza that is entirely composed of clichés, including woo-woo Indian attack music over shots of the nomad cavalry.[7]

All this is coupled with an overearnest performance by Stewart Granger, now bereft of his MGM Hollywood contract and lacking the athletic prowess of his Gainsborough days and MGM productions such as *Scaramouche* (1952), and the film is now mostly forgotten. However, it is far more viewable than *4 for Texas* and *The Frisco Kid,* which are both individually far better candidates for Aldrich's definition of a "terrible film." *Sodom and Gomorrah* also merits further attention. But it is not of interest as merely illustrating an authorship conflict between Aldrich and Butler, regarding which Krohn argues that "the director's very personal reading of the screenplay is erected over the bleached bones of Butler's Marxist parable."[8] Aldrich certainly undermines the generic aspects of the DeMille syndrome by bringing a different kind of complexity to the film. But he did this with every genre he approached. There is also no real reason to believe that he and Butler had different ideas about the film.

As William Aldrich has pointed out, his father had deep sympathy with those suffering from the blacklist.[9] He offered Butler work whenever the opportunity arose. Although the film may differ from the screenplay in several instances, this does not necessarily mean disagreement between director and scenarist. Aldrich often departed from screenplays for reasons of length and commercial exhibition. Aldrich and Butler's collaboration may have been more complementary than antagonistic. As in other Hollywood productions, Aldrich often expressed radical ideas indirectly and obliquely, knowing the problems any explicit approach would face. The Enterprise years were over. But the director still found ways of keeping faith with a cultural heritage virtually destroyed by the blacklist.

As critics notice, the film's opening scene of the camera dollying over the post-orgy bodies of glamorous Sodomite citizens ironically parallels later shots of half-naked bodies of used and abused slaves piled onto carts destined for the desert rubbish heap outside the city. Although the original criticism by Sodomite abolitionist Alabias (Feodor Chaliapin) in Butler's original script, which Krohn cites as involving "the denunciation of the economic system which sustains the Sodomite empire and perverts its inhabitants' ideas of right and wrong," becomes altered to emphasize lust, these two aspects are not mutually exclusive. Both are part of the same corrupt economic system. The film's publicity tended to emphasize lust rather than economics to reach a wider audience. But Butler's message remains central to the film.

Despite Aldrich dropping several explicit Marxist lines from Butler's screenplay, such as the emphasis on human beings as "commodities" in Alabias's original denunciation and Lot's stated desire to make his people compete economically with the Sodomites by becoming democratic middle-class businesspeople, such parallels do exist in the final film. For example, the mise-en-scène comparing the half-naked bodies of decadent citizens with those of their slaves needs no emphatic dialogue. Also, although Alabias never mentions "commodities" in the final version of his speech, his reference to slaves being used for pleasure and then worked to death depicts them as commodities in all but name. Furthermore, in his first encounter with Ildith (Pier Angeli), "chief of the queen's body slaves," Lot learns not only about the economic importance of salt for the region but also about the associated sexual slavery that depends on this commodity for its very existence. As Lot's future wife, whom audiences know will suffer a well-known fate, Ildith combines economics and sexuality within her own persona. She is transporting slaves to her mistress, Queen Bera (Anouk Aimée), and has paid for these commodities with salt. Ildith informs Lot that she is also a slave. But Butler's screenplay appropriately recognizes that a class structure exists among slaves in the Sodomite social structure as it did in pre–Civil War American society, where house plantation slaves occupied the top of their particular hierarchy. Ildith's eventual fate in the film thus represents a Marxist form of poetic justice. Furthermore, she seduces Lot into the social structure of Sodom and Gomorrah by employing her sexual charms. As she tells him, "Everything that gives pleasure is good." When she learns that Lot has recently lost his wife, she comments coquettishly, "There is always someone to take the place of a wife." Aldrich's cutaway to Lot shows him fully aware of the implications of this statement, which is the first sign of his beginning to fall into temptation.

The film also depicts Lot as a fellow member of Aldrich's gallery of deluded male heroes. Although he accepts Bera's gift of Ildith by including her in a community of free people rather than treating her as a commodity, he also places her in a situation where she suffers racial abuse from the Hebrew women. Aldrich and Butler certainly do not glamorize the "chosen people" in the film. Both Ildith and Lot's daughter Sheeah (Rosanna Podesta) are fully aware of the sexual desires repressed within Lot's stern patriarchal persona, even though he may deny it. Wearing Ildith's revealing Sodomite dress before her father, Sheeah reveals that she knows the real reasons why her father has accepted Ildith into their community. Lot slaps her face after she makes a revealing remark, a gesture linking him with other dominating Aldrich patriarchs such as Sam Hollis in *Hush . . . Hush, Sweet Charlotte.* Like Sam, Lot wishes his daughter to remain a little girl. His eventual murder of Astaroth (who has slept with both of Lot's daughters) reveals dark incestuous desires as well as the self-righteous fury of an angry father. Lot also misreads Ildith's character in the same way as Mike Callahan does with Frennessey in *World for Ransom.* Attracted to the Sodomite woman, Lot deliberately ignores the danger signals given to him by someone who served Queen Bera in more ways than one. Like Callahan, Lot only wishes to see what he wants to. As Ildith comments, "You're more of a slave to your beliefs than any slave in Sodom."

She initially rejects Lot's offer of marriage. When he remarks, "You can't be sure?" Ildith replies, enigmatically, "*I* can't be sure." However, after warning Lot, she decides to acquiesce to his male desire like a willing slave in Sodom, commenting, "I was trained to give pleasure." Lot naturally understands this reply according to his own gendered perspective. Ildith further warns Lot that she cannot guarantee "what I might do one day." Although her remark implies returning to Sodom, it also intimates that she may return again to the type of bodily service she once gave to her former mistress. Lot decides to take a chance after she offers him "pleasure you never dreamed of." After their marriage ceremony, Sheeah warmly greets the bridal pair while Lot's other, "innocent" daughter Maleb (Claude Mori) expresses unhappiness at the event. Sheeah now sees her father exhibiting the same type of sexual desires she has for Astaroth (Stanley Baker), whom her father has threatened with death should he touch her again. Although marginal to the film, Lot's family exhibits the same type of dysfunctional tensions appearing in Aldrich's other family melodramas. During a later scene in the film, Lot, Ildith, and Queen Bera watch a dance routine performed by two women dressed in male and female costumes. Bera remarks to Ildith, "There was a time when you could dance as they do now," after the two dancers (the Kessler twins) kiss. Lot does not get the message either verbally or visually.

When Lot discovers salt on his territory following the defeat of the Helamites, it is not difficult to see the significance of this scene. Butler's screenplay explicitly reveals that Helamite resentment at Sodomite economic oppression represents the real reason for their

enmity toward Queen Bera. She strategically uses the Hebrews as a
buffer state to protect her territory from the Helamites. After the
Helamite attack, the Hebrews find that their desired agrarian society
has been destroyed after aiding their Sodomite allies. But, ironically,
they discover salt on their territory, enabling them to change rapidly
from an agricultural community into merchant capitalists. This decision follows acts of violence committed by the Hebrews in defense
of Sodomite territory. They destroyed the dam that nurtured their
original agrarian community, an action that leads to their next stage
in an evolution leading to capitalism. Lot believes that the discovery
of salt represents a divine message enabling the chosen people to
compete with the Sodomites. Parodying the pre–civil rights ideology of "separate but equal," Lot proclaims to his community: "We
shall live in Sodom—separate but in full sight." However, they will
not become separate but equal by becoming contaminated by the
decadent lifestyle of their allies. Lot ignores the opportunity of attacking a Sodom weakened by the Helamite attack and freeing the
slaves. Instead, both he and his community soon become trapped by
the economic lifestyle of their neighbors. They deny the democratic
values of their original society by engaging in the reformist attitudes
Lot voices in the second part of the film. He condemns the "radical"
ideas of his son-in-law Ishmael (Giacomo Rossi-Stuart) to pursue instead a bourgeois path of reformism by persuading the Sodomites to
change by moral example, a strategy doomed to failure. As a result,
the elimination of Butler's lines articulating the full implications of
Lot's strategy does not radically alter the film: "We will show them
that a society of free men can make more profit than a society based
on slavery. God chose to turn my people from shepherds into mer-
chants."[11] Lot deludes himself in both Aldrich's and Butler's versions of this scene. He is both politically and sexually deceived by
his own male arrogance.

It is incorrect to argue that Aldrich replaces "Butler's Marxist critique of Lot's errors with a moral critique of his own, which makes
Lot a surrogate for the filmmaker."[12] The two approaches are not really separate. Also, Lot is certainly no surrogate for the director, for
he is a deeply flawed individual like other Aldrich characters.
Aldrich's film emphasizes the personal, rather than economic, factors of human existence. But this does not rule out the latter, as the
influences of Clifford Odets and Abraham Polonsky reveal. After
Waiting for Lefty, Odets changed his critique to emphasize the crip-

pling aspects of psychological factors hindering any radical opposition to the status quo. Individuals may believe in free agency. But they are always influenced by the world around them. They make decisions that they believe are personal, but these really result from dubious economic and social value systems.

The same pattern operates in *Sodom and Gomorrah*, despite problems involving the leading actor. Stewart Granger's Lot is another one of the many casting problems that affected Aldrich throughout his career, as illustrated by Robert Mitchum in *The Angry Hills*, Kirk Douglas in *The Last Sunset*, Frank Sinatra in *4 for Texas*, Cliff Robertson in *Too Late the Hero*, and Peter Falk in . . . *All the Marbles*. However, other factors also exist that compensate for this problematic casting. Granger's overbearing Lot represents another flawed character in Aldrich's universe. Despite Krohn's evaluation, both director and scenarist complement each other in terms of recognizing this fact.

For example, Krohn argues that when Lot kills Astaroth in front of the court after he learns that he has seduced both of his daughters, Aldrich gave Butler's script a different twist. Where Butler has Queen Bera imprison Lot for killing a member of the royal family, Aldrich brings a moral dimension into play. Unlike his earlier intervention when he saves Astaroth from Ishmael during his failed attempt to return runaway slaves to Sodom, Lot now refuses the fallen Astaroth's plea for mercy and murders him in front of the court. Bera makes the following remarks: "Congratulations. How delicious it is to cause death, to see life leaking out of a body and to think, 'I did this.' You are a true Sodomite—welcome. Just look at your Hebrews—cutaways to shamefaced Hebrews who have witnessed the duel. Next only to the pleasure of giving death is the excitement of watching it. They were participants in every bloody moment."[13]

However, although these lines were added to the film, they are not contradictory when we consider the character of Queen Bera. Although a decadent lesbian, she is a shrewd politician. Despite her brother's reluctance, she rents part of her territory to the Hebrews at the beginning of the film so that the agrarian community can act as a buffer zone between Sodom and the aggressive Helamites. Defense of the realm is one part of the agreement. But by fulfilling this part of the bargain, the chosen people ironically begin a process that will eventually undermine their democratic lifestyle. By changing from feudalism to capitalism after the destruction of the dam, the

Hebrew community comes closer to the corrupting influence of Bera and her society. Bera already attempts this earlier in the film when she sends one of her emissaries to entice Hebrew women into buying consumer goods. Among the items on offer are commodities "to make your house better than your neighbors'," a line obviously parodying the type of 1950s affluence seen in the melodramas of Douglas Sirk, where consumerism causes misery rather than satisfaction. Lot does murder a member of the royal family. But he commits an act Bera wanted in the first place. She uses Lot's emotionally arrogant feelings against him. Her speech to Lot also contains another example of her strategy as a leader. She makes the victim blame himself not only by condemning his patriarchal arrogance but also by manipulating the self-indulgent masochistic feelings ingrained within his personality. Lot admits these personal flaws when he escapes from prison. Bera also condemns him for drowning the Helamites by destroying the dam. Although this was a final act of desperation brought about by the betrayal of Astaroth's men and two of Lot's treacherous Hebrews who went over to the other side, Bera uses it to condemn Lot for what Krohn describes as "gratuitous sadism." But Lot shows this when he murders Astaroth before everybody. He is also a possessive father having deep incestuous feelings for his daughter Sheeah, feelings that echo those between Bera and Astaroth. Like any shrewd politician, Bera finds flaws in her opponent's character and uses them to good advantage. Lot murders a brother she wanted out of the way. She then uses the incident to remove Lot by making him blame himself. After asking his judicial opinion concerning punishment, she condemns him to prison to await trial.

Krohn sees a lack of logic in "her indictment of his self-flagellating acts" in Aldrich's additions to Butler's screenplay.[14] But Aldrich characters rarely exhibit logical behavior. Already influenced by Ildith, who wants to mold him into a heroic leader, perhaps in revenge for her abandonment by Bera, Lot is doomed on several levels. As Bera concludes, "In the name of righteousness and your God, you have abandoned yourself to the lust for blood." Her condemnation ironically encompasses the historical legacy of the Bible past and present. She also condemns him for corrupting the chosen people by bringing them to Sodom. Her charge is valid in terms of Lot's bourgeois reformist attitudes seen in the second part of the film. He is no longer the agrarian social activist who once offered sanctuary to slaves but, rather, is now part of a system that oppresses them. Lot refuses to help his son-in-law, Ishmael, free the slaves. Once in prison, Lot witnesses the torturing to death of slaves inspired to revolt by Ishmael. They were betrayed by greedy capitalist Hebrews already corrupted by Sodom who violated the traditional laws of giving sanctuary to fugitive slaves.[15]

When the angels free Lot, they mention Bera's corruption of "God's people."[16] The film assigns this social and economic corruption to a dominating female who affronts patriarchal norms. She is also a heroic figure who defies Lot's announcement of heavenly justice but faces her death bravely (or at least until she sees a pillar descending on her). According to Butler's original screenplay, Bera again seduces her former lover, Ildith, once she returns to Sodom as Lot's wife. She also successfully shows her the differences between her former role as a "free woman" in Sodom and her present submissive role as Lot's wife. Ildith had also warned Lot about the real nature of her character in an earlier scene in his tent. The deleted scene thus forms an inverse parallel to the one when Astaroth tells Sheeah that he has also seduced her sister Maleb. Astaroth and Sheeah's relationship exhibits sadomasochistic tendencies that occur in the earlier incestuous scene between Bera and Astaroth when she confronts her brother plotting in their father's tomb. Suspecting his allegiance to the Helamites, she begins sexual foreplay by inserting her finger into his mouth. The act follows a political discussion she has with her brother, establishing her power over him. Astaroth bites her finger, eliciting her pleasure. But when she returns the favor, he remains unemotional. Bera asks, "It doesn't give you any more pleasure?" He responds, "Neither pleasure . . . not even pain." When Astaroth earlier attempts to seduce Sheeah in the Hebrew camp, he makes a revealing comment about her reticence: "What restrains you? Is it rough treatment you expect?" The encounter between Bera and Astaroth occurs in their father's tomb, thus suggesting that their political and sexual conflicts result from a malign patriarchal influence similar to those operating in Aldrich's "Safari at Sea" contribution to *Adventures in Paradise, Attack! Autumn Leaves, What Ever Happened to Baby Jane?* and *Hush . . . Hush, Sweet Charlotte.* Astaroth later responds petulantly to his sister's power over him: "Why must I always be treated like a child?" His comment foreshadows Jane's resentment at Blanche in *Baby Jane* as well as the unequal power politics dominating the relationship between June and Childie in *The Killing of Sister George.*

Bera has also successfully engineered the corruption of Lot as well as his people. After Ishmael rejects Lot's reformist attitude concerning freeing the slaves, countering the latter's, "Slaves are the queen's property," with, "Are human beings property?" the sequence ends with Lot kissing Ildith, his back to camera. Aldrich significantly uses a quick match cut to the next scene, showing Astaroth kissing Sheeah in the same position as Lot in the previous scene. When he informs her about his successful seduction of her "innocent" sister Maleb, he further taunts her with the remark, "Do I remind you of your father?" As a product of an incestuous family, Astaroth clearly recognizes similar kinship patterns. His remarks suggest his knowledge of the fact that Sheeah has become attracted to him as a surrogate figure for her own father. After humiliating her by more "rough treatment" by offering her body to the captain of the guard (Antonio De Teffe), he masochistically expresses a death wish, envisaging his death in her arms. When this later happens, Sheeah turns on her own father, who not only has murdered someone who encroached on his own incestuous possessiveness (in a manner similar to John Mayhew in *Hush . . . Hush, Sweet Charlotte*) but also has killed a surrogate alter ego she has taken pleasure from. This violent spectacle occurs before both Sodomites and Hebrews. As Bera correctly recognizes, most of the chosen people have become little better than voyeurs gratuitously indulging in the spectacle before them. While some corrupted members of the chosen people have violated their ethical code by refusing to give sanctuary to escaped slaves, others have become little better than the devouring audiences seen at the end of *What Ever Happened to Baby Jane?* and *Hush . . . Hush, Sweet Charlotte,* who receive appropriate symbolic representation in the carnivorous dogs that appear in the final sequence of *The Legend of Lylah Clare*. Bera's condemnation of Lot may equally apply to each individual member of this contaminated Hebrew community: "You are a true Sodomite."

As a manipulative woman, Bera parallels other Aldrich female characters such as Frennessey in *World for Ransom,* Nicole in "Safari at Sea," and Lily Carver in *Kiss Me Deadly.* They all oppose male control and often use men who are victims of their own limited perception that they are supposedly in control, such as Mike Callahan and Mike Hammer. Lot falls into this category, especially when he murders Astaroth in an act of vengeful patriarchal possessiveness. As Krohn notes, "We are not far from Aldrich's portrayal of Mickey

Spillane's revenge-driven hero Mike Hammer as a sadist in *Kiss Me Deadly*, where the story of Lot's wife turning to salt after looking back at the destruction of Sodom is one of the cautionary myths Albert Dekker pretentiously trots out in response to an uncomprehending Gaby Rodgers's stubborn insistence on knowing 'what's in the box.'"[17]

However, the traditional end of Lot's wife at the climax contains other meanings. Looking back, Ildith's close-up resembles Bera's first significant close-up in the film when she exchanges a dominating look with an attractive female slave dancer. It suggests that Ildith also wishes to exercise her own form of control. She attempts to display a powerful controlling look like that of her former mistress now that her husband has lost his nerve. By looking back and defying the divine curse, Ildith hopes to be in the same powerful position as Lily Carver after disposing of two men threatening her autonomy (Soberin and Hammer). Lily believes that Pandora's box contains economic wealth. Ildith hopes to prove her husband wrong in believing that an unseen deity controls everything. By working on her husband's egotistic character, she hoped to become the dominant partner in the chosen people's new slaveholding society that will oppose Bera's rule. Instead, Ildith witnesses a conjunction of past and future. A nuclear explosion wipes out Sodom, just like Los Angeles in the future world of *Kiss Me Deadly*. Whereas Lily perishes in a fiery furnace after opening Pandora's box, Ildith changes into the traditional pillar of salt. By doing so, she ironically becomes a commodity herself. Lot is finally reduced to despair and humiliation. Now dependent on Sheeah, who has vengefully announced her intention of remaining with him to witness his fall, he mourns the departure of a female who not only gave him sexual pleasure and boosted his male ego but did not really belong to him. By looking back, Ildith reveals that her body and soul remain firmly committed to the sexual and economic structure of Sodom, which depended on slaves for its existence. After enslaving Lot by sexual techniques, she now finally loses her humanity and ends up a dead fetishistic commodity. Lot witnesses the final culmination of the folly of his involvement in a dehumanized social structure ending in apocalypse. The climax of *Sodom and Gomorrah* looks back to *Kiss Me Deadly* as well as forward to the devastating implications of *Twilight's Last Gleaming*. With the end of Sodom, "all that is solid melts into air."

NOTES

1. Ian Cameron and Mark Shivas, "Interview with Robert Aldrich," *Movie* 9 (1963): 8.

2. Alain Silver and James Ursini, *What Ever Happened to Robert Aldrich? His Life and His Films* (New York: Limelight Editions, 1995), 20. They refer to the Pierre Sauvage typescript of an interview that eventually appeared in *Movie* (1976–77). Aldrich's comment does not appear in the published version.

3. Edwin T. Arnold and Eugene I. Miller, *The Films and Career of Robert Aldrich* (Knoxville: University of Tennessee Press, 1986), 95; Silver and Ursini, *What Ever Happened to Robert Aldrich?* 22; Richard Combs, ed., *Robert Aldrich* (London: British Film Institute, 1978), 44.

4. Although Bill Krohn sees little reason to "revise contemporary evaluations of the picture today" ("*Sodom and Gomorrah*: The Auteur and the Potboiler," available at www.latrobe.edu.au/screeningthepast/firstrelease/fr0600/bkfr10d.htm, 30 June 2000, 1), he finds Hugo Butler's screenplay instructive in illustrating Aldrich's involvement in this genre.

5. Cameron and Shivas, "Interview with Robert Aldrich," 8.

6. Arnold and Miller, *The Films and Career of Robert Aldrich*, 96.

7. Krohn, "*Sodom and Gomorrah*," 1.

8. Krohn, "*Sodom and Gomorrah*," 5.

9. Arnold and Miller, *The Films and Career of Robert Aldrich*, 13–14.

10. Krohn, "*Sodom and Gomorrah*," 3.

11. Quoted in Krohn, "*Sodom and Gomorrah*," 3.

12. Krohn, "*Sodom and Gomorrah*," 5.

13. Krohn, "*Sodom and Gomorrah*," 5.

14. Krohn, "*Sodom and Gomorrah*," 5.

15. The contemporary parallels that Krohn sees in the scenes obliging "the director to show Jews as cowards who refuse to help, when in fact the American Jewish community was disproportionately numerous in the sit-ins and on the freedom buses that were mounting an assault on Jim Crow laws in the South" are redundant ("*Sodom and Gomorrah*," 4). Aldrich and Butler really criticize capitalist greed, for the Hebrews are already Sodomites in more senses than one. When the Sodomites and renegade Hebrews attempt to escape Sodom at the climax, they are often shot looting and stealing from others.

16. As Silver and Ursini note, the two angels are "mirror images of each other," expressing Aldrich's "disaffection with the self-righteous" (*What Ever Happened to Robert Aldrich?* 93). According to Jean Rouverol (telephone conversation, 8 May 2003), one of them was a well-known pimp from the Via Venuto whom Aldrich and Butler took pleasure in casting. For Aldrich's comments concerning scenes deleted by the British censor, see Robert

Aldrich, "Aldrich: Censor in Sodom," *Movie* 6 (1963): 19. The director commented that the fire-wheel sequence was meant to substitute for the sexual references removed from the film, all of which were later restored to the 154-minute laserdisc and video release versions.

17. Krohn, *"Sodom and Gomorrah,"* 6.

FILMOGRAPHY

A detailed filmography of the director's work may be found in Alain Silver and Elizabeth Ward's *Robert Aldrich: A Guide to References and Resources* and Alain Silver and James Ursini's *What Ever Happened to Robert Aldrich?* to which the reader is directed. This section is necessarily selective because it refers to works covered in the text. Hopefully, more examples of Aldrich's television work will surface in the future, so listings in this area are provisional.

1952. "The Guest." *The Visitor* (syndication title for *The Doctor*). Producer: Marion Parsonet; Director of Photography: Joseph Biroc; Teleplay: Don Ettinger; Host: Warner Anderson. Cast: Beulah Bondi (Mrs. West); Charles Buchinski/Bronson (Joe Langan); Joan Camden (Gwen West); James Brown (Bob); Bill Pille (Cop). 22 minutes.

1952. "Shanghai Clipper." *China Smith.* Producer: Bernard Tabakin; Director of Photography: Robert DeGrasse; Teleplay: Robert C. Dennis. Cast: Dan Duryea (China Smith/David Fitzgerald); Douglas Dumbrille (Inspector Hobson); Marian Carr (Anya Kerenski); Marc Krah (Pilok); Marya Marco (Miss Soong); Lewis Russell (Lord Ratcliffe); John Deering (Hexter). 22 minutes.

1952. "Straight Settlement." *China Smith.* Producer: Bernard Tabakin; Director of Photography: Robert DeGrasse; Teleplay: Lindsay Hardy, based on a story by Robert C. Dennis. Cast: Dan Duryea (China Smith); Myrna Dell (Shira); Douglas Dumbrille (Inspector Hobson), Paul Guilfoyle (Sing Ho); Susan Alexander (Maria Torres); Clarence Lung (Johnny Fong); Lucian Prival (Krantz). 22 minutes.

1953. *Big Leaguer.* Metro-Goldwyn-Mayer. Producer: Martin Rapf; Screenplay: Herbert Baker, based on a story by John McNulty and

Louis Morheim; Director of Photography: William Mellor; Musical Director: Alberto Colombo; Editor: Ben Lewis. Cast: Edward G. Robinson (John Lobert); Vera-Ellen (Christy); Jeff Richards (Abraham Polachuck); Richard Jaeckel (Bobby Bronson); William Campbell (Julie Davis); Lalo Rios (Chuy Aguilar); Bill Crandall (Tippy Mitchell); Frank Ferguson (Wally Mitchell); Mario Siletti (Mr. Polachuk). 71 minutes.

1953. "The Gift." *Four Star Playhouse*. Producer: Charles Boyer; Teleplay: John Baghi and Gwen Baghi, from a story by Amory Hare; Director of Photography: George Diskant. Cast: Charles Boyer (Carl Baxter); Maureen O'Sullivan (Minna Baxter); Dan Tobin (George Lennox); Joan Camden (Mrs. Mitchell); Amy Doran (Salvation Army Woman); Eddie Firestone (Young Father); Virginia Christine (Clerk). 22 minutes.

1953. "The Hard Way." *Four Star Playhouse*. Producer: Dick Powell; Teleplay: Blake Edwards; Director of Photography: George Diskant. Cast: Dick Powell (Willy Dante); Jack Elam (Vick); Robert Osterloh (Stan the Stickman); Regis Toomey (Lt. Waldo); Herb Vigram (Monte); Elizabeth Fraser (Janice Howl); Lennie Breman (Tino). 22 minutes.

1953. "The Squeeze." *Four Star Playhouse*. Producer: Dick Powell; Teleplay: Blake Edwards; Director of Photography: George E. Diskant. Cast: Dick Powell (Willy Dante); Joan Camden (Susan); Herb Vigran (Monte); Regis Toomey (Lt. Waldo); Richard Jaeckel (Stan); Mario Siletti (Deras); Karl Lukas (Ernie). 22 minutes.

1953. "The Witness." *Four Star Playhouse*. Producer: Dick Powell; Teleplay: Seeleg Lester and Merwin Gerard; Director of Photography: George Diskant. Cast: Dick Powell (Mike Donegan); James Millican (District-Attorney); Charles Buchinsky/Bronson (Frank Dana); Marian Carr (Alice Blair); Strother Martin (Ted Blair); Robert Sherman (Philip Baedeker); Walter Sande (Peterson); Charles Evans (Judge); Nick Dennis (Nick). 22 minutes.

1954. *World for Ransom*. Monogram. Producers: Robert Aldrich and Bernard Tabakin; Screenplay: Hugo Butler; Director of Photography: Joseph Biroc; Music: Frank DeVol; Editor: Michael Luciano. Cast: Dan Duryea (Mike Callahan); Marian Carr (Frennessey); Patric

Knowles (Julian March); Gene Lockhart (Alexis Pederas); Reginald Denny (Major Bone); Nigel Bruce (Governor Coutts); Douglas Dumbrille (Inspector McCollum); Keye Luke (Wing); Clarence Lung (Chan). 82 minutes.

1954. *Apache.* United Artists. Producers: Hecht–Lancaster Productions; Screenplay: James R. Webb; Directors of Photography: Ernest Laszlo and Stanley Cortez (uncredited); Music: David Raksin; Editorial Supervision: Alan Crosland Jr. Cast: Burt Lancaster (Massai); Jean Peters (Nalinle); John McIntire (Al Sieber); Charles Buchinsky/Bronson (Hondo); John Dehner (Weddle); Paul Guilfoyle (Santos); Walter Sande (Lt. Col. Beck); Morris Ankrum (Dawson); Monte Blue (Geronimo). 89 minutes.

1954. "The Bad Streak." *Four Star Playhouse.* Producer: Charles Boyer; Teleplay: John Bagni and Gwen Bagni; Director of Photography: George Diskant. Cast: Charles Boyer (Renneck); Virginia Grey (Angela); Robert R. Arthur (David); Esther Dale (Mrs. Weston); John Hoyt (Bentridge); Horace McMahon (Chick). 22 minutes.

1954. *Vera Cruz.* United Artists. Producer: James Hill; Screenplay: Roland Kibbee and James R. Webb, based on an original story by Borden Chase; Director of Photography: Ernest Lazlo; Music: Hugo Friedhofer; Editor: Alan Crosland Jr. Cast: Gary Cooper (Ben Trane); Burt Lancaster (Joe Erin); Denise Darcel (Countess Davarre); Cesar Romero (Marquis); Sarita Montiel (Nina); George Macready (Maximilian); Ernest Borgnine (Donnegan); Morris Ankrum (Ramirez); Henry Brandon (Danette); Charles Buchinsky/Bronson (Pittsburgh); Jack Lambert (Charlie); Archie Savage (Ballard). 94 minutes.

1955. *The Big Knife.* United Artists. Producer: Robert Aldrich; Screenplay: James Poe, based on the play *The Big Knife* by Clifford Odets; Director of Photography: Ernest Laszlo; Music: Frank DeVol; Art Direction: William Glasgow; Editor: Michael Luciano. Cast: Jack Palance (Charlie Castle); Ida Lupino (Marian Castle); Wendell Corey (Smiley Coy); Jean Hagen (Connie Bliss); Rod Steiger (Stanley Hoff); Shelley Winters (Dixie Evans); Ilka Chase (Patty Benedict); Everett Sloane (Nat Danziger); Wesley Addy (Hank Teagle); Paul Langton (Buddy Bliss); Nick Dennis (Mickey Feeney); Michael Fox (Announcer); Richard Boone (Narrator). 111 minutes.

1955. *Kiss Me Deadly.* United Artists. Producer: Robert Aldrich; Screenplay: A. I. Bezzerides, based on the novel *Kiss Me Deadly* by Mickey Spillane; Director of Photography: Ernest Lazlo; Music: Frank DeVol; Art Direction: William Glasgow; Editor: Michael Luciano. Cast: Ralph Meeker (Mike Hammer); Albert Dekker (Dr. Soberin); Paul Stewart (Carl Evello); Maxine Cooper (Velda); Gaby Rodgers (Gabrielle/Lily Carver); Wesley Addy (Pat Murphy); Juano Hernandez (Eddie Yeager); Nick Dennis (Nick); Cloris Leachman (Christina); Marian Carr (Friday); Jack Lambert (Sugar); Jack Elam (Charlie Max); Jerry Zinneman (Sammy); Percy Helton (Morgue Doctor); Fortunio Bonanova (Carmen Trivago); Silvio Minciotti (Old Mover); Leigh Snowden (Girl at Pool); Madi Comfort (Singer); Mort Marshall (Ray Diker); Strother Martin (Truck Driver). 105 minutes.

1956. *Attack!* United Artists. Producer: Robert Aldrich; Screenplay: James Poe, based on the play *Fragile Fox* by Norman Brooks; Director of Photography: Joseph Biroc; Music: Frank DeVol; Art Direction: William Glasgow; Editor: Michael Luciano. Cast: Jack Palance (Lt. Costa); Eddie Albert (Captain Cooney); Lee Marvin (Colonel Bartlett); William Smithers (Lt. Woodruff); Robert Strauss (Private Bernstein); Richard Jaeckel (Private Snowden); Buddy Ebsen (Sergeant Tolliver); Jon Sheppodd (Corporal Jackson); Strother Martin (Sergeant Ingersoll); Peter Van Eyck (German Captain); Steven Geray (German Orderly). 107 minutes.

1956. *Autumn Leaves.* Columbia. Producer: William Goetz; Screenplay: Jean Rouverol Butler; Director of Photography: Charles Lang Jr.; Music: Hans Salter; Art Direction: William Glasgow; Editor: Michael Luciano. Cast: Joan Crawford (Millicent Wetherby); Cliff Robertson (Burt Hanson); Vera Miles (Virginia); Lorne Greene (Mr. Hanson); Ruth Donnelly (Liz); Sheppard Strudwick (Dr. Couzzens); Selmer Jackson (Mr. Wetherby); Maxine Cooper (Nurse Evans); Frank Gerstle (Mr. Ramsey). 107 minutes.

1957. *The Garment Jungle.* Columbia. Producer: Harry Kleiner; Directors: Vincent Sherman and Robert Aldrich (uncredited); Screenplay: Harry Kleiner; Director of Photography: Joseph Biroc; Music: Leith Stevens; Art Direction: Robert A. Peterson; Editor; William Lyon. Cast: Lee J. Cobb (Walter Mitchell); Kerwin Matthews (Alan Mitchell); Gia Scala (Theresa Renata); Richard Boone (Artie

Ravidge); Valerie French (Lee Hackett); Robert Loggia (Tullio Renata); Joseph Wiseman (Tony); Adam Williams ("Ox"); Wesley Addy (Mr. Paul); Willis Bouchey (Dave Bronson); Celia Lovsky (Tullio's Mother). 88 minutes.

1957. *The Ride Back.* United Artists. Directors: Allen H. Miner and Oscar Rudolph (uncredited); Producer: William Conrad; Executive Producer: Robert Aldrich; Screenplay: Anthony Ellis; Director of Photography: Joseph Biroc; Music: Frank DeVol; Art Direction: William Glasgow; Editor: Michael Luciano. Cast: Anthony Quinn (Kallen); William Conrad (Hamish); George Trevino (Border Guard); Lita Milan (Elena); Victor Millan (Padre); Ellen Hope Monroe (the Girl). 79 minutes.

1959. *The Angry Hills.* Metro-Goldwyn-Mayer. Producer: Raymond Stross; Screenplay: A. I. Bezzerides, based on the novel *The Angry Hills* by Leon Uris; Director of Photography: Stephen Dade; Music: Richard Bennett; Art Direction; Ken Adam; Editor: Peter Tanner. Cast: Robert Mitchum (Mike Morrison); Elisabeth Mueller (Lisa); Stanley Baker (Conrad Heisler); Gia Scala ("Lefty"); Theodore Bikel (Tassos); Sebastian Cabot (Chesney); Peter Illing (Leonides); Leslie Phillips (Ray Taylor); Donald Wolfit (Dr. Stergion); Marius Goring (Commander Oberg). 105 minutes.

1959. "The Black Pearl." *Adventures in Paradise.* Producer: Richard Goldstone; Teleplay: James A. Michener and Thelma Schnee; Director of Photography: Maury Gertsman. Cast: Gardner McKay (Adam Troy); Patricia Medina (Celeste); Anthony Steel (Charles Remley); Kurt Kasznar (Wagner); Lon Chaney Jr. (One-Arm); Abraham Sofaer (Timaui); Weaver Levy (Oliver); Hal Baylor (Thompson). 47 minutes.

1959. "Safari at Sea." *Adventures in Paradise.* Producer: Richard Goldstone; Teleplay: James A. Michener and Bill Barrett. Cast: Gardner McKay (Adam Troy); Diana Lynn (Nicole Hazen); John Ericson (Jeff Hazen); Weaver Levy (Oliver); Anthony Eustral (Doctor); Genevieve Aumont (Woman at Bar). 47 minutes.

1959. *Ten Seconds to Hell.* United Artists. Producer: Michael Carreras; Screenplay: Robert Aldrich and Teddi Sherman, based on the novel *The Phoenix* by Lawrence Bachman; Director of Photography: Ernest

Laszlo; Music: Kenneth V. Jones; Editor: Henry Richardson. Cast: Jack Palance (Koertner); Jeff Chandler (Wirtz); Martine Carol (Margot); Robert Cornthwaite (Loeffler); Dave Willock (Tillig); Wesley Addy (Sulke); Jimmy Goodwin (Globke); Virginia Baker (Frau Bauer); Richard Wattis (Major Haven). 93 minutes.

1961. *The Last Sunset.* Universal–International. Producers: Eugene Frenke and Edward Lewis; Screenplay: Dalton Trumbo, based on the novel *Sundown at Crazy Horse* by Howard Rigsby; Director of Photography: Ernest Lazslo; Music: Ernest Gold; Art Direction: Alexander Golitzen and Alfred Sweeney; Editors: Edward Mann and Michael Luciano. Cast: Kirk Douglas (Brendan O'Malley); Rock Hudson (Dana Stribling); Dorothy Malone (Belle Breckenridge); Carol Lynley (Missy); Joseph Cotten (John Breckenridge); Neville Brand (Frank Hobbs); Regis Toomey (Milton Wing); Adam Williams (Calverton); Jack Elam (Ed Hobbs); George Trevino (Manuel). 112 minutes.

1961. *Sodom and Gomorrah.* Twentieth Century–Fox. Producer: Goffredo Lombardo; Screenplay: Hugo Butler; Directors of Photography: Silvio Ippoliti, Mario Montuori, and Cyril Knowles; Music: Miklos Rosza; Art Direction: Ken Adam and Giovanni D'Andrea; Editor: Peter Tanner. Cast: Stewart Granger (Lot); Pier Angeli (Ildith); Stanley Baker (Astaroth); Rosanna Podesta (Sheeah); Anouk Aimée (Queen Bera); Claude Mori (Maleb); Rik Battaglia (Melchior); Giacomo Rossi-Stuart (Ishmael); Feodor Chaliapin (Alabias); Antonio De Teffe (Captain). 154 minutes. Released in 1963.

1962. *What Ever Happened to Baby Jane?* Warner Bros. Producer: Robert Aldrich; Screenplay: Lukas Heller, based on the novel *Whatever Happened to Baby Jane?* by Henry Farrell; Director of Photography: Ernest Haller; Music: Frank DeVol; Art Direction: William Glasgow; Editor: Michael Luciano. Cast: Bette Davis (Jane Hudson); Joan Crawford (Blanche Hudson); Victor Buono (Edwin Flagg); Marjorie Bennett (Delia Flagg); Maidie Norman (Elvira); Anna Lee (Mrs. Bates); Barbara Merrill (Liza Bates); Julie Aldred (Jane as a Child); Gina Gillespie (Blanche as a Child); Dave Willock (Ray Hudson); Ann Barton (Cora Hudson); Bert Freed (Producer); Wesley Addy (Director); Maxine Cooper (Bank Teller); Michael Fix (Television Announcer). 132 minutes.

1963. *4 for Texas.* Warner Bros. Producer: Robert Aldrich; Screenplay: Teddi Sherman and Robert Aldrich, from an original story by Robert Aldrich; Director of Photography: Ernest Lazslo; Music: Nelson Riddle; Art Direction: William Glasgow; Editor: Michael Luciano. Cast: Frank Sinatra (Zack Thomas); Dean Martin (Joe Jarrett); Anita Ekberg (Elya Carlson); Ursula Andress (Maxine Richter); Charles Bronson (Matson); Victor Buono (Harvey Burdon); Edric Connor (Prince George); Nick Dennis (Angel); Richard Jaeckel (Mancini); Mike Mazurki (Chad); Wesley Addy (Trowbridge); Jack Elam (Dobie); Marjorie Bennett (Miss Ermaline); Percy Helton (Ansel); Jack Lambert (Monk); Fritz Feld (Maitre D'); the Three Stooges. 124 minutes.

1964. *Hush . . . Hush, Sweet Charlotte.* 20th Century–Fox. Producer: Robert Aldrich; Screenplay: Henry Farrell and Lukas Heller, from an original story by Henry Farrell; Director of Photography: Joseph Biroc; Music: Frank DeVol; Art Direction: William Glasgow; Editor: Michael Luciano. Cast: Bette Davis (Charlotte Hollis); Olivia de Havilland (Miriam Deering); Joseph Cotten (Dr. Drew Bayliss); Agnes Moorehead (Velma Cruther); Cecil Kellaway (Harry Willis); Victor Buono (Sam Hollis); Mary Astor (Jewell Mayhew); William Campbell (Paul Marchand); Wesley Addy (Sheriff); Bruce Dern (John Mayhew); George Kennedy (Foreman). 133 minutes.

1966. *The Flight of the Phoenix.* 20th Century–Fox. Producer: Robert Aldrich; Screenplay: Lukas Heller, based on the novel *The Flight of the Phoenix* by Elleston Trevor; Director of Photography: Joseph Biroc; Music: Frank DeVol; Art Direction: William Glasgow; Editor: Michael Luciano. Cast: James Stewart (Frank Towns); Richard Attenborough (Lew Moran); Peter Finch (Captain Harris); Hardy Kruger (Heinrich Dorfmann); Ernest Borgnine (Trucker Cobb); Ian Bannen (Crow); Ronald Fraser (Sergeant Watson); Christian Marquand (Dr. Renaud); Dan Duryea (Standish); George Kennedy (Bellamy); Gabrielle Tinti (Gabriele); Alex Montoya (Carlos); Peter Bravos (Tassos); William Aldrich (Bill); Barrie Chase (Farida). 148 minutes.

1967. *The Dirty Dozen.* Metro-Goldwyn-Mayer. Producer: Kenneth Hyman; Screenplay: Nunnally Johnson and Lukas Heller, based on the novel *The Dirty Dozen* by E. M. Nathanson; Director of Photography: Edward Scaife; Music: Frank DeVol; Art Direction: W. E.

Hutchinson; Editor: Michael Luciano. Cast: Lee Marvin (Major Reisman); Ernest Borgnine (General Worden); Charles Bronson (Joseph Wladislaw); Richard Jaeckel (Sergeant Bowren); John Cassavetes (Victor Franko); Jim Brown (Robert Jefferson); George Kennedy (Major Armbruster); Trini Lopez (Jimenez); Ralph Meeker (Captain Kinder); Robert Ryan (General Everett Dasher Breed); Telly Savalas (Maggott); Donald Sutherland (Pinkney); Clint Walker (Posey); Robert Webber (General Denton); Al Mancini (Bravos). 149 minutes.

1968. *The Legend of Lylah Clare.* Metro-Goldwyn-Mayer. Producer: Robert Aldrich; Screenplay: Hugo Butler and Jean Rouverol; Director of Photography: Joseph Biroc; Music: Frank DeVol; Art Direction: George W. Davis and William Glasgow; Editor: Michael Luciano. Cast: Kim Novak (Lylah Clare/Elsa Brinckmann); Peter Finch (Lewis Zarkan); Ernest Borgnine (Barney Sheean); Milton Selzer (Bart Langner); Rosella Falk (Rosella); Gabriele Tinti (Paolo); Coral Browne (Molly Luther); Valentina Cortese (Countess Bozo Bedoni); Jean Carroll (Becky Langner); Nick Dennis (Nick); Michael Fox (Premiere Announcer). 130 minutes.

1968. *The Killing of Sister George.* ABC/Palomar International. Producer: Robert Aldrich; Screenplay: Lukas Heller, based on the play *The Killing of Sister George* by Frank Marcus; Director of Photography: Joseph Biroc; Music: Gerald Fried; Art Direction: William Glasgow; Editor: Michael Luciano. Cast: Beryl Reid (June Buckridge); Susannah York (Alice "Childie" McNaught); Coral Browne (Mercy Croft); Ronald Fraser (Leo Lockhart); Patricia Medina (Betty Thaxter); Hugh Paddick (Freddie); Cyril Delavanti (Ted Baker). 138 minutes.

1969. *The Greatest Mother of 'Em All.* Promotional Short Film. Producer: Robert Aldrich; Screenplay: A. I. Bezzerides and Leon Griffiths; Director of Photography: Joseph Biroc; Art Direction: James Vance; Editors: Frank Urioste and Albert Nalpas (montage). Cast: Peter Finch (Sean Howard); Ann Sothern (Dolly Murdock); Alexandra Hay (Tricia Murdock); Kate Woodville (Eva Frazer); Barry Russo (Gene Frazer); Michael Fox (Nightclub Comic). 20 minutes.

1970. *Too Late the Hero.* Cinerama Releasing Corporation. Producer: Robert Aldrich; Screenplay: Robert Aldrich and Lukas Heller, from an original story by Robert Aldrich and Robert Sherman; Director of

Photography: Joseph Biroc; Music: Gerald Fried; Art Direction: James Vance; Editors: Michael Luciano and Albert Nalpas (montage). Cast: Michael Caine (Private "Tosh" Hearne); Cliff Robertson (Lt. Sam Lawson); Henry Fonda (Captain Nolan); Ian Bannen (Private Thornton); Harry Andrews (Lt. Col. Thompson); Denholm Elliot (Captain Hornsby); Ronald Fraser (Private Campbell); Lance Perceval (Corporal McLean); Percy Herbert (Sergeant Johnstone); Takakura Ken (Major Yamaguchi). 133 minutes.

1971. *The Grissom Gang.* Cinerama Releasing Corporation. Producer Robert Aldrich; Screenplay: Leon Griffiths, based on the novel *No Orchids for Miss Blandish* by James Hadley Chase; Director of Photography: Joseph Biroc; Music: Gerald Fried; Art Direction: James Vance; Editors: Michael Luciano and Frank Urioste. Cast: Kim Darby (Barbara Blandish); Scott Wilson (Slim Grissom); Tony Musante (Eddie Hagen); Robert Lansing (Dave Fenner); Irene Dailey (Ma Grissom); Connie Stevens (Anna Borg); Wesley Addy (John Blandish); Joey Faye (Woppy); Don Keefer (Doc); John Steadman (Old Man). 128 minutes.

1972. *Ulzana's Raid.* Universal. Producer: Carter DeHaven; Screenplay: Alan Sharp; Director of Photography: Joseph Biroc; Music: Frank DeVol; Art Direction: James Vance; Editor: Michael Luciano. Cast: Burt Lancaster (McIntosh); Bruce Davidson (Lt. DeBuin); Richard Jaeckel (Sergeant); Jorge Luke (Ke-Ni-Tay); Joaquin Martinez (Ulzana); Lloyd Bochner (Captain Gates); Douglass Watson (Major Wainwright); Karl Swenson (Rukeyser); Dran Hamilton (Mrs. Riordan); Gladys Holland (Mrs. Rukeyser); Dean Smith (Trooper Horowitz). 103 minutes.

1973. *Emperor of the North.* 20th Century–Fox. Producer: Stanley Hough; Screenplay: Christopher Knopf; Director of Photography: Joseph Biroc; Music: Frank DeVol; Art Direction: Jack Martin Smith; Editors: Michael Luciano, Roland Gross, and Frank Capacchione. Cast: Lee Marvin (A No. 1); Ernest Borgnine (Shack); Keith Carradine (Cigaret); Charles Tyner (Cracker); Malcolm Atterbury (Hogger); Harry Caesar (Coaly); Simon Oakland (Cop). 118 minutes.

1974. *The Longest Yard.* Paramount. Producer: Albert S. Ruddy; Screenplay: Tracy Keenan Wynn, from a story by Albert S. Ruddy;

Director of Photography: Joseph Biroc; Music: Frank DeVol; Art Direction: James S. Vance; Editors: Michael Luciano, Frank Capacchione, Allan Jacobs, George Hively (football sequences), and Steve Orfanos (montage). Cast: Burt Reynolds (Paul Crewe); Eddie Albert (Warden Hazen); Ed Lauter (Captain Knauer); Harry Caesar (Granville); Ray Nitschke (Bogdanski); Mike Henry (Rassmeusen); John Steadman (Pop); Bernadette Peters (Hazen's Secretary); Michael Conrad (Nate Scarboro); James Hampton (Caretaker); Anitra Ford (Melissa); Richard Kiel (Samson); Charles Tyner (Unger); Dino Washington (Mason); Michael Fox (Announcer). 121 minutes.

1975. *Hustle.* Paramount. Producer: Robert Aldrich; Screenplay: Steve Shagan; Director of Photography: Joseph Biroc; Music: Frank DeVol; Art Direction: Hillyard Brown; Editor: Michael Luciano. Cast: Burt Reynolds (Phil Gaines), Catherine Deneuve (Nicole Britton); Ben Johnson (Marty Hollinger); Paul Winfield (Louis Belgrave); Eileen Brennan (Paula Hollinger); Eddie Albert (Leo Sellars); Ernest Borgnine (Santoro); Jack Carter (Herbie Dalitz); Sharon Kelly (Gloria Hollinger); James Hampton (School Bus Driver); David Spielberg (Bellamy); Don "Red" Barry (Airport Bartender); Dave Willock (Liquor Store Clerk); Robert Englund (Holdup Man). 120 minutes.

1977. *The Choirboys.* Universal. Producers: Merv Adelson, Lee Rich; Screenplay: Christopher Knopf and Joseph Wambaugh (uncredited), based on the novel *The Choirboys* by Joseph Wambaugh; Director of Photography: Joseph Biroc; Music: Frank DeVol; Art Direction: Bill Kenney and Sid Tinglof; Editor: Maury Weintrobe. Cast: Charles Durning (Whalen); Louis Gosset Jr. (Calvin Potts); Perry King (Baxter Slate); Burt Young (Sergeant Dominic Scuzzi); Randy Quaid (Proust); Clyde Kusatsu (Tanaguchi); Don Stroud (Lyles); James Woods (Bloomgard); Robert Webber (Deputy Chief Riggs); George Dicenzo (Lt. Grimley); John Steadman (John). 119 minutes.

1977. *Twilight's Last Gleaming.* Allied Artists. Producer: Merv Adelson; Screenplay: Ronald M. Cohen, Edward Huebsch, and Tom Mankiewicz, based on the novel *Viper Three* by Walter Wager; Director of Photography: Robert Hauser; Music: Jerry Goldsmith: Art Direction: Werner Achmann; Editor: Michael Luciano. Cast: Burt Lancaster (Lawrence Dell); Richard Widmark (General Martin MacKenzie); Charles Durning (President David Stevens); Melvyn

Douglas (Zachariah Guthrie); Paul Winfield (Willis Powell); Burt Young (Augie Garvas); Joseph Cotten (Victor Renfrew); Roscoe Lee Browne (James Forrest); Gerald S. O'Laughlin (General Michael O'Rourke); Richard Jaeckel (Captain Towne); William Marshall (Klinger); Charles Aidman (Colonel Bernstein); Leif Erickson (Ralph Whittaker); Charles McGraw (General Crane); Simon Scott (Phil Spencer); William Smith (Hoxey); Phil Brown (the Reverend Cartwright). 143 minutes.

1979. *The Frisco Kid.* Warner Bros. Producer: Marc Neufeld; Screenplay: Michael Elias and Frank Shaw; Director of Photography: Robert B. Hauser; Music: Frank DeVol; Art Direction: Terence Marsh; Editors: Maury Winetrobe, Irving Rosenblum, and Jack Horger. Cast: Gene Wilder (Rabbi Avram Belinski); Harrison Ford (Tommy Lillard); George Dicenzo (Darryl Diggs); William Smith (Matt Diggs); Clyde Kusatsu (Ping). 122 minutes.

1981. *. . . All the Marbles.* Metro-Goldwyn-Mayer/United Artists. Producer: William Aldrich; Screenplay: Mel Frohman; Director of Photography: Joseph Biroc; Music: Frank DeVol; Art Direction: Carl Anderson; Editors; Irving C. Rosenblum and Richard Lane. Cast: Peter Falk (Harry); Vicki Frederick (Iris); Laurene Landon (Molly); Burt Young (Eddie Cisco); Tracy Reed (Diane); Ursuline Bryant-King (June); Richard Jaeckel (Reno Referee); John Hancock (John Stanley); Lenny Montana (Jerome); Clyde Kusatsu (Yamashito); Faith Minton (Big Mama). 112 minutes.

BIBLIOGRAPHY

Aldrich, Robert. "The High Price of Independence." *Films and Filming* 4, no. 9 (1958): 7, 35.

———. "Learning from My Mistakes." *Films and Filming* 6 (1960): 9, 33.

———. "Mes Deboires en Europe." *Cahiers du Cinema* 107 (1960): 2–6.

———. "Aldrich: Censor in Sodom." *Movie* 6 (1963): 19.

———. "American Report." *Cahiers du Cinema* 150–51 (1963–64): 24–25.

———. "La Fonction de Producer: Cinq Questions à Robert Aldrich." *Cahiers du Cinema* 150–51 (1963–64): 79–84.

———. "What Ever Happened to American Movies?" *Sight and Sound* 33 (1963–64): 21–22.

———. "The American Film Institute Seminar with Robert Aldrich." Transcript, Center for Advanced Film Studies, 2 November 1971. Beverly Hills: American Film Institute, 1978.

———. "The American Film Institute Seminar." Transcript, Center for Advanced Film Studies, 26 April 1978. Beverly Hills: American Film Institute, 1979.

Aldrich, Robert, and Lukas Heller. *Too Late the Hero.* Screenplay, 21 January 1969.

Anderson, Thom. "Red Hollywood." In *Literature and the Visual Arts in Contemporary Society,* ed. Suzanne Ferguson and Barbara Goseclose, 141–96. Columbus: Ohio State University Press, 1985.

Apstein, Theodore. *Rebellion.* Third-draft screenplay, 6 October 1969.

Arnold, Edwin T., and Eugene I. Miller. *The Films and Career of Robert Aldrich.* Knoxville: University of Tennessee Press, 1986.

Associates and Aldrich Co. *The Plaza.* Los Angeles: Associates and Aldrich Co., Inc., 20 January 1967.

Bachmann, Lawrence. *The Phoenix.* London: Collins, 1955.

Ball, Eve, with Norma Henn and Lynda Sánchez, eds. *Indeh: An Apache Odyssey.* Salt Lake City: Brigham Young University Press, 1980.

Baritz, Loren. *Backfire: A History of How American Culture Led Us into Vietnam and Made Us Fight the Way We Did.* Baltimore: Johns Hopkins University Press, 1998.

Barzman, Norma. *The Red and the Blacklist: The Intimate Memoir of a Holly-
    wood Expatriate*. New York: Thunder's Mouth Press/Nation Books, 2003.
Basinger, Jeanine. *Anthony Mann*. Boston: Twayne, 1979.
Belton, John. *Cinema Stylists*. Metuchen, N.J.: Scarecrow Press, 1983.
Berman, Marshall. *All that Is Solid Melts into Air: The Experience of Modernity*.
    New York: Simon & Schuster, 1982.
Betinez, Jason. *I Fought with Geronimo*. Harrisburg, Pa.: Stockpole Co., 1959.
Bezzerides, A. I. *The Greatest Mother of 'Em All*. Screenplay, 3 February 1965.
Bezzerides, A. I., and Leon Griffiths. *The Greatest Mother of 'Em All*. Screen-
    play, 19 May 1969.
Bigbsy, C. W. E. "*Awake and Sing!* and *Paradise Lost*." In *Critical Essays on Clif-
    ford Odets*, ed. Gabriel Miller, 153–64. Boston: G. K. Hall, 1991.
Blum, Daniel. *Theatre World: Season 1954–1956*. New York: Greenburg, 1955.
Boettcher, Thomas D. *Vietnam: The Valor and the Sorrow*. Boston: Little,
    Brown, 1985.
Bogdanovich, Peter. *Who the Devil Made It: Conversations with Legendary Film
    Directors*. New York: Ballantine Books, 1997.
Boreil, Jean. "Qu'est-il Arrivé à Baby Jane?" *Positif* 5, no. 6 (1963): 6–7.
Bratton, Jack, Jim Cook, and Christine Gledhill, eds. *Melodrama: Stage, Pic-
    ture, Screen*. London: British Film Institute, 1994.
Brenman-Gibson, Margaret. *Clifford Odets, American Playwright: The Years
    from 1906–1940*. New York: Athenaeum, 1981.
Brinckmann, Christine Noll. "The Politics of *Force of Evil*: An Analysis of
    Abraham Polonsky's Preblacklist Film." In *Prospects: The Annual of Amer-
    ican Cultural Studies*, vol. 6, ed. Jack Salzman, 356–86. New York: Burr
    Franklin, 1981.
Britton, Andrew. "Sideshows: Hollywood in Vietnam." *Movie* 28–29 (1981):
    2–23.
———. "Blissing Out: The Politics of Reaganite Entertainment." *Movie* 31–32
    (1986): 1–42.
Brooks, Jodi. "Fascination and the Grotesque: *What Ever Happened to Baby
    Jane?*" *Continuum* 5, no. 2 (1992): 225–34.
Brooks, Norman. *Fragile Fox*. New York: Dramatists Play Service, 1955.
Brooks, Peter. *The Melodramatic Imagination: Balzac, Henry James, Melodrama
    and the Mode of Excess*. New Haven: Yale University Press, 1976.
Brooks, Tim, and Earle Marsh. *The Complete Directory to Prime Time Network
    TV Shows 1946–Present*. 5th ed. New York: Ballantine Books, 1992.
Buhle, Paul, and Dave Wagner. "Jean Rouverol Butler." In *Tender Comrades:
    A Backstory of the Hollywood Blacklist*, ed. Patrick McGilligan and Paul
    Buhle, 155–76. New York: St. Martin's Press, 1999.
———. *A Very Dangerous Citizen: Abraham Lincoln Polonsky and the Hollywood
    Left*. Berkeley: University of California Press, 2001.
———. *Radical Hollywood: The Untold Story behind America's Favorite Movies*.
    New York: New Press, 2002.

Burman, Mark. "Abraham Polonsky: The Most Dangerous Man in America." In *Projections,* vol. 8, ed. John Boorman and Dennis Donahue, 229–72. London: Faber and Faber, 1998.

Butler, Hugo. *Sodom and Gomorrah.* Screenplay, 18 July 1961.

Butler, Hugo, and Jean Rouverol. *The Legend of Lylah Clare.* Screenplay, 1 May 1967.

Butler, Terence. "Polonsky and Kazan: HUAC and the Violation of Personality." *Sight and Sound* 57, no. 4 (1988): 262–67.

Byron, Stuart. "I Can't Get Jimmy Carter to See My Movie! Robert Aldrich Talks with Stuart Byron." *Film Comment* 13 (1977): 46–52.

Cabrera Infante, G. *A Twentieth Century Job.* Trans. Kenneth Hall and G. Cabrera Infante. London: Faber and Faber, 1991.

Calendo, John. "Robert Aldrich Says 'Life Is Worth Living.'" *Andy Warhol's Interview* 3 (1973): 30–33.

Cameron, Ian, and Mark Shivas. "Interview with Robert Aldrich." *Movie* 9 (1963): 8–11.

Cantor, Harold. "The Family as Theme in Odets's Plays." In *Critical Essays on Clifford Odets,* ed. Gabriel Miller, 127–40. Boston: G. K. Hall, 1991.

———. *Clifford Odets: Playwright, Poet.* 2d ed. Metuchen, N.J.: Scarecrow Press, 2000.

Capp, Rose. "B-Girls, Dykes and Doubles: *Kiss Me Deadly* and the Legacy of 'Late Noir.'" Available at www.latrobe.edu.au/screeningthepast/firstrelease/fr0600/rc1fr10m.htm, 30 June 2000.

Caputo, Raffaele. "*Film Noir*: You Sure Don't See All You Hear." *Continuum* 5, no. 2 (1992): 276–301.

Caputo, Rolando. "Aldrich, Leone, and *Vera Cruz*: Style and Substance over the Border." Available at www.latrobe.edu.au/screeningthepast/first release/fr0600/rcfr10g.htm, 30 June 2000.

Cates, Gilbert. "Robert Aldrich 1918–1983." *Directors Guild of America News* 8, no. 1 (1984): 1–3.

Caughie, John. *Theories of Authorship.* London: British Film Institute, 1981.

Caute, David. *Joseph Losey: A Revenge on Life.* New York: Oxford University Press, 1994.

Chabrol, Claude. "Evolution du Film Policier." *Cahiers du Cinema* 54 (1955): 27–33.

———. "Directed By." *Cahiers du Cinema* 150–151 (1964): 113–14.

———. "B.A., or A Dialectic of Survival." In *Projections,* 4&1/2, ed. John Boorman and Walter Donahue, 37–39. London: Faber and Faber, 1995.

Chase, Anthony. "The Strange Romance of 'Dirty Harry' and Mary Ann Deacon." *The Velvet Light Trap* 17 (1997): 13–18.

Chase, James Hadley. *No Orchids for Miss Blandish.* New York: Howell and Soskin, 1942.

———. *No Orchids for Miss Blandish.* Rev. ed. London: Avon Books, 1961.

Ciment, Michel. *Conversations with Losey.* London: Metheun, 1985.

Clurman, Harold. "Introduction." In *Night Music*, by Clifford Odets, vii–xiii. New York: Random House, 1940.

———. *The Fervent Years: The Story of the Group Theatre and the Thirties.* New York: Hill and Wang, 1957.

Cochran, David. *America Noir: Underground Writers and Filmmakers of the Postwar Era.* Washington, D.C.: Smithsonian Institution Press, 2000.

Cohen, Ronald M., and Edward Huebsch. *Twilight's Last Gleaming.* Second-draft screenplay, 9 January 1976.

Combs, Richard. "Worlds Apart: Aldrich since *The Dirty Dozen*." *Sight and Sound* 45 (1976): 112–15.

———. "Aldrich's *Twilight*." *Sight and Sound* 46 (1977): 186–97.

———. "*Big Leaguer*." *Monthly Film Bulletin* 44, no. 527 (December 1977): 266.

Combs, Richard, ed. *Robert Aldrich.* London: British Film Institute, 1978.

Cook, Jim, and Kingsley Canham. "Interview with Abraham Polonsky." *Screen* 11, no. 3 (1970): 57–77.

Coursodon, Jean-Pierre, with Pierre Sauvage. *American Directors,* vol. 2. New York: McGraw-Hill, 1983.

Cunningham, Frank. "*Night Music* and *Clash by Night*: Clifford Odets and Two Faces of Modernism." In *Critical Essays on Clifford Odets,* ed. Gabriel Miller, 227–37. Boston: G. K. Hall, 1991.

Curtiss, Ursula. *The Forbidden Garden.* New York: Dodd, Mead, and Co., 1962.

Danks, Adrian. "The Hunter Gets Captured by the Game: Robert Aldrich's Hollywood." Available at www.latrobe.edu.au/screeningthepast/first release/fr0600/adfr10h.htm, 30 June 2000.

de Baecque, Antoine. "La boîte atomique." *Cahiers du Cinema* 425 (1989): 50–51.

Delahaye, Michel. "Entretien avec Abraham Polonsky." *Cahiers du Cinema,* September 1969: 69.

Demonsablon, Philippe. "*World for Ransom*." *Cahiers du Cinema* 40 (1955): 49–50.

Denning, Michael. *The Cultural Front: The Laboring of American Culture in the Twentieth-Century.* London: Verso, 1997.

Derry, Charles. "The Horror of Personality." *Cinefantastique* 3, no. 4 (1974): 15–19.

———. *Dark Dreams: A Psychological History of the Modern Horror Film.* London: Thomas Yoseloff, 1977.

"Dialogue: Bertolucci and Aldrich." *Action* 9 (1974): 23–25.

Dimendberg, Edward. "From Berlin to Bunker Hill: Urban Space, Late Modernity, and Film Noir in Fritz Lang's and Joseph Losey's *M*." *Wide Angle* 19, no. 4 (1997): 62–93.

Drew, Bernard. "Leo Roars Again." *Film Comment* 17 (1981): 34.

"*Du Pont Show of the Week,* May 22, 1963." In *Variety Television Reviews 8, 1963–1965.* New York: Garland, 1987.

Durgnat, Raymond. "The Apotheosis of Va-va-voom." *Motion* 1, no. 3 (1962): 30–34.

———. "Paint It Black: The Family Tree of Film Noir." *Cinema* 6–7 (1970): 48–56.

Duval, Bruno. "Aldrich le Rebelle." *Image et Son* 306 (1976): 25–44.

Dyer, Peter John. "Meeting Baby Jane." *Sight and Sound* 32 (1963): 118–20.

Eisenschitz, Bernard. *Nicholas Ray: An American Journey.* Trans. Tom Milne. London: Faber and Faber, 1993.

Elley, Derek. "Experiences: An Interview with Susannah York." *Focus on Film* 9 (1972): 25–30.

Erickson, Todd. "Kill Me Again: Movement Becomes Genre." In *Film Noir Reader,* vol. 2, ed. Alain Silver and James Ursini, 307–30. New York: Limelight Editions, 1996.

Erskine, Thomas L., and James M. Welsh, eds. *Video Versions: Film Adaptations of Plays on Video.* Westport, Conn.: Greenwood Press, 2001.

Evans, Richard J. *In Defense of History.* New York: W. W. Norton, 1997.

Eyles, Allan. "The Private War of Robert Aldrich." *Films and Filming* 13 (1967): 4–9.

———. "Films of Enterprise." *Focus on Film* 35 (1980): 13–27.

Falsetto, Mario. *Stanley Kubrick: A Narrative and Stylistic Analysis.* 2ed ed. Westport, Conn.: Praeger, 2001.

Farber, Stephen. "New American Gothic." *Film Quarterly* 20 (1966): 22–27.

Fenin, George N. "An Interview with Robert Aldrich." *Film Culture* 2, no. 4 (1956): 8–9.

Fenin, George N., and William K. Everson. *The Western: From the Silents to the Seventies.* New York: Penguin, 1973.

Fleischman, Beth. "Clifford Odets." In *Twentieth Century Dramatists: Dictionary of Literary Biography,* vol. 7, ed. John McNicholas, 126–39. Detroit: Gale Research Press, 1981.

Flinn, Carol. "Sound, Woman, and the Bomb." *Wide Angle* 8, nos. 3–4 (1988): 115–27.

French, Philip. "*The Flight of the Phoenix.*" *Sight and Sound* 35, no. 2 (1966): 94.

Freud, Sigmund. "A Child Is Being Beaten." In *On Psychopathology: The Pelican Freud Library,* vol. 10, 159–94. London: Penguin, 1979.

Fussell, Paul. *Wartime: Understanding and Behavior during the Second World War.* New York: Oxford University Press, 1989.

Gallefent, Edward. "*Kiss Me Deadly.*" In *The Book of Film Noir,* ed. Ian Cameron, 240–46. New York: Continuum, 1993.

Gellman, Howard. *The Films of John Garfield.* Secaucus: Citadel Press, 1975.

Gill, Glenda E. "Canada Lee: Black Actor in Non-traditional Roles." *Journal of Popular Culture* 25, no. 3 (1991): 78–89.

Goodwin, James. "Clifford Odets." In *Dictionary of Literary Biography, vol. 26: American Screenwriters,* ed. Robert E. Monsberger, Stephen O. Lesser, and Randall Clark, 235–39. Detroit: Gale Research Co., 1984.

Greenberg, Joel. "Interview with Robert Aldrich." *Sight and Sound* 38, no. 1 (1968–69): 8–12.

Griffiths, Leon. *The Grissom Gang.* First-draft screenplay, 5 January 1970.

———. *The Grissom Gang.* Third-draft screenplay, 6 May 1970.

Grost, Michael. "*Kiss Me Deadly* and *World for Ransom.*" Classic Film and Television Home Page, available at www.members.aol.com/MGM 4273a.6/23/2001, 23 June 2001.

Halberstam, Judith. *Female Masculinity.* Durham: Duke University Press, 1998.

Hankin, Kelly. "Lesbian Locations: The Production of Lesbian Bar Space in *The Killing of Sister George.*" *Cinema Journal* 41, no. 4 (2001): 3–27.

Heller, Lukas. *What Ever Happened to Baby Jane?* Screenplay, 7 August 1962.

———. *The Flight of the Phoenix.* Revised final screenplay, 22 April 1965.

Heller, Lukas, and Robert Aldrich. *Hush . . . Hush, Sweet Charlotte.* Revised final screenplay, 11 May 1964.

Henderson, Brian. "The Searchers: An American Dilemma." *Film Quarterly* 34, no. 2 (1980–81): 19–34.

Hess, Judith. "Genre Films and the Status Quo." *Jump Cut* 1 (1974): 1, 16, 18.

Higham, Charles. "Robert Aldrich." *Action* 9, no. 6 (1974): 16–21.

Higham, Charles, and Joel Greenberg. *The Celluloid Muse: Hollywood Directors Speak.* London: Angus and Robertson, 1969.

Hill, Rodney. "Remembrance, Communication, and *Kiss Me Deadly.*" *Literature/Film Quarterly* 23, no. 2 (1995): 146–49.

Hirsch, Foster. *Joseph Losey.* Boston: Twayne, 1980.

———. *Detours and Lost Highways: A Map of Neo Noir.* New York: Limelight Editions, 1999.

Hoberman, J. "The Great Whatzit." *The Village Voice,* 15 March 1994: 43.

Humphries, Reynold. "When Crime Does Not Pay: Abraham Polonsky's *Force of Evil* (1948)." *Q/W/E/R/T/Y* 11 (2001): 205–10.

Hussey, Sally. "Scene 176: Recasting the Lesbian in Robert Aldrich's *The Killing of Sister George.*" Available at www.latrobe.edu.au/screeningthepast/ firstrelease/fr0600/shfr10d.htm, 30 June 2000.

Jarvie, Ian. "Hysteria and Authoritarianism in the Films of Robert Aldrich." *Film Culture* 22–23 (1965): 95–111.

Knopf, Christopher. *Emperor of the North Pole.* Final screenplay, 16 May 1972.

Krohn, Bill. "Adorno on Aldrich." Available at www.latrobe.edu.au/screening thepast/firstrelease/fr0600/bk2fr10b.htm, 30 June 2000.

———. "*Sodom and Gomorrah*: The Auteur and the Potboiler." Available at www.latrobe.edu.au/screeningthepast/firstrelease/fr0600/bkfr10d.htm, 30 June 2000.

Krueger, Eric. "Robert Aldrich's *Attack!*" *Journal of Popular Film* 2, no. 3 (1973): 262–76.

Kuntzel, Thierry. "The Film Work, 2." *Camera Obscura* 5 (1980): 7–69.

Lang, Robert. "Looking for the 'Great Whatzit': *Kiss Me Deadly* and Film Noir." *Cinema Journal* 27, no. 3 (1988): 32–44.

Lawrence, Jerome. *Actor: The Life and Times of Paul Muni.* New York: G. P. Putnam's Sons, 1974.

Leavis, F. R. *The Great Tradition.* New York: Doubleday, 1954.

Levy, Shawn. *Rat Pack Confidential.* New York: Doubleday, 1998.

Lowry, Ed. "Robert Aldrich." In *International Directory of Films and Filmmakers, vol. 2: Directors,* ed. Tom Prendergast and Sara Prendergast, 5–8. 4th ed. New York: St. James Press, 2000.

Loynd, Ray. "Director Robert Aldrich: Emperor of an Empty Studio." *Los Angeles Herald Examiner,* 1 July 1973: D1, D6.

Lyons, Donald. "Dances with Aldrich." *Film Comment* 27 (1991): 72–76.

Maltby, Richard. "'The Problem of Interpretation . . .': Authorial and Institutional Intentions in and around *Kiss Me Deadly.*" Available at www.latrobe .edu.au/screeningthepast/firstrelease/fr0600/rmfr10e.htm, 30 June 2000.

Martin, Adrian. "The Body Has No Head: Corporeal Figuration in Aldrich." Available at www.latrobe.edu.au/screeningthepast/firstrelease/fr0600/rmfr10e.htm, 30 June 2000.

May, Elaine Tyler. *Homeward Bound: American Families in the Cold War Era.* New York: Basic Books, 1988.

———. "Explosive Images: Sex, Woman, and the Bomb." In *Recasting America: Culture and Politics in the Age of Cold War,* ed. Lary May, 154–71. Chicago: University of Chicago Press, 1989.

May, Lary. *The Big Tomorrow: Hollywood and the Politics of the American Way.* Chicago: University of Chicago Press, 2000.

Mayersburg, Paul. "Robert Aldrich." *Movie* 8 (1963): 4–5.

McGarry, Eileen. "*Dirty Harry.*" In *Film Noir: An Encyclopedic Reference to the American Style,* 3d ed., ed. Alain Silver and Elizabeth Ward, 91–92. New York: Overlook Press, 1992.

McGilligan, Patrick, and Paul Buhle, eds. *Tender Comrades: A Backstory of the Hollywood Blacklist.* New York: St. Martin's Press, 1999.

Meikle, Denis. *A History of Horrors: The Rise and Fall of the House of Hammer.* Lanham, Md.: Scarecrow Press, Inc., 1996.

Mendelsohn, Michael J. "Odets at Center Stage." *Theatre Arts* 47 (May 1963): 16–19, 74–76.

———. "Odets at Center Stage." *Theatre Arts* 47 (June 1963): 28–34, 78–80.

———. *Clifford Odets: Humane Dramatist.* Deland, Fla.: Everett/Edwards, Inc., 1969.

Miller, Arthur. *Timebends.* New York: Grove Press, 1987.

Miller, Gabriel. *Clifford Odets.* New York: Continuum, 1989.

———. "*The Flowering Peach.*" In *Critical Studies on Clifford Odets,* ed. Gabriel Miller, 252–62. Boston: G. K. Hall, 1991.

Miller, Gabriel, ed. *Critical Studies on Clifford Odets.* Boston: G. K. Hall, 1991.

Mills, Bart. "Last Gleaming of Admiral X—Overlay of a Crack Up." *Los Angeles Times Calendar*, 6 June 1976: 36.

Moullet, Luc. "Le Poète et le Géometre." *Cahiers du Cinema* 101 (1959): 53–54.

Murray, Edward. *Clifford Odets: The Thirties and After.* New York: Frederick Ungar, 1968.

Myrick, Martin C. "John Lewis and the Film Score for *Odds against Tomorrow*." In *Odds against Tomorrow: The Critical Edition,* ed. John Schultheiss, 299–307. Northridge: California State University Press, 1999.

Naremore, James. *More than Night: Film Noir in Its Contexts.* Berkeley: University of California Press, 1998.

Nathanson, E. M. *The Dirty Dozen.* New York: Random House, 1965.

Nelson, Thomas Allan. *Kubrick: Through a Film Artist's Maze.* Bloomington: Indiana University Press, 2000.

Nevins, Francis M. *Cornell Woolrich: First You Dream, Then You Die.* New York: Mysterious Press, 1982.

———. "From the Dawn of Television: *China Smith*." Unpublished MS.

O'Brien, Geoffrey. *Hardboiled America: Lurid Paperbacks and the Masters of Noir.* New York: Da Capo, 1997.

Odets, Clifford. *Night Music.* New York: Random House, 1940.

———. *Clash by Night.* New York: Random House, 1942.

———. *The Big Knife.* New York: Random House, 1949.

———. *The Country Girl.* New York: Viking Press, 1951.

———. *The Flowering Peach.* New York: Dramatists Play Service, 1954.

———. *Waiting for Lefty and Other Plays.* New York: Grove Press, 1979.

Ophuls, Marcel. "De Noir Vertu." *Cahiers du Cinema* 130 (1962): 58–60.

Osteen, Mark. "The Big Secret: Film Noir and Nuclear Fear." *Journal of Popular Film and Television* 22, no. 2 (1994): 79–90.

Peary, Gerald. "Odets of Hollywood." *Sight and Sound* 56, no. 1 (1986): 59–63.

Pechter, William. "Abraham Polonsky and *Force of Evil*." *Film Quarterly* 15, no. 3 (1962): 47–54.

Petitclerc, Denne Bart. *Rage of Honor.* Screenplay, 7 September 1969.

Polonsky, Abraham. "Introduction." In *The Films of John Garfield,* by Howard Gellman, 7–9. Secaucus: Citadel Press, 1975.

———. "Abraham Polonsky." In *Tender Comrades: A Backstory of the Hollywood Blacklist,* ed. Patrick McGilligan and Paul Buhle, 481–94. New York: St. Martin's Press, 1999.

Powers, James. "Dialogue on Film: Robert Aldrich." *American Film* 4 (1978): 51–62.

Pye, Douglas. "*Ulzana's Raid*." *Movie* 27–28 (1981): 78–84.

Rappaport, Mark. "Abraham Polonsky's *I Can Get It for You Wholesale* (1951) Reconsidered." *Senses of Cinema,* available at www.sensesofcinema.com/contents/02/20/polonsky.html, 2002.

Reik, Theodor. *Masochism in Sex and Society.* Trans. Margaret H. Beigel and Gertrud M. Kurth. New York: Grove Press, 1962.

Ringel, Harry. "The Director as Phoenix." *Take One* 4 (1974): 9–16.

———. "Up to Date with Robert Aldrich." *Sight and Sound* 53, no. 3 (1974): 166–69.

Robinson, George. "Three by Aldrich." *The Velvet Light Trap* 9 (1974): 46–49.

Rogin, Michael. *Ronald Reagan, the Movie and Other Episodes in Political Demonology.* Berkeley: University of California Press, 1987.

Rosenbaum, Jonathan. *Movies as Politics.* Berkeley: University of California Press, 1997.

———. *Placing Movies: The Practice of Film Criticism.* Berkeley: University of California Press, 1997.

Ross, T. J. "Dark Legend." *December* 13 (1971): 196–201.

Rouverol, Jean. *Refugees from Hollywood: A Journal of the Blacklist Years.* Albuquerque: University of New Mexico Press, 2000.

Russo, Vito. *The Celluloid Closet: Homosexuality in the Movies.* Rev. ed. New York: Harper and Row, 1987.

Sanjek, David. "Fear Is a Man's Best Friend: Deformation and Aggression in the Films of Robert Aldrich." Available at www.latrobe.edu.au/screening thepast/firstrelease/fr0600/dsfr10b.htm, 30 June 2000.

Sarris, Andrew. "Whatever Happened to Baby Jane?" *Movie* 8 (1963): 6–7.

———. *The American Cinema: Directors and Directions 1929–1968.* New York: Dutton, 1968.

———. "What Ever Happened to Bobby Aldrich?" *Village Voice* 29 (28 October 1981): 49.

Sauvage, Pierre. "Aldrich Interview." *Movie* 23 (1976–77): 50–64.

Schlesinger, Arthur, Jr. *The Age of Roosevelt: The Crisis of the Old Order.* Boston: Houghton Mifflin, 1957.

Schultheiss, John, ed. *Body and Soul: The Critical Edition.* Northridge: Center for Telecommunication Studies, California State University, 2002.

Schultheiss, John, and Mark Shaubert, eds. *Force of Evil: The Critical Edition.* Northridge: California State University, 1996.

Setlowe, Rick. "Bob Aldrich and Dick Lester Have Differing Views of War Films." *Daily Variety,* 25 October 1967: 6.

Shadoian, Jack. *Dreams and Dead Ends: The American Gangster Film.* 2d ed. New York: Oxford University Press, 2003.

Shagan, Steve. *Hustle.* Screenplay, 20 August 1974.

Sharp, Alan. "White Man Unforks Tongue for Ulzana." *Los Angeles Times,* 14 May 1972: 20.

Sherman, Eric, ed. *Directing the Film: Film Directors on Their Art.* Boston: Little Brown, 1976.

Sherman, Eric, and Martin Rubin. *The Director's Event: Interviews with Five American Filmmakers.* New York: Athenaeum, 1970.

Sherman, Vincent. *Studio Affairs: My Life as a Film Director.* Lexington: University Press of Kentucky, 1996.

Shuman, R. Baird. *Clifford Odets.* New York: Twayne, 1962.

Silver, Alain. "*The Big Night.*" In *Film Noir: An Encyclopedic Reference to the American Style,* 3d ed., ed. Alain Silver and Elizabeth Ward, 32–33. New York: Overlook Press, 1992.

———. "*Kiss Me Deadly*: Evidence of a Style." In *Film Noir Reader,* vol. 2, ed. Alain Silver and James Ursini, 209–36. New York: Limelight Editions, 1996.

———. "Son of *Noir*: Neo–*Film Noir* and the Neo–B Picture." In *Film Noir Reader,* vol. 2, ed. Alain Silver and James Ursini, 331–38. New York: Limelight Editions, 1996.

Silver, Alain, and James Ursini. *What Ever Happened to Robert Aldrich? His Life and His Films.* New York: Limelight Editions, 1995.

Silver, Alain, and Elizabeth Ward. *Robert Aldrich: A Guide to References and Resources.* Boston: G. K. Hall, 1979.

Silver, Alain, and Elizabeth Ward, eds. *Film Noir: An Encyclopedic Reference to the American Style.* 3d ed. New York: Overlook Press, 1992.

Sklar, Robert. *City Boys.* Princeton: Princeton University Press, 1990.

Slotkin, Richard. *Regeneration through Violence: The Mythology of the American Frontier, 1600–1860.* Middletown, Conn.: Wesleyan University Press, 1973.

———. *The Fatal Environment: The Myth of the Frontier in the Age of Industrialization, 1800–1890.* New York: Athenaeum, 1985.

———. *Gunfighter Nation: The Myth of the Frontier in Twentieth-Century America.* New York: Athenaeum, 1992.

Spada, James. *Peter Lawford: The Man Who Kept the Secrets.* New York: Bantam Books, 1991.

Spiegelman, Judith. "Interview with Abraham Polonsky." In *Contemporary Authors 104,* ed. Frances C. Locher, 372–74. Detroit: Gale Research Co., 1982.

Sterrit, David. "Films." *Los Angeles Herald-Examiner California Living,* 30 May 1976: 4–5.

Stevens, Brad. "Variant Versions of Robert Aldrich's Films: A Case Study." Available at www.latrobe.edu.au/screeningthepast/firstrelease/fr0600/bsfr10c.htm, 30 June 2000.

Straayer, Chris. *Deviant Eyes, Deviant Bodies: Sexual Re-orientation in Film and Video.* New York: Columbia University Press, 1996.

Suid, Lawrence H. *Guts and Glory: The Making of the American Military Image in Film.* Rev. and expanded ed. Lexington: University of Kentucky Press, 2002.

Swindell, Larry. *Body and Soul: The Life of John Garfield.* New York: Morrow, 1975.

Tailleur, Roger. "Avènement du Cinema Américain." *Positif* 11 (1956): 11–23.

Telotte, J. P. "Talk and Trouble, *Kiss Me Deadly*'s Deadly Discourse." *Journal of Popular Film and Television* 2 (1985): 69–79.

———. *Voices in the Dark: The Narrative Patterns of Film Noir.* Urbana: University of Illinois Press, 1989.

Thompson, R. J. "Robert Aldrich: An Independent Career." Available at www.latrobe.edu.au/screeningthepast/firstrelease/fr0600/rtfr10a.htm, 30 June 2000.

Tibbetts, John C., and James M. Welsh, eds. *The Encyclopedia of Stage Plays into Film.* New York: Facts on File, Inc., 2001.

Truffaut, Francois. "Le Derby des Psaumes." *Cahiers du Cinema* 48 (1955): 42–45.

———. "Rencontre avec Robert Aldrich." *Cahiers du Cinema* 64 (1956): 2–11.

———. "Rencontre avec Robert Aldrich." *Cahiers du Cinema* 82 (1958): 4–10.

Tusher, William. "'Twilight's' and Controversy: They Wanted It and Got It." *Daily Variety,* 20 January 1977: 1, 23, 38.

Wambaugh, Joseph. *The Choirboys.* New York: Dell, 1975.

———. *The Choirboys.* First-draft screenplay, 8 July 1975.

Weales, Gerald. *Clifford Odets: Playwright.* New York: Pegasus, 1971.

Weiss, Andrea. *Vampires and Violets: Lesbians in the Cinema.* London: Jonathan Cape, 1992.

Wellman, Paul Isselin. *Broncho Apache.* New York: Doubleday, 1936.

Wells, Jeffrey. "Peter Falk and Robert Aldrich Tell It Straight re. MGM's 'All the Marbles.'" *The Film Journal* (October 1981): 10.

Whatling, Claire. *Screen Dreams: Fantasying Lesbians in Film.* Manchester: Manchester University Press, 1997.

Whitfield, Stephen. *The Culture of the Cold War.* Baltimore: Johns Hopkins University Press, 1991.

Williams, Tony. "Narrative Patterns and Mythic Trajectories in Mid-1980s Vietnam Movies." In *Inventing Vietnam,* ed. Michael Anderegg, 114–26. Philadelphia: Temple University Press, 1991.

———. *Hearths of Darkness: The Family in the American Horror Film.* Cranbury, N.J.: Fairleigh Dickinson University Press, 1996.

———. "The Big Knife." In *The Encyclopedia of Stage Plays into Film,* ed. John C. Tibbetts and James M. Welsh, 31–32. New York: Facts on File, Inc., 2001.

———. "The Big Knife." In *Video Versions: Film Adaptations of Plays on Video,* ed. Thomas L. Erskine and James M. Welsh, 29–30. Westport, Conn.: Greenwood Press, 2001.

———. "Ceiling Zero." In *The Encyclopedia of Stage Plays into Film,* ed. John C. Tibbetts and James M. Welsh, 46–47. New York: Facts on File, 2001.

———. "Fragile Fox." In *The Encyclopedia of Stage Plays into Film,* ed. John C. Tibbetts and James M. Welsh, 117–18. New York: Facts on File, 2001.

———. "The Killing of Sister George." In *The Encyclopedia of Stage Plays into Film,* ed. John C. Tibbetts and James M. Welsh, 169–70. New York: Facts on File, Inc., 2001.

Williams, Tony, and Jean-Jacques Malo, eds. *Vietnam War Films: Over 600 Feature, Made-for-TV, Pilot and Short Movies, 1939–1992, from the United States, Vietnam, France, Belgium, Australia, Hong Kong, South Africa, Great Britain and Other Countries.* Jefferson, N.C.: McFarland, 1994.

Windeler, Robert. "Aldrich: To Shut Up and Take Your Lumps." *New York Times,* 3 September 1967: II, X9.

Wood, Michael. *America in the Movies.* New York: Dell, 1970.

Wood, Robin. "Ideology, Genre, Auteur." *Film Comment* 13, no. 1 (1977): 46–51.

———. "80s Hollywood: Dominant Tendencies." *cineACTION!* 1 (1985): 2–5.

———. *Hollywood: From Vietnam to Reagan.* New York: Columbia University Press, 1986.

———. *Hitchcock's Films Revisited.* New York: Columbia University Press, 1989.

———. "Creativity and Evaluation: Two Film Noirs of the 1950s." In *Film Noir Reader,* vol. 2, ed. Alain Silver and James Ursini, 99–106. New York: Limelight Editions, 1999.

Wynn, Tracy Keenan. *The Longest Yard.* Revised final screenplay, 6 September 1973.

Zheutlin, Barbara, and David Talbot, eds. *Creative Differences.* Boston: South End Press, 1978.

Index

About the Author

Tony Williams is a professor in the English Department of Southern Illinois University, where he is the head of film studies. His books include *Jack London: The Movies* (Los Angeles: David Rejl, 1992), *Hearths of Darkness: The Family in the American Horror Film* (Cranbury, N.J.: Fairleigh Dickinson University Press, 1996), *Larry Cohen: Radical Allegories of an American Filmmaker* (Jefferson, N.C.: McFarland Sons Co., 1997), *Structures of Desire: British Cinema (1939–1955)* (New York: State University of New York Press, 2000), and *The Cinema of George A. Romero: Knight of the Living Dead* (London: Wallflower Press, 2003). He has recently completed coediting a collection of essays on international horror films with Steven Jay Schneider, and will soon begin coediting another collection on political horror films with Reynold Humphries.